THE FATHERS
OF THE CHURCH

A NEW TRANSLATION

VOLUME 68

THE FATHERS
OF THE CHURCH

A NEW TRANSLATION

SAINT JOHN CHRYSOSTOM

DISCOURSES AGAINST JUDAIZING CHRISTIANS

Translated by
PAUL W. HARKINS
Xavier University
Cincinnati, Ohio

THE CATHOLIC UNIVERSITY OF AMERICA PRESS
Washington, D.C.

NIHIL OBSTAT:

REV. HERMIGILD DRESSLER, O.F.M.
Censor Deputatus

IMPRIMATUR:

✝ WILLIAM CARDINAL BAUM
Archbishop of Washington

The *Nihil obstat* and *Imprimatur* are official declarations that a book or pamphlet is free of doctrinal or moral error. No implication is contained therein that those who have granted the *Nihil obstat* and *Imprimatur* agree with the contents, opinions, or statements expressed.

CONTENTS

PREFACE

This translation of St. John Chrysostom's eight *Discourses Against Judaizing Christians* presents to English readers some very important documents from fourth-century Antioch in Syria. Their importance stems from two factors. First, Judaizing must have caused a perilous situation for the Antiochene Christians; hence, the *Discourses* offer evidence for the Church historian. Second, these *Discourses* have occasioned subsequent charges of anti-Semitism which make Chrysostom a contributing cause to every argument and weapon used against the Jews in every pogrom for the last sixteen hundred years. Hence, Chrysostom's accusers have given to the *Discourses* a relevance which transcends any anti-Semitic situation local to Antioch.

Antioch was a most important city all during the fourth century as well as long before and after it. Therefore, it seems important for the whole history of anti-Semitism to publish these contemporary documents, which reflect so vividly the climate of that metropolis at that time. It is in this spirit that they are here offered for the first time in an English translation in book form.

Every translation should, in some sense, be a new creation. I shall create only insofar as I attempt to offer these discourses in a new idiom which is as faithful to Chrysostom's Greek as current English usage permits. My introduction and notes will try to present Chrysostom's position at Antioch and the problem he faced from those members of his flock who were leading their religious life on two fronts. The notes will also try to show Chrysostom's use of Scripture in the light of the latest advances in biblical scholarship.

Not only is the idiom new but so also is the title, although this has not come into being out of absolute nothing. Traditionally these homilies have been called *Kata Ioudaiōn*, which in Latin becomes *Adversus Iudaeos*, i.e., *Against the Jews*. This title misrepresents the contents of the *Discourses*, which clearly show that Chrysostom's primary targets were members of his own congregation who continued to observe the Jewish feasts and fasts.

Since the *Discourses* were delivered in a Christian church to a Christian congregation with few, if any, Jews actually present, I have not hesitated to add "Christians" to the title. That Chrysostom's polemics are aimed at Judaizers is borne out also in titles found in earlier editions and in the manuscripts. All these points will be discussed in their proper place in the introduction.

It is true that Chrysostom could hardly have delivered the *Discourses* in their present form after Vatican II's "Declaration on the Church's Attitude Toward Non-Christian Religions" (Cf. *Acta apostolicae sedis* 58 (1966) 740-44). Chrysostom held the position, which was common for centuries, that all Jews are responsible for Christ's passion and death, that they have been repudiated and cursed by God, and that they stand condemned out of the mouths of their own prophets. His position on these points is no longer tenable. Even if he was motivated by an overzealous pastoral spirit, many of his remarks are patently anti-Semitic. For these objectively unchristian acts he cannot be excused, even if he is the product of his times.

Nonetheless, the *Discourses* are of great relevance both for an understanding of the Judaizing movement in the Church and for the history of the whole question of anti-Semitism. It is to this purpose that they are here published.

Paul W. Harkins

Xavier University
Cincinnati, Ohio

SELECT BIBLIOGRAPHY

Texts and Translations of the Discourses (see below,*Introduction* III Sect. 6-8)

Erasmus, Desiderius. *Divi Iohannis Chrysostomi et Divi Athanasii . . lucubrationes aliquot* etc. [containing *Discourses* IV-VIII in a Latin translation] (Basle 1527).

Hoeschel, David. *Contra Iudaeos homiliae VI* (Augsburg 1602).

Duc, Fronton du (Fronto Ducaeus). *Ad populum Antiochenum, adv. Iudaeos, De incomprehensibili Dei natura, De sanctis deque diversis eiusmodi argumentis homiliae LXXVII* (Paris 1609).

Savile, Henry. *S. Iohannis Chrysostomi opera omnia* [title actually in Greek only] (8 vols., Eton 1612).

Duc, Fronton du (Fronto Ducaeus). *S. Iohannis Chrysostomi opera omnia* (12 vols., Paris 1636-42).

Montfaucon, Bernard de. *S. Iohannis Chrysostomi opera omnia* (13 vols., Paris 1718-38 and Venice 1734-41). Second edition by Th. Fix (Paris 1834-39; reprinted by J.-P. Minge in PG 47-61; Paris 1863 [earlier printings of vol. 48: 1859]).

Bareille, J. *Oeuvres complètes de S. Jean Chrysostome* [Montfaucon's text with French translation] (12 vols., Paris 1865-73).

Schatkin, Margaret. "St. John Chrysostom's Homily on the Protopaschites [the third discourse *Adv. Iud.*]: Introduction and Translation," *Orientalia christiana analecta* 195 (= The Heritage of the Early Church [Essays in Honor of . . . G.V. Florovsky]; Rome 1973) 167-86.

Other Patristic Texts and Translations

The Apostolic Fathers, trans. F.X. Glimm *et al.* (FC 1; New York 1946; rev. 1948; repr., Washington, D.C., 1962, 1969).

Cyprian, St. *Ad Quirinum testimonia,* trans. R.E. Wallis (Ante-Nicene Library 13; Edinburgh 1869).

Cyril of Jerusalem, St. *The Works of Saint Cyril of Jerusalem,* trans. L.P. McCauley and A.A. Stephenson (FC 64; Washington, D.C., 1970).

The Didache, The Epistle of Barnabas etc. trans. J.A. Kleist (ACW 6; Westminster, Md., 1948).

Jerome, St. *Lettres,* trans. J. Labourt, 7 (Paris 1961).

John Chrysostom, St. *Sur l'incompréhensibilité de Dieu [De incomp. 1-5],* introd. F. Cavallera and J. Daniélou; trans. R. Flacelière (SC 28bis; Paris 1951).

—————— *Huit catéchèses baptismales,* ed., trans. A. Wenger (SC 50bis; Paris 1957; new ed. 1970).

—————— *Homilies on the Gospel of St. John,* trans. Sister Thomas Aquinas Goggin (FC 33 and 41; New York 1957, 1960).

—————— *Baptismal Instructions,* trans. P.W. Harkins (ACW 31; Westminster, Md., 1963).

Josephus. *Jewish War,* trans. H. St. J. Thackeray, in The Loeb Classical Library *Josephus,* vols. 2-3 (London 1927, 1928).—*Jewish Antiquities,* trans. Thackeray, R. Marcus et al., *ibid.,* vols. 4-9 (London 1928-65).

Justin Martyr, St. *Writings,* trans. T.B. Falls (FC 6; New York 1948; repr., Washington, D.C., 1965).

xiii

_____ *The Dialogue with Trypho*, trans. A.L. Williams (London 1931).

Tertullian. *Adversus Iudaeos*, trans. S. Thelwell (Ante-Nicene Library 18; Edinburgh 1870).

Theodore of Mopsuetia. *Les Homélies catéchétiques . . .*, ed. R. Tonneau and R. Devreesse (Studi e testi 145; Vatican City 1949).

Bible

Septuaginta, ed. A. Rahlfs (2 vols., Stuttgart 1935).

The Septuagint Bible, trans. Charles Thomson, as edited, revised, and enlarged by C.A. Muses (Indian Hills, Colo., 1954).

The Jerusalem Bible, ed. A. Jones (Garden City, N.Y., 1966).

St. Joseph Edition of the Holy Bible: Confraternity Version (New York 1963).

The New American Bible . . ., trans. Members of the Catholic Biblical Association of America, sponsored by the Bishops' Committee of the Confraternity of Christian Doctrine (Paterson, N.J., 1970).

Brown, Raymond E., S.S. Fitzmeyer, Joseph A., S.J., Murphy, Roland E., O. Carm. edd. *The Jerome Biblical Commentary* (Englewood Cliffs, N.J., 1968).

Fuller, R.E., Johnston, L., Kearns, C., edd. *A New Catholic Commentary on Holy Scripture* (London 1969).

McKenzie, J.L. *Dictionary of the Bible* (Milwaukee 1965).

Orchard, B., Sutcliffe, E., edd. *A Catholic Commentary on Holy Scripture* (London 1953).

Other Works

Albert, P.S. *Jean Chrysostome considéré comme orateur populaire* (Paris 1858).

Attwater, D. *St. John Chrysostom* (Milwaukee 1939).

Baur, Chrysostom. *S. Jean Chrysostome et ses oeuvres dans l'histoire littéraire* (Louvain 1907).

_____ *John Chrysostom and His Time:* Vol. 1, *Antioch*, Vol. 2, *Constantinople,* trans. Sister M. Gonzaga, R.S.M. (Westminster, Md., 1960-61).

Brightman, F.E. *Liturgies Eastern and Western* (Oxford 1896).

Burger, D.C. *A Complete Bibliography of the Scholarship on the Life and Works of St. John Chrysostom* (Evanston 1964).

Bury, J.B. *History of the Later Roman Empire* (London 1923, repr. New York 1958).

Croiset, A. *Histoire de la littérature grecque* 5 (Paris 1899).

Daniélou, J. *The Bible and the Liturgy* (Notre Dame, Ind., 1956).

Downey, G. *A History of Antioch in Syria* (Princeton 1961).

_____ *Antioch in the Age of Theodosius the Great* (Norman, Okla., 1962).

Festugière, A.J. *Antioche païenne et chrétienne: Libanius, Chrysostome et les moines de Syrie* (Paris 1959).

Graetz, H. *History of the Jews* 2 (Philadelphia 1967).

Guignebert, C. "Les demi-chrétiens et leur place dan l'église antique," *Revue de l'histoire des religions* 88 (1903) 65–102.

Heer, F. *Gottes erste Liebe* (Munich 1967).

Hefele, C.J. *Histoire des conciles* 1.1–2 (Paris 1907).

Jaeger, Werner. *Early Christianity and Greek Paideia* (Cambridge, Mass., 1961).

Kraeling, C.H. "The Jewish Community at Antioch," *Journal of Biblical Literature* 51 (1932) 130–60.

Krauss, S. "Antioche," *Revue des études juives* 45 (1902) 27–49.

Ladner, G.B. "Aspects of Patristic Anti-Judaism," *Viator* 2 (1971) 355–63.

Malkowski, J. "The Element of *akairos* in John Chrysostom's Anti-Jewish Polemic" *Studia Patristica* 12 (1975) 222–231.

Musurillo, H.A. *The Fathers of the Primitive Church* (New York 1966).

Neusner, J. *Aphrahat and Judaism* (Leiden 1971).

Pelikan, J. *The Preaching of Chrysostom* (Philadelphia 1967).

Petit, P. *Libanius et la vie municipale à Antioche au IVe siècle après J.-C.* (Paris 1955).

———— *Les Etudiants de Libanius: un professeur de faculté et ses élèves au bas empire* (Paris 1956).

Quasten, J. *Patrology* (3 vols., Westminster, Md., 1950–60).

Reine, F. *The Eucharistic Doctrine and Liturgy of the Mystagogical Catecheses of Theodore of Mopsuetia* (Studies in Christian Antiquity 2; Washington, D.C., 1942).

Schwartz, E. *Christliche und jüdische Ostertafeln* (Berlin 1905).

Simon, M. "La polémique antijuive de saint Jean Chrysostome et le mouvement judaisant d'Antioche," *Annuaire de l'Institute de philologie et d'histoire orientales et slaves* 4 (1936) 140–53.

———— *Verus Israel* (Paris 1948).

Van de Paverd, Frans. *Zur Geschichte der Messliturgie in Antiocheia und Konstantinopel gegen Ende des vierten Jahrhunderts: Analyse der Quellen bei Johannes Chrysostomus* (Orientalia christiana analecta 187; Rome 1970.)

Wilde, R. *The Treatment of the Jews in the Greek Writers of the First Three Centuries* (Catholic University of America Patristic Studies 81; Washington, D.C., 1949).

Wilken, R.L. *Judaism and the Early Christian Mind* (New Haven and London 1971).

Williams, A.L. *Adversus Judaeos* (Cambridge 1935).

ABBREVIATIONS

ACW	*Ancient Christian Writers.* Westminster, Md.–London 1946–.
ACW 31	Harkins, P.W. *St. John Chrysostom: Baptismal Instructions.* Westminster, Md., 1963.
Adversus Iudaeos	John Chrysostom. *Discourses against Judaizing Christians.*
Baur	Baur, C. *John Chrysostom and His Time:* Vol. 1, *Antioch,* Vol. 2, *Constantinople,* tr. Sister M. Gonzaga, R.S.M. Westminster, Md., 1960–61.
CCHS	Orchard B., Sutcliffe, E., edd. *A Catholic Commentary on Holy Scripture.* London 1953.
Confr.	*St. Joseph Edition of the Holy Bible: Confraternity Version.* New York 1963.
DACL	*Dictionnaire d'archéologie chretiénne et de liturgie.* Paris 1907–53.
DB	McKenzie, J.L. *Dictionary of the Bible.* Milwaukee 1965.
De incomp.	John Chrysostom. *De incomprehensibili Dei natura.* PG 48, 701–812. Homilies 1–5 also SC 28bis.
Demonstration	John Chrysostom. *Demonstration against Jews and Pagans on the Divinity of Christ,* PG 48, 813–38.
Disc.	*Discourse* (any one of the eight discourses *Adversus Iudaeos*).
Downey, *History*	Downey, G. *A History of Antioch in Syria.* Princeton 1961.
DTC	*Dictionnaire de théologie catholique.* Paris 1903–50.
EJ	*Encyclopaedia Judaica.* New York 1972.
FC	*The Fathers of the Church: A New Translation.* New York (later Washington, D.C.) 1947–.
Graetz	Graetz, H. *History of the Jews* 2. Philadelphia 1967.
Guignebert	Guignebert, C. "Les demi-chrétiens et leur place dans l'église antique," *Revue de l' histoire des religions 88* (1903) 65–102.
JB	Jones, A., ed. *The Jerusalem Bible.* Garden City, N.Y. 1966.
JBC	Brown, R.E., Fitzmeyer, J.A., Murphy, R.E., edd. *The Jerome Biblical Commentary.* Englewood Cliffs, N.J., 1968.
Kraeling	Kraeling, C.H. "The Jewish Community at Antioch," *Journal of Biblical Literature* 51 (1932) 130–60.
LXX	Rahlfs, A. *Septuaginta.* 2 vols., Stuttgart 1935.
NAB	Members of the Catholic Biblical Association of America. *The New American Bible.* New York 1970.
NCCHS	Fuller, R.C., Johnston, L., Kearns, C., edd. *A New Catholic Commentary on Holy Scripture.* London 1969.
NCE	*New Catholic Encyclopedia.* New York 1967.
NT	New Testament.

OT	Old Testament.
PG	Migne, J.-P., ed. *Patrologiae cursus completus: Series Graeca.* 161 vols., Paris 1857-66.
Quasten	Quasten, J. *Patrology.* 3 vols., Westminster, Md., 1950-60.
SC	*Sources chrétiennes.* Paris 1942-.
Simon	Simon, M. "La polémique antijuive de saint Jean Chrysotome et le mouvement judaisant d'Antioche," *Annuaire de l'Institut de philologie et d'histoire orientales et slaves* 4 (1936) 140-153.
Williams	Williams, A.L. *Adversus Judaeos.* Cambridge 1935.

DISCOURSES AGAINST JUDAIZING CHRISTIANS

(Logoi kata Ioudaiōn)

Translated by
PAUL W. HARKINS
Xavier University
Cincinnati, Ohio

INTRODUCTION

I

HE PRESENT VOLUME has no need to offer any lengthy biographical notice on St. John Chrysostom. Two previous volumes of this series have already presented information on his life and work,[1] and still further data are easily found in readily available sources.[2] A brief sketch, however, may be in place here, to give some notion of Chrysostom's oratorical talent, his background in scriptural exegesis, his own position in the Church of Antioch, and the place in the Antiochene community of the people who are, in this volume, the targets of his polemics, namely, the Jews and Judaizing Christians.

(2) The date of Chrysostom's birth is uncertain, but A.D. 347 cannot be too far wrong. His widowed mother, Anthusa, saw to it that he received an excellent education in the Greek *paideia*,[3] and he soon became the most famous student of the pagan rhetorician Li-

1 Sister Thomas Aquinas Goggin, S.C.H., *St. John Chrysostom: Homilies on the Gospel of St. John* (FC 33 and 41; New York 1957, 1960). FC is also preparing a volume to contain two apologetic treatises of Chrysostom.

2 For biographies of Chrysostom see D. Attwater, *St. John Chrysostom* (Milwaukee 1939) and C. Baur, O.S.B., *John Chrysostom and His Time*: Vol. 1, *Antioch*, Vol. 2, *Constantinople*, tr. Sister M. Gonzaga, R.S.M. (Westminster, Md., 1960–61). For shorter accounts see P.W. Harkins, "Chrysostom (John)," *Encyclopaedia Britannica* 5 (1961) 665–66; "John Chrysostom, St.," *New Catholic Encyclopedia* 7 (1967) 1041–44. For bibliographies on Chrysostom and his works up to 1959 see J. Quasten, *Patrology* 3 (Westminster, Md., 1960) 424–82.

3 For the absorption of the Hellenic tradition into Christianity and the formation of a Hellenic-Christian culture see Werner Jaeger, *Early Christianity and Greek Paideia* (Cambridge, Mass., 1961).

banius.[4] After his baptism in 370 he saw the shallowness of the
current rhetoric and philosophy; he abandoned the world and devoted himself to the study of Scripture as both monk and hermit. The
imprudence of his austerities broke his health and forced him to
leave the desert and return to Antioch. Here he immediately became
associated with Bishop Meletius and served the Church as lector and
deacon. In 386, Flavian, successor to Meletius, ordained John a
priest, and the aged bishop seems to have entrusted to him the task
of preaching to the Christians of Antioch and instructing them in the
faith.

(3) In this office he welded into one his early rhetorical training
and his years of scriptural study. Chrysostom is not an orator[5] in the
image of Demosthenes and Cicero or even of Libanius, his teacher.
Their speeches showed careful divisions, developments, proofs, and
refutations, all ordered to a single end which gave unity to their
entire argument. We find no such unity in Chrysostom's homilies.
We do see in them divisions and parts, but they are often burdened
with repetitions, or subjects may be dropped before they are adequately discussed. The bonds between part and part are often flimsy,
and an announced topic may suddenly be forgotten in favor of some
other.[6]

(4) Despite their lack of structural unity, despite their frequent
digressions, his sermons do cohere with a spiritual unity because
there is never a word, a period, an argument, or a digression which
swerves from the purpose he has set for himself: he must confirm

---

4 G. Downey, *Antioch in the Age of Theodosius the Great* (Norman, Okla.,
  1962) 85–102, gives an excellent appreciation of Libanius. Exhaustive
  studies are found in A. J. Festugière, *Antioche païenne et chrétienne:
  Libanius, Chrysostome et les moines de Syrie* (Paris 1959) and P. Petit, *Les
  Etudiants de Libanius: Un Professeur de faculté et ses élèves au bas empire*
  (Paris 1956). Some doubt has been raised as to whether or not Chrysostom
  studied under Libanius. Festugière assembles the evidence but comes to no
  conclusion (*op. cit.* 409–10). See also A. H. M. Jones "Chrysostom's
  Parentage and Education," *Harvard Theological Review* 46 (1953) 171–73.
5 For a study of Chrysostom as a pulpit orator see Baur 1.206–30.
6 A. Croiset, *Histoire de la littérature grecque* (Paris 1899) 5.960–68, sees
  nothing deplorable in these failings but finds they add to Chrysostom's
  charm as a speaker.

the faith of his flock and correct their faults so that they may be truly members of one another and of Christ, their Head.

(5) As an exegete,[7] Chrysostom, naturally enough, belonged to the School of Antioch, which gave to the Scriptures their literal, historical, and grammatical sense, as opposed to the allegorical interpretation of the School of Alexandria. [8] This did not mean that the Antiochenes rejected all and any allegorical meaning in Scripture. But for the most part, they restricted it to those passages for which no other explanation seemed possible. Chrysostom did see allegory in the sacred writings, but it generally was of a simple kind which sees a reality foreshadowed in a type.

(6) Chrysostom had learned his exegesis under Diodorus, bishop of Tarsus, with whom he had studied for four years.[9] His grasp of both Testaments was astounding. His works contain no less than 18,000 citations—about 7,000 from the Old Testament and 11,000 from the New.[10] But still more impressive is the reverence and esteem with which he regarded the sacred writings. In them he found the infallible word of God in which the Holy Spirit speaks to men of all ages. That he had no Hebrew hurt him as a scientific exegete, but his insight into God's word and the needs of his flock made his great scriptural commentaries valuable not only for their exegesis but also for their instructions in morality and their exhortations to the life of virtue.

(7) John's importance in the Church of Antioch may have been due in part to the age and ill health of his bishop.[11] Flavian could not have carried on the arduous duties of his pastoral office alone. No doubt he was delighted to have someone as able and eloquent as

---

7 Baur 1.315–29 treats of Chrysostom as an exegete. For a study of Chrysostom as an Antiochene exegete see J. Pelikan, *The Preaching of Chrysostom* (Philadelphia 1967) 12–19.

8 An important study of the two schools has been made by J. Guillet, "Les Exégèses d'Alexandrie et d'Antioche," *Recherches de science religieuse* 34 (1947) 252–302.

9 For the school see V. Ermoni, "Antioche, Ecole théologique d'," DTC 1, pt. 2 (1937) 1435–39. See also Baur 1.89–103.

10 The figures are from Baur 1.316.

11 See Baur 1.390–95 for the relationship between Chrysostom and his bishop.

Chrysostom to whom he could delegate the tasks of preaching and instruction or with whom he could at least share these burdens.

(8) The celebration of the liturgy was usually limited to Sundays, yet during Lent, Eastertide, and the week of Pentecost it was celebrated every day.[12] At other times, too, we have evidence that the Mysteries were celebrated three or four times or even oftener each week.[13] And at each celebration of the Eucharist Chrysostom would preach, as well as at other services. These sermons, for the most part, were most favorably received; in fact he was often interrupted by the applause of the congregation.[14] So successful was he in his pastoral work at Antioch that he would no doubt have become bishop there if he had not been spirited off to become Patriarch of Constantinople, a post of distinction which ultimately led to his death in exile.[15]

(9) Besides his homiletic commentaries on the Scriptures, Chrysostom's pastoral efforts took him into the areas of moral theology and dogma[16] as well as apologetics and polemics. Since this volume is concerned with his work as a polemist against the Judaizing Christians and the Jews, it will be well now to turn to the position in Antioch of these primary and secondary targets of his attack.

(10) It was sometime after A.D. 40 that, in Antioch, the followers of Christ were first called Christians.[17] This name served to set them apart from both pagans and Jews. But it took almost three hundred years more before the Church came into any real ascend-

---

12 *Ibid.* 190, 197.

13 *Disc.* 3.4.3. All references to the eight *Discourses* are by *Discourse* number, section number (taken from the MSS and editions), and paragraph number (which I have introduced in my translation for convenience of cross-reference).

14 See P. Albert, *S. Jean Chrysostome considéré comme orateur populaire* (Paris 1858), esp. Chap. 7; Baur 1.207.

15 The tragedy of Chrysostom is recounted in Baur 2.

16 For Chrysostom as a dogmatist see Baur 1.355–72; as a moralist, *ibid.* 373–89.

17 Acts 11.26. See E.J. Bickerman, "The Name of Christians," *Harvard Theological Review* 42 (1949) 109–24; H.B. Mattingly, "The Origin of the Name Christiani," *Journal of Theological Studies 9* (1958) 26–37; J. Moreau, "Le Nom des chrétiens," *Nouvelle Clio* 1–2 (1949–50) 190–92.

ancy under Constantine, the first Christian Emperor (324–37).[18] Christianity, with its stress on a new city, the heavenly Jerusalem, posed a real threat for the old ways of life. Julian the Apostate (361–63), who saw the Church as a danger to the security of the state and society, did much to favor Judaism and to restore paganism.[19] The Arian Emperor Valens (364–78), one of Julian's successors, persecuted the orthodox Christians, permitted public pagan worship, and protected the Jews.[20]

(11) By 386, the year of Chrysostom's ordination to the priesthood, the devout Emperor Theodosius (379–95) had issued imperial legislation enforcing Christianity as the official religion. But both paganism and Judaism were far from dead. In fact most of the educated classes and civil administrators at Antioch were still pagan.[21] It is impossible to determine the population of Antioch at this time because the evidence is not reliable. In the year 363, when Libanius speaks of a population of 150,000 human beings, he may

---

18 Constantine was baptized shortly before he died but had long before identified himself with the Christian Church and creed. At the time of his death Antioch could look back on some six centuries of pagan influence and culture. It had more pagan temples than churches, more statues to the gods than altars to God when Constantine became emperor. The educational system was still basically the Greek *paideia,* and brilliant pagan teachers such as Libanius and Themistius fought hard to retain it. They saw in paganism not only a way of life for the individual but the salvation of the city, the *polis,* as well. For Libanius see above n. 4. For the attitude of Themistius, especially in the time of Emperor Julian, see three articles by G. Downey, "Education in the Christian Roman Empire: Christian and Pagan Theories under Constantine and his Successors," *Speculum* 32 (1957) 48–61; "Themistius and the Defense of Hellenism in the Fourth Century," *Harvard Theological Review* 50 (1957) 259–74; "The Emperor Julian and the Schools," *Classical Journal* 53 (1957–58) 97–103. For the political and social importance of the educational system in preserving the pagan traditional life of the *polis* also see Downey, "Ancient Education," *ibid.* 52 (1956–57) 337–45.

19 For Julian at Antioch see G. Downey, *History of Antioch in Syria* (Princeton 1961) 380-97; this work is hereinafter referred to as Downey, *History.*

20 For Valens see *ibid.* 399–413 and Festugiere, *Antioche païenne* 271.

21 See P. Petit, *Libanius et la vie municipale à Antioche au IVe siècle après J.-C.* (Paris 1955) 200–203. Petit has an interesting chapter (191-216) on religious life and municipal life.

not have counted slaves, and J. B. Bury seems quite correct in considering this estimate much too small.[22] For example, about the year 390, when Chrysostom says there were 100,000 Christians "here," he may have meant only those who worshipped in the Great Church.[23] What does seem reasonable is Chrysostom's statement that the majority of Antioch's people were Christians.[24] We may guess, then, that pagans and Jews together made up at least one third of the population. In any event both groups numbered in the thousands.

(12) One of the chief problems with which Chrysostom, as a pastor, would have to contend was the fact that the Christians, despite their greater number, were living in a decidedly pluralistic metropolis. Everywhere they encountered the distractions and temptations of the pagan and Jewish world; they were surrounded on all sides by perils calculated to endanger their souls and their hope in the new Jerusalem. They had to associate with, work with, even live in the same homes with pagans and Jews. Their Christian commitment demanded of them not only that they lead a life different from these non-Christians but that they also live the better and more perfect life to which Christ had called all men. Hence it was important to Chrysostom that he convince the weak ones in his flock that Christ is more than mere man, that he is the God who redeemed them and whom they must serve.

(13) However, Chrysostom's problems with pagans and Jews were not altogether the same. First, the pagans do not seem to have proselytized; the Jews did.[25] Second, the Christians found much

---

22 *History of the Later Roman Empire* (London 1923, repr. New York 1958) 1.88 n. 1.
23 Cf. *Hom. In Matthaeum* 85.4 (PG 58,762–63) and the discussion of the whole question by G. Downey, "The Size of the Population of Antioch," *Transactions of the American Philological Association* 89 (1958) 84–91. For the "Great Church" see *Disc.* 4 title and n. 2.
24 *Disc.* 1.4.4.
25 On the important question of Jewish proselytism in the Talmudic era see I. Levi, "Le Proselytisme juif," *Revue des études juives* 50 (1905) 1–9, continued *ibid.* 51 (1906) 1–31. Ed. Schwartz, *Christliche und Jüdische Ostertafeln* (Berlin 1905) 170, also has some penetrating remarks on Jewish proselytism.

about Judaism and synagogue worship that was attractive to them, and Chrysostom spoke of those who followed these attractions as sick with the Judaizing disease.[26] The desire of some Christians to celebrate Easter as a Passover, to regard Lent as a preparation for the Pasch,[27] and to fast on the Jewish fast days[28] caused him the gravest concern. Chrysostom seems to have feared the Jewish influence on Christians more than the pagan.[29]

(14) The Jews had a long history in Antioch and were, perhaps, numbered among the city's earliest inhabitants.[30] They had had their ups and downs. They had been subjected to a third captivity under Antiochus Epiphanes (175–163 B.C.),[31] but seem to have risen to prominence by the days of Herod the Great (37–4 B.C.) who was high in the favor of the Roman authorities.[32] This rise to prominence must have included a concomitant economic prosperity, as may be judged by the costly gifts sent to the Temple of Jerusalem by the Jewish Antiochenes of that day.[33]

(15) But their prominence and prosperity did not last long. They reacted violently to Emperor Caligula's decree that a statue to him

---

26 See, e.g., *Disc.* 1.1.5 and 1.4.4; see also *Disc.* 2.3.3, where he calls it the Galatians' disease.
27 *Disc.* 3.4.3.
28 *Disc.* 1.4.7.
29 R.L. Wilken, *Judaism and the Early Christian Mind* (New Haven and London 1971) 19, states that the purpose of the *Discourses* was to warn of the dangers of association with the Jews; G.B. Ladner, "Aspects of Patristic Anti-Judaism," *Viator* 2 (1971) 358, suggests that when Chrysostom does attack the Jews, the immediate cause was "none other but the very real attraction that the synagogues of the Jews of Antioch, with their feasts and fasts and other rites, had for the Christians of that city."
30 See the excellent articles by C.H. Kraeling, "The Jewish Community at Antioch," *Journal of Biblical Literature* 51 (1932) 130–160 (hereinafter referred to as Kraeling); S. Krauss, "Antioch," *Jewish Encyclopedia* 1 (1901) 632–33; "Antioche," *Revue des études juives* 45 (1902) 27–49.
31 Chrysostom speaks of this in *Disc.* 5.6.7 and 6.2.1.
32 See Kraeling 147.
33 Herod the Great had begun to build a new temple at Jerusalem in 19 B.C. Although the outer structure was finished in 10 B.C., the interior decorations were not completed until A.D. 64, six years before its destruction under Titus. Josephus, *Jewish War* 7.45 (trans. H. St. J. Thackeray, Loeb Libr. *Josephus* 3.519), in a flash-back review of the history of the Jews of Antioch, says that the Antiochene Jews' "richly designed and costly offer-

be erected in the Temple of Jerusalem. This reaction seems to have started at Antioch, where the decree had been transmitted to Petronius, governor of Syria (A.D. 40). Even though Claudius, Caligula's successor, countermanded the decree and restored a comparative tranquillity, the rebellion of the Palestinian Jews against Rome[34] roused the anger of almost all non-Jewish Syrians against their Jewish countrymen.[35]

(16) After the Jewish disaster under Vespasian and Titus (A.D. 70), which entailed the destruction of Jerusalem and its temple, and that under Hadrian (117–38), who rebuilt Jerusalem as a pagan city, Aelia Capitolina, but forbade the Jews to enter it, little is known of the Jewish community at Antioch for almost two centuries. The Emperor Constantine (324–37) both protected and restricted the Jews. His edict of toleration gave the same privileges to pagans, Christians, and Jews; he also protected the Jews from their former coreligionists who had been converted to Christianity. But he later reenacted Hadrian's law which closed Jerusalem to the Jews and restricted them in other ways.[36] Constantius II (337–61)

---

ings formed a splendid ornament to the temple," but Josephus gives no exact date. Kraeling *(ibid.)* mentions these votive offerings just before he speaks of the collection made by the Christians at Antioch "for the benefit of their brethren in Jerusalem at the time of the famine under Claudius." See Acts 11.27–30 and NAB note *ad loc.,* which dates this famine in 46–48. The sending of the temple offerings from Antioch would most probably have preceded the famine.

34 The revolt started in A.D. 66 at Jerusalem, which was crowded with Passover pilgrims. A combined force of Zealots (under Eleazar) and Sicarii (under Menahem) drove the Roman troops from Jerusalem. See H. Graetz, *History of the Jews* (Philadelphia 1967) 2.251–61 (hereinafter referred to as Graetz). Reprisals resulted in massacres of the Jews by the Romans at Caesarea and Jerusalem, which touched off a full-scale national revolt of the Judaeans, who forced the Roman governor of Syria, Cestius Gallus, and his troops to withdraw from the Holy City. See Downey, *History* 199. Ultimately Roman legions under Titus razed Jerusalem and destroyed the temple.

35 Only at Antioch, Sidon, and Apamea were the Jewish inhabitants spared according to Josephus, *Jewish War* 2.479 (trans. Thackeray, Loeb Libr. *Josephus* 2.509), but even in these cities there was tension and bitterness. See Kraeling 150.

36 For a strongly pro-Jewish account see Graetz 2.291–310 (on the fall of Jerusalem); 393–420 (on Hadrian); 561–64 (on Constantine). Chrysostom

continued restrictions on the Jews, prohibiting their worship, burdening them with taxes, and punishing all Christians who joined the communities of the Jews.[37]

(17) Under Julian (361–63) there was a revival of Jewish national ambition connected with the attempt to rebuild the temple. The Jews of Antioch were certainly involved in this revival. In fact, the Jews fitted well into Julian's plans to restore paganism. When he sought the aid of non-Christian groups in Antioch, the Jews came forward with the proposal that they would resume their sacrificial observances if the Emperor would give his approval to the restoration of the temple at Jerusalem. In fact, Chrysostom is at pains to recall to them both the enterprise and its failure.[38]

(18) Jovian (363–64) and Valens (364–78), Julian's successors, both showed toleration to the Jews. In his short reign of less than eight months Jovian allowed his subjects to declare allegiance to any religion they chose. Valens, an Arian, persecuted the orthodox Christians with great severity but protected the Jews and bestowed honors upon them.[39] Theodosius I (379–95), successor to Valens, restored some measure of peace to the Church in Antioch by bringing to an end the Arian disorders.[40] Although harsh to the heretics, he consistently protected the Jews and confirmed by law the rights of the Jewish Primates and Patriarchs and prevented the secular arm from interfering with the domestic affairs of the Jews.[41] And it was during the reign of Theodosius that Chrysostom was

---

mentions an attempted revolt against Constantine when the seditionists were mutilated by having their ears cut off and being paraded around like runaway slaves (Disc. 5.11.3). He also says (ibid.) that the incident was well known to old men among the Antiochenes, but strangely Graetz makes no mention of such an incident. Although Chrysostom speaks of the temple's destruction and various attempts to rebuild it in Demonstration, chapters 16 and 17 (PG 48.834–38), he neither mentions Constantine specifically nor does he allude to the mutilation of the rebel Jews.

37 See Graetz 2.571–72.
38 Disc. 5.11.4–9. Cf. also Kraeling 158 and M. Adler, "The Emperor Julian and the Jews," Jewish Quarterly Review 5 (1893) 591–651.
39 Cf. Graetz 2.602–603; Downey, History 398–99, 410–13.
40 See Downey, History 414–19.
41 See Graetz 2.612–13. One of these rights was to excommunicate members of their community.

ordained a priest at Antioch and took up pastoral duties which involved him in both apologetics and polemics with both pagans and Jews.

(19) It must be kept in mind that the decree *Cunctos populos* of February 27, 380, established orthodox Christianity as the religion of the Empire.[42] But this did not make all the imperial subjects ardent Christians. There were many demi-Christians, who were really demi-pagans.[43] The same political reason that brought many pagans into the Church, it would seem, brought many Jews into the fold. But a goodly number of these must have been demi-Christians, in the sense that they were demi-Jews.[44]

(20) The perils to the faith of Judaizing demi-Christians must have been particularly dangerous throughout Syria as well as in Antioch during the latter portion of the 4th century. Ephraem of Syria, according to Krauss, surpassed all the Church Fathers "in passionate hatred of the Jews," for which, he says, it is difficult to find an adequate reason, "especially as Ephraem hardly ever came into contact with the Jews, and therefore could never have been insulted by them." He then attributes Ephraem's animosity to the "marvellous power of resistance shown by the old creed."[45] Perhaps this resistance was being shown by Judaizing Christians, and they were the butt of Ephraem's attacks.

(21) Chrysostom, too, had to face perils from Judaizing Christians in Antioch. The movement there was very distinctly marked with popular syncretism and strongly colored by superstition and preoccupation with practices of magic. These were

---

42 See T. Mommsen and P.M. Meyer, edd., *Theodosiani libri XVI* (Berlin 1905) 16.1.2.
43 There is an important study on this question by C. Guignebert, "Les Demi-chrétiens et leur place dans l'église antique," *Revue de l'histoire des religions* 88 (1923) 65–102; hereinafter referred to as "Les Demi–chrétiens."
44 See M. Simon, "La Polémique antijuive de saint Jean Chrysostome et le mouvement judaisant d'Antioche," *Annuaire de l'Institut de philologie et d'histoire orientales et slaves* 4 (1936) 140–53, especially 143; hereinafter referred to as Simon.
45 See S. Krauss, "The Jews in the Works of the Church Fathers," *Jewish Quarterly Review* 6 (1894) 88–92.

characteristic of the fourth century, when the triumph of the Church led to wholesale conversions of people who would be Christians only on the surface.[46]

II

It was in such circumstances that Chrysostom delivered his eight discourses *Adversus Iudaeos,*[47] which are clearly polemical in character. In them Chrysostom often speaks with the bitterness of John the Baptist calling the Pharisees and Sadducees a brood of vipers; there is little of the gentle Christ weeping over Jerusalem.[48] If we look for eloquence in these homilies, we shall find it; if we look for a zeal which sears his adversaries, we shall not be

---

46 See Simon 143.
47 This is the Latin translation of the title given to the homilies in PG 48.843. The Benedictine editor, Montfaucon, gives a footnote (reprinted *ibid.*) which states that six MSS and [Henry] Savile [in his edition (1612) of Chrysostom] have at the head of this homily: "A discourse against the Jews; but it was delivered against those who were Judaizing and keeping the fasts with them [i.e., the Jews]." This note is not altogether accurate because Savile, for *Hom.* 27 of Vol. 6 (which is *Disc.* I among the *Adversus Iudaeos* in PG and in this translation), gives (p. 366) the title: "Chrysostom's Discourse Against Those Who Are Judaizing and Observing Their Fasts." In Vol. 8 (col. 798) Savile states that he has emended Hoeschel's edition of this homily with the help of two Oxford MSS, one from Corpus Christi College and the other from New College; he must have gotten his title from any or all of these sources. Savile gives all eight of the homilies *Adversus Iudaeos* (Vol. 6.312–88) but in the order IV–VIII (which are entitled *Kata Ioudaiōn,* i.e., *Adversus Iudaeos),* I (with the title given above), III and II (with the titles affixed to them in our translation). Because of the titles in both some MSS and editions and because of the arguments which will be set forth in this *Introduction,* we feel justified in calling this work *Against Judaizing Christians* rather than giving it the less irenic and somewhat misleading traditional title *Against the Jews.* See above, Preface and *Disc.* 1.1.4, where Chrysostom says: "Another very serious illness [Judaizing] calls for any cure my words can bring, an illness which has become implanted in the body of the Church. We must root this ailment out and then take thought for matters outside; we must cure those who are our own and then be concerned for others who are strangers." We shall often refer to the *Discourses* under the traditional title *Adversus Iudaeos* for brevity's sake.

48 Mt. 3.7; cf. Lk 13.34

disappointed. However, as Williams points out, neither the eloquence nor the zeal are necessarily tempered by any deep and thorough knowledge of the true position of Judaism in fourth-century Antioch.[49] Chrysostom knows the Jews and their synagogues rather as a risk to the faith of his Christian community, and he meets their threat with every weapon in his rhetorical arsenal.

(2) In fact, the whole Judaeo-Christian problem is a thorny one. Certainly in its earliest days there existed in the Church a spirit which saw the New Covenant as a fulfillment rather than an abrogation of the Old. Prior to the "Council of Jerusalem" of A.D. 55,[50] entrance into the earliest Christian community required the Old Law ritual of circumcision as well as the bath of regeneration through baptism. The first Christians at Jerusalem attended the temple worship while also participating in the Eucharistic sacrifice. The infant Church saw the synagogue with its prayer and explication of the Law and the prophets as necessary even if this had to be supplemented by hearing Christ's kerygma from the lips of his Apostles.[51]

(3) This, of course, presented problems if Christ's Church was to grow and preach his gospel to every creature. But the Holy Spirit showed clearly that Christ's Church must be truly catholic. Witness Stephen's discourse to the Sanhedrin before his martyrdom,[52] Peter's triple vision and the baptism of Cornelius,[53] the Council of Jerusalem,[54] and Paul's three missionary journeys to the Gentiles.[55] Here we have not only a demonstration of the growth of the Church in numbers but also of its increasing awareness of its catholic character.

---

49 A. L. Williams, *Adversus Judaeos* (Cambridge 1935) 132. (Hereinafter referred to as Williams).
50 Cf. Acts 15 and Gal. 2, with NAB notes *ad loc.*
51 See H.A. Musurillo, S.J., *The Fathers of the Primitive Church* (New York 1966) 12–17, 32–34.
52 Acts 7.
53 Acts 10.9–23; *ibid.* 44–48.
54 Acts 15.1–35.
55 Acts 13.1–14. 27; 15.36–18.22; 18.23–21.26.

(4) Although the majority of proselytes came from among pagans, there was never any doubt that the new dispensation had its roots in the covenant of the Old Law and there was a constant effort to convert the Jews to Christianity. This effort, as it has come down to us in literature, is to be seen in the new literary genre of the apology, which so often featured a dialogue between a Christian and a Jew. These dialogues showed the New Covenant as either a fulfillment or abrogation of the Old, and almost invariably left the Jewish disputant embarrassed and frequently unconvinced.

(5) The treatment of the Jews in the Greek Christian writers of the first three centuries has been discussed often and adequately.[56] The Christian authors recognized that the Jews played a chosen part in God's plan of salvation history. But just as they had often rejected God in the Old Testament, so, too, they had rejected his Anointed One. Not only did they reject Christ but they persecuted him and put him to death. They also persecuted his Church and calumniated his followers. The apologists maintained that the Jews' rejection of Christ led to their rejection by God, and the promises God made to them have now passed to all those who are willing to receive Christ.

(6) Still the Jews can be saved. Although the apologists of the first three centuries are often hostile to the Jews, it would not be fair to say that these Christian writers hated them. Judaism is opposed as a religion which has been supplanted by Christianity and as an institution responsible for Christ's crucifixion. But now that the Cross has triumphed, the Jews should see that there is a new Jerusalem in Christianity and be converted to it. They had played their part in God's redemptive plan and must no longer look for a temporal messiah who would restore the old Jewish commonwealth and way of life.[57]

(7) Much of this is also true of fourth-century authors, including

---

56 For an objective and careful review of this early Christian literature from St. Clement of Rome through Origen and his successors see R. Wilde, *The Treatment of the Jews in the Greek Writers of the First Three Centuries* (Catholic University of America Patristic Studies 81; Washington 1949). See also Wilken, *op. cit.* 9–18.

57 Cf. Wilde, *op. cit.* 229–32.

Chrysostom, but their hostility to Jews and Judaizers often descended from theological opposition to what is undisguised or poorly disguised anti-Semitism. There is no denying this fact; what is needed is some explanation for this opposition and hostility where it does go beyond the bounds of Christian charity.[58] A partial explanation for Chrysostom's bitterness may be found by drawing an analogy between the position of many pagans in the early Church and that of the Jews in fourth-century Antioch. C. Guignebert, in an illuminating article,[59] points out that for the first five centuries many converts from paganism to Christianity lived a sort of double religious life, which made them what he calls demi-Christians. Among the reasons he gives for this situation are syncretism, poor instruction in the faith, and the scandal of Christian converts who lapsed back into either partial or total paganism.

(8) As mentioned above (Introduction I 19), Theodosius I, by his decree of February 27, 380, established Christian orthodoxy as the official religion of the Empire. Naturally, this decree, as had the conversion of Constantine, brought many converts from both paganism and Judaism into the Church, which at last seemed free from official persecution. All too often the converts were politically motivated to accept the Christian faith rather than committed to its way of life. Although Theodosius' edict was renewed in six rescripts of increasing severity, many of these converts risked the ill will of the imperial authorities and the severity of the law to reject the Church more or less completely and, under one form or another, to take up again their ancestral religious practices.[60] Even after its triumph, therefore, the Church had borderline members whose Christian commitment was more or less solid but hardly exclusive. They kept their attachment to paganism or Judaism and were loath to abandon all their former practices.[61]

---

58 Wilken, op. cit. 19, calls Chrysostom's homilies "the most vituperative and vindictive attack on the Jews from Christian antiquity." Chrysostom's purpose, he says, was to warn Christians that association with Jews was dangerous.

59 "Les Demi-chrétiens" 65–102.

60 Cf. ibid. 72–74.

61 Chrysostom himself warned the Christians and demi-Christians of Antioch

(9) When Chrysostom puts pagans and Jews on a par,[62] he seems to recognize the analogy between the demi-Christians who held on to pagan practices and the demi-Christians who held fast to Jewish ways and ritual. Both constitute dangers to the faith of his flock, but the dangers from the Jews were more subtle,[63] and, hence, Chrysostom's hostility against the Jews is greater. Therefore, in the eight *Discourses*, he frequently and accusingly addresses the Jews, and his uncomplimentary comments smack of an anti-Semitic sentiment. But in this he is not entirely removed from the literary genre developed by many apologists who preceded and followed him in attacking Jewish claims to be God's chosen ones.[64]

(10) If we look to the basis of their argumentation and the exegetical method of interpreting the Old Testament, Chrysostom's series of sermons belongs to the tradition of polemic literature which

---

to avoid the suburban sanctuary at Daphne, the cave called Matrona's, and the place in Cilicia called sacred to Cronos. Cf. Guignebert 88, and see below *Disc.* 1.6.2–3. For the place in Cilicia sacred to Cronos see *In Epistolam ad Titum* 3.3 (PG 62.679).

62 *Disc.* 1.6.4–7. The same point is made by Simon 143.

63 *Disc.* 1.6.4–5. Wilken, *op. cit.* 19, says: "Apparently Christians found Jewish rites and practices very attractive and had begun to observe some Jewish customs in their homes or in the synagogue." See also Ladner, *op. cit.* 359–60, who suggests that Christian anti–Semitism had historical antecedents as well as socioeconomic, anthropological, and psychological preconditions. He rejects the explanation that Christian anti–Semitism is an externalization of the need for a scapegoat or of an oedipal wish to kill one's own father in the guise of the Jewish Father God and of every Jew. However, he knows of no one reason which will serve as a general explanation but thinks that assertion of identity may have some relevance. Throughout history, he says, groups of men [such as Christians] have found it difficult to gain and maintain their own identity merely by loving those within the group without hating those on the outside.

64 Ladner, *op. cit.* 358–59, finds Chrysostom's anti–Jewish polemical method very repellent when he applies the vituperations of Israel by its prophets to the Jews of his own time. It is repellent to current tastes and, furthermore, as good argumentation, it is of dubious efficacy unless Chrysostom knew that the Antiochene Jews of his time were acting much as their ancestors did in Jeremiah's day. To equate the synagogue with the theater and the bordello seems to be a rhetorical *tour de force* which aims more at proving that all three offer grave risks to the Christian rather than, as Ladner says, that all Jews are impure animals and demons.

begins, perhaps before A.D. 100, with the *Epistle of Barnabas*[65] and is continued in the second century by Justin Martyr in his *Dialogue with Trypho*.[66] The chief Latin polemics of the third century are in the same tradition: Tertullian's *Adversus Iudaeos*[67] and Cyprian's *Ad Quirinum testimonia*.[68] In the fourth century, but earlier than Chrysostom, we have two Greek anti-Semitic dialogues: one between Timothy and Aquila and another between Athanasius and Zacchaeus.[69] About the same time, in the Syriac-speaking Church, we have an important collection of twenty-three addresses by Aphrahat; about twelve of these constitute in whole or part a critique of Judaism and show many parallels with Chrysostom's homilies.[70]

---

65 For English translations see F.X. Glimm, *The Apostolic Fathers* (FC 1; New York 1947) 191–222 and J.A. Kleist, S.J., *The Didache, the Epistle of Barnabas*, etc. (ACW 6; Westminster, Md., 1948). The Epistle is discussed by Quasten 1.85–92; and by Wilde, *op. cit.* 87–91; and by Williams 14–27. Williams also gives a detailed examination of the date in "The Date of the Epistle of Barnabas," *Journal of Theological Studies* 34 (1933) 337–46.

66 For English translations see A.L. Williams, *Justin Martyr, The Dialogue with Trypho* (Society for Promoting Christian Knowledge; London 1931) and T.B. Falls, *St. Justin Martyr* (FC 6; New York 1948) 147–366. The *Dialogue* is discussed in Quasten 1.202–4; at greater length, by R. Wilde, *op. cit.* 105–30; and by Williams 31–42. For the attitude toward the Jews of other Christian authors prior to Justin see Wilde, *op. cit.* 78–97 and Williams 3–30.

67 For an English translation see S. Thelwall in the *Ante-Nicene Library* 18 (Edinburgh 1870) 201–58. The treatise is discussed in Quasten 2.268–69 and in Williams 43–52.

68 For an English translation see R. E. Wallis in the *Ante-Nicene Library* 13 (Edinburgh 1869) 78–198; *Ante–Nicene Fathers* 5 (Buffalo 1886) 507-57. The work is discussed in Quasten 2.362–63 and in Williams 56–64.

69 Williams (117 n. 1) mentions an English translation of the *Dialogue of Athanasius and Zacchaeus* made from a fifth–century Armenian version by F.C. Conybeare in *The Expositer* 5 (1897) 300–20 and 443–46. The Greek texts of both dialogues have been published by Conybeare in *The Dialogues of Athanasius and Zacchaeus and of Timothy and Aquila* (Anecdota Oxoniensia, Classical Series 8; Oxford 1898). Williams discusses both dialogues: *Timothy and Aquila* (which he dates about A.D. 200) 67–78, and *Athanasius and Zacchaeus* (which he dates about A.D. 325) 117–23.

70 Williams discusses Aphrahat's homilies (which he dates about A.D. 345)

(11) Chrysostom's discourses, however, have a special interest and importance for the history of the anti-Semitic question because of their undoubted novelty and originality. Although he may be using merely rhetorical devices in his direct attacks against Judaism, its beliefs, and practices, his argumentation could at times be called offensive. Here he goes far beyond any earlier Christian polemicist. Also, his predecessors for the most part wrote in a conventional form; Chrysostom's sermons[71] were actually delivered before publication and aimed at a definite adversary. Earlier authors had opposed Judaism in itself; Chrysostom assails the Jews of Antioch, or more particularly the demi-Christians who were jeopardizing their faith by their participation in Jewish practices.

(12) These Judaizing Christians must be reclaimed for the Church; others who were weak and on the brink must be frightened to keep them from falling. Hence, Chrysostom's language must be strong in his instruction of the sick and his denunciation of their disease. But what must not be forgotten is that his many direct addresses to and accusations of the Jews must have been chiefly rhetorical. After all, the eight sermons were preached in a Christian church and to a Christian congregation; one can hardly expect that many, if any, unconverted Jews were present to hear themselves attacked.[72]

(13) Even though these discourses are sermons and no Jews may have been present in the congregation, they have clearly played an

---

95–102. See also J. Neusner, *Aphrahat and Judaism* (Leiden 1971), who translates passages from the addresses which are relevant to Judaism and the Jews; he also adds three studies dealing with Aphrahat and Judaism, the rabbis, and the patristic critique of Judaism. Aphrahat is of special interest because he had a much better knowledge of Judaism than Chrysostom did. The similarities between Aphrahat and Chrysostom seem to have come from a common tradition rather than from direct influence since Chrysostom's knowledge of Syriac may have been limited.

71 Before Chrysostom only Aphrahat seems to have used the sermon form although the content of his discourses belongs more to the genre of the demonstration than the homily.

72 Wilken, *op. cit.* 18–19, maintains correctly that the mere fact that Christians wrote books in answer to the Jews does not prove that these works were necessarily aimed directly at the Jews. In some cases (and Chrysostom would be one) the audience is clearly Christian, and the author is trying to

important part in the history of the whole question of anti-Semitism. Once they were transcribed, published, and added to the stream of patristic literature, they not only marked an important moment in the Church's polemics against Judaism but they seem to have exercised an influence which went far beyond any specific occasion or local situation.

(14) In fact, as recently as 1967, Friedrich Heer[73] accused Chrysostom, along with Jerome and Augustine, of having presented a picture of the Jews which had its effect on neurotic anti-Semites in every historical crisis affecting the Jews for more than the next 1500 years. He further assigns to Chrysostom's eight *Discourses* an epoch-making significance because in them are found all the weapons used against the Jews down to the present day. They show the Jews as sensual, slippery, voluptuous, avaricious, and possessed by demons; the Jews are drunkards, harlots, and breakers of the Law; they are the people who murdered the prophets, Christ, and God.[74] It is true that Chrysostom does speak of the Jews in these coarse terms, but surely Heer has taken Chrysostom's accusations out of the context of sermons preached to a Christian congregation in a Christian church.[75]

(15) Whatever the effect of the sermons on the subsequent history of anti-Semitism, it is clear that the Judaizing movement in Antioch was a menace to orthodox Christianity. This is proved not only by the number and length of Chrysostom's homilies but especially by their tone, which unquestionably is often impetuous and sometimes even coarse.[76] There seems to be no doubt that they

give his hearers the information and arguments necessary to engage in discussion with the Jews.

73 Friedrich Heer, *Gottes erste Liebe* (Munich 1967) 63.

74 *Ibid.* 24 and below n. 76. Although Wilken's *Judaism and the Early Christian Mind* is basically a study of Cyril of Alexandria's exegesis and theology, he states (p. 1) that the bitterness of Cyril's attack against the Jews is rivalled only by St. John Chrysostom, "the notorious Jew-hater."

75 Chrysostom surely could not have intended the tragic future effects alleged by Heer. He was bent only on curing and reclaiming the Judaizing members of his own congregation.

76 E.g., in *Disc.* 1.3.1 he calls the synagogue a brothel, a theater, a den of

represent an energetic defense reaction or a vigorous counterattack which springs from an extremely disquieting local situation.

(16) It will be well, therefore, to state the symptoms and then the causes of this Judaizing movement at Antioch. Chrysostom himself gives us at least the essential symptoms;[77] since he says nothing of the causes, any discussion of these will have to rest on conjectures based on what is known about the history of Antioch and the Church there at the end of the fourth century.

(17) The Judaizing movement had become a strongly divisive force in the Church at Antioch.[78] Chrysostom speaks of the demi-Christians who participated in it as "sick with the Judaizing disease,"[79] or "sick with the Galatians' disease."[80] As far as can be reckoned from Chrysostom's words, the Judaizing sickness raged especially among women and slaves, who should be kept at home and away from the synagogues.[81]

(18) The synagogues were certainly centers for the celebration of the Jewish feasts, and participation by the demi-Christians was one of the principal symptoms of the Judaizing disease. Hence it is that Chrysostom speaks so harshly of the synagogue and says that it is no more than a theater into which the Jews drag effeminates, harlots,

---

robbers, and a lodging for wild beasts; in *Disc.* 1.4.1 he compares the Jews to pigs and goats; they are bent only on filling their bellies, getting drunk, and chasing after dancers and charioteers.

77 Much that I have to say on the symptoms and causes stems from the excellent study by M. Simon, "La Polémique antijuive" 140–53. See the same author's *Verus Israel* (Paris 1964) 256–63.

78 E.g., in *Disc.* 8.4.5–7 Chrysostom warns his congregation against broadcasting rumors about the number of Judaizing Christians, even if this number be large.

79 See *Disc.* 1.1.5 and 1.4.4.

80 See *Disc.* 2.2.3 and Gal 5.3. The point is that anyone who Judaizes by having himself circumcised must embrace the Jewish Law in its entirety.

81 See *Disc.* 2.3.4–6 and 4.7.3. Jerome also speaks of Judaizers among the women (*In Matt.* 23.5 [PL 26.175]) and ignorant and common people. Cf. *Epistola* 121 (*Ad Algasiam* 10) in J. Labourt, *Saint Jérôme: Lettres 7* (Paris 1961) 54. Josephus, the Jewish historian, also says that at Damascus all the women were Judaizers: *Jewish War* 2.20 (trans. Thackeray, Loeb Libr. *Josephus* 2.539).

and actors.[82] The chief feasts he mentions are the New Year, the Day of Atonement, and the Feast of Tabernacles.[83] He is just as harsh in what he has to say about the fasting of the Jews.[84]

(19) Of course, converts from Judaism might not have seen the same dangers which Chrysostom did if they were to continue to show veneration and respect for the rabbis, the solemnities, and the rituals of their old religion, even when this respect was tainted with superstition and magic. So it was that a man was dragging a woman into a synagogue to swear an oath because it was commonly believed that any oath sworn before the Jewish tribunal in a synagogue was more solemn and binding.[85] Chrysostom personally intervened and

---

82 See *Disc.* 1.2.7; 1.3.1; 4.7.3. Perhaps we should see in this identification of the synagogue with the theater an allusion to the fact that, under the Emperor Titus, a theater was built in the suburb of Daphne on the foundation of a synagogue which had been destroyed to make room for it. Kraeling (140–41) doubts that a synagogue was destroyed in order to build the theater of Titus (whom he mistakenly calls Tiberius), but see Downey, *History* 206–7.

83 All three of these feasts were celebrated in the seventh month, Tishri (Sept.–Oct.). The Jewish New Year falls on the first of Tishri and was characterized by trumpet blasts (cf. Lv 23.23–75). The Day of Atonement was on the tenth day of Tishri and involved a fast, the only one prescribed in Israelite cultic law (cf. Lv 16.29–34; 23.26–32). The feast of Tabernacles came on the fifteenth of Tishri and lasted a week during which the Jews danced and "made merry before the Lord" (cf. Lv 23.33–43); horns and trumpets were blown at all the great moments of the feast. For the New Year see DB 613–15; for Atonement, *ibid.* 65–70; for Tabernacles, *ibid.* 863–64.

84 Cf. *Disc.* 1.2.6–7. For a classification of Jewish fasts see the article "Fasting and Fast Days" in EJ 6.1195. Chrysostom seems, in most cases, to be talking about the fasting between the New Year (Rosh Ha-Shanah or Feast of Trumpets) and the Day of Atonement (Yom Kippur), a period known as the Ten Days of Penitence. For the latter see the article "Ten Days of Penitence," EJ 15.1001. For the laws and customs of Rosh Ha-Shanah see L. Jacobs, "Rosh Ha-Shanah," EJ 14.309–10. In the *Didache* (8.1) we read: "But do not let your fasts be with the hypocrites. They fast on Monday and Thursday; but you shall fast on Wednesday and Friday." The "hypocrites" would be the Pharisees, the Jews in general, or Jewish Christians who kept up the customs of the Pharisees. For the Jewish practice of fasting see H. Strack–P. Billerbeck, *Kommentar zum Neuen Testament aus Talmud und Midrasch* 2 (Munich 1924) 241–44 and 4.1 (Munich 1928) 77–114.

85 Cf. *Disc.* 1.3.4–5.

prevented the man from forcing the woman to swear an oath either in the synagogue or in any other place.[86]

(20) Chrysostom saw another symptom of the Judaizing disease in the eagerness of many demi-Christians to run to the synagogues and rabbis in search of cures.[87] The rabbis did enjoy a great reputation as physicians, and their therapeutic methods, at least in some instances, must have exercised a great fascination over the people they treated. But this fascination arose from the close association in the popular mind between physicians, magicians, and sorcerers. According to Chrysostom, Jewish therapy often depended on the use of incantations and amulets.[88]

(21) Of course the synagogues of Antioch may well have attracted the Christians or demi-Christians for reasons less demonic than those emphasized by Chrysostom. Perhaps they found the tribunal which sat in the synagogue more solemn and impartial than civil courts, just as they considered oaths sworn there more sacred and binding than those taken elsewhere. The Jewish rabbis did possess at least the reputation for curing diseases and expelling demons from the possessed. The synagogue worship may well have been more attractive than the lengthy services in the Christian churches. Perhaps the Christian homilies were so long that many were inclined to leave the churches after the readings of the Scriptures.[89]

(22) Indeed, demi-Christians of Antioch may have found genuine inspiration in the Jewish services, where they heard many of the

---

86 Cf. *ibid.* For Chrysostom's strong attitude against all oaths and swearing see ACW 31.143–49, 297–300.

87 Chrysostom says that to seek for such cures is to seek for help from demons; it would be better to remain in ill health or to die. *Disc.* 1.7.5–10 and 8.5.6 and 8.7.9.

88 *Disc.* 8.7.1–5. See Simon 143, who states that both Augustine and Jerome denounce these and analogous practices. The Jewish scholar S. Krauss, in his article "Antioche" in *Revue des études juives* 45 (1902) 44, states that the Jews in Antioch spread all sorts of superstitions and magic among the Christians.

89 As early as the year 341 the Synod of Antioch passed a decree which excommunicated those who attended the Christian services to hear the Scriptures but did not join in the prayers and dishonored the Eucharist. Cf. C.J. Hefele, *Histoire des conciles* 1.2 (Paris 1907) 715.

same Old Testament passages which were read in the Christian
churches. Furthermore, there must have been great attraction in the
solemnity of the great Jewish festivals which were celebrated with
various musical instruments and incense. Many saw Easter as a Passover and regarded Lent as a preparation for both the Jewish Pasch and
the feast of the unleavened bread.[90] Furthermore, they considered
the differences between Christians and Jews as slight and their disa-
greements as trivial.[91] As Kraeling points out, there was no sudden
demoralization of local Christianity; these practices represent a survi-
val of a tendency which pervaded the development of Christianity at
Antioch from the pre-Constantinian period.[92]

(23) This milieu may well lead to a sound conjecture on what was
the primary cause of the Judaizing movement at Antioch. There had
been a Jewish community in the city since the reign of Seleucus I in
the third century B.C.[93] Certainly this community, from its beginning, had been one of the most important centers of the diaspora.
Josephus reports that in A.D. 69 it was organized under an *archōn* or
chief executive officer, who probably worked with a council of elders.[94] The religious organization, as late as Chrysostom's day, was
subject to a patriarch[95] and had at least two important synagogues,

---

90 Cf. *Disc.* 3.3.6, where Chrysostom seems to refer to the Council of Nicaea,
   which, in the year 325, passed a decree on the date of Easter; see Hefele,
   op. cit. 1.1 450–77. The Council of Antioch made the same problem the
   subject of special legislation; see *ibid.* 1.2 714. Chrysostom also shows
   that conflict between the Christian and Jewish calendars can lead to the
   absurdity of Judaizers fasting during the whole week following Easter. See
   Disc. 3.5.7–8.
91 Cf. *Disc.* 4.3.6.
92 Kraeling 157. Ladner, *op. cit.* 358, makes the same point as does M. Simon
   in *Verus Israel* 379-80 and Krauss in "Antioche," *Revue des études juives*
   45 (1902) 43–44.
93 For the foundation of the city and the reign of Seleucus I see Downey,
   History 54–86. Downey points out that the Jews doubtless lived in their
   own community, with their own religious and political chiefs. Since full
   citizenship would have involved worship of the city gods, the Jews would
   be excluded from full citizenship; they may have enjoyed a form of poten-
   tial citizenship, i.e., a Jew could become a citizen on demand (*ibid.* 80).
94 *The Jewish War* 7.47 (trans. Thackeray, Loeb Libr. *Josephus* 3.519). See
   also Kraeling 137–39.
95 Cf. *Disc.* 6.5.6.

one within the city itself (in the quarter called Kerateion) and the other in the suburb of Daphne.[96] All the *Discourses* suggest that the Jewish community must have been numerous, influential, and active. It was not satisfied with gathering in the Judaizing Christians; their rabbis and congregations both solicited and supported this Judaizing custom.[97]

(24) The point would be that, despite the destruction of Jerusalem and even after the triumph of the Church, neither Jewish nationalism nor proselytism had been quenched. Antioch remained an important center for Judaism and posed a real peril for the Christian congregation. This leads to another conjecture on what may be another cause for the Judaizing movement—a cause which arises largely from the Church itself.

(25) Certainly, even after the triumph of the Church, throughout the Christian East and in Antioch in particular, the religious situation was very troubled and confused. Brief as it had been, the reign of Julian the Apostate (361–63) left its mark on the Church of Antioch.[98] His policy had been favorable to the Jews, and the memory of his benefactions, even twenty years after his death, gave the Jews a force and vitality which were dangerous for the local Church.

(26) Furthermore, Jewish monotheism offered certain contacts with Arianism and its anti-Trinitarian heresy. In fact, the first *Discourse* had interrupted a series of sermons which Chrysostom was giving against the Anomoeans, one of the branches of Arianism rampant at Antioch. But Chrysostom did not see this as a genuine

---

96 In *Disc.* 5.12.12 Chrysostom speaks in the plural of both urban and suburban synagogues, but the plural may be a generalizing one. In *Disc.* 1.6.2 he specifies a synagogue in town and one at Daphne.

97 In *Disc.* 4.1.2 Chrysostom, in speaking of the Jewish Pasch and fasts, says that the Jews, who are more dangerous than wolves, are bent on surrounding his flock; hence he must fight with them so that no sheep of his may fall victim to them. From what he says in *Disc.* 1.2.7 it would seem that the Jews bestowed a particular care on staging their religious ceremonies and heightened their pomp with music and dancing.

98 See Downey, *History* 380–97. Baur 1.331 says that by the time of Chrysostom the Jews had increased in number and importance at Antioch and even sought by preference to make proselytes among the Christians.

interruption, since the impiety of the Anomoeans was akin to that of the Jews because both rejected the sonship of Christ and denied that He is equal to God.[99]

(27) The third *Discourse* was again a quasi-interruption. In this sermon Chrysostom aimed his arguments against the Protopaschites because they had rejected the decisions of Nicaea and followed the Jewish norm for fixing the date of the Pasch. This Chrysostom saw as another Judaizing abuse and another close connection between the menaces threatening the Church from within and from without. Since the Jews had in some degree prepared the way for both the Anomoeans and the Protopaschites, Chrysostom feared both these groups because they were helpful to the Jews and the Judaizing movement.

(28) A further cause for Judaizing may be found in the Jewish influence on certain forms of Christian devotion. Pilgrimages to Palestine were becoming common. The Christian pilgrims showed their devotion not only to the holy places connected with the life and passion of Christ but equally to the memorials of the prophets, patriarchs, and kings of Israel. Here was an area where Jews and Christians shared in cultic practices and found an opportunity for what might prove to be a dangerous devotional syncretism.

(29) At Antioch, in all probability, there existed an analogous situation. For centuries the Jews there had had under their charge and protection the tombs of the seven Maccabees and their mother, who had been martyred for their Jewish faith under Antiochus Epiphanes (175–163 B.C.).[100] Their sepulcher was in the synagogue of Kenesheth Hashmunith, named for the mother of the seven brothers.[101]

---

99 Cf. *Disc.* 1.1.6. For Arianism see V.C. De Clercq, "Arianism" in NCE 1.791–94; the Anomoeans are mentioned *ibid.* 793.

100 Their martyrdom is recounted in 2 Mc 7. Dr. Margaret Schatkin (Dept. of Theology, Boston College) presented a most scholarly and illuminating paper, "The Maccabean Martyrs," to the meeting of the North American Patristic Society held under the auspices of the American Philological Association in December 1972. We hope her work will be published because it treats exhaustively the whole question of the Maccabean cult.

101 See Downey, *History* 110.

(30) Many Christians venerated the Maccabees and were attracted to their tomb because of their reputation for effecting cures. The Church authorities frowned on this interest shown by Christians in Jewish saints and solved the problem by taking over the synagogue, which they then turned into a Christian shrine.[102] The former synagogue, however, remained a center for the cult of the Maccabees, who were there honored equally with Christian saints. In Chrysostom's day the Maccabees had their own vigil and feast celebrated at the shrine; this elevation to the liturgical calendar of Antioch would certainly seem to argue to the existence of a cult which predated the conversion of the synagogue into a church.

(31) Surely, even before the synagogue became a shrine, the cult paid to the martyred Maccabees reflected both an official attitude on the part of the Church and a parallel attitude on the part of the faithful. The Church stressed in the case of these Jewish saints the continuity between the Old Law and the New Covenant. The Old Law showed prototypes of the great persons of the New, of Christ and his disciples. The seven Maccabees, who had died for their Jewish faith, were seen as precursors of the martyrs who had laid down their lives for Christ in the times of persecution.[103]

(32) When the parallel attitude on the part of the faithful had its beginning cannot be precisely fixed. Simon thinks it developed prior to the fourth century and on the very spot where tradition put their martyrdom and in the synagogue where their relics were preserved. The popular movement did not rest so much on symbolic precursors

---

102 Just when this happened is not sure; it may have been a reaction to the reign of Julian (d. 363) and must have been before Chrysostom's series *Adversus Iudaeos*, because he there speaks of another urban synagogue (cf. above, Introduction at n. 96). Simon 143 thinks that the Jews may have built a new edifice or had one put at their disposal by way of compensation. See also Downey, *History* 448.

103 Chrysostom preached a series of three short sermons *In sanctos Macchabaeos* (PG 50.617–28) in which he praised the martyrs' courage and exhorted his hearers to imitate their virtues; he also saw the seven brothers as examples of the connection between the Old and New Testaments. In the last of the three sermons he compares Eleazar (the old chief scribe who preceded the seven brothers in martyrdom [cf. 2 Mc 6]) to St. Peter (PG 50.627). See also Downey, *History* 448.

as it did on the addition of names to the list of holy ones on whose support the people might depend in time of need. The relics and the synagogue where they were preserved received greater veneration than the memory and example of the martyrs themselves.[104]

(33) The uncultivated people failed to see any risk to faith in what was becoming a dangerous superstition. They paid respect to the relics while forgetting the saints and what they had done. Little by little what had started out as a cult of local saints broadened into a Judaizing movement. What the people looked for principally from the seven brothers (as from all the saints and their relics) were miracles and cures. What were taken to be cures were performed by the rabbis around the martyrs' tomb and by the means which later Chrysostom denounced—incantations, amulets, and charms.[105]

(34) At first the cures were sought in the synagogue which sheltered the tomb of the Maccabees. The next step was to seek for help in any synagogue, and the rabbis were substituted for the martyrs as the agents who would perform the miracles. From there it was an easy thing for the demi-Christians to attribute an efficacious value to all cultic actions of the Jewish religion, which had proved itself so venerable and powerful in their eyes. After all, the Maccabees were held in honor because they preferred death to any violation of Jewish ritual. Could that ritual be out of date and no longer valid?[106] Hence, it would seem that the tomb of the Maccabees, because of the tenor of the times, may have proved to have been a strong force in supporting and spreading the Judaizing movement.

(35) Why did the Church convert the synagogue into a shrine? It is Simon's opinion that the seizure of the synagogue was motivated by two reasons: first, the Church wished to gain firm control of the relics of the holy martyrs, who were officially counted as precursors

---

104 Simon 150.
105 Cf. *ibid.* and see above, Introduction II 20. St. Augustine, in *De civitate Dei* 22.8–9 (PL 41.760–71; trans. G.G. Walsh and D.J. Honan, FC 24.431–51), testifies to numerous miraculous cures worked chiefly by the relics of St. Stephen. One of these cures involved a woman named Petronia, who had been previously persuaded by a Jew to seek a cure from her ailment by wearing an amulet on her person (FC 24.446).
106 Simon 150.

of Christianity; second, the Church saw the need to cut out at the roots the source of the Judaizing evil by suppressing, or, at least, controlling this opportunity for contact between Christians and Jews in their own synagogue.[107]

(36) The Maccabees were popular with both Jews and Christians. Their martyrdom offered a close analogy with the passions of Christian martyrs, their relics were at Antioch, and they were the only representatives of the Old Testament included in the martyrology of Antioch. Hence, the Church wished to give their cult a properly Christian label and to keep the veneration shown to them strictly orthodox. The Church recognized that, if not kept under control, the Maccabean cult was likely to spread the Judaizing tendency to a point dangerous to the faith. And so the synagogue was seized and converted into a Christian shrine.[108]

(37) Chrysostom's sermons, which were delivered after the synagogue became a shrine, offer proof that the Church's action had failed to stem the Judaizing tide. In the last *Discourse* of the series Chrysostom tells the demi-Christians that they have no excuse if for their fevers and hurts they run to the synagogues or even summon to their houses the rabbis, who are sorcerers and dealers in witchcraft. They must not run to God's enemies, the Jews, for cures; this will only rouse his anger against them still more. Rather they must run to the martyrs, to the saints, to those in whom he is well pleased and who can speak to him with great confidence and freedom.[109]

(38) If we take these words in the context of contemporary Antioch, Chrysostom is telling the Judaizers not to go to the rabbis or the synagogues for their cures but to the tomb of the local martyrs, the Maccabees, which is situated in what is now a Christian shrine. Put in this perspective, there is real meaning to the contrast which Chrysostom makes between true cures worked by the intercession of the holy martyrs and the cures wrought by the Jews and accomplished by the power of demons. [110]

---

107 *Ibid.* 150–51.
108 *Ibid.* 151.
109 Cf. *Disc.* 8.6.6.
110 Simon 151.

(39) Even though there is bitterness against the Jews in all eight *Discourses*, the tone changes considerably in the course of the series. The first, second and fourth do attack Jewish practices: their feasts and fasts are impious; their synagogues and souls are dwellings of demons; their circumcision is fruitless. But the third *Discourse* assails the Protopaschites for causing contentiousness in the Church, since they would date Easter by the Jewish Passover and fasts in defiance of the decree of the Council of Nicaea. However, all this is foolishness since the Christian Pasch and Lent have replaced the Jewish Passover and fasts.[111] As with *Discourses* I, II, and IV, Chrysostom again ends with a prayer that his wandering brethren may return to the fold.

(40) *Discourses* V–VII are far less vituperative and much more apologetic, exegetic, and instructional. In *Discourse* V, a theme found in Chrysostom's *Demonstration*[112] is repeated: the predictions of Christ are true, as are those of the prophets, and the temple will never be rebuilt. Chrysostom also speaks of the three captivities of the Jews and gives lengthy exegeses of the prophecies of Jeremiah and Daniel. Once more he ends with a plea to bring back those who are sick.

(41) *Discourses* VI and VII show that the Old Law has been supplanted by the New. Not only do the Jews have no temple, but they have no priesthood, no sacrifice. Again he ends both instruc-

---

111 The article "Fasting and Fast Days," EJ 6.1195, in its classification of fasts decreed by the rabbis, lists the first Monday and Thursday, and the following Monday after Passover and Sukkot. The fast was interpreted as an atonement for possible sins committed while in a state of drunkenness and gluttony during the holidays. L. Duchesne, "La Question de la Pâques au Concile de Nicée," *Revue des questions historiques* 28 (1880) 5–42, clearly shows that the Nicene decree was aimed at the Protopaschites. Quasten 3.340 cites Eusebius, *Vita Constantini* 3.18, who points out that Protopaschite practices led to the scandalous absurdity of some Christians fasting and other feasting on the selfsame days because, even after Easter, the Protopaschites were fulfilling their appointed fast while other Christians were present at banquets and amusements.

112 This is his apologetic treatise, *The Demonstration against Jews and Pagans on the Divinity of Christ* (PG 48.813–38).

tions with a plea for fraternal correction. The final *Discourse* (VIII) is almost entirely devoted to such a plea to help and correct those who have erred. He alludes to several of his earlier themes, such as avoiding the synagogues and cures of the Jews, but the burden of his exhortation is that his hearers must be Good Samaritans. Even if their brothers have already sinned, they must not be abandoned because their wounds can be healed.

(42) Any honest appraisal of Chrysostom's anti-Semitic sentiments as shown in the eight *Discourses* has to consider several factors. There is no question but that he speaks with extreme harshness against the Jews in several places. But when he condemns them, it is usually out of the mouths of their own prophets (as was customary in the genre) and because the Jews pose a peril to the faith of those Christians whose commitment was weak and who readily shared in Judaizing practices. The fact that all eight *Discourses* end with an exhortation to fraternal correction and a plea to bring back the sheep who have strayed from the Church makes it quite clear that not the Jews but the Judaizing Christians are Chrysostom's primary targets.

(43) Again, even after the triumph of the Church, Jewish proselytism and an energetic Judaizing movement persisted at Antioch because the Jewish community was strong and had a history reaching back to the foundation of the city. Here was the place where the Maccabees had been martyred; here was the site of their tomb. As local saints, these martyrs were popular with both Christians and Jews; the common veneration of their relics led to a syncretism which was perilous for the Christian faith. Even though the Church had taken over the synagogue which housed their tomb, it failed to root out this syncretism. Although many Christians saw little danger in the common cult, the Church recognized this syncretism as a very real peril and chose the middle course of venerating the Maccabees as saints of the Old Covenant and precursors of the Christian martyrs. This left Chrysostom in the strange position of facing two ways at the same time. He had to combat those who were blinded by an overly-rigid aversion for things Jewish[113] and, on the other side, he

---

113 E.g., in his *Homilia de Eleazaro et septem pueris* Chrysostom forcefully

had to attack the Judaizing disease and the damage it was doing to the demi-Christians. Obviously, the series *Adversus Iudaeos* is representative of this second side of his dilemma.

III

The series also presents problems which have nothing to do with anti-Semitism. How are the eight *Discourses* related to Chrysostom's apologetic treatise, the *Demonstration against Jews and Pagans on the Divinity of Christ*? Are the eight sermons in their proper sequence? When were they delivered? Have some sermons been lost? Do all the extant ones belong to the same series? What follows is an attempt to answer these questions.

(2) Is there a close bond between the *Demonstration* and the eight *Discourses*? Montfaucon, the Benedictine editor, not only thinks that there is such a bond, but that the *Discourses* were already under preparation when the *Demonstration* was written. He rests his opinion on the following questionable evidence.

(3) In Chapter 17 of the *Demonstration*,[114] Chrysostom says that, when he speaks against the Jews, he will give a clearer and fuller explanation of the abrogation of the Jewish cult. Montfaucon, in his preliminary remarks to *Adversus Iudaeos*,[115] not only quotes this promise but goes on to say that Chrysostom kept it when he proved at length, especially in *Discourses* IV-VIII, that the Jewish ritual had been rejected and destroyed. Williams[116] feels that a promise given in the *Demonstration* should have been made good within the *Demonstration*. The fact that this is not the case probably explains the incompleteness and abrupt ending of this treatise as it has come down to us.

---

attacked those Christians who were led into error by the enemies of the Church and refused to render fitting homage to the Maccabees. These anti–Semites would not give them their proper place in the choir of martyrs on the pretext that they had not shed their blood for Christ but for the Law and its prescriptions against eating pork (PG 63.525).
114 PG 48.836.
115 *Ibid.*
116 *Adversus Iudaeos* 135–36.

(4) We are inclined to agree with Williams for two reasons. First, it would be strange to make such a promise in a written treatise (which would not end so abruptly if the promise were kept there) and then fulfill the promise in the entirely different literary form of the spoken homily. Second, there is a problem of dating. Williams feels that the promise could not be looking forward to the *Discourses* because the *Demonstration* breathes an utterly different spirit from the sermons and shows little trace of their rancor. He considers the *Demonstration* as worthily eloquent but hardly indicative of an orator who had already won an assured position in Antioch. He therefore assigns the *Demonstration* to the year of Chrysostom's diaconate (381) rather than to the year of his ordination to the priesthood (386).[117] Montfaucon dates the *Demonstration* in 386 because it must have preceded the fulfillment of its promise in *Discourses* IV to VIII, which he assigns to 387.[118]

(5) Whether Montfaucon is right or wrong about the date of the *Demonstration*, his argument for it is weak because it rests on the assumption that there is an intrinsic connection between the *Demonstration* and the eight *Discourses*. If there is any connection, it would seem to be an accidental and tenuous one. Both works are by the same man but belong to different genres and show two different aspects of Chrysostom's pastoral activity. In the *Demonstration* he defends the divinity of Christ against the pagans; in the eight *Discourses* he attacks the Judaizing tendencies of the demi-Christians.

(6) The next problem deals with the sequence of the eight *Discourses* and arises from the fact that the order is not constant in the manuscripts and the editions. The editions of David Hoeschel (1602)[119] and Fronton du Duc (1609)[120] both follow the major-

---

117 *Ibid.*
118 PG 48.839.
119 *Contra Iudaeos homiliae VI.* Graece nunc primum . . . editae (Augsburg 1602), the *editio princeps* of the Greek text. Cf. Chrysostom Baur, *S. Jean Chrysostome et ses oeuvres dans l'histoire littéraire* (Louvain 1907) 103.
120 *Ad populum Antiochenum, adv. Iudaeos*, etc. (Paris 1609) 432–46. Cf. Baur, *op. cit.* 106. Presumably the same six sermons, in the same order, appear in the Ducaeus edition, Paris 1602 (listed by Baur, *op. cit.* 103).

ity of the manuscripts in giving a series of only six *Discourses,* viz., I, IV, V, VI, VII, VIII. Erasmus[121] and Savile,[122] following four manuscripts which omit the first *Discourse,* reduce the series to five, viz., IV, V, VI, VII, VIII. Savile publishes I, II, and III as well, and immediately following IV-VIII, but not as part of the series. In his 1636-42 edition of the *Opera omnia* Fronton du Duc also publishes II and III, but in a different volume from his set of six sermons.[123]

(7) Monfaucon[124] is responsible for the present order of the eight *Discourses.* His arguments for this sequence are not without cogency and, in their course, treat also the matters of date, the possibility of lost homilies, and his reasons for assigning all the extant ones to the one single series.

(8) We have just seen that the earlier editors considered the series as consisting of five or six *Discourses,* although the omitted sermons are published apart from the series in the editions of Savile and du Duc. All the earlier editors were merely following the sequences found in the manuscripts at their disposal; none examined by any editor, including Montfaucon, shows a series of eight *Discourses.* Some of the manuscripts, however, do contain the other *Discourses* without serial numbers but merely with titles such as: "Against Those Who Fast the Fast of the Jews" (II) and "Against Those Who Keep the First Paschal Fast" (III).

(9) Although Erasmus omits and Savile transfers the first homily (an ordering which Montfaucon says in his *Monitum* that Savile had found in three manuscripts), Montfaucon follows Hoeschel, du Duc,

---

121 In Latin (his own translation) only, *D. Io. Chrysostomi . . . et divi Athanasii . . . lucubrationes aliquot* etc. (Basle 1527). Cf. Baur, *op. cit.* 154.

122 H. Savile, *S. Iohannis Chrysostomi opera omnia,* 8 vols. (Eton 1612). Cf. Baur, *op. cit.* 106. In vol. VI the *Discourses* occupy pp. 312–66 (IV–VIII), 366–85 (I–III).

123 In the fifth volume (of 1616) *Disc.* II appears on pages 715–22, Disc. III on pages 702–15. The Latin translation is given as by du Duc himself.

124 B. de Montfaucon, *S Iohannis Chrysostomi opera omnia,* 12 vols. (Paris 1718–38 [the *Discourses* are found in vol. I, pp. 587–688] and Venice 1734–41); second edition by Th. Fix (Paris 1834–39); reprinted in J.P. Migne, *Patrologiae cursus completus: Series Graeca* (Paris 1836) 47–61 (the *Discourses* are found in 48.863–942).

and the majority of manuscripts in putting it as first in the series. He also finds internal evidence not only for this position but also for the date of the homily. Chrysostom says there that the Jewish feasts and fasts will soon be upon them, one after another and in quick succession. Since many so-called Christians will be joining the Jews in these observances, Chrysostom felt constrained to interrupt his series of sermons against the Anomoeans in order that he might combat the more immediate danger.[125]

(10) From this evidence Montfaucon dates the first homily toward the end of August 386. He argues for August because the feasts (Trumpets and Tabernacles) which Chrysostom specifically mentions fall in the month of Tishri (September–October),[126] and in the second homily Chrysostom says that the fast of the Jews will begin after five days and that he had anticipated this when he had delivered an exhortation to avoid the Jewish fasts and feasts some ten or more days before.[127] Montfaucon dates the first homily in 386 because the first five sermons of the series against the Anomoeans (which was interrupted by the first *Discourse*)[128] were delivered before Christmas 386.

(11) What we have just said also establishes by internal evidence a link between the second and the first. There is further evidence that the second is in its proper place because its title reads in part: "After the Other Discourse Had Been Given and Five Days Before the Jewish Fast." And again in the second he refers back to the first when he says: "Did you not hear in my previous discourse the argument which clearly proved to us that demons dwell in the very souls of the Jews and in the places in which they gather?"[129] But, as Montfaucon points out, Chrysostom gives a clear and lengthy proof of that point in the first *Discourse*.[130] The evidence, there-

---

125 *Disc.* 1.1.5. The series *De incomprehensibili Dei natura contra Anomoeos* is found in PG 48.701–812 and SC 28bis, and is discussed in Quasten 3.451.
126 See McKenzie, DB 114–15 (Calendar), 613–15 (New Year), and 863–64 (Tabernacles).
127 See *Disc.* 2.1.1.
128 See *Disc.* 1.1.4 and PG 48.699 and 840.
129 Cf. *Disc.* 2.3.5.
130 Cf. *Disc.* 1.4.1–2 and 1.6.6–7.

fore, would seem to indicate that the second is in its proper place and was delivered between September 1 and 15 in 386.

(12) Montfaucon has no hesitation in putting in the third place the homily which bears the title: "Against Those Who Keep the First Paschal Fast." Just as Chrysostom's first two *Discourses* had interrupted his series against the Anomoeans, this third is a later interruption of his attacks against these same heretics. At the very beginning of the third *Discourse* he says: "Once again a necessary and pressing need has interrupted the sequence of my discourses. I must put aside my struggles with the [Anomoean] heretics for today... But the untimely obstinacy of those who wish to keep the first Paschal fast forces me to devote my entire instruction to their cure."[131]

(13) From the second homily of his series against the Anomoeans it seems clear that this second interruption came after he had delivered at least two of the eight *Discourses*, after he had entertained a throng of "spiritual fathers,"[132] and after the celebration of many martyrs' feasts had occupied him.[133] These activities, according to Montfaucon, would have claimed so much of Chrysostom's time that he could not have resumed his series against the Anomoeans until the latter part of September 386.

(14) Montfaucon places the second interruption of the Anomoean series and the third of the eight *Discourses* at the very end of September or in early October. In support of this he adduces a text from the homily *In diem natalem Christi*, which Chrysostom preached on Christmas Day 386. There he says: "But that was the feast of the Tabernacles and the fasts... For at that time I took upon myself many lengthy sermons against the Jews, accusing them for their untimely fasting."[134] But that would put the "lengthy ser-

---

131 *Disc.* 3.1.1. That the heretics were the Anomoeans is clear because he says (*ibid.*): "I was ready to address your loving assembly again on the glory of the only-begotten Son of God."
132 According to the title prefixed to the homily these spiritual fathers were bishops but, according to a footnote *ad loc.* (PG 48.709), may have been monks from the neighborhood of Antioch.
133 See PG *ibid.*
134 PG 49.351–62. The quotation is found in cols. 357–58 and assigns the feast and fast to September. See also PG 48.840–41.

mons" in the month of September (Tishri); the Protopaschites, against whom the third *Discourse* is aimed, kept their Easter celebration on the date of the Jewish Passover, the 14th of Nisan (March-April). It seems more likely, therefore, that the *Discourse* against the Protopaschites would have been delivered closer to the Passover than to the feast of Tabernacles. If this be true, this *Discourse* would not be one of the "many lengthy sermons against the Jews;" furthermore, the Protopaschites were not Jews but Judaizing Christians.

(15) The difficulty does not seem to be so much in considering the third *Discourse* as a second interruption of the series *Contra Anomoeos* as in considering it as belonging to the series *Adversus Iudaeos*. True, Chrysostom speaks in the third *Discourse* of those who say the Pasch and the feast of unleavened bread are one; he admits that Christ observed the Jewish Pasch. But both the observance of time (14th of Nisan) and of place (Jerusalem) have been abrogated. The Christian Pasch is the celebration of the mysteries; its fast does not follow the feast of unleavened bread but encompasses the forty days of Lent.[135]

(16) Many of the sentiments of this sermon are found in the other *Discourses*, but the chief theme of the *Discourse* against the Protopaschites seems to be the grave danger of contentiousness within the Church. Their stubborn adherence to the Jewish reckoning of the Pasch is a symptom of this contentiousness, but there must have been other and more dangerous ones. In speaking about computing the exact date of Easter, Chrysostom says: "So let us stop fighting with shadows, let us stop hurting ourselves in the big things while we are indulging our rivalry over the small."[136]

(17) What are the big things? He goes on to say:

---

135 Cf. *Disc.* 3.4.3–8. Here Chrysostom shows his lack of concern with the technical side of computing the date. That aspect is, in his eyes, not only irrelevant but could and did prove to be fraught with harm for the Church. Although other authors were much concerned with justifying the Church's post–Nicene method of calculation, F. Floeri and P. Nautin, *Homélies pascales* 3 (Sources chrétiennes 48; Paris 1957) 77, much prefer Chrysostom's realism in the matter of computing the exact date. See M. Schatkin, *op. cit. infra* (n. 157) 168–9, 185 n. 36.

136 Cf. *Disc.* 3.6.12.

Fasting at this or that time is not a matter for blame. But to
rend asunder the Church, to be ready for rivalry, to create
dissension, to rob oneself continuously of the benefits of
religious meetings—these are unpardonable, these do demand
an accounting, these do deserve serious punishment.[137]

(18) If the Protopaschites were causing further dissensions within
the Church, Chrysostom would have good reason to interrupt his
series *Contra Anomoeos* to correct them—possibly even some six
months after the disputed date of Easter. But Montfaucon seems to
have less good reason for linking this sermon to *Discourses* I and II.
The only connection seems to rest on some similarity of content
and, possibly, on some contiguity in time. Even Chrysostom's exhortation to fraternal correction in this *Discourse* is different:

Let us all pray that our brothers come back to us. Let us pray
that they cling fondly to peace and stand apart from untimely
rivalry. Let us pray that they scorn this sluggish spirit of theirs
and find a great and lofty understanding. Let us pray that they
be set free from this observance of days so that all of us, with
one heart and one voice, may give glory to God and the Father
of our Lord Jesus Christ, to whom be glory and power now
and forever, world without end. Amen.[138]

(19) This exhortation, just as the rest of the sermon, shows considerable differences from *Discourses* I and II. It seems that Montfaucon would have done better to follow the example of the other
editors and publish this sermon separately from the series.

(20) Let us now return to Chrysostom's Christmas sermon of
386, where he says: "But that was the feast of the Tabernacles and
the fasts... For at that time I took upon myself many lengthy
sermons against the Jews, accusing them of untimely fasting."[139]

---

137 *Disc.* 3.6.13.
138 *Disc.* 3.6.14.
139 PG 49.351–62. See *ibid.* 48.840–41.

(21) Even if, after Chrysostom's manner, he is not overscrupulous in giving dates and "that time" may run from late August through September, October, or November, the words "many lengthy sermons against the Jews" would have to mean more than the first two (or three) of the series *Adversus Iudaeos*. Of course, these might be included, but there may well have been others which have been lost.[140] In fact, it even seems sure that some or all of the "many lengthy sermons" have not survived. At the end of the third *Discourse* he says: "But I make no account of it [i.e., the computation of the date for Easter], as I proved when I devoted many discourses to this subject."[141] This statement excludes the third *Discourse*, in which it is made. Neither of the first two treats specifically of computing the date of Easter or Passover. Even if this statement were to refer to the first two *Discourses*, could Chrysostom have said this if there had not been many other sermons on this subject—discourses which have not come down to us?

(22) Of course, the "many lengthy sermons against the Jews" might refer to the remaining five *Discourses* (IV–VIII) in the series. But this could not be true if those five were delivered after Christmas of 386 and belong to a second attack against the Judaizers made on the recurrence of the same feasts and fasts in the following year (387). And this seems to be the case.

(23) The fourth *Discourse* opens with the words: "Again the Jews, the most miserable and wretched of all men, are going to fast, and again we must secure the flock of Christ."[142] In the first, Chrysostom had said: "The festivals of the pitiful and miserable Jews are soon to march upon us one after another in quick succession: the feast of Trumpets, the feast of Tabernacles, the fasts."[143]

---

140 The second *Discourse,* for example, is found in only one MS and there with a considerable lacuna. See PG 48.841. See also J. Juster, *Les Juifs dans l' empire romain* (Paris 1914) 62.
141 *Disc.* 3.6.9. Since the content of this *Discourse* points to a time not far ı removed from the date of Easter and Passover (March–April), the "Many discourses" are not likely to be the same as the "many lengthy sermons against the Jews, accusing them for their untimely fasting," since the latter belong to the month of September. See above, Introd. III 14.
142 *Disc.* 4.1.1. But see my note on the title to this *Discourse.*
143 *Disc.* 1.1.5.

In the second, he says: "The wicked and unclean fast of the Jews is now at our doors."[144] The third states: "But the untimely obstinacy of those who wish to keep the first Paschal fast forces me to devote my entire instruction to their cure."[145] So it would seem that when in the fourth *Discourse* he says: "Again the Jews . . . are going to fast and again we must secure the flock of Christ," he can scarcely be referring to the festivals and fasts of 386 but to their recurrence in 387 or a later year.

(24) If *Discourses* IV–VIII are in proper sequence, as all the editors agree, there is another reason for assigning them to 387. In *Discourse* VI Chrysostom says: "Surely you all know and remember the time when some evil tricksters in our midst tore down the statues . . . And you remember that they all paid the supreme penalty."[146] This insurrection occurred in 387, probably in March, and Chrysostom delivered his famous series of twenty-one sermons *De statuis* (PG 49.15–222) in an effort to quiet his disaffected fellow citizens.[147] The last homily of this series was preached on Easter Sunday 387 and the preceding twenty during Lent of that year. Hence the sixth *Discourse* must have been delivered after Easter of 387.

(25) At the end of this same *Discourse*, Chrysostom speaks as if it were delivered just before or during the Jewish fast.[148] The fifth was given the day before the sixth, as the title of the latter *Discourse* states,[149] and after the fourth, because he speaks at the beginning of the fifth of a large throng gathered to see to it that he kept the promise he had made.[150] The fourth was delivered some ten days

---

144 *Disc.* 2.1.1.
145 *Disc.* 3.1.1.
146 *Disc.* 6.6.7. The statues were those of the Emperor Theodosius and his family.
147 Baur 1.259–83 discusses these days of terror in Antioch. See also Downey, *History* 426–33.
148 See *Disc.* 6.7.10. The fasts are those connected with the Ten Days of Penitence. See above, n. 84.
149 The title to *Discourse* 6 reads: "After He Had Delivered a Long Homily Against the Jews the Previous Day . . . ."
150 *Disc.* 5.1.1. The fourth makes no clear promise, but the fifth does continue the general theme found in the fourth: the exile which began

before the Jewish fast.[151] At the beginning of the seventh he states that the Jewish feasts are not yet over;[152] the eighth comes after the festivals and fasting,[153] and all that remains is to reclaim and rehabilitate those who have fallen into the Judaizing trap. It would seem, then, that *Discourses* IV–VIII are in proper sequence and may have been delivered within a span of three weeks in September 387.

(26) Since *Discourses* I–III belong to 386 and IV–VIII to 387 or later, they cannot all be assigned to a continuous series. *Discourses* I and II are intrinsically united and do belong to one series. The sermon against the Protopaschites was delivered at about the same time in 386, but its intrinsic links with *Discourses* I and II are too tenuous to place it with any strong certainty as the third in a series with the other two. *Discourses* IV–VIII are in proper sequence and they form, it would seem, a second series, given at the recurrence of the Jewish festivals and fasts, probably in September 387. In *Discourses* I and II (and possibly III) Chrysostom attacks and attempts to cure those sick with the Judaizing disease. In *Discourses* IV–VIII he returns, probably in the following year, to try to make the cure complete because some demi-Christians are still infected by the ailment to which he had turned his healing hand the year before.

(27) Some authorities (e.g., Baur and Altaner) assign no dates for the sermons. Quasten (3.452) agrees with Montfaucon in dating the eight *Discourses* in the years 386-87. Williams states that they were delivered at Antioch soon after Chrysostom's presbyterate (386). Perhaps Usener is the least cautious of all when he assigns to each of the eight its day, month, and year (387-89).[154] He also feels that a sermon preached on September 2, 388, has been lost.

---

with the destruction of the temple will never end because the temple will never be rebuilt. Hence, all the observances of the Law are abrogated.
151 *Disc.* 4.1.3. A similar anticipation is found in *Disc.* 2.1.1.
152 *Disc.* 7.1.1–2.
153 *Disc.* 8.1.1.
154 Juster, *op. cit.* 62, gives Usener's dates as follows:

I August 22, 387	V September 28, 388
II September 4, 387	VI September 30, 388
III January 24, 387	VII October 1, 388
IV September 2, 389	VIII September 11, 387

(28) We would follow Quasten, Williams, and Montfaucon in placing the sermons earlier, in the years 386–87. We disagree with any theory that there is only a single series. There seem to be at least two series in whole or in part. It also seems fairly sure that Montfaucon is correct in believing that some sermons have been lost, but we would be somewhat hesitant to put the third *Discourse* in its present position as part of an incomplete series.

(29) I have used Montfaucon's Greek text as reprinted in the Migne *Patrologia graeca* as the basis for this English translation.[155] The same edition has Latin translations printed on pages facing the Greek text. David Hoeschel translated the first *Discourse*, and Fronton du Duc the second and third. The Latin version of the last five is that of Erasmus. J. Bareille prints the eight *Discourses* in his *Oeuvres complètes de saint Jean Chrysostome* (Paris 1865) 2.352–513, with his own French translation accompanying the Greek text (a reprint of Montfaucon). There is also the slightly older rendering in the complete French Chrysostom produced largely under the direction of a M. Jeannin: Arras and Bar-le-Duc 1863–69. Somewhat more than ten years ago C. Mervyn Maxwell presented a doctoral dissertation to the University of Chicago entitled: *Chrysostom's Homilies Against the Jews: An English Translation.*[156] This work has not been published even on microfilm and I have never seen it. The present version would seem to be the first published translation of the homilies into English.[157]

---

155 The Migne column–numbers are given in square brackets.
156 Maxwell's dissertation is listed in *American Doctoral Dissertations 1965–66* (Ann Arbor n.d.) 129; it does not appear in *Dissertation Abstracts.*
157 Recently M. Schatkin has published "St. John Chrysostom's Homily on the Protopaschites [our third *Discourse*]: Introduction and Translation," *Orientalia christiana analecta* 195 (Rome 1973) 167–86. Comparison of her version with my own shows no substantial differences apart from the two translators' individual styles.
      I have not determined what Chrysostomic "fift Homelie against the Jewes" appears as the final element in a [1574] London printing in the British Museum (*Catalogue* . . . 143, s.v. London, IV. Appendix–Miscellaneous, col. 2141) which opens with a work entitled "The disclosing of a late conterfeyted possession by the deuyl . . ."

(30) Biblical texts have been translated directly from Chrysostom's Greek. I have found it useful to compare Chrysostom's citations from the Old Testament with the readings of the Septuagint, as given in A. Rahlfs' sixth edition (2 vols. Stuttgart 1935), here designated by the abbreviation LXX. It was also profitable to compare my translations from the LXX with an earlier English version.[158] In my renderings from both Testaments I have consulted *The Jerusalem Bible* (JB)[159] and *The New American Bible* (NAB).[160] Wherever "cf." precedes a Scriptural citation in my notes, it means either that the reader is referred to the text for confirmation of Chrysostom's argument, or that Chrysostom has quoted the text in an abridged form, or that his quotation varies from Rahlfs' LXX.

(31) Biblical proper names generally appear in the form used in NAB, from which I have drawn also the abbreviations for the books of Scripture. Where a given book of the Bible is differently designated in NAB and in the Septuagint (Vulgate), both forms are given, that from NAB first. Thus I give, e.g., 2 Kgs (4 Kgs), 1 Chr (1 Par), Sir (Ecclus), Rv (Apoc). In the enumeration of the Psalms (or of verses thereof), however, the Septuagint (Vulgate) number is given first; e.g., Ps 138 (139).14.

(32) I was fortunate to have available *The Jerome Biblical Commentary* (JBC), edited by R. Brown, J. Fitzmeyer, and R. Murphy (Englewood Cliffs, N.J., 1968) and have made extensive use of it in

---

158 For this purpose I made use of a monument of early American scholarship, Charles Thomson's translation of the Septuagint Bible, (published Philadelphia 1808), as edited, revised, and enlarged by C.A. Muses (Indian Hills, Colo., 1954).
159 Garden City, N.Y., 1966.
160 *The New American Bible.* Translated from the Original Languages with Critical Use of All the Ancient Sources by Members of the Catholic Biblical Association of America . . . (New York 1970). The reader is sometimes referred, especially for its notes, to an earlier Confraternity version, viz. the *Saint Joseph Edition of the Holy Bible* . . . 1963).

my notes to the eight *Discourses*.[161] My notes also have gained much from *A Catholic Commentary on Holy Scripture* (CCHS), edited by B. Orchard *et al.* (London 1953), and its successor, *A New Catholic Commentary on Holy Scripture* (NCCHS), edited by R. Fuller *et al.* (London 1969).

---

161 References to JBC are in the form employed in the book itself—by article and section numbers.

DISCOURSE I

ODAY I HAD INTENDED [843] to complete my discussion of the topic on which I spoke to you a few days ago; I wished to present you with even clearer proof that God's nature is more than our minds can grasp.[1] Last Sunday[2] I spoke on this at great length and I brought forward as my witnesses Isaiah, David, and Paul. For it was Isaiah who exclaimed: "Who shall declare his generation?"[3] David knew

---

1 This is a clear reference to the first sermon *De incomprehensibili Dei natura contra Anomoeos,* delivered in 386 (cf. PG 48.699–710; SC 28bis 72–110). Quasten 3.451 describes the Anomoeans as the most radical of the Arian sects, which pretended to know God as God knows Himself; they maintained not merely the inequality but the dissimilarity of the Son's nature to that of the Father. The bracketed 843 and the bracketed numbers that follow in sequence refer to (approximate) column-openings in PG 48.

2 Since last Sunday was only "a few days ago," Chrysostom must also have preached at weekday liturgies. See above, Introd. I 8.

3 Cf. Is 53.8 (LXX). The Hebrew text of this verse has been variously emended and translated. NAB reads: ". . . and who would have thought any more of his destiny?" JB gives: ". . .would anyone plead his cause?" and adds a note that the words "who will explain his generation (or descent)?" of the Greek and Latin has been taken by Christian tradition to refer to the mysterious origin of Christ. E. Power (CCHS 568) points out that the Hebrew noun *dôr* (the reading probably basic to LXX) usually means "generation" in the sense of lifetime or contemporaries, but it cannot indicate the act of generating, the eternal or temporal generation of Christ. Chrysostom, following the School of Antioch, takes the Greek word *genea* in its literal meaning of descent or generation. When he mentions the text in *De incomp.* 1.5 (PG 48.705–6; SC 28bis 94) he seems more interested in the future tense of the verb, because he says: "He did not say, 'Who declares (or explains)' but, 'Who shall declare (or explain)' his generation?" Thus he excluded any future declaration or explanation. Hence, the Anomoean can never define the substance of God (*ibid.* 1.4, PG 48.705; SC 28 bis 92).

1

God was beyond his comprehension and so he gave thanks to him and said: "I will praise you for you are fearfully magnified: wonderful are your works."[4] And again it was David who said: "The knowledge of you is too wonderful for me, a height to which my mind cannot attain."[5] Paul did not search and pry into God's very essence, but only into his providence; I should say rather that he looked only on the small portion of divine providence which God had made manifest when he called the gentiles. And Paul saw this small part as a vast and incomprehensible sea when he exclaimed: "O the depth of the riches and of the wisdom and of the knowledge of God! How incomprehensible are his judgments, and how unsearchable his ways!"[6]

(2) These three witnesses gave us proof enough, but I was not satisifed with prophets nor did I settle for apostles. I mounted to the heavens and gave you as proof the chorus of angels as they sang: "Glory to God in the highest, and on earth peace, good will among men."[7] Again, you heard the Seraphim as they shuddered and cried out in astonishment: "Holy, holy, holy, the Lord God of hosts, all the earth is filled with his glory."[8] And I gave you also the Cherubim who exclaimed: "Blessed be his glory [844] in his dwelling."[9]

---

4 Cf. Ps 138(139).14, which both here and where cited twice in *De incomp.* 1.4 (PG *ibid.*; SC 28 bis 90 92) follows the variant "you are fearfully magnified" for "I am etc." of Rahlfs' LXX and "I am fearfully, wonderfully made" of NAB.

5 Ps 138(139).6. The text also is found twice in *De incomp.* (*ibid.*).

6 Rom 11.33. Cited also in *De incomp.* 1.5 (PG 48.706; SC 28bis 96), where Chrysostom makes the same point about God's providence in calling the gentiles but adds the rejection of the Jews.

7 A common variant of Lk 2.14 found in many Greek NT MSS and in patristic writings. Chrysostom gives only the first part of the text in *De incomp.* 1.6 (PG 48.707; SC 28bis 100, 102).

8 Cf. Is 6.3. Again in *De incomp.* (*ibid.*) he gives only the first part: "Holy, holy, holy."

9 Cf. Ez 3.12 (LXX), which reads, "the glory of the Lord" for "his glory," as Chrysostom quotes the text both here and in *De incomp.* (PG *ibid.*; SC 28bis 102). NAB reads: ". . .the glory of the Lord rose from its place." E. Power (CCHS 605) seems to feel that the similarity of the Hebrew words for "rise" and "blessed" explains the omission of "blessed" and its replace-

(3) So there were three witnesses on earth and three in Heaven who made it clear that God's glory cannot be approached. For the rest, the proof was beyond dispute; there was great applause,[10] the audience warmed with enthusiasm, your assembly came aflame. I did rejoice at this, yet my joy was not because praise was coming to me but because glory was coming to my Master. For that applause and praise showed the love you have for God in your souls. If a servant loves his master and hears someone speak in praise of that master, his heart comes aflame with a love for him who speaks. This is because the servant loves his master. You acted just that way when I spoke: by the abundance of your applause you showed clearly your abundant love for the Master.

(4) And so I wanted again today to engage in that contest.[11] For if the enemies of the truth never have enough of blaspheming our Benefactor, we must be all the more tireless in praising the God of all. But what am I to do? Another very serious illness[12] calls for any cure my words can bring, an illness which has become implanted in the body of the Church. We must first root this ailment out and then take thought for matters outside; we must first cure our own and then be concerned for others who are strangers.

(5) What is this disease? The festivals of the pitiful and miserable Jews[13] are soon to march upon us one after the other and in quick succession: the feast of Trumpets,[14] the feast of Taberna-

---

ment by "rose" or "ascended." JB translates: "Blessed be the glory of Yahweh in his dwelling place," much as does Chrysostom.

10 Chrysostom was frequently applauded by his congregation. See P. Albert, *S. Jean Chrysostome considéré comme orateur populaire,* esp. ch. 7, and Baur 1.206–30, esp. 216.

11 Chrysostom often speaks of his attacks on Christ's enemies as contests. See, e.g., *De incomp.* 2.1 (PG 48.709; SC 28 bis 112), where he says: "Come, let us again enter the contest against the infidel Anomoeans." Since the ailment is "implanted in the body of the Church" and since "we must first cure our own," the homilies must clearly have been delivered against Judaizing Christians. See above, Introd. I 13; II 1.

12 The illness, of course, is the Judaizing disease. Again we have here evidence that he has interrupted his series against the Anomoeans.

13 Cf. below *Disc.* 1.2.1. and 4.1.1.

14 This is the New Year or Rosh Ha-Shanah, which falls on the first of Tishri (Sept.–Oct.). See McKenzie, DB 613–15 and L. Jacobs, "Rosh Ha-Shanah, EJ 14.309–10. *Disc.* 4 is (erroneously?) entitled: "Against the Jews and the Trumpets of their Pasch." But see *Disc.* 4.7.4–6; 7.1.2.

cles,[15] the fasts.[16] There are many in our ranks who say they think as we do. Yet some of these are going to watch the festivals, and others will join the Jews in keeping their feasts and observing their fasts. I wish to drive this perverse custom from the Church right now. My discourses [845] against the Anomoeans can be put off to another time,[17] and the postponement would cause no harm. But now that the Jewish festivals are close by and at the very door, if I should fail to cure those who are sick with the Judaizing disease, I am afraid that, because of their ill-suited association and deep ignorance, some Christians may partake in the Jews' transgressions; once they have done so, I fear my discourses on these transgressions will be in vain. For if they hear no word from me today, they will then join the Jews in their fasts; once they have committed this sin, it will be useless for me to apply the remedy.[18]

(6) And so it is that I hasten to anticipate this danger and prevent it. This is what physicians do. They first check the diseases which are most urgent and acute. But the danger from this sickness is very closely related to the danger from the other; since the Anomoeans' impiety is akin to that of the Jews, my present conflict is akin to my former one. And there is a kinship because the Jews and the Anomoeans make the same accusation. And what charges do the Jews make? That He called God His own Father and so made Himself equal to God.[19] The Anomoeans also make this charge—I should not say they make this a charge; they even blot out the phrase "equal to God" and what it connotes, by their

---

15 This falls on the fifteenth of Tishri and lasts a week, during which the Jews danced and "made merry before the Lord" (cf. Lv 23.33–43). See McKenzie, DB 863–64 and art. "Sukkot," EJ 15.495–501.

16 The fasts here referred to would seem to be the Ten Days of Penitence between Rosh Ha-Shanah and Yom Kippur (the Day of Atonement). See art. "Ten Days of Penitence," in EJ 15.1001. For Yom Kippur, which falls on the tenth of Tishri, see McKenzie, "Day of Atonement," DB 69-70. C. Stuhlmueller (JBC 22:54) sees Ez 42.20 and Neh 9.1 as witnesses to the effort of concentrating on one great day of fasting, Yom Kippur (cf. Lv. 16.29).

17 Another evidence that the series De incomp. was interrupted after the first homily of that series.

18 Is 58.3–5 shows how the Jews' fasting was unacceptable to God and involved transgressions. See below Disc. 1.2.6–7.

19 Cf. Jn 5.18.

resolve to reject it even if they do not physically erase it.

II

But do not be surprised that I called the Jews pitiable. They really are pitiable and miserable. When so many blessings from heaven came into their hands, they thrust them aside and were at great pains to reject them. The morning Sun of Justice arose for them, but they thrust aside its rays and still sit in darkness. We, who were nurtured by darkness, drew the light to ourselves and were freed from the gloom of their error. They were the branches of that holy root, but those branches were broken.[20] We had no share in the root, but we did reap the fruit of godliness. From their childhood they read the prophets, but they crucified him whom the prophets had foretold. We did not hear the divine prophecies but we did worship him of whom they prophesied. And so they are pitiful because they rejected the blessings which were sent to them, while others seized hold of these blessings and drew them to themselves. Although those Jews had been called to the adoption of sons, they fell to kinship with dogs; we who were dogs received the strength, through God's grace, to put aside the irrational nature which was ours and to rise to the honor of sons. How do I prove this? Christ said: "It is not fair to take the children's bread and to cast it to the dogs."[21] Christ was speaking to

---

20 Cf. Rom 11.16–17. A. Theissen (CCHS 1072) points out that "holy" refers to Israel's objective holiness, i.e., her election and being set apart for God. For St. Paul the root is the root of the olive tree, which is a metaphor for Israel in Jer 11.16 and Hos 14.7. In Rom 11.17–24 the olive tree is no longer the symbol of the OT church but of the OT church continued in the Church of Christ, where Gentile branches are grafted on the old tree and not planted as new trees. [The revised article by P. Byrne (NCCHS 1134) adds nothing new to Theissen.] But Chrysostom sees the Old Covenant as abrogated rather than fulfilled. The Jews rejected God's blessings and now God has rejected Israel.

21 Matt. 15.26. Chrysostom seems to miss the fact that Christ's reply to the Canaanite woman is a little parable turned into an allegory, and that his words are not as harsh as they seem. Cf. A. Jones (CCHS 880), who

the Canaanite woman when He called the Jews children and the Gentiles dogs.

(2) But see how thereafter the order was changed about: they became dogs, and we became the children. Paul said of the Jews: "Beware of the dogs, beware of the evil workers, beware of the mutilation. For we are the circumcision."²² Do you see how those who at first were children became dogs? Do you wish to find out how we, who at first were dogs, became children? "But to as many as received him, he gave the power of becoming sons of God."²³

(3) Nothing is more miserable than those people who never failed to attack their own salvation. When there was need to observe the Law, they trampled it under foot. Now that the Law has ceased to bind, they obstinately strive to observe it. What could be more pitiable than those who provoke God not only by transgressing the Law but also by keeping it? On this account Stephen said: "You stiff-necked and uncircumcised in heart, [846] you always resist the Holy Spirit,"²⁴ not only by transgressing the Law but

---

further points out that Christ used the diminutive form (*kynaria*), "pet dogs." Although Chrysostom quotes the text accurately, all his other references here to dogs (both Jew and Gentile) use a non-diminutive form, which implies some contempt.

22 Phil 3.2–3. This whole chapter of Phil is directed against Jews and Judaizers (cf. NAB note *ad loc.*). The word "dogs" (and Paul does not use the diminutive) is a term of contempt and, according to a note in Confr. *ad loc.*, means "false teachers," a term which the Jews of the time applied to the godless and to Gentiles. The phrase "evil workers" (cf. C. Lattey, CCHS 1130) means the Jews, especially as practicing and inculcating circumcision, which Paul implies has now become mere mutilation. The true circumcision is now circumcision of heart and soul. Cf. Acts 7.51.

23 Jn 1.12. W. Leonard (CCHS 980) points out that the "power" is the grace of faith. To receive the Word is an act of faith, and faith is the means of appropriating the dignity of divine sonship. Cf. Gal 3.26: "For you are all the children of God through faith in Christ Jesus."

24 Acts 7.51. Stephen suggests that the Jews are no better than pagans because their hearts are hardened and their ears closed to the spiritual meaning of their religion (cf. C.S. Dessain, CCHS 1029). Chrysostom discusses the Jews' opposition to the Holy Spirit in *Disc.* 4.4.3.

also by wishing to observe it at the wrong time. (4) Stephen was right in calling them stiff-necked. For they failed to take up the yoke of Christ, although it was sweet and had nothing about it which was either burdensome or oppressive. For he said: "Learn from me for I am meek and humble of heart," and, "Take my yoke upon you, for my yoke is sweet and my burden light."[25] Nonetheless they failed to take up the yoke because of the stiffness of their necks. Not only did they fail to take it up but they broke it and destroyed it. For Jeremiah said: "Long ago you broke your yoke and burst your bonds."[26] It was not Paul who said this but the voice of the prophet speaking loud and clear. When he spoke of the yoke and the bonds, he meant the symbols of rule, because the Jews rejected the rule of Christ when they said: "We have no king but Caesar."[27] You Jews broke the yoke, you burst the bonds, you cast yourselves out of the kingdom of heaven, and you made yourselves subject to the rule of men.[28] Please consider with me how accurately the prophet hinted that their hearts were uncontrolled. He did not say: "You set aside the yoke," but "You broke the yoke," and this is the crime of untamed beasts,

---

25 Cf. Mt 11.29–30. Chrysostom's quotation is neither complete nor precise. But it does give Christ's great invitation to faith in him and his Law. The "yoke" is a metaphor for the Law (cf. Jer 5.5 and Acts 15.10). Christ's Law is easy because he perfects the Law (Mt 5.17) and has joined to it the Beatitudes (Mt 5.3–12), which make outward appearance subject to inward spirit; this makes the New Law a Law of love. Since the Law is his, those who seek to follow it will have His help and will find the burden light (cf. A. Jones, CCHS 872). Stephen called the Jews stiff-necked because they failed to take up the yoke of Christ's New Law as they had broken the yoke of the Old.

26 Cf. Jer 2.20. See also *ibid.* 5.5 and Ps 2.3. Again, the "yoke" is the Law. From Jer 5.5 we see that even the great ones "had broken the yoke and torn off the harness." The theme of Ps 2 is the conflict of the forces of evil with God and his anointed King whom they reject.

27 Cf. Jn 19.15.

28 This is the first of many direct addresses to the Jews. Consistently, throughout the text of all eight homilies, Chrysostom uses the singular ("You, O Jew"), which I have in all cases translated in the plural because the rhetorical apostrophe seemed to single out no one individual but to address the Jewish people as a whole.

who are uncontrolled and reject rule.

(5) But what is the source of this hardness? It comes from gluttony and drunkenness. Who says so? Moses himself. "Israel ate and was filled and the darling grew fat and frisky."[29] When brute animals feed from a full manger, they grow plump and become more obstinate and hard to hold in check; they endure neither the yoke, the reins, nor the hand of the charioteer. Just so the Jewish people were driven by their drunkenness and plumpness to the ultimate evil; they kicked about, they failed to accept the yoke of Christ, nor did they pull the plow of his teaching.[30] Another prophet hinted at this when he said. "Israel is as obstinate as a stubborn heifer."[31] And still another called the Jews "an untamed calf."[32]

(6) Although such beasts are unfit for work, they are fit for killing. And this is what happened to the Jews: while they were making themselves unfit for work, they grew fit for slaughter. This is why Christ said: "But as for these my enemies, who did not want me to be king over them, bring them here and slay them."[33] You Jews should have fasted then, when drunkenness was doing those terrible things to you, when your gluttony was giving birth to your ungodli-

29 Cf. Dt 32.15. Chrysostom reads "Israel" for "Jacob" of LXX. JB gives: "Jacob ate and had his fill, Jeshurun grew fat, turned restive"; a note adds that Jeshurun (a word of uncertain derivation) is applied to Israel here and in 33.5. The verse is taken from the canticle of Moses (Dt 32.1–43); verses 15–18 show how Israel abused God's kindness. Chrysostom points this out in *Disc.* 3.3.8, where he quotes verse 18.

30 Chrysostom uses the same metaphor of the plow elsewhere (cf., e.g., P.W. Harkins in ACW 31.120) but here the point is that the Jews, like obstinate oxen, reject the yoke of Christ's Law and refuse to pull the plow of instruction.

31 Cf. Hos 4.16.

32 Cf. Jer 31.18 (38.18 in LXX) which reads: "Like a calf I was untamed."

33 Lk 19.27. This text is the climax of the parable of the gold pieces (*ibid.* 11-27). Both this and the parable of the talents (Mt 25.14–30) show a master who tests his servants, rewards the faithful, and punishes the wicked. Luke's words "who did not want me to be king over them" are made necessary by his addition in 19.14 ("We do not wish this man to be king over us"); they contain a formidable lesson for the Jewish leaders. Chrysostom refers to the parable from Matthew in *Disc.* 8.9.8–10 and quotes Lk 19.27 in the *Demonstration* 4 (PG 48.819).

ness—not now. Now your fasting is untimely and an abomination. Who said so? Isaiah himself when he called out in a loud voice: "I did not choose this fast, says the Lord." Why? "You quarrel and squabble when you fast and strike those subject to you with your fists."³⁴ But if your fasting was an abomination when you were striking your fellow slaves, does it become acceptable now that you have slain your Master? How could that be right?

(7) The man who fasts should be properly restrained, contrite, humbled—not drunk with anger. But do you strike your fellow slaves? In Isaiah's day they quarreled and squabbled when they fasted; now when they fast, they go in for excesses and the ultimate licentiousness, dancing with bare feet in the marketplace. The pretext is that they are fasting, but they act like men who are drunk. Hear how the prophet bid them to fast. "Sanctify a fast," he said.³⁵ He did not say: "Make a parade of your fasting," but "call an assembly; gather together the ancients."³⁶ But these Jews are gathering choruses of effeminates and a great rubbish heap of [847] harlots; they drag into the synagogue the whole theater, actors and all. For there is no difference between the theater and the synagogue.³⁷ I know that some suspect me of rashness because I said there is no difference between the theater and the synagogue; but I

---

34 Is 58.4–5 etc. The whole chapter deals with true fasting to which injustice and oppression are obstacles. The preoccupation of the Jews with the observance of fast days suggests a situation such as is indicated in Zec 7.3–14 where justice and charity are enjoined as more pleasing to God (cf. E. Power, CCHS 570). The fast days to which Isaiah refers appear to be those instituted to commemorate the fall of Jerusalem (cf. Zec 8.19 and NAB, note *ad loc.*).

35 Jl 1.14. verse 5 says: "Wake up, you drunkards, and weep; wail all you drinkers of wine, because the juice of the grape will be withheld from your mouths." A locust plague on the land of Judah is the occasion for Joel's call to penance.

36 *Ibid.*

37 See Introd. II 18. Cf. G. Ladner, in *Viator* 2 (1971) 358-59, who says: "John Chrysostom makes it appear as if Christians were attracted . . . merely by comparatively external paraphernalia and customs, especially by the sound of their tubas, by their fasting, followed by festive dancing and singing . . ." Cf. Also *Disc.* 2.3.4; 7.1.2.

suspect them of rashness if they do not think that this is so. If my declaration that the two are the same rests on my own authority, then charge me with rashness. But if the words I speak are the words of the prophet, then accept his decision.

III

Many, I know, respect the Jews and think that their present way of life[38] is a venerable one. This is why I hasten to uproot and tear out this deadly opinion. I said that the synagogue is no better than a theater and I bring forward a prophet as my witness. Surely the Jews are not more deserving of belief than their prophets. "You had a harlot's brow; you became shameless before all." [39] Where a harlot has set herself up, that place is a brothel. But the synagogue is not only a brothel and a theater; it also is a den of robbers and a lodging

---

38 For "way of life" Chrysostom uses *politeia,* which means, politically, citizenship or government; it is then extended to the citizen's daily life, conduct, or way of life. The adjective "venerable" seems to give it a religious sense as well. If "venerable" here means "impressive on account of age or history," the Jewish way of life was such at Antioch, because its government and institutions there could be traced back to Seleucus I (ca. 300 B.C.); under Antiochus IV the Jews were a quasi-autonomous unit who preserved their religious individuality and were judged by their own judges according to their own laws (see Downey, *History* 107–11 and Kraeling 138–39). Elsewhere I have translated *politeia* as "commonwealth and way of life" because it seems to imply citizenship in Jerusalem and the way of life of God's chosen nation. A developed analysis of the meaning of *politeia* is given by G. W. H. Lampe, *A Patristic Greek Lexicon* (Oxford 1961) 1113 (sect. F of the article).

39 Cf. Jer 3.3 (LXX). McKenzie, DB 700, points out that the infidelity of Israel to Yahweh is called prostitution a number of times by the prophets and cites, among other passages, Jer 3.1–4 and 6–10. Ladner, *ibid.,* finds Chrysostom's anti–Jewish polemical method very repellent when he applies the vituperations of Israel by its prophets to Jews of his own time. This is true; furthermore, as good argumentation, it is of dubious efficacy unless Chrysostom (and his congregation) knew that the Antiochene Jews of his time were acting much as their ancestors did in the days of Jeremiah and the other prophets. Equating the synagogue with the theater and the bordello is a rhetorical *tour de force* which seems aimed at proving that all three offer grave risks to the Christian rather than, as Ladner says, that all Jews are impure animals and demons.

for wild beasts. Jeremiah said: "Your house has become for me the den of a hyena."[40] He does not simply say "of a wild beast,"but "of a filthy wild beast," and again: "I have abandoned my house, I have cast off my inheritance."[41] But when God forsakes a people, what hope of salvation is left? When God forsakes a place, that place becomes the dwelling of demons.

(2) But at any rate the Jews say that they, too, adore God. God forbid that I say that. No Jew adores God! Who says so? The Son of God says so. For he said: "If you were to know my Father, you would also know me. But you neither know me nor do you know my Father."[42] Could I produce a witness more trustworthy than the Son of God?

(3) If, then, the Jews fail to know the Father, if they crucified the Son, if they thrust off the help of the Spirit, who should not make bold to declare plainly that the synagogue is a dwelling of demons? God is not worshipped there. Heaven forbid! From now on it remains a place of idolatry. But still some people pay it honor as a holy place.

(4) Let me tell you this, not from guesswork but from my own experience. Three days ago—believe me, I am not lying—I saw a free woman of good bearing, modest, and a believer. A brutal, unfeeling man, reputed to be a Christian (for I would not call a person who would dare to do such a thing a sincere Christian) was forcing her to enter the shrine of the Hebrews[43] and to swear

---

40 Chrysostom's citation is not accurate. It may be a conflation of Jer 7.11 (LXX), which reads: "Is my house a den of thieves . . .?" and Jer 12.9 (LXX), which reads: "Is not my inheritance to me a hyena's cave . . .?"
41 Cf. Jer 12.7. Chrysostom transposes the verbs of the LXX text. The note in JB points out that "house" here means "land," as in Zec 9.8.
42 Cf. Jn 8.19. NAB reads: "You know neither me nor my Father. If you knew me, you would know my Father too." Chrysostom not only inverts the two sentences but also the objects of the second. Because the Son is his witness, Chrysostom may put him first in both sentences. Unfortunately, where Chrysostom discusses the text in his *Commentary on John* (52.3–4; PG 59.290–91), he does not quote it but merely stresses that Father and Son are the same in nature and substance.
43 This would be the synagogue. As pointed out before (Introd. II 19) the Jews had their own courts and judges; even Christians may have found

there an oath about some matters under dispute with him. She came up to me and asked for help; she begged me to prevent this lawless violence—for it was forbidden to her, who had shared in the divine mysteries,[44] to enter that place. I was fired with indignation, I became angry, I rose up, I refused to let her be dragged into that transgression, I snatched her from the hands of her abductor. I asked him if he were a Christian, and he said he was. Then I set upon him virgorously, charging him with lack of feeling and the worst stupidity; I told him he was no better off than a mule if he, who professed to worship Christ, would drag someone off to the dens of the Jews who had crucified him. I talked to him a long time, drawing my lesson from the Holy Gospels;[45] I told him first that it was altogether forbidden to swear and that it was wrong to impose the necessity of swearing on anyone.[46] I then told him [848] that he must not subject a baptized believer to this necessity. In fact, he must not force even an unbaptized person to swear an oath.

(5) After I had talked with him at great length and had driven the folly of his error from his soul, I asked him why he rejected the Church and dragged the woman to the place where the Hebrews assembled. He answered that many people had told him that oaths sworn there were more to be feared. His words made me groan, then I grew angry, and finally I began to smile. When I saw the devil's wickedness, I groaned because he had the power to seduce men; I grew angry when I considered how careless were

---

these tribunals, which sat in the synagogues, more solemn and impartial than the civil courts, just as oaths sworn there were considered more sacred and binding than those taken elsewhere. Cf. Graetz 2.614 and Ladner, *ibid.*

44 The divine mysteries are the Mass. The Synod of Laodicea in Phrygia (ca. 360) had formulated important Canons for the discipline of clergy and laity. Canon 37 forbade anyone to take from Jews or heretics any gifts on feast days or to celebrate a feast with them; Canon 38 forbade anyone to accept unleavened bread from Jews or to participate in their sacrileges. See C. Hefele, *Histoire des conciles* 1.2 1019.

45 Cf., e.g., Mt 5.33–37.

46 For Chrysostom's strong attitude towards all oaths and swearing see ACW 31.143–49; 297–300.

those who were deceived; when I saw the extent and depth of the folly of those who were deceived, I smiled.

(6) I told you this story because you are savage and ruthless in your attitude toward those who do such things and undergo these experiences. If you see one of your brothers falling into such transgressions, you consider that it is someone else's misfortune, not your own; you think you have defended yourselves against your accusers when you say: "What concern of mine is it? What do I have in common with that man?" When you say that, your words manifest the utmost hatred for mankind and a cruelty which befits the devil. What are you saying? You are a man and share the same nature. Why speak of a common nature when you have but a single head, Christ? Do you dare to say you have nothing in common with your own members? In what sense do you admit that Christ is the head of the Church? For certainly it is the function of the head to join all the limbs together, to order them carefully to each other, and to bind them into one nature. But if you have nothing in common with your members, then you have nothing in common with your brother, nor do you have Christ as your head.[47]

(7) The Jews frighten you as if you were little children, and you do not see it. Many wicked slaves show frightening and ridiculous masks to youngsters—the masks are not frightening by their nature, but they seem so to the children's simple minds—and in this way they stir up many a laugh.[48] This is the way the Jews

---

47 The doctrine of Christ's Mystical Body, a favorite with Chrysostom. Cf., e.g., ACW 31. 177, 328, 329, where Chrysostom speaks of Christ as our head and us as His members and body. The classical text for this doctrine, 1 Cor. 12, is discussed in Chrysostom's *Commentary on 1 Corinthians* (PG 61.263D–264D). In his Fifth Baptismal Instruction (14), Chrysostom bases the mutual concern of Christians for the salvation of all members on 1 Cor. 12.27 and Eph. 4.25.

48 Chrysostom speaks of children frightened by masks and hobgoblins because of natural weakness. Cf. ACW 31.136. There the context is not the synagogue but the baths of the Jews (cf. Lv 15.5 and *passim*). He also speaks of mothers who frighten their children with masks so that they will run to their embrace (ACW 31.293). Cf. *Disc.* 3.1.8.

frighten the simpler-minded Christians with the bugbears and hob-goblins of their shrines. Yet how could their ridiculous and dis-graceful synagogues frighten you? Are they not the shrines of men who have been rejected, dishonored, and condemned?

IV

Our churches are not like that; they are truly frightening and filled with fear.[49] God's presence makes a place frightening be-cause he has power over life and death.[50] In our churches we hear countless discourses on eternal punishments, on rivers of fire, on the venomous worm, on bonds that cannot be burst, on exterior darkness. But the Jews neither know nor dream of these things. They live for their bellies, they gape for the things of this world, their condition is no better than that of pigs or goats because of their wanton ways and excessive gluttony. They know but one thing: to fill their bellies and be drunk, to get all cut and bruised, to be hurt and wounded while fighting for their favorite chario-teers.[51]

(2) Tell me, then, are their shrines awful and frightening? Who would say so? What reasons do we have for thinking that they are frightening unless someone should tell us that dishonored slaves, who have no right to speak and who have been driven from their Master's home, should frighten us, who have been given honor and the freedom to speak? Certainly this is not the case. Inns are not

---

49 Cf. Gen 28.17. The centuries-old adaptation of this verse (and of a phrase in verse 22) as the introit of the Mass in the Common for the Dedication of a Church has been preserved in the current *Missale Romanum* of Pope Paul VI; in English it runs as follows: "Terrible is this place: it is the house of God, and the gate of heaven; and it shall be called the court of God."
50 Cf., e.g., Jn 5.21.
51 For Chrysostom's attitude toward the theater and horse racing see Dow-ney, *History* 443–45. Cf. also G. La Piana, "The Byzantine Theater," *Speculum* 11 (1936) 171–211; B. H. Vandenberghe, "Saint Jean Chrysos-tome et les spectacles," *Zeitschrift für Religions- und Geistesgeschichte* 7 (1955) 34–46.

more august then royal palaces. Indeed the synagogue [849] is less deserving of honor than any inn. It is not merely a lodging place for robbers and cheats but also for demons. This is true not only of the synagogues but also of the souls of the Jews, as I shall try to prove at the end of my discourse.[52]

(3) I urge you to keep my words in your minds in a special way. For I am not now speaking for show or applause[53] but to cure your souls. And what else is left for me to say when some of you are still sick although there are so many physicians to effect a cure?[54]

(4) There were twelve apostles and they drew the whole world to themselves. The greater portion of the city is Christian, yet some are still sick with the Judaizing disease. And what could we, who are healthy, say in our own defense? Surely those who are sick deserve to be accused. But we are not free from blame, because we have neglected them in their hour of illness; if we had shown great concern for them and they had the benefit of this care, they could not possibly still be sick.

(5) Let me get the start on you by saying this now, so that each of you may win over his brother. Even if you must impose restraint, even if you must use force, even if you must treat him ill and obstinately, do everything to save him from the devil's snare and to free him from fellowship with those who slew Christ.

(6) Tell me this. Suppose you were to see a man who had been justly condemned being led to execution through the marketplace. Suppose it were in your power to save him from the hands of the public executioner. Would you not do all you could to keep him from being dragged off? But now you see your own brother being dragged off unjustly and wickedly to the depth of destruction. And it is not the executioner who drags him off, but the devil. Would you be so bold as not to do your part toward rescuing him

---

52 See below *Disc.* 1.6.6 and 2.3.5.
53 See the references to applause above, n. 10.
54 Chrysostom has many references to physicians and cures. Cf., e.g., *Disc.* 2.1.1–2. The "many physicians" are his non–Judaizing listeners who formed a majority of the city's population, as he will say in a moment.

from his transgression? If you don't help him, what excuse would you find? But your brother is stronger and more powerful than you. Show him to me. If he will stand fast in his obstinate resolve, I shall choose to risk my life rather than let him enter the doors of the synagogue.

(7) I shall say to him: What fellowship do you have with the free Jerusalem, with the Jerusalem above?[55] You chose the one below; be a slave with that earthly Jerusalem which, according to the word of the Apostle, is a slave together with her children.[56] Do you fast with the Jews? Then take off your shoes with the Jews, and walk barefoot in the marketplace, and share with them in their indecency and laughter. But you would not choose to do this because you are ashamed and apt to blush. Are you ashamed to share with them in outward appearance but unashamed to share in their impiety? What excuse will you have, you who are only half a Christian?[57]

(8) Believe me, I shall risk my life before I would neglect any one who is sick with this disease—if I see him. If I fail to see him, surely God will grant me pardon. And let each one of you consider this matter; let him not think it is something of secondary importance. Do you take no notice of what the deacon continuously calls out at the mysteries? "Recognize one another,"[58] he says. Do you not see how he entrusts to you the careful examination of your brothers? Do this in the case of the Judaizers, too. When you observe someone Judaizing, take hold of him, show him what he is doing, so that you may not yourself be an accessory to the risk he runs.

---

55 The contrast is between the earthly Jerusalem of the Old Covenant and the Jerusalem above of the New. See ACW 31.77, 132, 154, 247, 249, 284.

56 Cf. Gal 4.25–26 and notes in both NAB and Confr. *ad loc.,* which identify the present Jerusalem with the Old Testament and synagogue and the free Jerusalem above with the New Testament and the Church.

57 Cf. the notion of demi-Christian in the Introd. II 8–9.

58 This is the first of two passages in the sermons *Adversus Iudaeos* which reflect more or less exactly the language of small sections of the liturgy

(9) If any Roman soldier serving overseas[59] is caught favoring the barbarians and the Persians, not only is he in danger but so also is everyone who was aware of how this man felt and failed to make this fact known to the general. Since you are the army of Christ, be overly careful [850] in searching to see if anyone favoring an alien faith has mingled among you, and make his presence known—not so that we may put him to death as those generals did, nor that we may punish him or take our vengeance upon him, but that we may free him from his error and ungodliness and make him entirely our own.

(10) If you are unwilling to do this, if you know of such a person but conceal him, be sure that both you and he will be subject to the same penalty. For Paul subjects to chastisement and punishment not only those who commit acts of wickedness but also those who approve what they have done.[60] The prophet, too,

---

known to Chrysostom at Antioch toward the end of the fourth century (for the other passage see below, *Disc.* III nn. 87 and 88; and cf. *Disc.* III n. 52). On the earlier study of these texts made by F.E. Brightman, *Liturgies Eastern and Western* (Oxford 1896; repr. 1965, 1967) 470–481 (cf. p. liii), notable advance has recently been made by Frans van de Paverd, *Zur Geschichte der Messliturgie . . . : Analyse der Quellen bei Johannes Chrysostomos* (Rome 1970; see above, Select Bibliography), a work kindly brought to my attention by Dom Anselm Strittmatter, O.S.B. As regards the present passage, the deacon's proclamation *Epiginōskete allēlous* ("Recognize one another") appears in some contexts as part of the dismissal of the catechumens and has in effect the meaning advanced by Brightman (596–97), "See that no disqualified person is present." Van de Paverd (239–41) rightly holds, however, that Chrysostom intends the verb in a more positive sense, one reminiscent of the meaning given it by St. Paul in 1 Cor 16.18, 2 Cor 13.5.

59 Constantius made Antioch his headquarters during his war against the Persians, against whom he conducted almost annual campaigns (339–350). Gallus, appointed Caesar by Constantius in 351, came to Antioch and immediately organized a spy system to search out and execute the disaffected (Downey, *History* 355–63). The war was renewed in 359 (*ibid.* 368) and continued during the reign of Julian the Apostate and Valens, who defeated the Persians in 373 (*ibid.* 381, 391, 402).

60 Cf. Rom 1.32. Paul is speaking of the punishment of idolaters; he means that the pagan's abysmal state is shown not only in his own failure to honor God and live an upright life but in his approval of the same conduct in others.

brings to the same judgment not only thieves but those who run with the thieves.[61] And this is quite reasonable. For if a man is aware of a criminal's actions but covers them up and conceals them, he is providing a stronger basis for the criminal to be careless of the law and making him less afraid in his career of crime.

V

But I must get back again to those who are sick. Consider, then, with whom they are sharing their fasts. It is with those who shouted. "Crucify him, Crucify him,"[62] with those who said: "His blood be upon us and upon our children."[63] If some men had been caught in rebellion against their ruler and were condemned, would you have dared to go up to them and to speak with them? I think not. Is it not foolish, then, to show such readiness to flee from those who have sinned against a man, but to enter into fellowship with those who have committed outrages against God himself? Is it not strange that those who worship the Crucified keep common festival with those who crucified him? Is it not a sign of folly and the worst madness?

(2) Since there are some who think of the synagogue as a holy place, I must say a few words to them. Why do you reverence that

---

61 Cf. Ps 49 (50). 18.

62 Lk 23.21.

63 Mt 27.25. Chrysostom obviously holds the position, which was common for centuries, that all Jews are responsible for Christ's passion and death. Vatican II's "Declaration on the Relationship of the Church to Non-Christian Religions" (*Documents of Vatican II*, ed. W. Abbott, 666) states that these "cannot be blamed on all the Jews then living, without distinction, nor upon the Jews of today. Although the Church is the new people of God, the Jews should not be presented as repudiated or cursed by God, as if such views followed from the holy Sceiptures." A footnote at this point says that Cardinal Bea and others explained Mt 27.25 as the cry of a Jerusalem crowd that had no right to speak for the whole Jewish people. J. Fitzmeyer discusses the text in "Anti-Semitism and Matthew 27. 25," *Theological Studies* 26 (1965) 667-71. Chrysostom quotes the same text in *Disc.* 6.1.7 to prove that the martyrs have a special hatred for the Jews.

place? Must you not despise it, hold it in abomination, run away from it? They answer that the Law and the books of the prophets are kept there. What is this? Will any place where these books are be a holy place? By no means! This is the reason above all others why I hate the synagogue and abhor it. They have the prophets but do not believe them; they read the sacred writings but reject their witness—and this is a mark of men guilty of the greatest outrage.

(3) Tell me this. If you were to see a venerable man, illustrious and renowned, dragged off into a tavern or den of robbers; if you were to see him outraged, beaten, and subjected there to the worst violence, would you have held that tavern or den in high esteem because that great and esteemed man had been inside it while undergoing that violent treatment? I think not. Rather, for this very reason you would have hated and abhorred the place.

(4) Let that be your judgment about the synagogue, too. For they brought the books of Moses and the prophets along with them into the synagogue, not to honor them but to outrage them with dishonor. When they say that Moses and the prophets knew not Christ and said nothing about his coming, what greater outrage could they do to those holy men[64] than to accuse them of failing to recognize their Master, than to say that those saintly prophets are partners of their impiety? And so it is that we must hate both them and their synagogue all the more because of their offensive treatment of those holy men.

(5) Why do I speak about the books and the synagogues? In time of persecution, the public executioners lay hold of the bodies of the martyrs, they scourge them, and tear them to pieces.[65] Does it make the executioners' hands holy because they lay hold

---

64 Not only are the prophets without honor in their country (cf. Lk 4.24; Jn 4.44) but were not inspired by God when they predicted the coming of Christ; hence, their message was rejected by the Jews.

65 Chrysostom gives many vivid descriptions of the sufferings of the martyrs. See, e.g., ACW 31.111, 274–76 and G. Racle, "A la source d'un passage de la VIIᵉ Catéchèse Baptismale de S. Jean Chrysostome," *Vigiliae Christianae* 15 (1961) 46–53.

of the bodies of holy men? Heaven forbid! The hands which grasped and held the bodies of the holy ones still stay unholy. Why? Because those executioners did a wicked thing when they laid their hands upon the holy. And will those who [851] handle and outrage the writings of the holy ones be any more venerable for this than those who executed the martyrs? Would that not be the ultimate foolishness? If the maltreated bodies of the martyrs do not sanctify those who maltreated them but even add to their blood-guilt, much less could the Scriptures, if read without belief, ever help those who read without believing. The very act of deliberately choosing to maltreat the Scriptures convicts them of greater godlessness.

(6) If they did not have the prophets, they would not deserve such punishment; if they had not read the sacred books, they would not be so unclean and so unholy. But, as it is, they have been stripped of all excuse. They do have the heralds of the truth but, with hostile heart, they set themselves against the prophets and the truth they speak. So it is for this reason that they would be all the more profane and blood-guilty: they have the prophets, but they treat them with hostile hearts.

(7) So it is that I exhort you to flee and shun their gatherings. The harm they bring to our weaker brothers is not slight; they offer no slight excuse to sustain the folly of the Jews. For when they see that you, who worship the Christ whom they crucified, are reverently following their ritual, how can they fail to think that the rites they have performed are the best and that our ceremonies are worthless? For after you worship and adore at our mysteries, you run to the very men who destroy our rites. Paul said:

"If a man sees you that have knowledge[66] sit at meat in the idol's temple, shall not his conscience, being weak, be emboldened to eat

---

66 The knowledge here mentioned may be the Christian *gnosis* of Clement and Origen. There were at Corinth Jewish Christians pretending to have a charismatic knowledge of the Scripture and its application to practical living which made them superior to others.

those things which are sacrificed to idols?"[67] And let me say: If a man sees you that have knowledge come into the synagogue and participate in the festival of the Trumpets, shall not his conscience, being weak, be emboldened to admire what the Jews do? He who falls not only pays the penalty for his own fall, but he is also punished because he trips others as well. But the man who has stood firm is rewarded not only because of his own virtue but people admire him for leading others to desire the same things.[68]

(8) Therefore, flee the gatherings and holy places of the Jews. Let no man venerate the synagogue because of the holy books; let him hate and avoid it because the Jews outrage and maltreat the holy ones, because they refuse to believe their words, because they accuse them of the ultimate impiety.[69]

VI

That you may know that the sacred books do not make a place holy but that the purpose of those who frequent a place does make it profane, I shall tell an old story. Ptolemy Philadelphus[70] had collected books from all over the world. When he learned that the Jews had writings which treated of God and the ideal state, he sent for men from Judea and had them translate those books, which he then had deposited in the temple of Serapis, for he was

---

67 Cf. 1 Cor 8.10. Even though the "knowledge" be false or overconfident, it can be a stumbling block to the weak (8.9) and encourage them to act against their consciences.

68 In the Greek, many of the words in these last two sentences have athletic connotations from wrestling.

69 See above *Disc.* 1.5.4.

70 According to legend the Greek translation of the Pentateuch was the work of seventy (or rather seventy-two) translators; it was called, therefore, the Septuagint. The term was extended to include the translation into Greek of the entire OT. It is still the official Bible of both the Greek Orthodox Church and the Greek rite of the Catholic Church. See L.F. Hartman, "Septuagint," NCE 13.97. Montfaucon thinks it highly improbable that the books were still preserved "up to the present day" in the temple of Serapis (PG 48.851 n.).

a pagan.[71] Up to the present day the translated books remain there in the temple. But will the temple of Serapis be holy because of the holy books? Heaven forbid! Although the books have their own holiness, they do not give a share of it to the place because those who frequent the place are defiled.

(2) You must apply the same argument to the synagogue. Even if there is no idol there, [852] still demons do inhabit the place. And I say this not only about the synagogue here in town but about the one in Daphne as well;[72] for at Daphne you have a more wicked place of perdition which they call Matrona's.[73] I have heard that many of the faithful go up there and sleep beside the place.[74]

---

71 The Greek word for "pagan" is *Hellēn*, literally meaning a Hellene or Greek. Is 9.12 (LXX) uses it for gentile as opposed to Jew, as does Jn (7.35 [see NAB note *ad loc.*] and 12.20). In NT the word *ethos* (nation) is more frequently used for non—Jews, but we find *Hellēn* in Acts (eleven times) and in the Pauline Epistles (thirteen times) in the sense of gentile or pagan. In fact, Chrysostom uses the term *Hellēn* for pagan in the title to his *Demonstration against Jews and Pagans on the Divinity of Christ* and throughout the text.

72 In *Disc.* 5.12.12 Chrysostom speaks in the plural of both urban and suburban synagogues, but his plural may be a generalizing one; at an earlier time there may have been several more (cf. Downey, *History* 109–11). One synagogue at Daphne was destroyed under Titus (A.D. 79) to make room for a theater (p. 206) but must have been replaced by one which stood there in Chrysostom's day. Either that synagogue or a later one was plundered and burned in the riots of the Olympic Games of 507 (cf. pp. 505–506).

73 Chrysostom refers to this place in his commentary *In Epist. ad Titum* 3.3 (PG 62.679): "But if those who observe their diets are sick (Paul says 'For receive those who are weak in faith; do not enter into disputes about opinions with them' [cf. Rom 14.1]), what would you say of those who keep the same fasts with them, who observe their sabbaths? What would you say of those who go to places which are consecrated in their eyes? I mean the place in Daphne, the cave called Matrona's . . ." Montfaucon's note *ad loc.* refers to the text here, where the cave is called a shrine because sacred to Matrona (who some think is Juno) and Apollo. Juno is called *Matrona* by Horace, *Odes* 3.4.59 and in some inscriptions. It is interesting that Chrysostom transliterates the Latin word here as he does "Saturn" also in *In Epist. ad Titum* 3.3 (PG 62.679), referring to a shrine in Cilicia. Cf. Guignebert 88–89.

74 The reference is to "incubation," a practice wherein a suppliant would

(3) But heaven forbid that I call these people faithful. For to me the shrine of Matrona and the temple of Apollo [75] are equally profane. If anyone charges me with boldness, I will in turn charge him with the utmost madness. For, tell me, is not the dwelling place of demons a place of impiety even if no god's statue stands there? Here the slayers of Christ gather together, here the cross is driven out, here God is blasphemed, here the Father is ignored, here the Son is outraged, here the grace of the Spirit is rejected. Does not greater harm come from this place since the Jews themselves are demons? In the pagan temple the impiety is naked and obvious; hence, it would not be easy to deceive a man of sound and prudent mind or entice him to go there. But in the synagogue there are men who say they worship God and abhor idols, men who say they have prophets and pay them honor. But by their words they make ready an abundance of bait to catch in their nets the simpler souls who are so foolish as to be caught off guard.

(4) So the godlessness of the Jews and the pagans is on a par. But the Jews practice a deceit which is more dangerous. In their synagogue stands an invisible altar of deceit on which they sacrifice not sheep and calves but the souls of men.[76]

(5) Finally, if the ceremonies of the Jews move you to admiration, what do you have in common with us? If the Jewish ceremo-

---

lodge for a few days in the precincts of some sanctuary to entreat the god and obtain a divine oracle through a dream or in some other manner (Cf. T. Gaster, *Thespis* [Garden City, N.Y. 1961] 330). There might be a reference here to temple prostitution, which was, however, a pagan rather than a Jewish practice (cf. Dt 23.18–19). It is doubtful that "the women serving at the entrance of the meeting tent, " with whom the sons of Eli lay (cf. 1 Sm [1 Kgs] 2.22 and note *ad loc* in NAB) were temple prostitutes, but the sacred character of the servant women's duties aggravated the sin of Eli's sons. Cf. JBC 9:13. Tertullian speaks of one who sleeps in a temple as *incubator* in his *De anima* 49 (trans. E.A. Quain in FC 10.228).

75 The temple of Apollo at Daphne was both ancient and famous; it contained a statue of the god rivaling in size the statue of Zeus at Olympia. The statue and temple roof were burned when struck by lighting. See Downey, *History,* esp. 105, 364–65, 387–88, and 595–96.

76 Of course the synagogues, unlike the temples, could have neither altars nor sacrifices. Since, however, the godlessness of pagans and Jews is on a par, the synagogue destroys men's souls on its invisible altar of deceit.

nies are venerable and great, ours are lies. But if ours are true, as they *are* true, theirs are filled with deceit. I am not speaking of the Scriptures. Heaven forbid! It was the Scriptures which took me by the hand and led me to Christ.[77] But I am talking about the ungodliness and present madness of the Jews.

(6) Certainly it is the time for me to show that demons dwell in the synagogue, not only in the place itself but also in the souls of the Jews. As Christ said: "When an unclean spirit is gone out, he walks through dry places seeking rest. If he does not find it, he says: I shall return to my house. And coming he finds it empty, swept, and garnished. Then he goes and takes with him seven other spirits more wicked than himself and they enter into him and the last state of that man is made worse than the first. So shall it be also to this generation."[78]

(7) Do you see that demons dwell in their souls[79] and that these demons are more dangerous than the ones of old? And this is very reasonable. In the old days the Jews acted impiously toward the prophets; now they outrage the Master of the prophets. Tell me this. Do you not shudder to come into the same place with men possessed, who have so many unclean spirits, who have been reared amid slaughter and bloodshed? Must you share a greeting with them and exchange a bare word? Must you not turn away from them since they are the common disgrace and infection of the whole world? Have they not come to every form of wickedness? Have not all the prophets spent themselves making many and long speeches of accusation against them?[80] What tragedy, what manner of lawlessness have they not eclipsed by their blood-

---

77 Chrysostom began his study of Scripture in the School of Diodorus and continued it during his life as a monk. See Baur 1.89–114. Cf. also *Disc.* 2.2.7.

78 Cf. Mt 12.43–45 and Lk 11.24–26; Chrysostom omits "from a man" in verses 43 and 24, but gives, "So shall it be also to this generation," in Mt 12.45. Cf. also above, *Disc.* 1.4.2.

79 Cf. *Disc.* 2.3.5.

80 Cf., e.g., the tirades of Is 1.1–31; 2.6–4.6;9.8–10.4; 28.1–29.16; Jer 2.1–6.30; Ez 4.1–24.27. Chrysostom argues from the guilt of their forebears to the guilt of contemporary Jews.

guiltiness? They sacrificed their own sons and daughters to demons.[81] They refused to recognize nature, they forgot the pangs of birth, they trod underfoot the rearing of their children, they overturned from their foundations the laws of kinship, they became more savage than any wild beast.

(8) Wild beasts [853] oftentimes lay down their lives and scorn their own safety to protect their young. No necessity forced the Jews when they slew their own children with their own hands to pay honor to the avenging demons, the foes of our life. What deed of theirs should strike us with greater astonishment? Their ungodliness or their cruelty or their inhumanity? That they sacrificed their children or that they sacrificed them to demons? Because of their licentiousness, did they not show a lust beyond that of irrational animals? Hear what the prophet says of their excesses. "They are become as amorous stallions. Every one neighed after his neighbor's wife."[82] He did not say: "Everyone lusted after his neighbor's wife," but he expressed the madness which came from their licentiousness with the greatest clarity by speaking of it as the neighing of brute beasts.

VII

What else do you wish me to tell you? Shall I tell you of their plundering, their covetousness, their abandonment of the poor, their thefts, their cheating in trade?[83] The whole day long will

---

81 Cf. Ps 105(106).37; 2 Kgs (4 Kgs) 16.3. Child sacrifice was considered to be in honor of "demons" (cf. "demons" in Dt 32.17). Infant sacrifice imitates the Caananite practice; in 2 Kgs (4 Kgs) 21.6 Manasseh also has his son "immolated by fire" as Ahaz does *ibid.* 16.3; 23.10 shows that this constituted the consecration of the child to the pagan god Molech. The immolation of infants was practiced chiefly in lands where Baal was worshipped. Cases in Israel were exceptional, despite Chrysostom's generalization here and in *Disc.* 3.3.8. Cf. P. Ellis (JBC 10:50, 10:65).

82 Jer 5.8. In cataloguing the sins of Judah, particularly adultery, the prophet speaks in crude terms. Chrysostom alludes to this same text again in *Disc.* 4.6.3. Cf. Jer 13.27.

83 Stock charges against the Jews for which Chrysostom offers no proof.

not be enough to give you an account of these things. But do their festivals have something solemn and great about them? They have shown that these, too, are impure. Listen to the prophets; rather, listen to God and with how strong a statement he turns his back on them. "I have found your festivals hateful, I have thrust them away from myself."[84]

(2) Does God hate their festivals and do you share in them? He did not say this or that festival, but all of them together. Do you wish to see that God hates the worship paid with kettledrums, with lyres, with harps, and other instruments? God said: "Take away from me the sound of your songs and I will not hear the canticle of your harps."[85] If God said: "Take them away from me," do you run to listen to their trumpets? Are these sacrifices and offerings not an abomination? "If you bring me the finest wheaten flour, it is in vain: incense is an abomination to me."[86] The incense is an abomination. Is not the place also an abomination? And when was it an abomination? Before they committed the crime of crimes, before they killed their Master, before the cross, before the slaying of Christ, it was an abomination. Is it not now all the more an abomination? And yet what is more fragrant than incense? But God looks not to the nature of the gifts but to the intention of those who bring them; it is by this intention that he judges their offerings.

(3) He paid heed to Abel and then to his gifts. He looked at Cain and then turned away from his offering. For Scripture says:

84 Am 5.21. NAB (on 5.21–27) annotates as follows: "The Lord condemns, not ritual worship in itself, but the cult whose exterior rites and solemnity have no relation to interior morality and justice. The Israelites falsely worshipped him as neighboring nations adored Baal or Chamos, deities which were thought to protect their respective peoples against their enemies in return for ritual observances, without any relation to right conduct." See also M. Leahy, CCHS 663 and D. Ryan, NCCHS 698–99.
85 Am 5.23 (LXX). Chrysostom cites the same text in *Disc.* 7.3.4, in the same context as here. See also J. Quasten, "The Conflict of Early Christianity With the Jewish Temple Worship," *Theological Studies* 2 (1941) 481–87.
86 Is 1.13 (LXX). NAB reads "offerings" for "wheaten flour." JBC 16:8 points out that the Hebrew word for "offering" in this passage seems to mean any

"For Cain and his offerings he had no regard."[87] Noah offered to
God sacrifices of sheep and calves and birds. The Scripture says:
"And the Lord smelled a sweet odor,"[88] that is, he accepted the
offerings. For God has no nostrils but is a bodiless spirit. Yet what
is carried up from the altar is the odor and smoke from burning
bodies, and nothing is more malodorous than such a savor. But
that you may learn that God attends to the intention of the one
offering the sacrifice and then accepts or rejects it, Scripture calls
the odor and smoke a sweet savor; but it calls the incense an
abomination because the intention of those offering it reeked with
a great stench.

(4) Do you wish to learn that, together with the sacrifices and
the musical instruments and the festivals and the incense, God also
rejects the temple because of those who enter it? He showed this
mostly by his deeds, when he gave it over to barbarian hands,
and later when he utterly destroyed it.[89] But even before its destruction, through his prophet he shouted aloud and said: "Put not

---

kind of gift; the same word is later used to designate bloodless offerings,
such as cereal or meal offerings.
87 Gn 4.5. E. Sutcliffe (CCHS 188) deduces from God's displeasure that
Cain had already been guilty of sin. Cf. 1 Jn 3.12 and Heb 11.4. E. Maly
(JBC 2:31) and B. Vawter (NCCHS 182) both point out that the Yahwist
tradition in Gn gives no reason for God's acceptance of Abel's sacrifice and
his rejection of Cain's; the Lord shows favor and grants mercy to whom he
will (cf. Ex 33.19). The author of Gn 4.5 is probably interested in the
"younger son" motif (cf. Gn 25.23). Like Isaac with regard to Ishmael,
Jacob to Esau, and Judah to his older brothers, Abel is preferred to Cain.
Chrysostom discusses Cain's sin and its consequences in *Disc.* 8.2.6–10.
88 Gen 8.21. Cf. E. Maly, (JBC 2:42), who remarks that the flood story (Gn
7.1–8.22) ends with an emphasis on man and the restoration of his life
with God. The anthropomorphism is a persistent element of the ancient
flood tradition and occurs in the Babylonian account. "Altar" and "holocausts" are used in 8.20 for the first time in Scripture. Verses 21–22 (cf.
6.5–6) show that man's evil inclinations have not changed, but God's firm
salvific will now dictates mercy and the continuation of salvation history.
89 Solomon's temple was destroyed by the Babylonians in 587 B.C, Herod's
was ransacked and razed by the Romans under Titus in 70 A.D. Cf. *Demonstration 16* (PG 48.834–38) for Christ's prophecy of the temple's destruction and the failure of all attempts to restore it. See also *Disc.* 5.1.6–8;
5.4.1–6; 5.11.3–9.

your trust in deceitful words for it will not help you [854] when you say: 'This is the temple of the Lord! The temple of the Lord!' "⁹⁰ What the prophet says is that the temple does not make holy those who gather there, but those who gather there make the temple holy. If the temple did not help at a time when the Cherubim and the Ark were there, much less will it help now that all those things are gone, now that God's rejection is complete, now that there is greater ground for enmity. How great an act of madness and derangement would it be to take as your partners in the festivals those who have been dishonored, those whom God has forsaken, those who angered the Master?

(5) Tell me this. If a man were to have slain your son, would you endure to look upon him, or to accept his greeting?⁹¹ Would you not shun him as a wicked demon, as the devil himself? They slew the Son of your Lord; do you have the boldness to enter with them under the same roof? After he was slain he heaped such honor upon you that he made you his brother and coheir. But you dishonor him so much that you pay honor to those who slew him on the cross, that you observe with them the fellowship of the festivals, that you go to their profane places, enter their unclean doors, and share in the tables⁹² of demons. For I am persuaded to call the fasting of the Jews a table of demons because they slew God. If the Jews are acting against God, must they not be serving the demons? Are you looking for demons to cure you?⁹³ When Christ allowed the demons to enter into the swine,

---

90 Jer 7.4 (LXX). Chrysostom quotes LXX accurately but NAB repeats "temple" (or "sanctuary" in JB) three times. G. Couturier (JCB 19:25) sees in the triple repetition an illustration of the superstitions and magic significance attached to the temple in the popular mind. As the shelter of the Ark of the Covenant, Yahweh's throne, it was sacred and could not fall to the enemy; for the same reason, the whole country would be preserved.

91 Cf. a similar sentiment in ACW 31.59 and 234.

92 Cf. 1 Cor 10.21, although there St. Paul is talking about gentile (i.e. pagan) sacrifices, whereas Chrysostom states that by "the table of demons" he means the Jewish fasts. In *Disc.* 3.2.2 Chrysostom again uses Paul's words in speaking of the Corinthian Christians who ate meat offered to idols.

93 Cf. above, Introd. II 38. In *Disc.* 8.5.6, 8.6.4–6 and 8.7.1 Chrysostom has

straightway they plunged into the sea.[94] Will these demons spare the bodies of men? I wish they would not kill men's bodies, that they would not plot against them. But they will. The demons cast men from Paradise and deprived them of honor from above. Will they cure their bodies? That is ridiculous, mere stories. The demons know how to plot and do harm, not to cure. They do not spare souls. Tell me, then, will they spare bodies? They try to drive men from the Kingdom. Will they choose to free them from disease?

(6) Did you not hear what the prophet said? Rather, did you hear what God said through the prophet? He said that the demons can do neither good nor evil.[95] Even if they could cure and wanted to do so—which is impossible—you must not take an indestructible and unending punishment in exchange for a slight benefit which can soon be destroyed. Will you cure your body and destroy your soul? You are making a poor exchange. Are you angering God who made your body, and are you calling to your aid the demon who plots against you?

(7) If any demon-fearing pagan has medical knowledge, will he also find it easy to win you over to worship the pagan gods? Those pagans, too, have their skill. They, too, have often cured many diseases and brought the sick back to health. Are we going to share in their godlessness on this account? Heaven forbid! Hear what Moses said to the Jews. "If there arise in the midst of you a prophet or one that says he has dreamed a dream and he foretell a sign and a wonder, and that sign or wonder which he spoke come to pass, and he say to you: 'Let us go and serve strange gods whom our fathers did not know,' you shall not hear the words of

much to say of "demonic" cures by the Jews through the use of amulets, charms, and spells (see, e.g., *Disc.* 8.5.6–8; 8.6.11).

94 Cf. Mt 8.31–32.

95 Cf. Jer. 10.5 where the prophet points out that pagan idols are made of wood, adorned with silver and gold, mute; like scarecrows, they must be carried for they cannot walk. Therefore, they should not be feared, "they can do no harm, neither is it in their power to do good." In *Disc.* 4.1.6 and 4.2.1–7 Chrysostom says that both good and evil depend on God's will.

that prophet or dreamer."[96]

(8) What Moses means is this. If some prophet rises up, he says, and performs a sign, by either raising a dead man or cleansing a leper, or curing a maimed man, and after working the wonder calls you to impiety, do not heed him just because his sign comes to pass. Why? "The Lord your God is trying you to see whether you love him with all your heart [855] and all your soul."[97] From this it is clear that demons do not cure. If ever God should permit demons to cure, as he might permit a man to do, his permission is given to test you—not because God does not know what you are, but that he may teach you to reject even the demons who do cure.

(9) And why do I speak of bodily cures? If any man threatens you with gehenna[98] unless you deny Christ, do not heed his words. If someone should promise you a kingdom to revolt from the only-begotten Son of God, turn away from him and hate him. Be a disciple of Paul and emulate those words which his blessed and noble soul exclaimed when he said: "I am sure that neither death nor life, nor angels, nor principalities, nor powers, nor things present, nor things to come, nor height, nor depth, nor any other creature shall be able to separate us from the love of God, which is in Christ Jesus our Lord."[99]

(10) No angels, nor powers, nor things present, nor things to come, nor any other creature separated Paul from the love of Christ. Do you revolt to cure your body? And what excuse could we find? Certainly we must fear Christ more than gehenna and desire him more than a kingdom. Even if we be sick, it is better to

---

96 Cf. Dt 13.2–4 (LXX). R. Mackenzie (CCHS 267) states that in 18.22 unfulfilled prophecies indicate the false prophet. Here we see that prophecies which come true are not an infallible sign of a true prophet. He must also be tested by his doctrine. Chrysostom cites the same text in *Disc.* 8.5.7, to prove that the Jews' cures are not genuine.

97 Dt 13.4.

98 A valley of death and corruption, a fiery abyss where the impious will burn, a place of punishment where the wicked will be destroyed. See McKenzie, DB 299–300.

99 Rom 8.38–39.

remain in ill health than to fall into impiety for the sake of a cure; for even if a demon cures you, he has hurt more than he has helped. He has helped the body, which a short time later will altogether die and rot away. But he has hurt the soul, which will never die. Kidnappers often entice little boys by offering them sweets, and cakes, and marbles, and other such things; then they deprive them of their freedom and their very life. So, too, the demons promise cure of a limb and then dash the whole salvation of the soul into the sea.

(11) Beloved, let us not put up with that; in every way let us seek to keep ourselves free from godlessness. Could Job not have heeded his wife, blasphemed against God, and been free from the disaster which beset him? "Curse God and die," she said.[100] But he chose rather to suffer the pain and to waste away; he chose to endure that unbearable blow rather than to blaspheme and be free from the evils which beset him. You must emulate him. If the demon shall promise you ten thousand cures from the ills which beset you, do not heed him, do not put up with him—just as Job refused to heed his wife. Choose to endure your illness rather than destroy your faith and the salvation of your soul. God does not forsake you. It is because he wishes to increase your glory that oftentimes he permits you to fall sick. Keep up your courage so that you may also hear him say: "Do you think I have dealt with you otherwise than that you may be shown to be just?"[101]

VIII

I could have said more than this, but to keep you from forgetting what I have said, I shall bring my discourse to an end here with the words of Moses: "I call heaven and earth to witness against you."[102] If any of you, whether you are here present or

---

100 Jb 2.9 (LXX). The meaning is Job has nothing to hope for from God and, therefore, no reason to live. In *Disc.* 8.6.1–3 Chrysostom speaks of Job's pains and patience.
101 Cf. Jb 40.8 (LXX).
102 Dt 30.19 and cf. 4.26.

not, shall go to the spectacle of the Trumpets, or rush off to the synagogue, or go up to the shrine of Matrona,[103] or take part in the fasting, or share in the sabbath, or observe any other Jewish ritual great or small, I call heaven and earth as my witnesses that I am guiltless of the blood of all of you.

(2) These words will stand by your side and mine on the day of our Lord Jesus Christ.[104] If you heed them, they will bring you great confidence; [856] if you heed them not or conceal anyone who dares to do those things, my words shall stand against you as bitter accusations. "For I have not shrunk from declaring to you the whole counsel of God."[105]

(3) I have deposited the money with the bankers. It remains for you to increase the deposit and to use the profit from my words for the salvation of your brothers.[106] Do you find it an oppressive burden to denounce those who commit these sins? It is an oppressive burden to remain silent. For this silence makes you an enemy to God and brings destruction both to you who conceal such sinners and to those whose sins go unrevealed. How much better it is to become hateful to our fellow servants for saving them than to provoke God's anger against yourselves. Even if your fellow servant be vexed with you now, he will not be able to harm you but will be grateful later on for his cure. But if you seek to win your fellow servant's favor, if you remain silent and hurt him by concealing his sin, God will exact from you the ultimate penalty. Your silence will make God your foe and will hurt your brother; if you denounce him and reveal his sin, you will make God propitious and benefit your brother and you will gain as a friend one who was crazed but who learned from experience that you served him well.

---

103 See above, *Disc.* 1.6.2.
104 That is, Judgment Day.
105 Acts 20.27.
106 Chrysostom is fond of metaphors from business and commerce; e.g., faith is a contract (ACW 31.50, 222), the sponsors in baptism are spiritual sureties (*ibid* 49). Cf. *Disc.* 8.9.8-10.

(4) Do not think, then, that you are doing your brothers a favor if you should see them pursuing some absurdity and should fail to accuse them with all zeal. If you lose a cloak, do you not consider as your foe not only the one who stole it but also the man who knew of the theft and refused to denounce the thief? Our common Mother [the Church] has lost not a cloak but a brother. The devil stole him and now holds him in Judaism. You know who stole him; you know him who was stolen. Do you see me lighting, as it were, the lamp of my instruction and searching everywhere in my grief? And do you stand silent, refusing to denounce him? What excuse will you have? Will the Church not reckon you among her worst enemies? Will she not consider you a foe and destroyer?

(5) Heaven forbid that anyone who hears my words of advice should commit such a sin as to betray the brother for whom Christ died. Christ poured out his blood on his account. Are you too reluctant to utter a word on his account? I urge you not to be so reluctant. Right after you leave here, stir yourselves to the chase and let each of you bring me one of those suffering from this disease.

(6) But heaven forbid that so many be sick with it. Let two or three, or ten or twenty of you bring me one man. On the day you do and when I see in your nets the game you have caught,[107] I will set before you a more plentiful table.[108] If I see that the advice I gave today has been put to work, I shall be more zealous in undertaking the cure of those men, and this will be a greater boon both for you and them.

(7) Do not regard my words lightly. Be scrupulous in hunting out those who suffer from this sickness. Let the women search for the women, the men for the men, the slaves for the slaves, the freemen for the freemen, and the children for the children. Come all of you to our next meeting with such success that you win praise from me and, before any praises of mine, that you obtain

---

107 Ancient hunters used beaters to drive the game into nets stretched across forest paths. Once trapped the animals could be easily captured or killed. See *Disc.* 2.1.3–5.
108 Here the table is the table of instruction (cf. ACW 31.266, 282).

from God a great and indescribable reward which in abundant measure surpasses the labors of those who succeed. May all of us obtain this by the grace and loving-kindness of our Lord Jesus Christ, through whom and with whom be glory to the Father together with the Holy Spirit now and forever, world without end. Amen.

DISCOURSE II

Against those who fast the fast of the Jews and against the Jews themselves. Delivered after the other discourse had been given and five days before the Jewish fast.[1]

HE WICKED AND UNLCEAN FAST of the Jews [857] is now at our doors. Though it is a fast, do not wonder that I have called it unclean. What is done contrary to God's purpose, be it sacrifice or fast, is the most abominable of all things.[2] Their wicked fast will begin after five days. Ten days ago, or more than ten, I anticipated this and gave an exhortation with the hope it would make your brothers safe. Let no one find fault and say my discourse was untimely because I gave it so many days beforehand. When a fever threatens, or any other disease, physicians anticipate this and with many remedies make safe and secure the body of the man who will be seized by the fever; they hurry to snatch his body from the dangers which threaten it before the patient experiences their onset.[3]

---

1 Only *Disc.* 2, 3, 4, and 6 bear titles in PG. These, although not attributable to Chrysostom, are found in some MSS. In the present title, since "other discourse" seems to refer to *Disc.* I, the fast is again probably that connected with the Ten Days of Penitence (EJ 15.1001). See *Disc.* 1.1.5 and 1.2.7. For the internal links between *Discourses* I and II see above, Introd. III 10–11.

2 Since good and evil depend on God's will (see *Disc.* 4.1.6; 4.2.1–7), anything done against God's will is evil even if it seems to be good.

3 Chrysostom often refers to the physician's art. See, e.g., *Disc.* 1.1.4; 1.4.3; 3.2.4; ACW 31.38, 100, 106. Martyrs are spiritual physicians (*ibid.* 105–8). In *In Genesim hom.* 20 (PG 53.170) Chrysostom speaks of Christ as the physician whose skill is available to the sinner who will pay the fee of faith. In the present passage, the remedies are preventive; the illness is the Judaizing and the Galatian disease. See *Disc.* 1.1.5; 1.4.4; 2.2.3.

35

(2) Since I, too, see that a very serious disease is going to come upon you, long beforehand I gave you solemn warning so that you might apply corrective measures before the evil attacked. This was my reason for not waiting until just before the days of fasting to exhort you. I did not want the lack of time to stop you from hunting out your brothers;[4] I hoped that with the span of many days you might be able to track down with all fearlessness those who ate suffering from this disease and restore them to health.

(3) Men who are going to celebrate a wedding or prepare a sumptuous feast do this same thing. They do not wait for the day itself. Long beforehand they speak with the fishermen and bird hunters so that the brevity of time may present no obstacle to preparing for the banquet. Since I, too, am going to set a banquet[5] before you against the obstinacy of the Jews, I have gotten a head start in talking to you, the fishermen, that you may sweep up your weaker brothers in your nets and bring them to hear what I have to say.[6]

(4) Those of you who did fish and have your catch securely in your nets, remain steadfast and bind them tight with your words of exhortation. Those of you who have not yet taken this goodly catch have time enough in these five days to trap and overcome your prey. So let us spread out the nets of instruction; like a pack of hunting dogs let us circle about and surround our quarry; let us drive them together from every side and bring them into subjection to the laws of the Church. If you think it is a good idea, let us send to pursue them the best of huntsmen, the blessed Paul, who once shouted aloud and said: "Behold, I, Paul, tell you that if you be circumcised, Christ will be of no advantage to you."[7]

---

4 See *Disc.* 1.8.5–7.

5 The banquet is the banquet of instruction. See *Disc.* 1.8.6.

6 In *Disc.* 1.8.6 the nets are hunters'. Here the metaphor is extended to include fishermen's nets, which gather in their catch so as to exhort and instruct those they have caught. Thus the nets become means of salvation. Hunters' nets reappear in the following paragraph.

7 Gal 5.2. Judaizing Christians must have been telling the Galatian converts from paganism that circumcision was necessary for salvation. Cf. Acts 15.1.

(5) When wild beasts and savage animals are hiding under a thicket and hear the shout of the hunter, they leap up in fear. The loud clamor drives them from their hiding place and, even against their will, the hunter's cry forces them out, and many a time they fall right into the nets. So, too, your brothers are hiding in what I might call the thicket of Judaism. If they hear [858] the shout of Paul, I am sure that they will easily fall into the nets of salvation and will put aside all the error of the Jews. For it is not Paul who spoke, but Christ, who moved Paul's soul. So when you hear him shout and say: "Behold, I, Paul, tell you,"[8] consider that only the shout is Paul's; the thought and the teaching are Christ's, who is speaking to Paul from within his heart.

(6) But someone might say: "Is there so much harm in circumcision that it makes Christ's whole plan of redemption[9] useless?" Yes, the harm of circumcision is as great as that, not because of its own nature but because of your obstinacy. There was a time when the law was useful and necessary, but now it has ceased and is fruitless. If you take it on youself to be circumcised now, when the time is no longer right, it makes the gift of God[10] useless. It is because you are not willing to come to him that Christ will be of no advantage to you. Suppose someone should be caught in the act of adultery and the foulest crimes and then be thrown into prison. Suppose, next,

---

8 Cf. Gal 5.2. Chrysostom cites the same text in *Disc.* 3.3.9 and 8.5.5 to show that Christians are not subject to the Old Covenant.

9 Redemption is based on Christ's Incarnation; we participate in it by baptism, not by circumcision Cf. ACW 31.161–62, 232, 328. To accept circumcision is to embrace the Old Law in its entirety; but God has rejected the Old Covenant, and what God has rejected can no longer be good or useful becuase it is now contrary to his will. Aphrahat, the first great father of the Iranian Church and a contemporary of Chrysostom, also maintained that circumcision never had any salvific value except where combined with faith, and Israel was unfaithful, as the prophets themselves contended. See J. Neusner, "The Jewish-Christian Argument in Fourth-Century Iran: Aphrahat on Circumcision, the Sabbath, and the Dietary Laws," *Journal of Ecumenical Studies* 7 (1970) 282–90.

10 The gift of God is the grace of redemption given to us in baptism, the bath of regeneration. Cf., e.g., ACW 31.33, 42, 126, 130. See Neusner, *art. cit.* 286 and below *Disc.* 2.2.1.

that judgment was going to be passed against him and that he would be condemned. Suppose that just at that moment a letter should come from the Emperor[11] setting free from any accounting or examination all those detained in prison. If the prisoner should refuse to take advantage of the pardon, remain obstinate and choose to be brought to trial, to give an account, and to undergo punishment, he will not be able thereafter to avail himself of the Emperor's favor. For when he made himself accountable to the court, examination, and sentence, he chose of his own accord to deprive himself of the imperial gift.

(7) This is what happened in the case of the Jews. Look how it is. All human nature was taken in the foulest evils. "All have sinned,"[12] says Paul. They were locked, as it were, in a prison by the curse of their transgression of the Law. The sentence of the judge was going to be passed against them. A letter from the King came down from heaven. Rather, the King himself came. Without examination, without exacting an account, he set all men free from the chains of their sin.

II

All, then, who run to Christ are saved by his grace and profit from his gift. But those who wish to find justification[13] from the Law will also fall from grace.[14] They will not be able to enjoy the

---

11 Chrysostom speaks often of letters of the Emperor. Cf., e.g., ACW 31.138, 294–95, which quotes passages in the same vein from De incomp. 12 (PG 48.809–10) and In Genesim hom. 44 (PG 54.406).

12 Cf. Rom 3.23. All men are in need of justification and sanctifying grace. Cf. A. Theissen, CCHS 1053–54. St. Paul refers here not to habitual or original sin but to the fact that Christian salvation, embracing all men, copes with the universality of sin among them. See J. Fitzmeyer, JBC 53:39.

13 Cf. Rom 3.28, which states the converse: "For we reckon that a man is justified by faith independently of the works of the Law." Cf. Gal 5.4.

14 Cf. Rom 3.20 and Confr. note ad loc.: "It does not follow. . . that no man is justified by the works of the Law, that good works are not necessary for salvation. The justification of which St. Paul here speaks is the infusion of sanctifying grace which alone renders a person supernaturally pleasing in the sight of God. This cannot be obtained either by the observance of the Law or by any other work of unregenerate man." Cf. Ps 142 (143) 2.

King's loving-kindness because they are striving to gain salvation by their own efforts; they will draw down on themselves the curse of the Law because from the works of the Law no flesh will find justification. So it is that Paul says: "If you be circumcised, Christ will be of no advantage to you."[15] For the man who strives to gain salvation from the works of the Law has nothing in common with grace. This is what Paul hinted at when he said: "If out of grace, then not in virtue of works; otherwise grace is no longer grace. But if out of works, no longer is it grace: otherwise work is no longer work."[16] And again: "If justice be by the Law, then Christ died in vain."[17] And again: "You who are justified in the Law are fallen from grace."[18] You have died to the Law, you have become a corpse;[19] hereafter you are no longer under its yoke, you are no longer subject to its necessity. Why, then, do you strive to make trouble for yourself when it is all to no purpose and in vain?

(2) When Paul said: "Behold, I, Paul, tell you,"[20] why did he add his name? [859] Why did he not simply say: "Behold, I tell you"? He wanted to remind them of the zeal which he had shown with regard to Judaism. What he is saying is this: "If I were a gentile

---

15 Cf. Gal 5.2.
16 Cf. Rom 11.6. The second sentence is not given in the printed editions of the NT text, but it is found in some MSS and Chrysostom includes it in his *Commentary on Romans* (PG 60.578).
17 Cf. Gal 2.21. To return to the practice of the Law is to reject the gift of the life of grace and divine life. If the Law could give justification, then Christ's great redemptive act was unnecessary and a mockery. See B. Orchard, CCHS 1116 and NCCHS 1178.
18 Cf. Gal 5.4. Chrysostom cites the same text in *Disc.* 8.5.5 in the same words, but in slightly varied forms below in 2.3.8 and 6.7.4. NAB reads: "Any of you who seek your justification in the law have severed yourselves from Christ and fallen from God's favor!"
19 Cf. Rom 6.3–4: "Do you not know that all we who have been baptized into Christ Jesus have been baptized into his death? For we were buried with him by means of Baptism into death . . ." Confr. note *ad loc.* says that the allusion is to Baptism by immersion, where the descent into the water suggests the descent of the body into the grave as the ascent from the water suggests the resurrection to a new life. See also NAB note on verses 1–11.
20 Cf. Gal 5.2 (in part).

and knew nothing of Jewish matters, perhaps someone would say that, because I had no share in the Jewish plan and dispensation, because I did not know the power of circumcision, I reject it from the dogmas of the Church." This is why he added his name. He wished to remind them of what he had done in behalf of the Law. It is almost as if he were to say: "I do this not through hatred of circumcision but in full knowledge of the truth. I, Paul, say this, that Paul who was circumcised on the eighth day, who am an Israelite by birth, a Hebrew of the Hebrews, of the tribe of Benjamin, a Pharisee according to the Law, who zealously persecuted the Church,[21] who entered houses, dragged out men and women, and handed them over into custody.[22] All this could persuade even those who are very stupid that I set down this law not through any hatred nor in ignorance of things Jewish but in full knowledge of the surpassing truth of Christ. 'And I testify again to every man who has himself circumcised, that he is bound to observe the whole Law.' "[23]

(3) Why did he not say: "I exhort," or "I command," or "I say"? Why did he say: "I testify"? So that he might, by this word, remind us of the future judgment. Where there are witnesses who testify, there also are judgments and sentences. He is frightening his hearer, then, by reminding him of the royal throne and by showing him that those very words will be his witnesses on that day when each man will give an account of what he has done, what he has said, and what he has heard. The Galatians heard those words in days gone by. Let those who are sick with the Galatians' disease[24] hear them again today. If they are not now present, let them hear through you the

21 Cf. Phil 3.6-6. When Paul says, "a Hebrew of the Hebrews," he may be referring not only to racial descent but also to language and customs, which his parents retained even though living among gentiles in Tarsus. Cf. Acts 22.3 and 23.6. In *Disc.* 3.3.2 Chrysostom quotes Phil 3.5–6 in part and adds 7.

22 Cf. Acts 8.3; 9.1–2; 22.3–5.

23 Gal 5.3. J. Fitzmeyer, JBC 49:29, says: "The Judaizers in Galatia seem to have insisted on the adoption of certain Jewish customs (circumcision, observance of feasts, respect for angels, etc.). Paul warns: if you accept the 'sign' of a Jew, then you oblige yourself to the whole way of life (cf. Jas 2.10). But this is not to walk according to the truth of the Gospel."

24 The Galatians' disease was Judaizing but especially submitting to circumci-

words that Paul exclaimed and said: "I testify again to every man who has himself circumcised, that he is bound to observe the whole Law."[25]

(4) Do not tell me that circumcision is just a single command; it is that very command which imposes on you the entire yoke of the Law. When you subject yourself to the rule of the Law in one part, you must also obey its commands in all other things. If you do not fulfill it, you must be punished and draw its curse upon yourself. When a sparrow has fallen into the hunter's net, even if only its foot is caught, all the rest of its body is caught as well. So, too, the man who fulfills a single commandment of the Law, be it circumcision or fasting, through that one commandment, has given the Law full power over himself; as long as he is willing, and if he is willing to obey a part of the Law, he cannot avoid obeying the whole Law.

(5) We do not say this in accusation of the Law. Heaven forbid! We say it because we wish to show forth the surpassing riches of the grace of Christ. For the Law is not contrary to Christ. How could it be, when he is the one who gave the Law, when the Law leads us to him? But we are forced to say all these things because of the untimely contentiousness of those who do not use the Law as they should. The ones who outrage the Law are those who bid us stand apart from it once and for all and come to Christ, and then tell us to hold fast to it again.[26] The Law has profited our nature very much. I agree to that and would never deny it. But you Judaizers cling to it beyond the proper time and will not let us see how very useful it has been.

(6) It would be the greatest source of praise for a tutor if his young pupil no longer [860] needed him to keep watch over his conduct because the lad had advanced to greater virtue. So, too, it would be the greatest praise for the Law that we no longer had need

---

sion, which was a public pledge to practice the whole Law. Cf. Confr. note on Gal 5.3. For the Judaizing disease see *Disc.* 1.1.5 and 1.4.4.
25 Gal 5.3.
26 This sentence must refer to Judaizing Christians who made converts and then urged them to observe the practices of the Law.

of its help. For the Law has brought that very thing to pass for us: it has prepared our soul to receive a greater philosophy.[27]

(7) So it is that he who still sits at the feet of the Law and can see nothing greater than what is written therein derives no great profit from it. But I put the Law aside and ran to the loftier teachings of Christ; yet I could grant to the Law the greatest dignity because it made me such that I could go beyond the trivialities written therein and rise to the loftiness of the teaching which comes to us from Christ.[28]

(8) The Law did profit our nature greatly, but only if it led us sincerely to Christ. If this be not the case, it did us harm by depriving us of the greater things because of our close attention to those which are less; it also hurt us by still keeping us in the countless wounds of our transgressions. Suppose there were two physicians, one weaker, the other stronger. If the weaker one applied medicines to the ulcers but could not free the sick man once and for all from the pain coming from his sores . . .[29]

III

< "If therefore you are offering your gift at the altar, and there you remember that your brother has anything against you, > leave there your offering before the altar and go first to be reconciled to your brother, and then come and offer your gift."[30] Christ did not

---

27 The life of virtue according to the Gospel. Philosophy refers basically to the love of wisdom. In the Christian context, wisdom is the true doctrine, the Christian way of life.

28 See *Disc.* 1.6.5, where Chrysostom says the Scriptures took him by the hand and led him to Christ.

29 A prudent guess would see the Old Law in the weaker physician and Christ in the stronger. There follows a long lacuna, perhaps of eight columns in PG (judging from the average length of these Homilies). Montfaucon, in his preliminary remarks (*Monitum*) to the series, expresses his regret that this homily has come down to us in a mutilated state. Both he and his friends had searched practically every library in Europe for a MS containing the entire sermon, but their efforts were in vain (PG 48.839). The portion we do have came close to being lost, since it has been preserved, even in its mutilated condition, in only a single MS (*ibid.* 841).

30 Cf. Mt 5.23–24, from which the bracketed words are supplied. Toward the

say: "Submit your offering and then go away," but, "Let it stay there unoffered and go first to be reconciled to your brother."

(2) Nor did he do this[31] only here but again in another place. If a man has an infidel wife, that is, a gentile, he is not forced to put her away. For St. Paul said: "If any man has an unbelieving wife and she consents to live with him, let him not put her away."[32] But if he has a wife who is a harlot and an adulteress, there is nothing to stop him from putting her away. For Christ said: "Everyone who puts away his wife save on account of immorality, causes her to commit adultery."[33] And so he is allowed to put her away because of immorality.[34]

(3) Do you see God's loving-kindness and concern? He says: "If your wife be a gentile, do not put her away. But if she be a harlot, I

---

end of the lacuna, Chrysostom must have been making the point that God cares just as much or more about how a man treats his fellow man than he cares about how a man treats Him.

31 The context in Mt 5 is the New Spirit of Christ vs. the Old Law, which he has come not to destroy but to fulfill (Mt 5.17), and he shows the contrast by six examples: murder, adultery, divorce, oaths, revenge, and love of one's enemies. Chrysostom treats of the first three. Regarding murder, Jesus prohibits even anger, the passion that impels to murder and which is as guilty an action as murder itself. Should men yield to anger, the duty of reconciliation arises. Mt 5.23–24 makes clear how urgent this duty is. Worship (the most sacred action in the eyes of a Jew) must be postponed for reconciliation. Cf. J. McKenzie, JBC 43:34–36.

32 Chrysostom goes to the third example, divorce, but takes his first text from Paul (1 Cor 7.12) to show the primacy of personal relationship between man and man (or woman) over the cultic relationship between man and God.

33 Chrysostom returns to Mt and cites 5.32, which must be understood in the light of Mt 19.9. In both texts the Greek word for "immorality" is *porneia*, i.e., "fornication" or "prostitution," and designates unchaste conduct generally. McKenzie, JBC 43:38 argues that *porneia* may mean an unlawful union of concubinage; then 5.32 would mean: "Every one who sends away his woman [Greek has no distinct noun for "wife"] —except in the case of concubinage — makes her commit adultery."

34 Confr. note to 5.32 says that unfaithfulness justifies separation from bed and board, but the bond of marriage remains unbroken. This is clear from the conclusion of this verse and still clearer in Mk 10.11; Lk 16.18; Rom 7.2; 1 Cor 7. 10–11, 39.

do not stop you from doing so." What he means is this: "If she acts outrageously toward Me, do not put her away; if she outrages you, there is no one to stop you from putting her away." If God, then, showed us such honor, will we not deem him deserving of equal honor? Will we let him be outraged by our wives?[35] Will we permit this even though we realize that the greatest punishment and vengeance will be stored up for us when we neglect the salvation of our wives?

(4) This is why he made you to be head of the wife. This is why Paul gave the order: "If wives wish to learn anything, let them ask their own husbands at home,"[36] so that you, like a teacher, a guardian, a patron, might urge her to godliness. Yet when the hour set for the services summons you to the church, you fail to rouse your wives from their sluggish indifference. But now that the devil summons your wives to the feast of Trumpets and they turn a ready ear to his call, you do not restrain them. You let them entangle themselves in accusations of ungodliness, you let them be dragged off [861] into licentious ways. For, as a rule, it is the harlots, the effeminates, and the whole chorus from the theater who rush to that festival.[37]

(5) And why do I speak of the immorality[38] that goes on there? Are you not afraid that your wife may not come back from there after a demon has possessed her soul? Did you not hear in my previous discourse the argument which clearly proved to us that demons dwell in the very souls of the Jews and in the places in which they gather?[39] Tell me, then. How do you Judaizers have the boldness, after dancing with demons, to come back to the assembly of the apostles? After you have gone off and shared with those who

---

35 The Judaizing sickness raged especially among women. See Introd. II 17 and *Disc.* 4.7.3. See also NAB notes on Mt 5.27–32; 19.3–8.

36 Cf. 1 Cor 14.35 The rest of the verse reads: "for it is unseemly for a woman to speak in church." Chrysostom certainly quotes out of context.

37 Cf. *Disc.* 1.2.7.

38 Again the Greek word for "immorality" is *porneia;* see above, n. 33.

39 Cf. *Disc.* 1.4.1 and 1.6.7–8.

shed the blood of Christ, how is it that you do not shudder to come back and share in his sacred banquet, to partake of his precious blood? Do you not shiver, are you not afraid when you commit such outrages? Have you so little respect for that very banquet?[40]

(6) I have spoken these words to you. You will speak them to those Judaizers, and they to their wives. "Fortify one another."[41] If a catechumen is sick with this disease, let him be kept outside the church doors. If the sick one be a believer and already initiated, let him be driven from the holy table. For not all sins need exhortation and counsel; some sins, of their very nature, demand cure by a quick and sharp excision. The wounds we can tolerate respond to more gentle cures; those which have festered and cannot be cured, those which are feeding on the rest of the body, need cauterization with a point of steel. [862] So is it with sins. Some need long exhortation; others need sharp rebuke.

(7) This is why Paul did not enjoin us to exhort in every case but also to rebuke sharply: "Wherefore rebuke them sharply."[42] Therefore, I will now rebuke them sharply, so that they may accuse themselves and feel shame for what they have done. Then they will never again be hurt by that sinful fast.

(8) So I shall put aside exhortation henceforth as I testify and exclaim: "If any man does not love the Lord Jesus Christ, let a curse be upon him."[43] What greater evidence could there be that a man does not love our Lord than when he participates in the festival with those who slew Christ? It was not I who hurled the curse at them, but Paul. Rather, it was not Paul but Christ, who spoke through him and said earlier: "Those who are justified in the law have fallen away

---

40 The Judaizing Christians returned from the festivals of the Jews to participate in the Eucharistic banquet without thinking of Paul's admonition in 1 Cor 11.27–29. The article, "Fasting and Fast Days," EJ 6.1195, speaks of the following Monday after Passover and Sukkot as fast days and says this fast was interpreted as an atonement for possible sins committed while in the state of drunkenness and gluttony during the holidays.
41 Cf. 1 Thes 5.11.
42 Cf. Ti 1.13.
43 Cf. 1 Cor 16.22.

from grace."[44]

(9) So speak these words to them, read aloud[45] to them these texts. Show all your zeal in saving them. When you have snatched them from the devil's jaws, bring them to me on the day of the Jewish fast. Then, after I have kept the rest of my promise[46] to you, let us, with one accord and with one voice, join our brothers in giving glory to God and the Father of our Lord Jesus Christ, for to Him is glory forever. Amen.

---

44 Cf. Gal 5.4. Cited above, in *Disc.* 2.2.1 and below, in 6.7.4 and 8.5.5. In each instance Chrysostom is rebuking and warning Judaizing Christians.
45 I.e., recite these texts.
46 The promise must have been made in the missing portion of the sermon.

DISCOURSE III

Against those who keep the first Paschal Fast [1]

NCE AGAIN A NECESSARY and pressing need [861] has interrupted the sequence of my recent discourses.[2] I must put aside my struggles with the heretics for today and turn my attention to this necessary business. For I was ready to address your loving assembly again on the glory of the only-begotten Son of God. But the untimely obstinacy of those who wish to keep the first paschal fast[3] forces me to devote my entire instruction to their cure. For the good shepherd does more than drive away the wolves; he also is most diligent in caring

---

1 Quasten 3.452 says that this *Discourse* deals with those who held their Easter with the Jews on the 14th of Nisan, the so—called Protopaschites. The thrust of the work is more against the contentiousness of this group, which may have been a closely knit portion of the larger body of Judaizing Christians. Nowhere in the *Discourse* do we find evidence of a pre-Passover fast by the Jews; those who followed the Jewish calendar, however, to fix the date of Easter might find their lenten fast extending beyond the feast of the Resurrection.

2 Again the series *De incomp.* is interrupted, perhaps after the second, third, or fourth homily against the Anomoeans. See *Disc.* 1.1.1–6 and Montfaucon's *Monitum* (PG 48.840).

3 Chrysostom is not referring to Quartodecimanism but to a lenten fast preceding Easter which the Quartodecimans (who waned in the 3rd century) celebrated on the Jewish Passover. Cf. J. Ford, "Quartodeciman," NCE 12.13. During the first three centuries the period in preparation for Easter did not exceed two weeks. A forty-day period is first mentioned in Canon 5 of the Council of Nicaea (325) but not in connection with fasting. See C. Hefele, *Histoire des Conciles* 1.1 549; W. O'Shea, "Lent," NCE 8.634–36; E. Vacandard, "Carême," DACL 2.2.2139–58.

for his sheep who are sick. What does he gain if the flocks escape the jaws of the wild beasts but are then devoured by disease?

(2) The best general is the one who not only repels the siege engines of the enemy but first puts down rebellion within his own city. He knows well that there will be no victory over an outside foe as long as there is civil war within. Do you not know that there is no more destructive force than rebellion and obstinacy? Listen to the words of Christ: "A kingdom divided against itself shall not stand."[4] And yet, what is more powerful than a kingdom which possesses revenues of money, weapons, walls, fortresses, so large a number of soldiers, horses, and ten thousand other sources of strength?

(3) But even power as great as that is destroyed when it revolts against itself. Nothing produces weakness so effectively as contentiousness and strife; and nothing produces power and strength [862] so effectively as love and concord. When Solomon grasped this truth he said: "A brother that is helped by his brother is like a strong city and kingdom bolted and barred."[5] Do you see the great strength which comes from concord? And do you see the great harm caused by contentiousness? A kingdom in revolt destroys itself. When two brothers are bound together and united into one, they are more unbreakable than any wall.

(4) I know that, by God's grace, most members of my flock are free from this disease and that the sickness involves only a few. But this is no reason for me to relax my care. If only ten, or five, or two, or even one were sick, he must not be neglected. If there is only one worthless outcast, still he is a brother, and Christ died for him. And Christ made great account of the weak ones. He said: "Whoever causes one of these little ones who believe in me to sin, it were better for him to have a great millstone hung around his neck, and to be drowned in the sea."[6] And again: "As long as you did not do it

---

4 Cf. Mt 12.25 here cited in an abbreviated form.

5 Cf. Prv 18.19 (LXX).

6 Cf. Mt 18.6. Even though the Protopaschites are sick, they are brothers for whom Christ died and of whom, like the little ones, he makes great account.

for one of these little ones, you did not do it for me."[7] And again: "It is not the will of your Father in heaven that a single one of these little ones should perish."[8]

(5) Is it not absurd, when Christ shows such care for his little ones, that we should refuse to care for them? Do not say: "He is one person." Rather, you must say: "He is one, yes, but if we do not take care of him, he will spread the disease to the rest." Paul said: "A little leaven ferments the whole mass."[9] And our neglect of the little ones is what overturns and destroys everything. Neglected wounds become serious, just as the serious wounds would easily [863] become minor if they receive the proper care.

(6) Moreover, the first thing I have to say to the Judaizers is that nothing is worse than contentiousness and fighting, than tearing the Church asunder and rending into many parts the robe which the robbers did not dare to rip.[10] Are not all the other heresies enough without our tearing each other apart? You must listen to Paul when he says: "But if you bite and devour one another, take heed or you will be consumed by one another."[11]

(7) Tell me this. Do you stray outside the flock and have you no fear of the lion that prowls about outside the fold? "For your enemy, like a lion, goes about seeking whom he may seize."[12] Here you see a shepherd's wisdom. He does not let the lion in among the

---

7 Cf. Mt 25.45, which reads "least ones" for "little ones."

8 Mt 18.14.

9 Gal 5.9. This is a proverb which shows that if neglected, this manifestation of Judaizing has the power to spread; bad influence will cause total ruin (Confr. note *ad loc*). A similar proverb is found in 1 Cor 5.6, where the Confr. note says: "Fermentation was considered as a kind of corruption. Therefore leaven was removed from Jewish houses for the observance of the Passover to symbolize removal of sin, the corruption of the soul. Cf. Ex 12.15. . ."

10 Reference is to the seamless robe of Christ on Calvary. Chrysostom's "robbers" appear to be the Roman soldiers, who said: "Let us not tear it, but let us cast lots for it, to see whose it shall be" (Jn 19.24).

11 Gal 5.15. Confr. note says that this signifies the ruin of the Christian community.

12 Cf. 1 Pt 5.8. J. Fitzmeyer (JBC 58:26) points out that the lion's description is from Ps 21 (22).14.

sheep for fear the lion may terrify the flock. Nor does he drive the
lion away from outside the fold. Why? So that he may gather all the
sheep together inside the fold, because they are afraid of the wild
beast outside. Do you have no reverence and respect for your father?[13] Then fear your foe. If you separate yourself from the flock,
your enemy will surely catch you.

(8) Christ, too, could have driven the enemy away from the outside of the fold. But to make you sober and watchful,[14] to make
you constantly run to your Mother[15] for refuge, he permitted him
to roar outside the fold. Why did he do this? So that when those
within the fold hear his roar, they may take refuge together and be
more closely bound to one another. Mothers who love their children
also do this: when their children cry, they often threaten to throw
them to the jaws of the wolves. Of course, they would not throw
them to the wolves but they say they will, to stop the children
from bothering them. Everything Christ did was done to keep us
bound together and living at peace with one another.

II

And so it was that Paul could have accused the Corinthians of
many great crimes but he accused them of contentiousness before any
other. He could have accused them of fornication, of pride, of taking
their quarrels to the pagan courts, of banquets in the shrines of idols.
He could have charged that the women did not veil their heads and
that the men did. Over and above all this, he could have accused
them of neglecting the poor, of the pride they took in their charis-

---

13 The "father" may be Peter, who in 1 Pt 5. 1–4 instructs bishops and
priests, the shepherds, how to tend their flocks. More likely the father is
Flavian, bishop of Antioch, who may have been present at this discourse,
as he certainly was during *Disc.* 6.1.4. The father only wishes to inspire in
his flock fear and respect for the foe.

14 Cf. 1 Pt 5.8. The context of this verse implies trust in God, who is faithful to you. Fitzmeyer (JBC 58:26) says that the early Church's exhortation to watchfulness always implies a confidence and trust in God.

15 "Mother" is, of course, the Church. As in *Disc.* 1.3.7 (n 48), she must
frighten her children to make them run to her.

matic gifts, and in the matter of the resurrection of the body. But since, along with these, he could also find fault with them because of their dissensions and quarrels with one another, he passed over all the other crimes, and corrected their contentiousness first.

(2) If you will not think I am making a nuisance of myself on this point, I shall clarify it from Paul's own words. He did give top priority to correcting the Corinthians' obstinacy and contentiousness. And he did this even though he could charge them with all those other crimes. Hear what he says about their fornication: "It is actually reported that there is lewd conduct among you."[16] That they were puffed up and proud: "As if I were not coming to you, some are puffed up." [17] Again, that they would plead their cases in the pagan courts: "Dare any of you, having a matter against another, bring your case to be judged before unbelievers?"[18] That they ate meat offered to idols: "You cannot be partakers of the table of the Lord and of the table of devils."[19] Hear his words of reproach for the women who do not veil their heads and the men who do. "Every man praying or prophesying with his head covered, disgraces his head. But every woman praying or prophesying with her head uncovered, disgraces her head."[20] He showed that they neglected the poor when he said: "One is hungry and another drinks over-

---

16 Cf. 1 Cor 5.1. The lewd conduct (*porneia*) here referred to, unlike that mentioned in *Disc.* 2.3.2, is the incestuous union of a man with his stepmother. Cf. NAB note *ad loc.* and *Disc.* 8.3.6.

17 Cf. 1 Cor 4.18. The boastfulness of the Corinthians is not the true sign of God's sovereignty; Paul's power, given to him as minister of divine severity and mercy, is. Cf. R. Kugelman, JBC 51:26.

18 Cf. 1 Cor 6.1. NT reads "unjust," but Kugelman (JBC 51:30) says that "unbelievers" are meant, rather than simply corrupt or venal men. The abuse of such litigation before pagan courts was probably fomented by the rivalries of the various Corinthian factions. See NAB note *ad loc.*

19 Cf. 1 Cor 10.21. This prohibition may mean that a Christian must not go to a dinner if it involved his attendance at pagan rites. In *Disc.* 1.7.5 Chrysostom says that participating in the Jewish feasts and fasts, entering their synagogues or homes is to share in the table of demons.

20 Cf. 1 Cor 11.4–5. Prophesying means speaking by special inspiration, not necessarily about the future. Kugelman (JBC 51:69) points to an ambivalence in the word "head." The man who prays with covered head dishonors

much."²¹ And again: "or do you [864] despise the church of God and put to shame the needy?"²² When they were all jumping for the more important charismatic gifts and no one was satisfied with the less important, he said: "Are all apostles? Are all prophets?"²³ We can conclude that they were raising doubts about the resurrection because he says: "But someone will say: 'How do the dead rise? Or with what kind of body do they come? ''²⁴

(3) Although he could make so many accusations, his first charge against the Corinthians was dissension and contentiousness. At the very beginning of his letter he said: "I beseech you, brethren, by the name of our Lord Jesus Christ, that you all say the same thing, and that there be no dissensions among you."²⁵ For he knew, he know

---

himself by abdicating the dignity God has conferred on the man; he also dishonors Christ, his hierarchical head. The woman with uncovered head shames her feminine dignity and her husband by repudiating the sign of female subjection. Her shame (cf. 11.6) is that of a woman whose head has been shaved; this would be not only naturally repugnant but perhaps alludes to the shameful chastisement predicted by Is 3.24.

21 Cf. 1 Cor 11.21. NAB note on verses 17–34, says that the Eucharistic service was preceded by a light meal, the Agape, or love-feast. W. Rees (CCHS 1093) says that Paul here condemns the uneven sharing of food at the Agape. Latecomers and poorer members who belonged to no faction would not receive enough. So while some went hungry, others overindulged, even became drunk—if that be not a natural exaggeration caused by Paul's disgust at their selfishness.

22 Cf. 1 Cor 11.22. Cf. Jas 2.1–7, where H. Willmering (CCHS 1175) makes the point that true Christian spirit demands benevolence toward the poor and afflicted; hence, partiality to the rich in Christian assemblies is out of place and contradicts the principles of the Gospel. See also K. Condon, NCCHS 1242.

23 Cf. 1 Cor 12.29. As the human body's members serve the whole body, so all charismatic gifts were given for the good of the whole Church. The "higher" gifts contribute more to the Church's welfare, but the greatest gift is charity (cf. 1 Cor 13; see JBC 51:77).

24 1 Cor 15.35. Some Corinthians seem to have denied the resurrection of the dead. Paul shows that each will have a body adapted to the conditions of its existence; glorified man will have a body suited to his glorious state (cf. JBC 51:86).

25 Cf. 1 Cor 1.10 and NAB note ad loc. The Confr. note states that the dissensions were neither heretical nor schismatic but gave rise to cliques based on attachment to one or other of the apostles or teachers to the

clearly, that this problem was more urgent than the others. If the fornicator, or the braggart, or a man in the grip of any other vice comes frequently to the church, he will quickly draw profit from the instruction, thrust aside his sin, and return to health.

(4) But when a man has broken away from this assembly, when he has withdrawn from the instruction of the fathers, when he has fled from the physician's clinic, even if he appears to be in good health, he will soon fall sick.[26] The best physicians first quench the fires of fever and then cure the wounds and fractures. That is what Paul did. He first removed the dissension and then cured their wounds limb by limb. And so he spoke of dissension before the other sins, so that the Corinthians would not stand apart in strife, so that they would not choose the leaders whom they should follow, so that they would not divide up the body of Christ into many parts.[27]

(5) But he was talking not only to the Corinthians; he was also speaking to those who would come after them and suffer from the same Corinthian disease. I would be glad to ask those of us who are sick with this illness: What is the Pasch;[28] what is Lent?[29] What belongs to the Jews; what belongs to us? Why does their Pasch come once each year; why do we celebrate ours each time we gather to celebrate the mysteries?[30] What does the feast of unleavened bread mean?[31] And I would like to ask them many more questions which contribute to understanding this subject.

---

detriment of perfect Christian charity. Similar contentiousness on the part of the Protopaschites gives the main thrust to this *Discourse.*

26 The fathers who instruct are the priests or bishops who, in 1 Pt 5.2, have the obligation to "tend the flock." Again we have a medical metaphor. See *Disc.* 2.1.1 and n. 3

27 Cf. 1 Cor 1.12–13.

28 Here Chrysostom means the Jewish Pasch (14 Nisan) which the Protopaschites took as their date for Easter.

29 See above, n. 3.

30 "Mysteries" are the Eucharistic sacrfice.

31 The feast of Mazzoth, combined with Passover in Ex 12.15–20, Lv 23.6, Nm 28.17, Ez 45.21, commemorated the deliverance of Israel from Egypt. Cf. J. McKenzie, "Feast of Mazzoth," DB 556–57. Only unleavened bread was to be eaten for a week beginning with the evening of the feast of

(6) If I were to ask them, you would then clearly know how untimely the contentiousness of these men is. They cannot explain what they do. But they refuse to ask anybody, just as if they were wiser than anybody else. They deserve the strongest condemnation because they do not have the answers themselves, but they refuse to follow those who have been appointed to lead them. They have simply risked all they have on this silly practice and are throwing themselves head first down into the depths of danger.

III

When I have this to say against them, what argument of theirs will seem clever? They ask: "Did you not observe this fast before?"[32] It is not your place to say this to me, but I would be justified in telling you that we, too, fasted at this time in earlier days, but still we put more importance on peace than on the observance of dates.[33] And I say to you what Paul said to the Galatians: "Become like me, because I also have become like you."[34] What does this mean? He was urging them to renounce circumcision, to scorn the sabbath, the feast days, and all the other observances of the Law. When he saw they were frightened and afraid that they might be subjected to chastisement and punishment for their transgression, he gave them

---

Passover. Cf. Mt 26.17; Mk 14.12; Lk 22.1,7 for NT references to this feast.

32 Prior to the Council of Nicaea (325), which rejected the Quartodeciman date for Easter on 14 Nisan. See above, n. 3.

33 Three factors had entered into fixing the date for observing Easter: the month of Nisan, the fourteenth lunar day of that month, and the closest Sunday either preceding or following that day. The Christians, differently from the Jews, chose Sunday for their Pasch, although this observance of Sunday was not at first universally established because of past aversion and local opposition (cf. Hefele, *Histoire des conciles* 1.1 451). Nicaea put peace above contentiousness in fixing the date of Easter.

34 Cf. Gal 4.12. Although most of the Galatian converts were Gentiles, they were observing the Jewish calendar (verses 8–10). Chrysostom here makes the same plea for unity which Paul does.

courage by the example of his own actions when he said: "Become like me, because I also have become like you."

(2) For, he said, I did not come from the Gentiles, did I? I was not [865] without experience of the Jewish way of life under the Law and the punishment set for those who transgress it, was I? "I am a Hebrew of the Hebrews; as regards the Law, a Pharisee; as regards zeal, a persecutor of the Church. But the things that were gain to me, these, for the sake of Christ, I counted loss."[35] That is, once and for all I stood aloof from them. Therefore, become like me, for I, too, was as you are.

(3) But why do I speak on my own account? Three hundred Fathers or even more gathered together in the land of Bithynia and ordained this by law;[36] yet you disdain their decrees. You must choose one of two courses: either you charge them with ignorance for their want of exact knowledge on this matter, or you charge them with cowardice because they were not ignorant, but played the hypocrite and betrayed the truth. When you do not abide by what they decreed, this is exactly the choice you must make. But all the events of the Council make it clear that they showed great wisdom and courage at that time. The article of faith[37] they set forth at the Council show how wise they were, because they blocked up the mouths of heretics and, like an impregnable wall, they repelled the treachery of every hostile attack. They proved their

---

35 Cf. Phil 3.5–6,7. Chrysostom quotes 5–6 in *Disc.* 2.2.2 and 7 below (*Disc.* 3.6.2). The point here seems to be that Paul is more Jewish than the Judaizing Philippians. After his conversion, however, he is the thorough Christian and rejects all Judaizing, be it practiced by converts from Judaism or paganism. See J. Greehy, NCCHS 1196.

36 According to Eusebius' *De vita Constantini* 1.3.8 (PG 20.1061) 250 bishops, accompanied by a throng of priests and others, attended the Council. The Synodal Book says the bishops numbered 318 (cf. Hefele, *op. cit.* 396). For a thorough discussion of the solution to the Paschal question see *ibid.* 450–77. The canon concerning Easter is quoted *ibid.* 467. The synod of Antioch (341), in its first canon, threatened with excommunication those who did not adopt the decree of Nicaea (*ibid.* 477–79).

37 This refers to the Nicene Creed. The heretics are the Arians. See Hefele, *op. cit.* 442–48.

courage during the war waged on the Churches and the persecution
which had but lately come to an end.[38]

(4) Like champions in battle who have set up many memorials of
victory and have suffered many wounds, so, too, these champions of
the Churches, who could count the many tortures they had endured
for their confession of the faith, came together from every side,
bearing on their bodies the marks of Christ's wounds. Some could
tell of their hardships in the mines, others of the confiscation of all
their possessions, and still others of starvation and continuous flog-
gings. Some could show where the flesh had been torn from their ribs,
some where their backs had been broken, some where their eyes had
been dug out, and still others where they had lost some other part of
their bodies for the sake of Christ.[39] At that time the whole synodal
gathering, welded together from these champions, along with their
definition of what Christians must believe, also passed a decree that
they celebrate the paschal feast in harmony together. They refused
to betray their faith in those most difficult times [of persecution];
would they sink to pretense and deceit on the question of the Easter
observance?

(5) Look what you do when you condemn Fathers so great, so
courageous, so wise. If the Pharisee lost all the blessings he possessed
because he condemned the publican,[40] what excuse will you have,
what defense will you make for rising up against these great teachers
beloved of God, especially since your attack is so unjust and irra-

---

38 The persecution must have been that begun under Diocletian (303–5) and
continued under Maximus (305–13). Eusebius' *De vita Constantini* 1.3.9
(PG 20.1064) states that some of the bishops at Nicaea (325) were very
old, others in the freshness of their youth.

39 Theodoret, *Historia ecclesiastica* 1.1.7 (PG 82.920), says that many of the
bishops bore on their bodies the scars of Christ.

40 See Lk 18.10–14 for the parable of the Pharisee and the publican. Chrysostom's exegesis is strange because the Pharisee despises rather than condemns the publican. The Pharisee's lost blessings (the Greek is *agatha*)
are, it seems, both spiritual (because he did not go home justified) and
material (because everyone who exalts himself shall be humbled or placed
in a lowly condition). Cf. Jas 1.9–11; also Lk 14.11; Mt 23.12. Lk 18.9
says the parable is spoken to some who trusted in themselves as being just
and despised others. This fits the Protopaschites.

tional? Did you not hear Christ himself say: "Where two or three are gathered together in my name, there am I in the midst of them?"⁴¹ But if Christ is in their midst where two or three are gathered together, was not his presence all the more pervasive among the more than three hundred Fathers at Nicaea? Christ was present there, it was Christ who formulated and passed the laws. Yet you condemn not only the Council Fathers but the whole world which approved their judgment.

(6) Do you consider that the Jews are wiser than the Fathers who came from everywhere in the world? How can you do that when the Jews have been driven from their ancestral commonwealth and way of life and have no sacred festival to celebrate? I hear many say that the Pasch and the feast of unleavened bread are one. But there is no feast of unleavened bread among them, nor is there a Pasch. Why is there no feast of unleavened bread among them? Hear the words of the Lawgiver: "You may not sacrifice the Passover in any one of the cities which the Lord your God gives you, but only in the place in which [866] His name shall be invoked."⁴² And Moses was here speaking of Jerusalem.⁴³

(7) Do you see how God confined the festival to one city, and later destroyed the city so that, even if it was against their wills, he might lead them away from that way of life? Surely, it is clear to everybody that God foresaw what would come to pass. Why, then, did he bring them together to that land from all over the world if he foresaw that their city would be destroyed? Is it not very

---

41 Cf. Mt 18.20.
42 Cf. Dt 16.5, 6. Chrysostom perhaps conflates verse 6 of LXX which reads: "but only there in the place which the Lord your God shall choose that his name be invoked will you offer the paschal sacrifice. . . . "
43 Although Dt describes events prior to the Jews' crossing of the Jordan and the founding of any sacred city, it fits Chrysostom's favorite argument that there was to be no true Passover or sacrifice except in Jerusalem. There is a similar historical inaccuracy in Chrysostom's insistence that the festivals be observed in Jerusalem in *Disc.* 4.4.3–9. If the temple will not be rebuilt, there can be no Jewish commonwealth and way of life; sacrifices and ritual were forbidden during the exiles. See e.g., *Demonstration* 16–17 (PG 48.834–38); *Disc.* 4.4.4–9; 5.4.1–5.12.12. Their priesthood is gone, so there can be no sacrifice (cf. *Disc.* 6.6.1–6; 7.2.1–9; 7.3.1–6).

obvious that he did this because he wished to bring their ritual to
an end? God did bring the ritual to an end, but you go along with
the Jews, of whom the prophet said: "Who is blind but my children,
or deaf but those who lord it over them?"[44]

(8) And against whom did they show their want of sense and
feeling? Was it not against the apostles, the prophets, and their
teachers? Why must I mention teachers and prophets when they
slaughtered their own children? For they did sacrifice their sons and
daughters to demons.[45] When they ignored the voice of nature, were
they going to observe the festival days? Tell me this. Did they not
trample kinship under foot, did they not forget their children, did
they not forget the very God who created them? Moses said: "You
have forsaken the God that begot you, and have forgotten the God
that nurtured you."[46] Were they going to keep the festivals after
they had forsaken God? Who could say that?

(9) Christ did keep the Pasch with them. Yet he did not do so
with the idea that we should keep the Pasch with them. He did so
that he might bring the reality to what foreshadowed the reality. He
also submitted to circumcision, kept the sabbath, observed the festival days, and ate the unleavened bread. But He did all these things
in Jerusalem. However, we are subject to none of these things, and
on this Paul spoke out loud and clear: "If you be circumcised, Christ
shall be of no advantage to you."[47] And again, speaking of the
feast of unleavened bread, he said: "Therefore let us keep festival,
not with the old leaven, not with the leaven of malice and wickedness, but with the unleavened bread of sincerity and truth."[48] For

---

44 Cf. Is 42.19 (LXX). The reference is to Israel "my children," the blind
    servant. NAB reads: "or deaf like the messenger I send," a deaf servant. A
    blind and deaf servant could no longer be a light to the nations (49.6).
    Chrysostom's LXX reading would seem to refer to Israel's Babylonian cap-
    tors.
45 Cf. Ps 105(106).37; see *Disc.* 1.6.7 and notes.
46 Cf. Dt 32.18 (LXX).
47 Gal 5.2. Cf. *Disc.* 2.1.4; 2.2.1; 8.5.5.
48 1 Cor 5.8, on which R. Kugelman (JBC 51:28) comments: "The Christian
    life should be joyful because Christ has become 'for us redemption' (1 Cor
    1.30), and at his parousia the faithful will be glorified with him (Phil

our unleavened bread is not a mixed flour but an uncorrupted and virtuous way of life.

IV

Why did Christ keep the Pasch at that time? The old Pasch was a type of the Pasch to come, and the reality had to supplant the type. So Christ first showed the foreshadowing and then brought the reality to the banquet table.[49] Once the reality has come, the type which foreshadowed it is henceforth lost in its own shadow and no longer fills the need. So do not keep pleading this excuse, but show me that Christ did command us to observe the old Pasch. I am showing you quite the opposite. I am showing you that Christ not only did not command us to keep the festival days but even freed us from the obligation to do so.

(2) Hear what Paul had to say. And when I speak of Paul, I mean Christ; for it is Christ who moved Paul's soul to speak. What, then, did Paul say? "You are observing days, and months, and seasons, and years. I fear for you, lest perhaps I have labored in vain among you."[50] And again: "As often as you shall eat this bread and drink this cup, you shall proclaim the death of the Lord."[51] When he said: "As often as," Paul gave the right and power to decide this to those who approach the mysteries, and freed them from [867] any obligation to observe the festival days.

4.4–7). In 5.7 the unleavened bread symbolizes the Christians; in this verse, the virtues that should characterize them. 'Sincerity,' single-mindedness or purity of intention, as well as 'truthfulness' should distinguish the Christian."

49 Chrysostom's use of allegorical interpretation is always simple; it sees a reality through a type. Here the Paschal supper is the type, the Lord's Supper is the reality.

50 Cf. Gal 4.10–11. Because the Galatian converts from paganism are following the Jewish calendar of feasts, Paul is afraid his work among them may have utterly failed. Col 2.16–17 show that Christians have no need or obligation to observe abrogated Judaic rites and practices.

51 Cf. 1 Cor 11.26. In 11.23–25, Paul, in recalling the original Last Supper, gives the earliest extant testimony on the institution of the Eucharist (about eight years before Mark's gospel). In 11.26 he reminds the Corinthians of the close connection between the Mass and Calvary. Chry-

(3) Now our Pasch and Lent are not one and the same thing: the Pasch is one thing, Lent another. Lent comes once each year; our Pasch is celebrated three times each week, sometimes even four times, or rather as often as we wish.[52] For the Pasch is not a fast but the offering and sacrifice which is celebrated at each religious service That you may know that this is true, listen to Paul when he says: "For Christ, our passover, has been sacrificed,"[53] and again: "As often as you shall eat this bread and drink the cup, you proclaim the death of the Lord."[54]

(4) So as often as you approach the sacrificial banquet with a clean conscience, you celebrate the Pasch. You celebrate it not when you fast but when you share in that sacrifice. "For as often as you shall eat this bread and drink this cup, you proclaim the death of the Lord." Our Pasch is the proclamation of the Lord's death. The sacrifice which we offer today, that which was offered yesterday, and each day's sacrifice is alike and the same as the sacrifice offered on that Sabbath day;[55] the sacrifice offered on that Sabbath is no more solemn than today's, nor is today's of less value than that; they are one and the same, alike filled with awe and salvation.

(5) Why, then, do we fast for forty days? In the past, and espe-

sostom omits the last part of the verse "until he comes," i.e., the Church must proclaim, by celebrating the Eucharist, the Lord's redemptive death until the day of the parousia. Cf. R. Kugelman, JBC 51:71.

52 Montfaucon notes (PG 48.867) that at Alexandria the Liturgy was celebrated three times a week. At Antioch there would seem to have been no restriction. St. Augustine says that his mother, Monica, had attended Mass daily (*Confessions*, 9.13.36; trans. V. Bourke in FC 21.261). Also see Introd. I 8. Van de Paverd, *op. cit.* (above, *Disc.* I n. 58) 61–62, analyses the present passage (sects. 3–5).

53 Cf. 1 Cor 5.7. The Church is always engaged in a Paschal celebration because Christ, by his death and resurrection, has accomplished the salvation foreshadowed in the exodus. Paul sees in the lamb sacrificed at Passover and eaten at the festal dinner a type of Christ's redemptive sacrifice. See JBC 51:28.

54 Cf. 1 Cor 11.26.

55 The reference seems clearly to be to the sacrifice offered by Christ at the Passover supper. Perhaps Chrysostom calls the Passover a Sabbath because the Sabbath was a day holy to Yahweh, as the Passover obviously was Cf. J. McKenzie, DB 752 ("Sabbath") and 365–67 ("Holy").

cially at the time when Christ entrusted to us these sacred mysteries, many a man approached the sacrificial banquet without thought or preparation. Since the Fathers[56] realized that it was harmful for a person to approach the mysteries in this heedless fashion, they came together and marked out forty days for people to fast, pray, and gather together to hear the word of God. Their purpose was that we might all scrupulously purify ourselves during this time by our prayers, almsgiving, fasting, vigils tears, confessions, and all the other pious practices, so that we might approach the mysteries with our consciences made as clean as we could make them.

(6) And they did well when they came to our aid and established for us the practice of this lenten fast.[57] This is clear because, if we keep shouting and proclaiming a fast the whole year through, no one listens to what we say. But as soon as the season of Lent draws near, even the laziest of men rouses himself, even though no one counsels or advises him. Why? He gets advice and counsel from the season of Lent.

(7) So if a Jew or pagan ask you why you are fasting, do not tell him that it is because of the Pasch or because of the mystery of the cross. If you tell him that, you give him an ample grip upon you.[58] Tell him we fast because of our sins and because we are going to approach the mysteries. The Pasch is not a reason for fasting or grief;

---

56 That the "Fathers. . .came together" seems to imply a Council, perhaps, Nicaea. Since we have only the Creed, twenty canons, and the synodal decree of that Council, if any mention of a lenten fast was made, it must have been in a lost portion of the conciliar acts. The Council of Antioch (341) threatened with excommunication those who rejected the Nicene decree on Easter (Hefele, *Histoire des conciles* 1.1 477–79).

57 Chrysostom speaks often enough of Lent and fasting in his Baptismal Instructions (ACW 31.80, 86, 93, 215, 217, 305) and elsewhere, but the fast may have been a recommendation rather than an obligation. Cf. T. Finn, *The Liturgy of Baptism in the Baptismal Instructions of St. John Chrysostom* (Washington 1967) 48, who cites the Lenten practice at Antioch by drawing on Chrysostom's sermons *De statuis*, delivered during Lent of 387.

58 Here Chrysostom may be using a term from wrestling; it is just as likely, however, that he has in mind a proverbial expression in which to "give a *labēn*," means to give an opponent in argument an opportunity for refutation. Cf. Dionysius of Halicarnassus, *Ars rhetorica* (edd. H. Usener and L. Radermacher, Leipzig 1904) 8.15.

it is a reason for cheerfulness and joy. The cross has taken away sin; it was an expiation for the world, a reconciliation for the ancient enmity.[59] It opened the gates of heaven, changed those who hated into friends; it took our human nature, led it up to heaven, and seated it at the right hand of God's throne. And it brought to us ten thousand other blessings.

(8) There is no need, then, to grieve or be downcast; we must rejoice and glory in all these things. This is why Paul said: "But God forbid that I should glory save in the cross of our Lord Jesus Christ."[60] And again: "But God commends his charity towards us, because when as yet we were sinners, Christ died for us."[61] [868] John put it like this: "God so loved the world."[62] Tell me, how did God love the world? John passed over all the other signs of God's love and put the cross in first place. For after he said: "God so loved the world," he said:"That he gave his only-begotten Son," that he be crucified,[63] "that those who believe in him may not perish but may have life everlasting."[64] If, then, the cross is the basis and boast of love, let us not say that it is a cause for grief. Heaven forbid that we grieve because of the cross. We grieve for our sins, and this is why we fast.

---

59 In the *Demonstration* Chrysostom has two beautiful chapters (9–10) on the power of the cross (PG 48.825–27). Here he states that it is the means of our redemption, justification, and salvation.

60 Cf. Gal 6.14. J. Fitzmeyer (JBC 49:32) says that Paul's boast is opposed to the vanity of the Judaizing Galatians (6.12). Paul is not self-reliant but dependent on the grace and favor of God. "Cross" here means the whole Christ-event.

61 Cf. Rom 5.8–9. God's (i.e., the Father's) love, poured out through the Spirit (5.5), is now demonstrated in Christ's gratuitous death for us, his enemies. This is Paul's starting point for the Trinitarian dogma. In 4.25 man's justification was ascribed to Christ's resurrection; here it is attributed to his death on the cross. Cf. Fitzmeyer, JBC 53:48,51.

62 Cf. Jn 3.16.

63 "That he be crucified" fits the context of the cross, but these words are found in no MS of Jn 3.16. They may be here Chrysostom's explanation of "that he gave his only-begotten Son," which he omits.

64 Cf. Jn 3.16. The text stresses the gratuity of God's love for the world, which is the only explanation for the gift of eternal life made possible for us in the redemption achieved in Christ's death on the cross. Cf. B. Vawter, JBC 63:71.

V

Although the catechumen keeps the fast each year, he does not celebrate the Pasch since he does not share in the sacrifice.[65] But even though a man is not observing the lenten fast, he does celebrate the Pasch as long as he comes to the altar with a clean conscience and shares in the sacrifice—whether it be today, tomorrow, or any day whatsoever. The best time to approach the mysteries is determined by the purity of a man's conscience and not by his observance of suitable seasons.[66]

(2) Yet we do just the opposite. We fail to cleanse our conscience and, even though we are burdened with ten thousand sins, we consider that we have celebrated the Pasch as long as we approach the mysteries on that feast day. But this is certainly not the case. If you approach the altar on the very day of the Sabbath[67] and your conscience be bad, you fail to share in the mysteries and you leave without celebrating the Pasch. But if you wash away your sins[68] and share in the mysteries today,[69] you do celebrate the Pasch in precisely the proper way.

(3) Therefore you must safeguard this exactness and vigor of spirit, not in the observance of the proper times but in your approach to the altar. Now you would elect to endure all things rather than change this practice.[70] So, too, you must disdain it and choose

---

65 The catechumens left the church before the *arcani disciplina,* the rule of the secret. Only the baptized could remain for the sacrifice. See Finn, *op. cit.* 38–39.

66 This seems to indicate that the lenten fast was a recommendation rather than an obligation.

67 Here the Sabbath would seem to be Easter Sunday.

68 Baptism of course washes away sins but thereafter we need "tears, repentance, confession, almsgiving, prayer, and every other kind of reverence." See Chrysostom, *De sancta Pentecoste* 1 (PG 50.463). Confession *(exomologēsis)* is opposed to denial *(arnēsis).* Chrysostom is singularly unspecific on the practice of auricular confession. Cf. Baur 1.361–62. See above *Disc.* 3.4.5.

69 If one's conscience is clean, he may participate in the Eucharist today or any day. He need not wait for Easter. See above, *Disc.* 3.4.3–4.

70 The practice of observing the suitable seasons.

to do or suffer anything so as not to approach the mysteries when you are burdened with sins.

(4) Be sure that God takes no account of such observance of special seasons. Hear him as he passes judgment on those at his right hand: "You saw me hungry and gave me to eat; you saw me thirsty and gave me to drink; you saw me naked and you covered me."[71] But he charged with quite different conduct those on his left hand. At another time he brought forward another man in a parable and castigated him because He remembered the evil the man had done. For he said: "You wicked servant, I forgave you all the debt. Should not you then have had compassion also on your fellow servant, even as I had compassion on you?"[72] Again, when the virgins had no oil in their lamps, he locked them out of the bridechamber.[73] And he cast out another man who came into the feast without a wedding garment because this man was garbed in filthy clothes and was wearing the cloak of his fornication and uncleanness.[74] But no one was ever punished or accused because he observed the Pasch in this or that month.

(5) But why speak of ourselves since we have been set free from all such necessity? We are citizens of a city above in heaven, where there are no months, no sun, no moon, no circle of seasons. If you wish to give exact attention to the matter, you will see that, even among the Jews, little account was made of the season of the Pasch, but they cared greatly about the place for it, namely, Jerusalem. Some men came up to Moses and said to him: "We are unclean through touching the dead body of a man. [869] How shall we

---

71 Cf. Mt 25.35–36. Also see *ibid.* 44–45. Mt is talking of the Last Judgment.
72 Cf. Mt 18.32–33. The debtor is heartless and merciless.
73 Cf. Mt 25.7–13. The foolish virgins were unprepared for the groom's coming.
74 Cf. Mt 22.11–13. The ill-garbed guest is as unfit as the children of the kingdom in 8.12, the weeds in the field (which are the sons of the wicked one and sown by the devil) in 13.36–42, and the wicked servant in the parable of the talents in 25.14–30. All will know the weeping and gnashing of teeth. Chrysostom sees more in the parable since he calls the guest's unfit garb the cloak of his fornication and uncleanness.

avoid failing in the Lord's offering?"[75] He said to them: "Wait here and let me report it to God."[76] Then, after he reported it, he brought back the law which says: "If any man be unclean through touching a dead body, or be afar on a journey and be unable to keep the Pasch in the first month, he shall keep it in the second."[77]

(6) And so is not the observance of the time annulled among the Jews so that the Pasch may be observed in Jerusalem? Will you not show greater concern for the harmony of the Church than for the season? So that you may seem to be observing the proper days, will you outrage[78] the common Mother of us all and will you cut asunder the Holy Synod?[79] How could you deserve pardon when you choose to commit sins so enormous for no good reason ?

(7) But why must I speak of the Jews? No matter how eagerly and earnestly we wish it, it is not altogether possible for us to observe that day on which He was crucified. This will make it clear. Let us suppose the Jews had not sinned, that they were not hard of heart, nor senseless, nor indifferent, nor despisers; suppose they had not fallen from their ancestral way of life but were still carefully observing it. Even if this was the case, we could not, by following in

---

75 Cf. Nm 9.7. Contact with a dead body made a person unclean for seven days (cf. Nm. 19.11–13, 16). The same incident occurs again in *Disc.* 4.4.6.
76 Cf. Nm. 9.8 (LXX).
77 Cf. *ibid.* 10–11. The uncleanness did not prohibit an Israelite from taking part in the Passover rites unless the period of his uncleanness coincided with the 14th of Nisan. If it did, or if a man was on a journey and far from the rest of the Israelites at the prescribed time, after being cleansed or after his return, the rites were to be observed at the second Passover, one month later. At the time of Nm 9, the Israelites celebrated the Passover in the Sinai desert (*ibid.* 5); they had not yet reached the promised land nor had Jerusalem come into Judah's possession until David's time (ca. 1000 B.C.). Chrysostom, therefore, is guilty of anachronism regarding the place. Nor was the time annulled; it was postponed.
78 The Greek verb is *emparoineō*, to behave like one who is drunk, and therefore, to act offensively or outrageously. Chrysostom describes such outrageous conduct in *Disc.* 8.1.2–4; the drunkard is worse than a demoniac (cf. ACW 31.84, 255–56).
79 I.e., bring disunion to the Church by ignoring the Easter canon of Nicaea. The Greek text might also admit the meaning: "bring disunion to the holy gathering," i.e., the Antiochene congregation.

their footsteps, put our finger on the very day on which He was crucified and fulfilled the Pasch. Let me tell how this is the case. When He was crucified it was the first day of the feast of unleavened bread and the day of preparation.[80]

(8) But it is not possible for both of these to fall always on the same day. This year the first day of the feast of unleavened bread falls on Sunday, and the fast must still last for a whole week.[81] According to this, after Passiontide, after the cross and resurrection have come and gone, we are still fasting. And it has often happened that, after the cross and resurrection, our fast is still being observed because the week is not yet over. This is why no observance of the exact time is possible.

VI

Let us not quarrel, let us not say: "After fasting these many years, am I to change now?" Change for that very reason. Since you have been so long severed from the Church, come back now to your Mother. No one says: "After I lived as her enemy so long a time, I am ashamed to be reconciled now." You have grounds for shame if you do not change for the better but persist in your untimely contentiousness. That is what destroyed the Jews. While they always kept looking for the old customs and life, these were stripped from

---

80 Cf. Mt 26.17–19; Mk 14.12–16; Lk 22.7–13, who all identify the first day of the unleavened bread with preparation for the Passover meal; Mk 15.42 and Jn 19.14, 31 also speak of "the day of preparation" before the Sabbath of the Passover, i.e., Good Friday. The passion chronology of the Gospels is confusing. See McKenzie, "Passion," DB 640–43. Chrysostom seems to mean that the first day of Mazzoth (which is combined with, but follows, Passover in Lv 23.6) and the day of preparation for the Passover Sabbath cannot always fall on the same day.

81 This is a difficult passage. If the first day of Mazzoth fell on Sunday, for those who calculated by the Jewish system, the Pasch would have fallen on Saturday and been celebrated then. For those following the reckoning of Nicaea, Easter would have been the Sunday following Mazzoth. Thus, Christians would be fasting after Good Friday and Easter as reckoned by the Protopaschites by the Jewish calendar. Actually, Christians may have fasted only on Good Friday and Holy Saturday, but see above, *Disc.* 3.4.5–6 and nn.

them and they turned to impiety.

(2) But why do I speak of fasting and the observance of special days? Paul continued to observe the Law and to endure many a toil; he patiently put up with many journeys and hardships; he surpassed all his contemporaries in the exact observance of that way of life. But after he achieved the heights of that life and came to realize that he was doing all this for his own hurt and destruction, he immediately changed. He did not say to himself: "What is this? Am I to lose the reward for this great zeal of mine? Am I to waste all this work?" Rather he was the quicker to change for the very reason that he might continue to suffer that loss. He scorned justification by the Law so that he might receive the justification of faith. And so he loudly proclaimed: "The things that were gain to me I have counted as loss for Christ."[82] And Christ said: "If you offer your gift [870] at the altar, and there you remember that your brother has anything against you, go first and be reconciled to your brother and then come and offer your gift."[83]

(3) What do you mean? If your brother has something against you, Christ does not permit you to offer your sacrifice until you are reconciled to your brother. When you have the whole Church and so many Fathers against you, do you have the hardihood to dare to approach the divine mysteries before you put aside that unseemly enmity? Since this is the way you feel, how could you celebrate the Pasch?

(4) I say this not only to those who are sick but also to you who are in good health. When you who are well see how many are sick, you will show them great care and kindness, you will pick them out, gather them together, and bring them back to their Mother. Whatever they say against us, however they jump at us, no matter what else they do to us, we must not grow weary and stop until we win them back. For there is nothing comparable to peace and harmony.

(5) It is for this reason that, when the Father[84] enters the

---

82 Cf. Phil 3.7.

83 Mt 5.23–24. Cf. *Disc.* 2.3.1.

84 I.e., the bishop (Flavian).

church, he does not mount to this chair[85] until he has prayed for all of you; when he rises from this chair, he does not begin his instruction until he has first given the peace to all. And when the priests are going to give the blessing, they first pray for peace for you and then begin the blessing.[86]

(6) And when the deacon bids you to pray all together, he also enjoins you in his prayer to ask for the Angel of Peace, and that everything which concerns you be blessed with peace.[87] As he dismisses you from the assembly, he petitions [peace] for you and says: "Go in peace."[88] And without this peace, it is altogether impossible for us to say or do anything. For peace is our nurse and mother, she is very careful to cherish us and foster us. I am not speaking of what is merely called by the name of peace, nor of the peace which comes from sharing meals together, but of the peace which accords with God, the peace which comes from the harmony sent by the Spirit. Many are now tearing this peace asunder by destroying us and exalting the Jews. These men consider the Jews as more trustworthy teachers than their own Fathers; they believe the account of Christ's passion and death which is given by those who slew Him. What could be more unreasonable than this?

(7) Do you not see that their Passover is the type, while our Pasch is the truth? Look at the tremendous difference between them. The Passover prevented bodily death, whereas the Pasch quelled God's anger against the whole world; the Passover of old freed the Jews

---

85 Since Chrysostom was not yet a bishop, he probably pointed to the episcopal throne when he said "this chair."

86 The Liturgy contains constant petitions for peace.

87 The translation takes into account the recent discussion of sects. 5–6 given by Van de Paverd, op. cit. (above, Disc. I n. 58), especially 83–86, 210–12 (for the Angel of Peace, see references assembled on p. 545, s.v. Engel des Friedens). Cf. Brightman, op. cit. 473, lines 9–10 (cf. 478 n. 14); also 381, line 17, where, in the liturgy that bears Chrysostom's name, we read: "Let us ask from the Lord the Angel of Peace, faithful leader, guardian of our souls and bodies."

88 On this sentence see Van de Paverd 406; cf. Brightman 475, line 26 (cf. 481 n. 35).

from Egypt, while the Pasch has set us free from idolatry; the Passover drowned the Pharaoh, but the Pasch drowned the devil;[89] after the Passover came Palestine, but after the Pasch will come heaven.

(8) Why, then, do you sit beside a lamp after the sun has appeared? Why do you wish to nourish yourself on milk when solid food is being given to you? You were nourished with milk so that you might not remain satisfied with milk; the lamp shone for you that it might guide you and lead you by the hand into the light of the sun. Now that the era of more perfect things has come, let us not run back to the former times, let us not observe the days and seasons and years; rather, let us everywhere be careful to follow the Church by paying heed to charity and peace before all things.

(9) Suppose the Church were to be tripped up and fall. The accurate computation of dates would not succeed in making her slip as much as this division and schism would deserve the blame. [871][90] But I make no account of the exact date, since God makes no account of it, as I proved when I devoted many discourses to this subject.[91] But the one thing I seek is that we do all things in peace and concord. If we do so, you will not stay home and get drunk[92] while we are fasting with the rest of the people, and the priests are praying together for the whole world.

(10) Note well that this is of the devil's doing and that it is not a single sin, nor two, nor three, but far more than three. It cuts you off from the flock, it makes you ready to hold so many Fathers in scorn, it hurls you into contentiousness, it thrusts you over to the Jews, and furthermore it makes you a scandal both to your own family and to strangers. How can we blame the Jews for waiting for you in their houses when it is you who go running to them?

---

89 A reference to baptism (by immersion) which was ordinarily conferred at Easter. See ACW 31.64 for the same use of type and reality.
90 Again, we can see that the main thrust of this homily is against contentiousness. See above, *Disc.* 3.1.6–2.6.
91 See Introd. II 21–23.
92 During the Church's Lent, the Protopaschites, along with other Christians, should devote themselves to avoiding pleasures, fasting (whether required or only recommended), and attending church for prayers and services.

(11) These sins are not the only problem. During those days of the fast great harm could come to you from your failure to take advantage of the Scripture readings, the religious meetings in the church, the blessing, and the prayers said in common. Great harm could come to you while you and your bad conscience are spending this whole time in fear and dread that, like some foreigner or stranger, you may be caught in your sinful act. And during all this time, in common with the Church, you should be discharging all your religious duties in a spirit of confidence, pleasure, good cheer, and full freedom.

(12) The Church does not recognize the exact observance of dates. In the beginning the Fathers decided to come together from [872] widely separated places and to fix the Easter date; the Church paid respect to the harmony of their thinking. loved their oneness of mind, and accepted the date they enjoined. My earlier remarks have proved adequately that it is impossible for us or you or any other man to arrive at the exact date of the Lord's day. So let us stop fighting with shadows, let us stop hurting ourselves in the big things while we are indulging our rivalry over the small.

(13) Fasting at this or that time is not a matter for blame. But to rend asunder the Church, to be ready for rivalry, to create dissension, to rob oneself continuously of the benefits of religious meetings—these are unpardonable, these do demand an accounting, these do deserve serious punishment.

(14) I could have said much more than this. What I have said is enough for those who heed me; those who fail to heed my words will not be helped even if I should have much more to say. So let me finish my discourse at this point, and let us all pray together that our brothers come back to us. Let us pray that they cling fondly to peace and stand apart from untimely rivalry. Let us pray that they scorn this sluggish spirit of theirs and find a great and lofty understanding. Let us pray that they be set free from this observance of days so that all of us, with one heart and with one voice, may give glory to God and the Father of our Lord Jesus Christ, to whom be glory and power now and forever, world without end. Amen.

DISCOURSE IV

Against the Jews and the trumpets¹ of their Pasch

Delivered at Antioch in the Great Church²

GAIN³ THE JEWS, [871] the most miserable and wretched of all men,⁴ are going to fast,⁵ and again we must make secure the flock of Christ. As long as no wild beast disturbs the flock, shepherds, as they stretch out under an oak or pine tree and play their flutes, let their sheep go off to graze with full freedom. But when the shepherds feel that the

---

1 The title presents a problem when it speaks of the "trumpets of their Pasch," since Montfaucon and others seem to prove that *Discourses* IV–VIII form a series relating to the September feasts and fasts of 387. The Passover (which fell on April 25 in 387) or its continuation, the feast of unleavened bread, are mentioned several times in this *Discourse* (e.g., 4.4.3–8; 4.5.2–4) but always in a generic sense in support of the sermon's main thrust against the Judaizers, who would now observe the Law so exactly but at the wrong time and place. Fasting is also frequently mentioned (e.g. 4.1.1; 4.1.3; 4.1.5; 4.5.2–4; 4.5.6). The opening three paragraphs anticipate by ten days or more the coming of the fast as it was anticipated by fifteen or more in *Disc.* 1 (see *Disc.* 2.1.1) and by five in *Disc.* 2 (*ibid.*). This seems to favor Montfaucon's argument and indicate the September fasts on the Day of Atonement and the Ten Days of Penitence following Rosh Ha-Shanah (EJ 15.1001), as also does Chrysostom's clear statement that the Jews were not permitted to fast during the feast of the unleavened bread, which included Passover (*Disc.* 4.5.3). Furthermore, we find in the present sermon several echoes of *Discourses* I and II which were certainly aimed at the September feasts and fasts. Trumpets did have a cultic use. The NAB note on Nm 10.10 says they were blown at the great annual feasts of Passover, Pentecost (see below, n. 36), and Tabernacles. There is no mention of trumpets or trumpeters until toward the end of this *Discourse* (4.7.4–5). The title does not appear in all MSS or editions and may be a later intrusion.

71

wolves will raid, they are quick to throw down the flute and pick up their slingshots; they cast aside the pipe of reeds and arm themselves with clubs and stones. They take their stand in front of the flock, raise a loud and piercing shout,[6] and oftentimes the sound of their shout drives the wolf away before he strikes.

(2) I, too, in the past, frolicked about in explicating the Scriptures, as if I were sporting in some meadow; I took no part in polemics because there was no one causing me concern.[7] But today the Jews, who are more dangerous than any wolves, are bent on surrounding my sheep; so I must spar with them and fight with them so that no sheep of mine may fall victim to those wolves.

(3) That fast will not be upon us for ten days or more.[8] But do not be surprised that from today on I am taking up my tools and building a fence around your souls. This is what the hard-working farmer does. When he has a rushing stream nearby which may wash away the fields he has tilled, he does not [872] wait for winter.

---

2 The Great Church, octagonal in shape, and with a gilded roof, was begun by Constantine in 327, completed by his son Constantius, and dedicated in 341. It was closed by Julian the Apostate in 362, in reprisal for the burning of Apollo's temple at Daphne. The Arians later occupied it until Bishop Meletius, who had acknowledged the Nicene creed, recovered it in 364 (cf. Downey, *History* 342–46, 388, 396, 399).

3 Montfaucon interprets this as marking the beginning of a new series (*Monitum*, PG 48.841).

4 The adjectives echo "the pitiful and miserable Jews" of *Disc.* 1.1.5 and 1.2.1.

5 The Ten Days of Penitence between Rosh Ha-Shanah and Yom Kippur. See *Disc.* 1.1.5.

6 The shepherd's shout is an appropriate simile because Chrysostom is the shepherd who hopes the shout of his instruction will frighten off the Jewish proselytizers and protect the Judaizing Christians of his flock.

7 Either he refers to lost commentaries or to exegetical instructions given when he was a deacon. The only commentary which surely predates the homilies *Adversus Iudaeos* is the series of nine homilies on Genesis which belongs to Lent of 386. He may mean some of his treatises and the series, *De incomp.* 1–5, which was twice interrupted by the present series. However, he may have felt that these were more apologetic than polemic. But he surely felt concern about the Anomoeans, whose impiety he found akin to the Jews'. Cf. *Disc.* 1.1.6. He uses Scripture liberally in all his works. See above, Introd. I 6.

8 He anticipated the fast by fifteen or more days in *Discourse* I (cf. *Disc.* 2.1.1) and by five in *Discourse* II (cf. *ibid.*). Therefore the present hom-

Long beforehand he fences in the banks, builds up dikes, digs ditches, and makes every preparation against the flood. While the stream runs quietly and is low in its bed, it is a simpler matter to restrain it; when it has become swollen and is swept along with a violent rush of waters, it is no longer so simple to oppose the flood. And so it is that long beforehand the farmer anticipates the surge of the torrent and contrives by every means to keep his fields secure in every way.

(4) As well as farmers, every soldier, sailor, and reaper makes it a practice to prepare ahead. Before the hour of battle, the soldier cleans off his breastplate, examines his shield, makes ready the bridle and bit, feeds and cares for his horse, and sees to it that he is well prepared in every way. Before the sailor launches his ship into the harbor's waters, he prepares the keel, repairs the sides, hews and shapes the oars, stitches together the sails, and makes ready all the other equipment of his ship.[9] Many days before the harvest, the reaper sharpens his sickle, gets ready the threshing-floor, his oxen, his wagon, and everything else which may help him in the harvest. Indeed you can see men everywhere making preparations for their business beforehand so that, when the time does come, it is an easy matter for them to carry on their enterprise.

(5) I am following the example of these men. Many days beforehand I am making your souls secure by exhorting [873] you to flee from that accursed and unlawful fast. Do not tell me that the Jews are fasting; prove to me that it is God's will that they fast. If it be not God's will, then their fasting is more unlawful than any drunkenness.[10] For we must not only look at what they do but we must also seek out the reason why they do it.

---

ily can hardly belong to the same series as *Discourses* I and II.

9 Sailors kept their ships in drydock during the stormy winter months. Before the sailing season, keels had to be scraped, hulls patched, and new oars hewn and shaped from tree trunks; cf., e.g., Vergil, *Aeneid* 4.397–400.

10 Cf. *Disc.* 1.2.5–6. The fasting of the Jews is an untimely abomination. When drunkenness and gluttony made them reject God's yoke, then they should have fasted. Now the Old Law is abrogated and its fasts and feasts are accursed because rejected by God.

(6) What is done in accordance with God's will is the best of all things even if it seems to be bad. What is done contrary to God's will and decree is the worst and most unlawful of all things—even if men judge that it is very good. Suppose someone slays another in accordance with God's will. This slaying is better than any loving-kindness. Let someone spare another and show him great love and kindness against God's decree. To spare the other's life would be more unholy than any slaying. For it is God's will and not the nature of things that makes the same actions good or bad.[11]

II

Listen to me so that you may learn that this is true. Ahab[12] once captured a king of Syria and, contrary to God's decree, saved his life. He had the Syrian king enjoy a seat by his side and sent him off with great honor. About that time a prophet came to his companion and "said to him: 'In the word of the Lord, strike me.' But his companion was not willing to strike him. And the prophet said to him: 'Because you would not hearken to the word of the Lord, behold, you will depart from me and a lion will strike you.' And he departed from him, and the lion found him and struck him. Then the prophet found another man and said: 'Strike me.' And the man did strike him and wounded him, and the prophet bandaged up his face."[13]

(2) What greater paradox than this could there be? The man who struck the prophet was saved; the one who spared the prophet was punished. Why? That you may learn that, when God commands, you must not question too much the nature of the action; you have only to obey. So that the first man might not spare him out of reverence, the prophet did not simply say: "Strike me" but said: "Strike me

---

11 Cf. *Disc.* 1.7.6.
12 Ahab was king of Israel 869–50 B.C. See 1 Kgs (3 Kgs) 16.29–22.39. Cf. McKenzie, "Ahab," DB 15–16. The Syrian king was Ben–hadad (or Benadad); cf. 1 Kgs (3 Kgs) 20.35–43.
13 For this piece of narration Chrysostom adheres fairly closely to 1 Kgs (3 Kgs) 20.35–38 (LXX 21.35–38). He must be using a punctuation different from that of LXX 21.35 when he joins "in the word of the Lord"

in the word of God."[14] That is, God commands it; seek no further. It is the King who ordains it; reverence the rank of him who commands and with all eagerness heed his word. But the man lacked the courage to strike him and, on this account, he paid the ultimate penalty. But by the punishment he subsequently suffered, he encourages us to yield and obey God's every command.

(3) But after the second man had struck and wounded him, the prophet bound his own head with a bandage, covered his eyes, and disguised himself. Why did he do this? He was going to accuse the king and condemn him for saving the life of the king of the Syrians.[15] Now Ahab was an impious man and always a foe to the prophets. The prophet did not wish Ahab to recognize him and then drive him from his sight; if the king drove him away, he would not hear the prophet's words of correction. So the prophet concealed his face and any statement of his business in the hope that this would give him the advantage when he did speak and that he might get the king to agree to the terms he wanted.[16]

(4) "When the king was passing by, the prophet called aloud [874] to him and said: 'Your servant went forth to the campaign of

---

with "strike me" and thus gives to the prophet's command a divine sanction. NAB reads: "One of the guild prophets was prompted by the Lord [i.e. in the word of the Lord] to say to his companion, 'Strike me.' " JB: "At Yahweh's order [i.e. in the word of the Lord] a member of the brotherhood of prophets said to a companion of his, 'Strike me' . . . . ," both in substantial agreement with Chrysostom. But both Confr. and LXX read: "One of the prophets said to his companion in the word of the Lord: 'Strike me,' " thus designating the companion as a fellow-prophet but giving no divine sanction to the command. P. Ellis (JBC 10:43) speaks of a "son of a prophet," i.e., a disciple of the prophets or a member of one of the prophetic guilds (cf. 2 Kgs [4 Kgs] 2.3).

14 JBC 10:43 says that the man is obliged to obey because the prophet speaks "in the word of the Lord" and that for his disobedience he is killed by the lion.

15 The second man does obey and so sets the stage for the prophet to teach Ahab a lesson such as Nathan taught David in 2 Sm (2 Kgs) 12.1–12.

16 Chrysostom's quotation of verse 38 above was abbreviated and (with Rahlfs' LXX text) omitted the element of disguise, which he here includes. The bandage was necessary to cover both the wound and any marks such as tatoos, incisions, or a shaven head (cf. Zec 13.16; Ez 9.4;

war. Behold, a man brought another man to me and said to me: "Guard this man for me. If he shall leap away and bound off, it will be your life for his life, or you will pay a talent of silver." And it happened that as your servant turned his eyes this way and that, the man was not there.' And the king of Israel said to him: 'This is your judgment before me:[17] You slew the man.' And the prophet hurried to take the bandage from his eyes, and the king of Israel recognized that he was one of the sons of the prophets. And he said to the king: 'So says the Lord: "Because you let go from your hand a man worthy of death, it will be your life for his life, and your people for his people." ' "[18]

(5) Do you see how not only God but men make this kind of judgment because both God and men heed the end and the causes rather than the nature of what is done? Certainly even the king said to him: "This is your judgment before me: you slew the man." You are a murderer, he said, because you let an enemy go. The prophet put on the bandage and presented the case as if it were not the king but somebody else on trial, so that the king might pass the proper sentence. And, in fact, this did happen. For after the king condemned him, the prophet tore off the bandage and said: "Because you let go from your hand a man worthy of death, it will be your life for his life, and your people for his people."[19]

(6) Did you see what a penalty the king paid for his act of kindness? And what punishment he endured in return for his untimely sparing of his foe? The one who spared a life is punished; another, who slew a man, was held in esteem. Phinehas certainly slew two people in a single moment of time—a man and his wife; and after he slew them, he was given the honor of the priesthood.[20] His

---

1Kgs [3 Kgs] 18.28; 2 Kgs [4 Kgs] 2.23) which would have identified him as a prophet and made Ahab suspicious of the story he is about to tell.

17 I.e., you are judging yourself for me. Ahab is made to condemn himself for releasing Ben—hadad, as David condemned himself in 2 Sm (2 Kgs) 12.5—6.

18 Cf. 1 Kgs (3 Kgs) 20.39—42 (LXX 21.39—42). The prediction of Ahab's death is fulfilled in 22.34—38.

19 1 Kgs (3 Kgs) 20.42 (LXX 21.42).

20 Nm 25.6—13 and see J. McKenzie, "Phinehas," DB 674.

act of bloodshed did not defile his hands; it even made them cleaner. (7) So you see that he who struck the prophet goes free, while he who refused to strike him perishes; you see that he who spared a man's life is punished, while he who refused to spare a life is held in esteem. Therefore, always look into the decrees of God before you consider the nature of your own actions. Whenever you find something which accords with His decree, approve that—and only that.

III

Let us examine the matter of fasting and apply this rule to it. Suppose we should not apply this rule but merely take the act of fasting and consider it with no reference to anything else. The result will be great tumult and confusion. It is true that highwaymen, grave-robbers, and sorcerers have their sides torn to pieces; it is also true that the martyrs undergo this same suffering. What is done is the same, but the purpose and reason why it is done is different. And so it is that there is a great difference between the criminals and martyrs.

(2) In these cases we not only consider the torture but we first look for the intention and the reasons why the torture is inflicted. And this is why we love the martyrs—not because they are tortured but because they are tortured for the sake of Christ. But we turn our backs on the robbers—not because they are being punished but because they are being punished for their wickedness.

(3) So, too, in the matter of fasting, you must pass a judgment. If you see people fasting for the sake of God, approve what they do; if you see that they do this against God's will, turn your back on them and hate them more than you do those who drink, revel, and carouse. And in the case of this fasting [875] we must inquire not only into the reason for fasting but we must consider also the place and the time.

(4) But before I draw up my battle line against the Jews, I will be glad to talk to those who are members of our own body, those who seem to belong to our ranks although they observe the Jewish rites

and make every effort to defend them.[21] Because they do this, as I see it, they deserve a stronger condemnation than any Jew. Not only the wise and intelligent but even those with little reason and understanding would agree with me in this. I need no clever arguments, no rhetorical devices, no prolix periodic sentences to prove this. It is enough to ask them a few simple questions and then trap them by their answers.

(5) What, then, are the questions? I will ask each one who is sick with this disease: Are you a Christian? Why, then, this zeal for Jewish practices? Are you a Jew? Why then, are you making trouble for the Church? Does not a Persian side with the Persians? Is not a barbarian eager for what concerns the barbarians? Will a man who lives in the Roman empire not follow our laws and way of life? Tell me this. If ever anyone living among us is caught in collusion siding with the barbarians, is he not immediately punished? He is given neither hearing nor examination, even if he has ten thousand arguments in his own defense. If ever anyone living among the barbarians is clearly following Roman custom and law, again, will he not suffer the same punishment? How, then, do you expect to be saved by defecting to that unlawful way of life?[22]

(6) The difference between the Jews and us in not a small one, is it? Is the dispute between us over ordinary, everyday matters, so that you think the two religions are really one and the same? Why are you mixing what cannot be mixed?[23] They crucified the Christ

---

21 Cf. *Disc.* 1.1.5, where, as here, he means the Judaizing Christians.

22 Cf. *Disc.* 1.4.9–10. Roman armies made almost annual campaigns against the Persians ("barbarians") between 339 and 373; Antioch, which was the Roman headquarters, had an elaborate spy system to search out and punish disaffected citizens (cf. Downey, *History* 355–63, 368, 381, 391, 402). There were other wars after these *Discourses* were delivered, and Antioch was captured by the Persians in 540 and 611 (cf. Downey, *History* 505, 533–46, 575). Chrysostom's hearers would have remembered some of the campaigns and the espionage network.

23 Simon 142 n. 7 quotes this and explains it in the light of *Disc.* 2.3.5, where Chrysostom asks: "After you have gone off and shared with those who shed the blood of Christ, how is it that you do not shudder to come back and share in his sacred banquet, to partake of his precious blood?"

whom you adore as God. Do you see how great the difference is? How is it, then, that you keep running to those who slew Christ when you say that you worship him whom they crucified? You do not think, do you, that I am the one who brings up the law on which these charges are based, nor that I make up the form which the accusation takes? Does not the Scripture treat the Jews in this way?

(7) Hear what Jeremiah says against those same Jews: "Go off to Kedar and see; send off to the islands of the Kittim and find out if such things have happened."[24] What things? "If the gentiles will change their gods, and indeed they are not gods, but you have changed your glory and from it you will derive no profit."[25] He did not say: "You have changed your God," but, "your glory."[26] What he means is this. Those who worship idols and serve demons are so unshaken in their errors that they choose not to abandon them nor desert them for the truth. But you, who worship the true God, have cast aside the religion of your fathers and have gone over to strange ways of worship. You did not show the same firmness in regard to the truth that they did in regard to their error. That is why Jeremiah says: "Find out if such things have happened, if the gentiles will change their gods, and indeed they are not gods; but you have changed your glory and from it you will derive no profit."[27] He did not say: "You have changed your God," for God does not change. But he did say: "You have changed your glory." You did no harm to me, God says, because no harm has come to me. But you did dis-

---

24 Cf. Jer 2.10 (LXX). Kedar was a nomad tribe of the Syrian desert; Kittim refers to a Phoenician colony in Cyprus. The two names represent East and West.
25 Cf. Jer 2.11. In verse 8 the priests have become specialists in the Law, but have no real knowledge of Yahweh or their religion. Hosea reproached them earlier in a similar way (Hos 4.4–10) for exchanging Yahweh for shame (i.e., idols).
26 Both C. Lattey (CCHS 576) and G. Couturier (JBC 19:16) say that "glory" here does mean God (cf. Nm 14.21; Dt 10.21; Is 6.3). Then Jer 2.10 will mean that the Israelites have changed their God and will derive no profit or help from him while they go after empty idols (ibid. 5). This is substantially Chrysostom's interpretation.
27 Ibid. 10–11.

honor yourselves. You did not make my glory less, but you did diminish your own.

(8) Let me also say this to those who are our own—if I must call our own those who side with the Jews. Go to the synagogues and see if the Jews have changed their fast; see if [876] they kept the pre-Paschal fast with us; see if they have taken food on that day.[28] But theirs is not a fast; it is a transgression of the law, it is a sin, it is trespassing. Yet they did not change.[29] But you did change your glory and from it you will derive no profit; you did go over to their rites.

(9) Did the Jews ever observe our pre-Paschal fast? Did they ever join us in keeping the feast of the martyrs? Did they ever share with us the day of the Epiphanies?[30] They do not run to the truth, but you rush to transgression. I call it a transgression because their observances do not occur at the proper time. Once there was a proper time when they had to follow those observances, but now there is not. That is why what was once according to the Law is now opposed to it.

IV

Let me say what Elijah said against the Jews. He saw the unholy life the Jews were living: at one time they paid heed to God, at another they worshipped idols. So he spoke some such words as these: "How long will you limp on both legs? If the Lord our God is with you, come, follow Him; but if Baal, then follow him."[31] Let me, too, now say this against these Judaizing Christians. If you judge that Judaism is the true religion, why are you causing trouble to the Church? But if Christianity is the true faith, as it really is, stay in it

---

28 Apparently, Good Friday, when Christians usually fasted. Of course the Jews would have eaten on that day.

29 The Jews are as steadfast in their error as were the pagans of Jer 2.11.

30 "The Epiphanies" (ta epiphania) was used both of the Nativity or Christmas and also of a celebration commemorating the baptism of Christ. The Jews would have no reason for solemnizing either day.

31 Cf. 1 Kgs (3 Kgs) 18.21 (LXX). P. Ellis (JBC 10:41) says of this text that the Israelites cannot make up their minds, faced as they are with the dilemma of choosing between the traditional worship of Yahweh and

and follow it. Tell me this. Do you share with us in the mysteries, do you worship Christ as a Christian, do you ask him for blessings, and do you then celebrate the festival with his foes? With what purpose, then, do you come to the church?

(2) I have said enough against those who say they are on our side but are eager to follow the Jewish rites. Since it is against the Jews that I wish to draw up my battle line, let me extend my instruction further. Let me show that, by fasting now, the Jews dishonor the law and trample underfoot God's commands because they are always doing everything contrary to his decress. When God wished them to fast, they got fat and flabby;[32] when God does not wish them to fast, they get obstinate and do fast; when he wished them to offer sacrifices, they rushed off to idols; when he does not wish them to celebrate the feast days, they are all eager to observe them.[33]

(3) This is why Stephen said to them: "You always oppose the Holy Spirit."[34] This is the one thing, he says, in which you show your zeal: in doing the opposite to what God has commanded. And they are still doing that today. What makes this clear? The Law itself. In the case of the Jewish festivals the Law demanded observance not only of the time but also the place. In speaking about this feast of the Passover, the Law says to them something such as this: "You will not be able to keep the Passover in any of the cities

---

the Baal worship of Jezebel. For Baal and his worship, which reduced Yahweh to a personified natural force and made religion a mere means of securing the goods of nature, see J. McKenzie, "Baal," DB 72–73.

32 Cf. *Disc.* 1.2.5. Now that the Old Law is abrogated, the Jews are obstinate in observing its precepts.

33 Cf. e.g., Jer 2.5, where the Israelites turn to idols. Below (*Disc.* 4.6.2–3) Chrysostom suggests that God took no pleasure in sacrifice but permitted it to the Jews because of their weakness and sinful ways.

34 Cf. Acts 7.51. This sums up Stephen's main accusation against his Jewish opponents (cf. Nm 27.14; Is 63.10; 2 Chr [2 Par] 30.7–8).See also *Disc.* 1.2.3, where Chrysostom quotes the entire verse from Acts.

which the Lord your God gives to you."[35] The Law bids them keep the feast on the fourteenth day of the first month and in the city of Jerusalem. The Law also narrowed down the time and place for the observance of Pentecost,[36] when it commanded them to celebrate the feast after seven weeks, and again, when it stated:"In the place which the Lord your God chooses."[37] So also the Law fixed the feast of Tabernacles.[38]

(4) Now let us see which of the two, time or place, is more necessary, even though neither the one nor the other has the power [877] to save. Must we scorn the place but observe the time? Or should we scorn the time and keep the place? What I mean is something such as this. The Law commanded that the Passover be held in the first month and in Jerusalem,[39] at a prescribed time and in a prescribed place. Let us suppose that there are two men keeping the Passover. Suppose one of them neglects the place but observes the time; suppose the other observes the place but neglects the time. Let the one who observes the time but neglects the place celebrate the Passover in the first month, but far away from Jerusalem; and let the one who observes the place but neglects the time celebrate the feast in Jerusalem but in the second month instead of the first.

(5) Next, let us see which of these two is charged and accused, and which receives approval and esteem. Will it be the one who

---

35 Cf. Dt 16.5 (LXX). However, Chrysostom is wrong if he means that the Passover sacrifice must at this time be offered in Jerusalem, which will not come into Judah's possession until David's day (ca. 1000 B.C.). He is guilty of the same anachronism in *Disc.* 3.3.6 and 3.5.5. What Dt insists on is that the Israelites come to a central shrine for the sacrifice (cf. 12.11; 14.2, 6, 7). See J. Blenkinsopp, JBC 6:40.

36 Cf. Dt 16.10. NAB note *ad loc.* says that the feast of Weeks was later known more commonly as Pentecost. See J. McKenzie, "Pentecost," DB 657–58.

37 For the reckoning of seven weeks cf. Lv. 23.15–21; Dt 16.9. For the place cf. Dt 12.11; 16.11.

38 Cf. Dt 16.13–15 and J. McKenzie, "Feast of Tabernacles," DB 863–64.

39 Only after David's day did Jerusalem become the central shrine for sacrifice to which each male had to go for the three feasts of Mazzoth, Pentecost, and Tabernacles or Sukkot (cf. Dt 16.16).

transgressed in the matter of time but observed the place, or the one who neglected the place but observed the time? If the man who transgressed about the time so as to celebrate the feast in Jerusalem clearly deserves esteem, but the one who observed the time while neglecting the place deserves to be charged and accused for his impious action, it is quite obvious that those who do not keep the Passover in the proper place are transgressing the Law, even if they maintain a thousand times over that they are observing the proper time.

(6) Who will make this clear to us? Moses himself. As he tells it, even after some men had observed the Passover outside Jerusalem, "they came up to Moses and said: 'We are unclean through touching the body of a dead man. We should not fail to offer the Lord's offering at its proper time among the sons of Israel, should we?' And Moses said to them: 'Stay here and I shall listen to what the Lord will command in your regard.' And the Lord spoke to Moses and said: 'Speak to the sons of Israel and say: "If any man be unclean through the body of a dead man, or if he be afar off on a journey, whether he be one of you or of your descendants, he shall keep the Pasch in the second month." ' "⁴⁰

(7) He means something such as this. If anyone be away from home in the first month, let him not keep the Passover outside the city; but let him return to Jerusalem and keep it in the second month. Let him disregard the time so as not to fail in the matter of the city. In this way he shows that observance of the place is more necessary than observance of the time.

---

40 The narrative is taken from Nm 9.7–11 (LXX). Here no mention is made that the defiled men had observed the Passover. To have observed it in Jerusalem at that time is anachronistic. They are to keep the feast in the second month, after they have become ritually clean, but at a central shrine (cf. Dt 12.11; 14.2, 6, 7). Since the text from Scripture and the argument are so much the same as in *Disc.* 3.3.6 and 3.5.5, it may be that this homily belongs to a different series and time. Nor do we have a necessary argument here that this homily is concerned chiefly with Passover because Pentecost and Sukkot were equally connected with a fixed time and place (Dt 16.10–11, 13–15).

(8) But what could the Jews say if they observe the Passover outside the city of Jerusalem? Since they transgress in the more necessary matter of place, their observance in the less important matter of time cannot be urged in their defense. The result is that they are guilty of the worst transgression of the Law, even if it is obvious a thousand times over that they are not neglecting the matter of time.

(9) This is certain not only from what I have said but also from the prophets. What excuse would the Jews of today have when it is clear that the Jews of old never offered sacrifice, nor sang hymns in an alien land,[41] nor did they observe any such fasts as they do today? To be sure, the Jews of old were expecting to recover the way of life in which they could observe these rituals. Therefore, they remained obedient to the Law and did what it commanded, for the Law told them to expect this.[42] But the Jews of today have no hope of recovering their forefathers' way of life. In what prophet can they find proof that they will?[43] They have no hope, but they cannot bear to give up these practices. And yet, even if they were expecting to recover the old way of life, even so they ought to be imitating those holy men of old by neither fasting nor observing any other such ritual.[44]

V

To prove to you that the Jews in exile observed none of these rituals, hear [878] what they said to those who asked them to do so. For their barbarian captors were urging them by force and demand to play their musical instruments. "Sing to us a hymn of the

---

41 Cf. Ps 136 (137).4. The verse hints that the land of their Babylonian captors was not only hostile but unclean; Chrysostom understands it as unfit for ritual observance. Cf. *Demonstration* 16–17 (PG 48.835–36).

42 Namely, that one day they would return from exile to their Holy City and be able to resume their rituals.

43 The present bondage of the Jews, although foretold by Josephus and Daniel, will never end nor will their temple be rebuilt. Cf. *Disc.* 5.9.1–5.11.10 and *Demonstration* 16–17 (PG 48.834–38).

44 Cf. *Demonstration* 17 (PG 48.835–36).

Lord,"[45] they said. But the Jews clearly understood that the Law
commanded them not to do so. Therefore, they said: "How shall we
sing the song of the Lord in a strange land?"[46] And, again, the three
boys who were captives in Babylon said: "At this time we have no
prince or prophet nor place to offer sacrifice in your sight and find
mercy."[47] Certainly there was much room for a place of sacrifice
in the country, but since the temple was not there, they steadfastly
refrained from offering sacrifice.

(2) And again God spoke to his people through the lips of
Zechariah: "For these seventy years you have not kept a fast for me,
have you?[48] He was speaking of the captivity. Tell me. By what
right, then, do you Jews fast today, when your ancestors neither
offered sacrifices, nor fasted, nor kept the feasts? And this makes it
especially clear that they did not observe the Passover. Where there
was no sacrifice, there no festival was held, because all the feasts had
to be celebrated with a sacrifice.

(3) Let me provide proof for this very point. Listen to the words
of Daniel: "In those days I, Daniel, was mourning for three weeks. I
ate not desirable bread, and neither flesh nor wine entered my
mouth, nor did I anoint myself with ointment in those weeks. And it
came to pass on the twenty-fourth day of the first month that I saw
the vision."[49] Pay careful heed to me here, for this text makes it
clear that they did not observe the Passover. Let me tell you how
this is. The Jews were not permitted to fast during the days of the
feast of unleavened bread.[50] But for twenty-one days Daniel took
no food at all. And what proves that the twenty-one days included

---

45 Ps 136(137).3.
46 *Ibid.* 4 and above, Disc. 4.4.9.
47 Cf. Dn 3.38. Chrysostom quotes the text somewhat differently in *Demonstration* 17 (PG 48.836) but to the same point.
48 Zec 7.5 (LXX). C. Stuhlmueller (JBC 23:33) points out that the fast was not for God but for the disaster of the Babylonian captivity, which resulted from Israel's own failure and sinfulness.
49 Cf. Dn 10.2–4 (LXX). L. Hartman (JBC 26:32) says that Daniel's fasting is not penance for sin but in preparation for mystical knowledge.
50 They had to abstain from leavened bread, but there was no obligation to fast during the seven days of the feast of unleavened bread, which started with sunset of Passover (14th of Nisan).

the days of the feast of unleavened bread? We learn this from what he said, namely, that it was on the twenty-fourth day of the first month.[51]

(4) But the Passover comes to an end on the twenty-first of that month. If they began the feast on the fourteenth day of the first month and then continued it for seven days, they then come to the twenty-first. Nonetheless, Daniel steadfastly continued his fast even after the Passover had come and gone. For if Daniel had begun his fast on the third day of the first month and then continued through a full twenty-one days, he passed the fourteenth, went on for seven days after that, and then kept fasting for three more days.

(5) How, then, do the Jews of today avoid being cursed and defiled? The holy ones of old followed no such observances of what the Law prescribed, because they were in a strange land. Are today's Jews doing just the opposite so that they may stir up contentiousness and strife? If some of the holy ones of old who spoke and acted this way were lax and irreverent, perhaps we would have considered their failure to observe these precepts as a sign of their laxity. But they loved and revered God, they gave their very lives for what God had decreed.[52] So it is abundantly clear that failure to keep the Law was not the result of their laxity. Rather, their failure to keep the Law was prompted by the Law itself, because the Law said they must not observe those rituals outside Jerusalem.

(6) This brings us to a conclusion on another matter of great importance. The observances regarding sacrifices, sabbaths, new moons, and all such things prescribed by the Jewish way of life of that day were not essential.[53] Even when they were observed they

---

51 I.e., on the 24th of Nisan (the first month) the vision came to Daniel (cf. Dn 10.1–3) and he stopped fasting. But if he fasted for three weeks prior to that, he must have ignored the feasts of Passover and Mazzoth (unleavened bread).

52 Chrysostom seems to have had in mind the incident of the three boys in the fiery furnace (Dn 3), whom he will mention in a moment and again in *Disc.* 5.6.1. They did not die in the furnace but, more importantly, they did love and revere God and his Law.

53 For God's rejection of the Jewish festivals see *Disc.* 1.7.2–4 F. Moriarty (JBC 16:8) points out that sacrifice is worthless without the proper in-

could make no [879] great contribution to virtue; when neglected they could not make the excellent man worthless, nor degrade in any way the sanctity[54] of his soul. But those men of old, while still on earth, manifested by their piety a way of life that rivals the way the angels live. Yet they followed none of these observances, they slew no beasts in sacrifice, they kept no feast, they made no display of fasting. But they were so pleasing to God that they surpassed this human nature of ours and, by the lives they lived, they drew the whole world to a knowledge of God.

(7) Who could match a Daniel? Who could match the three boys in Babylon? Did they not anticipate the greatest commandment which the Gospels give, the commandment which is the chief source of all blessings? Had they not already proved this by their deeds? For John says: "Greater love than this no one has, that one lay down his life of his friends."[55] But they laid down their lives for God.[56]

(8) We must admire them for this. But we must also admire them because they were not doing it for any reward. This is why the boys in Babylon said: "There is a God in heaven, and he can save us; but if he will not, be it known, O king, that we will not worship your gods."[57] The prophet means: The reward is sufficient for us that we are dying for God. And they gave proof of this great virtue even though they were observing none of the Law's prescriptions.

---

terior dispositions—an idea common to the prophets (Am 5.21–24; Hos 6.6; Jer 7.21–23), who condemn the hypocrisy of the abuse but not the institution of sacrifice. The ritual for celebrating the new moon is found in Nm 28.11–15. J. Castelot (JBC 76:128–31) gives the origin, significance, and observance of the Sabbath. Aphrahat holds there is nothing spiritually essential in keeping it (see J. Neusner, *art. cit. supra* [*Disc.* II n. 9] 290–94).

54 I have translated *philosophia* as sanctity. Cf. *Disc.* 2.2.6
55 Jn 15.13.
56 In Dn 3.19–23 the boys are bound and thrown into the fiery furnace, but it is their executioners who are devoured by the flames. The boys miraculously go unscathed. They do give witness to their God and, hence, are martyrs; they do not, however, lay down their lives for him.
57 Dn 3.17 (LXX).

VI

You Jews will say: "Why, then, did God impose these prescriptions if he did not wish them observed?" And I say to you: If he wished them observed, why, then, did he destroy your city? God had to do one or the other of two things if he wished these prescriptions to remain in force: either he had to command you not to sacrifice in one place, since he intended to scatter you to every corner of the world; or, if he wished you to offer sacrifice only in Jerusalem, he was obliged not to scatter you to every corner of the world and he should have made that one city impregnable, because it was there alone that sacrifice has to be offered.

(2) Again the Jews will say: "What is this, then? Was God contradicting himself when he ordered the Jews to sacrifice in one place but then barred them from that very place?" By no means! God is very consistent. He did not wish you to offer sacrifices from the beginning, and I bring forward as my witness of this the very prophet who said: "Hear the word of the . . . Lord, you rulers of Sodom, give ear to the law of our God, you people of Gomorrah."[58] But it was really to the Jews the prophet spoke, not to those dwelling in Sodom and Gomorrah. Yet he calls the Jews by the names of these people because, by imitating their evil lives, the Jews had developed a kinship with those who dwelt in those cities.[59]

(3) In fact Isaiah called the Jews dogs[60] and Jeremiah called them mare-mad horses.[61] This was not because they suddenly changed

---

58 Is 1.10 (LXX).
59 Cf. *ibid.* 9. Cf. Neusner, *art. cit.* 285, who says that Aphrahat, in discussing verse 10, demonstrates the spiritual character of prophecy. A Sodomite is one who does the deeds of the Sodomites, not one born in Sodom. Likewise, a true Israelite is one who does God's will, not merely one born of Israel after the flesh.
60 Cf. Is 56.10, which thus contemptuously refers to Israel's watchmen, who are blind leaders in the attack against either the apostate Samaritan cult or even the religious excesses at Jerusalem. Cf. C. Stuhlmueller, JBC 22:52.
61 Cf. Jer 5.8 and see *Disc.* 1.6.8.

natures with those beasts but because they were pursuing the lustful habits of those animals. " 'What care I for the number of your sacrifices?' says the Lord. But it is clear that those who dwelt in Sodom never offered sacrifices. Isaiah is aiming his remarks against the Jews when he calls them by the name of those brute animals, and he does so for the reason I just mentioned. " 'What care I for the number of your sacrifices' says the Lord 'I am filled up with your holocausts of rams I desire not the fat [880] of sheep, and the blood of bulls, not even if you come to appear before me. For who required all these things from your hands?' "[63] Did you hear his voice clearly saying that he did not require these sacrifices from you from the beginning? If he had made sacrifice a necessity, he would also have subjected the first Jews to this way of life and all the patriarchs who flourished before the Jews of Isaiah's day.[64]

(4) Then the Jews will ask: "How is it that he straightway did permit the Jews to sacrifice?"[65] He was giving in to their weakness. Suppose a physician sees a man who is suffering from fever and finds him in a distressed and impatient mood. Suppose the sick man has his heart set on a drink of cold water and threatens, should he not get it, to find a noose and hang himself, or to hurl himself over a cliff. The physician grants his patient the lesser evil, because he wishes to prevent the greater and to lead the sick man away from a violent death.

(5) This is what God did. He saw the Jews choking with their mad yearning for sacrifices. He saw that they were ready to go over to

---

62 Is 1.11. NAB notes that, however numerous, sacrifices are not acceptable without the right disposition on the part of the worshipper (cf. Am 5.21–24; Hos 6.6; Jer 7.21–23 and above, *Disc.* 4.5.5.
63 Is 1.11–12 (LXX). God is really condemning not the sacrifices but the hypocrisy of those who offer them.
64 If Chrysostom means "patriarchs" in the technical sense (the generations between Adam and Noah), there were no sacrifices prior to Noah's sacrifice after the flood (Gn 8.20), and his statement is correct. If he uses the term more generally to include the holy men who flourished before Isaiah's day, he is wrong.
65 Is 40.16 more than hints that sacrifices will be restored after the exile in Babylon. Cf. NAB note *ad loc.*

idols if they were deprived of sacrifices. I should say, he saw that they were not only ready to go over, but that they had already done so. So he let them have their sacrifices. The time when the permission was granted should make it clear that this is the reason. After they kept the festival in honor of the evil demons, God yielded and permitted sacrifices. What he all but said was this: "You are all eager and avid for sacrifices. If sacrifice you must, then sacrifice to me." But even if he permitted sacrifices, this permission was not to last forever; in the wisdom of his ways, he took the sacrifices away from them again.

(6) Let me use the example of the physician again—there is really no reason why I should not. After he has given into the patient's craving, he gets a drinking cup from his home and gives instructions to the sick man to satisfy his thirst from this cup and no other. When he has gotten his patient to agree, he leaves secret orders with the servants to smash the cup to bits; in this way he proposes, without arousing the patient's suspicion, to lead him secretly away from the craving on which he has set his heart.

(7) This is what God did, too. He let the Jews offer sacrifice but permitted this to be done in Jerusalem and nowhere else in the world. After they had offered sacrifices for a short time, God destroyed the city. Why? The physician saw to it that the cup was broken. By seeing to it that their city was destroyed, God led the Jews away from the practice of sacrifice, though it was against their will. If God were to have come right out and said: "Keep away from sacrifice," they would not have found it easy to keep away from this madness for offering victims. But now, by imposing the necessity of offering sacrifice in Jerusalem, he led them away from this mad practice; and they never noticed what he had done

(8) Let me make the analogy clear. The physician is God, the cup is the city of Jerusalem, the patient is the implacable Jewish people, the drink of cold water is the permission and authority to offer sacrifices. The physician has the cup destroyed and, in this way, keeps the sick man from what he demands at an ill-suited time. God destroyed the city itself, made it inaccessible to all, and in this way led the Jews away from sacrifices. If he did not intend to make

ready an end to sacrifice, why did God, who is omnipresent and fills the universe, confine so sacred a ritual to a single place? Why did he confine worship to sacrifices, the sacrifices to a place, the place to a time, and the time to a single city, and then destroy the city? It is indeed a strange and surprising thing. The whole world is left open to the Jews, but [881] they are not permitted to sacrifice there; Jerusalem alone is inaccessible to them, and that is the only place where they are permitted to offer sacrifice.

(9) Even if a man be completely lacking in understanding, should it not be clear and obvious to him why Jerusalem was destroyed? Suppose a builder lays the foundation for a house, then raises up the walls, arches over the roof, and binds together the vault of the roof with a single keystone to support it. If the builder removes the keystone, he destroys the bond which holds the entire structure together. This is what God did. He made Jerusalem what we might call the keystone which held together the structure of worship. When he overthrew the city, he destroyed the rest of the entire structure of that way of life.

VII

Let then my battle with the Jews wait awhile. I did fight a skirmish of words with them today, but I said only what was enough to save our brothers from danger. Perhaps I said much more than that. But I must now exhort those of you who are here in church to show great concern for the fellow members of our body.[66] I do not want to hear you say: "What concern is this of mine? Why interfere and meddle in other people's affairs?"

(2) Our Master died for us. Will you not take the trouble to say a single word? What excuse or defense will you find for this? Tell me this. If you look the other way when so many souls are perishing,

---

66 There is some variety in the MSS and editions here. Some read: "to show great concern for the days which have passed;" others have: "to show great concern for the days which are with us;" both would seem to refer to Jewish feast days. We prefer Montfaucon's reading, which better fits the context of an exhortation to fraternal correction.

how will you find the confidence to stand before the judgment seat of Christ? I wish I could know which ones are running off to the synagogue. Then I would not have needed your help but I would have straightened them out with all speed.

(3) Whenever your brother needs correction, even if you must lay down your life, do not refuse him. Follow the example of your Master. If you have a servant or if you have a wife, be very careful to keep them at home. If you refuse to let them go to the theater, you must refuse all the more to let them go to the synagogue. To go to the synagogue is a greater crime than going to the theater. What goes on in the theater is, to be sure, sinful; what goes on in the synagogue is godlessness. When I say this I do not mean that you let them go to the theater, for the theater is wicked; I say it so that you will be all the more careful to keep them away from the synagogue. [67]

(4) What is it that you are rushing to see in the synagogue of the Jews who fight against God?[68] Tell me, is it to hear the trumpeters?[69] You should stay at home to weep and groan for them, because they are fighting against God's command, and it is the devil who leads them in their revels and dance.[70] As I said before, if there once was a time when God did permit what is against his will, now it is a violation of his law and grounds for punishments beyond number. Long ago, when the Jews did have sacrifices, they did sound their trumpets;[71] now God does not permit them to do this.

(5) At least listen to the reason why they got the trumpets. God said to Moses: "Make for yourself trumpets of beaten silver."[72]

---

67 See above *Disc.* 1.2.7; 1.6.7; 2.3.3–4; and Introd. I.18.
68 The words: "in the synagogue of the Jews who fight against God" are missing in some MSS.
69 This is the first mention of trumpeters in the homily, although the title reads; "Against the Jews and the Trumpets of their Pasch;" see above, n.1. "Trumpets" will be mentioned four times in this and the following two paragraphs. The Feast of Trumpets is mentioned in *Disc.* 1.1.5.
70 Cf. *Disc.* 1.2.7–1.3.1–3.
71 Trumpets were blown over holocausts and peace offerings on days of celebration and festivals (cf. Nm 10.10).
72 Nm 10.2, which continues: "which you shall use in assembling the community and in breaking camp."

Next God explained how the trumpets were to be used, for he went on to say: "You will sound them over the holocausts, and the sacrifices for your deliverance."[73] (6) But where is the altar? Where is the ark? Where is the tabernacle and the holy of holies? Where is the priest? Where are the cherubim of glory? Where is the golden altar of incense? Where is the mercy-seat? Where is [882] the bowl? Where are the drink offerings? Where is the fire sent down from heaven?[74] Did you lose all those and keep only the trumpets? Do you Christians not see that what the Jews are doing is mockery rather than worship?

(7) I blame the Jews for violating the Law. But I blame you much more for going along with the lawbreakers, not only those of you who run to the synagogues but also those of you who have the

---

73 Chrysostom's explanation shows a conflation of verses 2 and 10.
74 These all belong to the temple and its sacrificial equipment. J. McKenzie, DB, is very useful for all the following items. For the altar see esp. J. Castelot, JBC 76:72-76; for the ark, *ibid.* 76:46–48; for the tent or tabernacle, *ibid.* 76:44–45. On the priesthood see *ibid.* 76:3–38 and *Disc.* 6.4.6–6.6.6. The Cherubim of glory (i.e., of God ?) shielded with their wings the mercy-seat (*ibid.* 76:46, 59); for the incense altar see *ibid.* 76:73; for the mercy-seat or propiatiatory (from which God dispensed his mercy to his people) see *ibid.* 76:46, Although the bowls may have been for carrying incense (so Chrysostom's word *phialē* is used in Rv 6.8), it seems more likely they were for libations or drink offerings, which constituted part of the later holocaust ceremony (JBC 76:78). In Lv 10.1 the word *pyreion* is used for censer. The fire is the fire for the holocaust, which was to burn perpetually (Lv 6.2–6), probably as a symbol of divine presence. The "fire sent down from heaven" was a theophany such as in Lv 9.23–24, which issued down from the meeting tent to consume the offerings already burning on the altar, to show that Aaron's holocausts are approved as sacred and acceptable to Yahweh. All sacred fire had to come from the altar itself (Lv 16.12). Cf. R. Faley, JBC 4:22. The "fire of God" (Jb 1.16), "fire from heaven" (2 Kgs [4 Kgs] 1.10–14) and "the fire of Yahweh" (Nm 11.1; 1 Kgs [3 Kgs] 18.38) is lightning. But fire is an element of the theopanies of Sinai (Ex 19.16–18) and the burning bush (Ex 3.2–4). The pillar of fire (Ex 13.21; 14.24; Nm 14.14) is a symbol of the divine presence in Israel. Fire may be a sign of his good pleasure and acceptance of sacifice (Gn 15.7; Lv 9.24; Jgs 6.21; 1 Kgs [3 Kgs] 18.38) or the element by which he destroys the wicked (Gn 19.24; Lv 10.2). Chrysostom speaks of the ark, temple etc. again in *Disc.* 6.7.2–6.

power to stop the Judaizers but are unwilling to do so. Do not say to me: "What do I have in common with him? He is a stranger, and I do not know him." I say to you that as long as he is a believer, as long as he shares with you in the same mysteries, as long as he comes to the same church, he is more closely related to you than your own kinsmen and friends. Remember, it is not only those who commit robbery who pay the penalty for their crime; those, too, who could have stopped them but did not, pay the same penalty. Those guilty of impiety are punished, and so, too, are those who could have led them from godless ways but did not, because they were too timid or lazy to be willing to do so.

(8) To be sure, the man who buried his talent gave it back to his master whole and entire; yet he was punished because he did not make a profit from it.[75] Suppose, then, that you yourself remain pure and free from blame; if you fail to make a profit from your talent, if you fail to bring back to salvation your brother who is perishing, you will suffer the same punishment which he does.

(9) Is it some great burden I am asking of you, my beloved? Let each one of you bring back for me one of your brothers to salvation. Let each one of you interfere and meddle in your brother's affairs so that we may come to tomorrow's service[76] with great confidence, because we are bringing gifts more valuable than any others, because we are bringing back the souls of those who have wandered away. Even if we must suffer revilement, even if we must be beaten, even if we must endure any other pain whatsoever, let us do everything to win these brothers back. Since these are sick brothers who trample us underfoot, revile us, and rail against us, we are not stung by their insults; we want to see one thing and only one thing: the return to health of him who behaved in this outrageous way.

(10) Many a time a sick man tears the physician's clothes. But the physician does not let this stop him from trying to cure his patient.

---

75 Cf. Mt 25.24–30 and *Disc.* 8.9.8–10.
76 "Tomorrow's service" may merely mean "the next service." The opening of the next homily offers no sure clue as to the exact meaning. We do find such a clue in *Disc.* 6.1.3, which shows that this sermon was delivered one day after *Discourse* V.

It is normal, then, for physicians to show such concern for their patients' bodily health. When so many souls are perishing, is it right for us to slacken our efforts and to think we are suffering no terrible harm, even if our own members are rotting with disease? Paul did not think so. What did he say? "Who is weak, and I am not weak? Who is scandalized, and I am not on fire?"[77] See to it that you catch this fire.

(11) Suppose you see your brother perishing. Even if he reviles you, if he insults you, if he strikes you, if he threatens to become your foe, if he menaces you in any other way, show your courage and endure all these insults so that you may win his salvation. If he should become your foe, God will be your friend and will give you in return many great blessings on that day.[78]

(12) May the prayers of the saints save those who have wandered into error, may you who are faithful be successful in your hunt, may those who have blasphemed God be freed from their ungodliness and come to know Christ, who died for them on the cross, so that all of us may, with one accord and one voice, give glory to God and the Father of our Lord Jesus Christ, to whom be glory and power together with the Holy Spirit for ever and ever. Amen.

---

77 2 Cor 11.29. See below *Disc.* 7.6.3.
78 I.e., the day of judgment, when you will stand at his right hand. Cf. *Disc.* 3.5.4.

DISCOURSE V

 OW IS IT THAT we have [883] a larger throng assembled here today? Surely, you have come together to demand that I keep my promise;[1] you are here to receive the silver tried in the fire which I pledged to pay over to you. For as the Psalmist says: "The words of the Lord are pure words: silver tried by the fire, purged from the earth."[2] Blessed be God because he has put in your hearts the yearning to hear words good for your souls.

(2) When wine-tipplers get up each morning, they start their meddlesome probing to discover where they will find the day's drinking-bouts, carousals, parties, revels, and drunken brawls; they busy themselves searching for bottles, mixing bowls, and drinking cups. But when you get up each day, you go around asking where you will find exhortation and counsel, encouragement, and instruction, the kind of discourse which draws you to give glory to Christ.

---

1 The promise he will keep is not altogether clear from *Discourse* IV. "Tomorrow's service" in 4.7.9 may have meant merely "the next service." "Today" need not necessarily mean the day after *Disc.* IV was delivered. One or more sermons may have been lost (cf. Introd. III 21). If a promise was made in *Disc.* IV it must have been vague: e.g., in 4.7.1 Chrysostom says: "Let then my battle with the Jews wait awhile. I did fight a skirmish of words with them today, but I said only what was enough to save our brothers from danger. Perhaps I said much more than that." What he had said was by way of condemning the Jews for observing their ritual at the wrong time and place. He will continue this general theme in *Discourse* V by showing that they will never have the right place because their temple will never be rebuilt, they will never recover their sacrifice, priesthood, or kings. This could be the fulfillment of his promise.

2 Ps 11 (12).7 (LXX).

This makes me the more eager to hold fast to my topic and, from the fullness of my heart, to keep the promises I have made.

(3) My battle against the Jews did come to a fitting end. The monument marking their rout has been set up, the victory crown belongs to me, and I have captured the prize I sought from my previous discourse. For the task I had undertaken was to prove that what the Jews now do by way of ritual transgresses and violates the Law. It was my desire to show that in these rites we have men doing battle with God, creatures waging war against him. And with God's help, I did give precise proof of this. For even if the Jews were going to recover their own city, if they were about to return to their old commonwealth and way of life and see their temple rebuilt—an event which will never come to pass—even so, they have no defense for their present practices.[3]

(4) The three boys in Babylon, Daniel, and all the others who spent their days in captivity kept expecting to recover their own city and, after seventy years, to see the soil of their fatherland; they kept looking forward to living again under their ancestral laws.[4] They had a clear pledge and promise that this would come to pass. However, until the promise was fulfilled, until they did return, they did not dare to perform any of the prescribed rites the way the Jews of today do.[5]

(5) This is the way you, too, can silence and gag the Jews. Ask the Jew why he observes the fast when he has no city. If he shall say: "Because I expect to recover my city," you say to him: "Stop fasting, then, until you do recover it. Certainly, until the holy ones of old returned to their own fatherland, they practiced none of the

---

3 This does summarize much that was said in *Discourse* IV, of which there are further echoes in the present homily, which also has much in common with the *Demonstration.*

4 Cf. Dn 1–6. The modern reader must realize that the stories in these chapters are apocalyptic. God possesses the attributes revealed in them; those faithful to his Law and confident in his power may be assured he will deliver them from their danger and restore them from bondage. The seventy years prophecied by Jer 25.11 are changed to seventy weeks of years (cf. Dn 9.24 and NAB note) but Jerusalem will be restored.

5 See *Disc.* 4.5.3.

rites which you now practice. From this it is clear that you are violating the law, even if you are going to recover your city, as you say; you are transgressing your convenant with God and outraging that old commonwealth and way of life." What I have said to your loving assembly both here and in my previous discourse is enough to silence and gag the shameless arguments of the Jews and to prove that they are transgressing the Law.[6]

(6) It was not my sole purpose to stitch shut the mouths of the Jews. I also was anxious [884] to give you more extensive instruction in the teachings of the Church.[7] Come now, and let me give you abundant proof that the temple will not be rebuilt and that the Jews will not return to their former way of life. In this way you will come to a clearer understanding of what the Apostles taught, and the Jews will be all the more convicted of acting in a godless way. As witness I shall produce not an angel, not an archangel, but the very Master of the whole world, our Lord Jesus Christ. When he came into Jerusalem and saw the temple, he said: "Jerusalem will be trodden down by many nations, until the times of many nations be fulfilled."[8] By this he meant the years to come until the consummation of the world. And again, speaking to his disciples about the temple, he made the threat that a stone would not remain upon a stone in that place until the time when it be destroyed.[9] His threat was a prediction that the temple would come to a final devastation and completely disappear.

(7) But the Jew totally rejects this testimony. He refuses to admit what Christ said. What does the Jew say? "The man who said this is my foe. I crucified him, so how am I to accept his testimony?" But

---

6 Because their city has been destroyed and their present bondage will never end. Cf. below *Disc.* 5.9.1–5.11.10 and *Demonstration* 16–17 (PG 48.835–38).

7 Chrysostom here turns from polemics and more to apologetics and instruction in Christian doctrine. For the rest of this chapter and all of 3 and 4 he will take all but one of his texts from NT.

8 Cf. Lk 21.24. The nations are the Gentiles who are to take the place of the Jews in the divine plan (cf. Lk 20.16 and Rom 11.25).

9 Cf. Mt 24.2. The text is quoted in *Demonstration* 16 (PG 48.834); the prediction was fulfilled under Titus in 70. Christ's power is proved by his own predictions which have been realized.

this is the marvel of it. You Jews did crucify him. But after he died on the cross, he then destroyed your city; it was then that he dispersed your people; it was then that he scattered your nation over the face of the earth. In doing this, he teaches us that he is risen, alive, and in heaven.

(8) Because you were not willing to recognize his power through his benefactions, he taught you by his punishment and vengeance that no one can struggle with or prevail against his might and strength. But even so, you do not believe in him, you do not recognize that he is God and Master of all the world, but you consider him just another man.[10]

(9) Come then and let us conduct a test as we would in the case of a man. How do we test human beings? If we see that a man tells the truth in all things and never in any way lies to another, we accept his word, even if he happens to be a foe. At least we do so if we have any sense. In the same way, when we see that a man is a liar, even if he tells the truth in some instances, we do not readily accept his word.

II

Let us look, then, at the character and habits of Christ. Not only did he predict and foretell the destruction of the temple but he also prophesied during his life many other things which were going to come to pass a long time afterwards. Let us, then, bring these predictions into the open. If you see that he is lying in these predictions, then do not accept his prediction about the temple, nor consider it deserving of your belief. But if you see that he tells the truth in all things and that this prediction has been fulfilled, if you see that long years have passed but still testify to the truth of what he foretold, let us have no more of your impudence and stubbornness in matters which are clearer than the light of the sun.

---

10 In the *Demonstration* the phrase "a mere man" (i.e., not divine) occurs often; e.g., in 9 we read: "From this you may understand that the Crucified One was no mere man" (PG 48.825). Also see *Disc.* 5.3.2, 3 and 11 for the expression "mere man."

(2) Let us see what else he predicted. There once came up to him a woman with an alabaster jar of precious ointment and she poured it on him. His disciples were indignant at what happened and said: "Why was this not sold [885] for three hundred denarii and given to the poor?"[11] He reproved them, however, and said "Why do you trouble the woman. She has done a good deed. For I say to you, wherever on the whole earth this gospel is preached, this also that she has done shall be told in memory of her."[12] Did he lie or did he tell the truth? Was his prediction fulfilled or did it fail to come true? Put these questions to the Jew. Even if he counts his shameless acts in the tens of thousands, he will not be able to look at this prophecy in the face and stare it down.

(3) Certainly we do hear her story told in all the churches. Consuls have stood listening to it, and generals, too; men, women, the renowned, the distinguished, the famous ones in every city. Wherever in the world you may go, everyone respectfully listens to the story of her good service; her action is known in every corner of the earth.

(4) How many kings brought many and great blessings on their cities, how many kings waged successful wars, set up many trophies of victory, saved nations, built cities, and in addition, acquired countless revenues? Yet they, for all their great exploits, are buried in the silence of oblivion. Many queens and great ladies have conferred benefits beyond number on those subject to them. Yet some people do not even know them by name. But this worthless woman, who only poured out her ointment, is praised everywhere in the world; the long passage of years has failed to blot out the memory of her, and the time to come will never quench her fame.

---

11 Cf. Mt 26.9. The supper at Bethany takes place six days before the Passover in Jn 12.1; Mt places it two days before the Passover (26.3) to bring together the narratives of the anointing and the betrayal by Judas. Chrysostom conflates the accounts of Mt 26.6--13 and Jn 12.1--8. Jn gives the detail of the 300 denarii (12.5). A denarius was a day's wage according to the parable of the laboreres in the vineyard (Mt 20.2).

12 Mt. 26.10,13; cf. Mk 14.6,8--9; Jn 12.7. Jn omits the promise concerning Mary; Lk omits the whole Bethany incident.

(5) And yet hers was not a deed of renown. For what renown was there in pouring out some ointment? Nor was she a distinguished person, for she was a low woman and an outcast.[13] Nor was there a large audience to see, for only the disciples were gathered around her. Nor was the place one where she could be easily seen. She made no entrance onto a theater stage to perform her service but did her good deed in a house with only ten[14] people present.

(6) Nonetheless, even though she was a lowly person, even though only a few were there to witness it, even though the place was undistinguished, neither these facts nor any others could obscure the memory of that woman. Today, she is more illustrious than any king or queen; no passage of years has buried in oblivion the service she performed.

(7) Tell me, now. How do you explain this? Who brought this about? Is it not the work of the God to whom this service was paid? Is it not God who has spread the story of her deed to every corner of the earth? Is it within the scope of human power to predict such things as these? Who in his right mind could say that? We marvel and are astounded when Christ foretells what he, himself, will do. But when he predicts what others will do and then makes these actions of others clear to all the world and worthy of every man's belief, it is still more astounding and marvellous.

(8) Again, he said to Peter: "Upon this rock I will build my Church, and the gates of hell shall not prevail against it."[15] You Jews tell me how you can attack this prediction of his. How can you

---

13 Only Jn 12.3 identifies the woman at Bethany as Mary, sister of Martha and Lazarus (11.1–2). It is presumed that this Mary was the Mary Magdalene who stood on Calvary (Mt 27.56), sat at the sepulcher (ibid. 61) and came to the tomb on the first day of the week (28.1). If so, and the tradition is constant, she is the Magdalene from whom seven devils had gone out (Lk 8.2).

14 Not to be taken literally. Ten was the perfect Pythagorean number but here seems to be used, as it is in Latin, to mean a few or an indefinite number. Cf. the following sentence.

15 Mt 16.18. Cf. Demonstration 12–13 for Christ's prediction on the founding of the Church and the miraculous spread of the Gospel message (PG 48.829–33).

show that this prophecy is false? The testimony of the facts will not allow it, even if you are obstinate and dispute it ten thousand times. How many conflagrations of war have been kindled against the Church? Many armies have taken the field, many weapons have been used, every form of punishment and torture has been contrived. There were [886] frying-pans, racks caldrons, ovens, cisterns, cliffs, fangs of wild beasts, seas, confiscations, and ten thousand other means of torture, unmentionable and unendurable.[16] And these were used not only by foreigners but by our own countrymen. Indeed, a sort of civil war held everything in its grip; rather, it was more bitter than any civil war. Not only did citizens do battle with citizens but kinsmen with kinsmen, members of the same household with each other; friends fought friends. Yet none of these things destroyed the Church nor made it weaker.[17]

(9) Certainly, the wonderful and unexpected thing about this is that all these attacks were made against the Church when it was just beginning.[18] If these dread persecutions were let loose against it after it had taken root and after the Gospel message had been planted everywhere in the world, it would not be so strange that the Church had resisted these attacks. But it was at the beginning of her teaching mission, when the seed of faith had just been sown and the understanding of those who heard the word was still somewhat weak, that these violent wars broke out in all their fury. The fact that they did not weaken our position but even made us prosper all

---

16 For the persecutions of the early Church cf. *Demonstration* 13–15 (PG 48.832–33). For the frying-pans cf. 2 Mc 7.3, where in describing the preparation for the martyrdom of the seven brothers LXX uses the same Greek word *(tēgana)*. Many similar tortures are mentioned also in the apocryphal 4 Mc and discussed by G. Racle, "A la source d'un passage de la VIIe catèchese baptismale de S. Jean Chrysostome," *Vigiliae christianae* 15 (1961) 46–53.

17 Cf. Mt 10.35. Ignatius was Antioch's most famous martyr; he was thrown to the lions in 116 under Trajan. Other persecutions which affected Antioch with greater or less severity were those under Marcus Aurelius (161–80), Maximinus the Thracian (235–38), Decius (249–51), Valerian (257–60), Diocletian (303), and Maximinus (311–313).

18 Cf. *Demonstration* 15 (PG 48.833).

the more is the miracle that surpasses all miracles.

(10) You may say that the Church now stands firm because of the peace granted to it by the emperors.[19] To keep you from saying this, God permitted the Church to be attacked and persecuted at a time when it was smaller and seemed to be weaker. God wanted you to learn that the security the Church enjoys today does not come to it from the peace granted by emperors, but from the power of God.

III

To help you see the truth of this, consider how many men wished to introduce their teachings among the Greeks and to establish a new commonwealth and way of life. Think of such men as Zeno,[20] Plato,[21] Socrates,[22] Diagoras,[23] Pythagoras,[24] and countless others. Yet they fell so far short of success that many people do not even now know them by name. But Christ not only wrote a constitution but even brought a new way of life to the whole world.[25] How many miracles do they say that Apollonius of Tyana[26] worked? But

---

19 Cf. *ibid.* During Chrysostom's life, all the emperors after Constantine (324–37) except Julian the Apostate (361–63) were Christians, although Valens favored Arianism.

20 There were four Greek philosophers of this name. From the preceding sentence we may suspect that the founder of the Stoic school, Zeno of Citium (fl. ca. 300 B.C.) is meant because among his pupils was Sphaerus, who inspired the revolution and institution of a new government at Sparta under Cleomenes III in 227 B.C.

21 Plato in his *Republic* and *Laws* teaches that the good of a state depends on the moral value of its citizens, on the prevalence of justice and harmony between higher and lower elements.

22 Socrates taught Plato, who is thought to represent much of Socrates' doctrine.

23 Diagoras of Melos (5th cent. B.C.), a member of the Sophistic movement, was an outspoken atheist. Nothing is known of his political philosophy.

24 Pythagoras (b. ca. 580 B.C.) founded a school or brotherhood at Croton in southern Italy. His political influence was exercised in favor of oligarchy. He greatly advanced the mathematical, geometrical, and astronomical sciences. None of his writings has survived.

25 Of course Chrysostom means the Kerygma of the Gospels. This point is treated and developed in the *Demonstration* 12–14 (PG 48.829–33).

26 A Neopythagorean philosopher and alleged wonder-worker of the 1st cent.

all his deeds were a fraud, a vain show, and devoid of truth. And you may learn this from the fact that, in an instant, they vanished and disappeared.

(2) Let no one consider it an insult to Christ that, while speaking of him, I mentioned Pythagoras, Plato, Zeno and the man from Tyana. I am not doing this of my own choice but out of consideration for the weakness of the Jews, who see in Christ a mere man. This is what Paul did when he came to Athens. On entering the city, he took the topic for his exhortation not from the prophets or the gospels, but from the Athenians' altar to the unknown God.[27] He did not consider their altar more deserving of faith than the gospels, nor did he account the inscription on it more worthy of honor than the prophets. But he was speaking to pagan Greeks, who believed in none of our sacred books, and so he used arguments from their own beliefs to subdue them. He did the same thing at Corinth when he said: "I have become to the Jews a Jew, to those without the Law, as one without the Law (though I am not without the law of God, but am under the law of Christ)."[28]

(3) The Old Testament does this, too, in speaking to the Jews about God. It says: "Who is like to you among the gods, O Lord?"[29] What do you mean, Moses? Is there any comparison at all

---

after Christ. An unreliable *Life* (in Greek) by Philostratus II describes Apollonius as an ascetic, and miracle-worker, transforming him into a pagan Christ. There is no precise information extant on his doctrine. Cf. M.R.P. McGuire, "Apollonius of Tyana," NCE 1.669.

27 Cf. Acts 17.23. Paul's speech is probably an example of an inserted discourse composed by Luke; it mirrors the reaction of a Christian missionary, who speaks from the depths of his faith when confronted with pagan religious culture. Pausanias (1.1.4) speaks of Athenian altars to "unknown gods" (i.e., to whatever god needed thanking or placating) but no altar has yet been found at Athens with precisely this dedication. Cf. J. Fitzmeyer, JBC 45:86.

28 Cf. 1 Cor 9.20–21. Chrysostom has Paul mean that, as a speaker, he is "all things to all men." R. Kugelman (JBC 51:60) says that while Paul is freed from the Jewish Law in Christ, and living among the Gentiles, he knows only the law of Christ, which is charity (Jn 15.12).

29 Ex 15.11. As Chrysostom suggests, the gods are the objects of heathen worship. The verse, however, is from the paean of victory sung by Moses and the Israelites together to celebrate Pharaoh's defeat. By their

between the true God and false gods? Moses would reply: "I did not say this to make a comparison; but since I was talking to the Jews, who had a lofty opinion of demons, I condescended to their weakness and [887] brought in the lesson I was teaching in this way." Let me also say that since my discussion is with the Jews, who consider that Christ is mere man and one who violated their Law, I compared him with those whom the pagan Greeks admire.

(4) If you wish me to make a comparison with men from among the Jews themselves, men who tried to do what Christ did, men who gathered disciples and were proclaimed as leaders and chiefs but who were immediately forgotten, let me try to prove it in this way. Surely this was what Gameliel[30] did to stop their mouths. When he saw the Sanhedrin in a rage and eager to shed the blood of the disciples, he wished to put a stop to their ungovernable anger. So he gave orders for the apostles to be put outside for a little while and then had this to say to the Jews.

(5) "Take care what you are about to do to these men. For some time ago there rose up Theudas, claiming to be somebody, and four hundred men followed him, but he perished and all his followers were scattered abroad. And after him there rose up Judas the Galilean, who drew a considerable crowd; he too died and his disciples perished. So now I say to you, Take care, for if this work is of men, it will be overthrown; but if it is of God, you will not be able to overthrow it. Else perhaps you may find yourselves fighting even against God."[31]

(6) Where, then, is the proof that if this is the work of men, it will perish? You had proof of this, said Gamaliel, from the cases of Judas and Theudas. So if the man whom the Apostles proclaim is a leader such as Judas and Theudas, if he does not do all he does by the power of God, wait a little while, and the outcome of events will give credibility to what you say. You will know from the way things

---

deliverance Yahweh has clearly proved his dominion over all gods and shown himself the savior of Israel. Hence, the reply Chrysostom presently puts in the mouth of Moses is highly questionable and characterizes the orator rather than the exegete.

30 Cf. Acts 5.34–41.

31 Cf. ibid. 35–39.

turn out whether he is a deceiver, as you say, and one who violates the Law, or the God who rules all things and, with ineffable power, orders and arranges our affairs.

(7) And this did come to pass. They did wait. The very outcome of events did prove that his power was divine and unconquerable. That trick which had deceived many men was turned around and back on the devil's own head. When Satan saw that Christ had come, he wished to cover up the reality of his coming[32] and to hide the true purpose of his Incarnation. So he brought on stage the rogues whom we mentioned, so that Christ might be considered one of them. And he did this on the cross, too, when he had two thieves crucified with Christ; he did the same thing in the case of Christ's coming when he strove to conceal the truth by putting it alongside the false. But he failed in both cases, and his very effort provided the strongest proof of Christ's power.

(8) Tell me this. If three men were crucified in the same place, at the same time, by the same judges, why have the two thieves been lost in silence, while He alone is worshipped? Again, if many men introduced new governments, got themselves adherents, and today not even their names are known, how is it that Christ is paid divine service throughout the world?

(9) Comparison makes facts especially clear. You Jews make this comparison, then, and learn how the truth has prevailed. What deceiver has gotten for himself so many churches all over the world, what rogue extended his worship to the ends of the earth, what imposter has every man [888] bowing down before him, and this in the face of ten thousand obstacles?[33] No one did. It is clear, then, that Christ was not a deceiver; he has saved us, he confers blessings upon us, he takes care of us, he protects our lives.

---

32 The Greek word for "coming" is *parousia* for which see J. McKenzie, DB 638–40. Here it seems to mean either Christ's first coming, his Incarnation (cf. 2 Tm 1.10), or his second, but imminent, coming. From the second century on, when it was clear that his second coming was not imminent, *parousia* was understood as meaning Christ's presence among and within the members of his Church.

33 Cf. *Demonstration* 15 (PG 48.833).

(10) Let me add one more prediction before I return to the topic on which I proposed to speak. Christ said: "I did not come to send peace upon the earth, but a sword."[34] However, he did not speak of what he would himself desire but he was foretelling the end to which things would come. He went on to say: "For I have come to set a man at variance with his father, and a daughter-in-law with her mother-in-law, and a daughter with her mother."[35]

(11) Tell me this. How did he foretell this if he was a mere man and one of the crowd? For this is what he meant. It sometimes happened that in one and the same house one person would believe, and another would not; then the father would want to lead his own son to deny his faith. This is why Christ predicted this very thing. What he was saying was this: "The power of the gospel will be so strong that sons despise their fathers, daughters their mothers, and parents their children. For they will choose not only to scorn members of their own household, but even to lay down their lives, to endure and suffer all things rather than deny their religion."

(12) How could he have managed to know this if he was just another man out of the crowd? How did it occur to him to reach the conclusion that sons would pay greater veneration to him than to their fathers, that parents would find him dearer than their own children, that wives would have a more ardent love for him than for their own husbands? And how did he know that this would happen not in one home only, nor in two, nor three, nor ten, nor twenty, nor a hundred, but in every corner of the world, in every city and country, on land and sea, in populous places and in those with few, if any, dwellings? No one can say that he foretold this and then failed to fulfill his prediction. Certainly it was not only at the very beginning but it is true even today that, because of their religion, many are hated and cast forth from their fathers' houses. However, they pay no heed to this; the fact that they suffer it for the sake of Christ is consolation enough for them.

---

34 Cf. Mt 10.34.
35 Cf. *ibid.* 35 and above, *Disc.* 5.2.8.

(13) Tell me this. What human being ever had the power to do this? Yet this man made all these predictions about that woman, about the Church, and about the wars which would be waged against it. He also predicted that the temple would be destroyed, that Jerusalem would be captured, and that the city would no longer be the city of the Jews as it had been in the past.[36]

(14) If he was wrong and deceived you in all those other predictions, and they did not come true, then refuse to believe what he foretold of Jerusalem and the temple. But you do see those other predictions gloriously fulfilled and their truth waxing stronger with each passing day. The gates of hell did not prevail against the Church, after so many years the story of what that woman did is still told all over the world, and men who believed in him did pay greater veneration to him than to their own parents, wives, and children. If this is true, tell me, why do you reject this one prediction about the temple, especially since the testimony of time puts the gag of silence on your shameless words?

(15) Suppose a mere ten, twenty, thirty, or fifty years were to have passed since the capture of Jerusalem. Even then you would have absolutely no right to show your impudence by rejecting his prediction, but if you wished to be obstinate, you might have had some pretext for protest left to you. But not only fifty years but many more than one, two, or three centuries[37] have passed since Jerusalem was captured. And never has there been seen a single trace or shadow of the change for which you are waiting. Why, then, are

---

36 Cf. Mt 24.1–23. The discourse is eschatological and apocalyptic, intertwining the two themes of the passing of Israel and the end of the world. Mt also merges the apocalyptic and prophetic with the historical. For Palestinian Judaism, even for the Jewish Christian, the collapse of Jerusalem was truly the end of the world. A world in which Yahweh was not worshipped by his people, in his land, in his temple was not for them the world of history. The gentile Christian was less aware of the magnitude of the crisis, both historical and theological, involved in the fall of Palestinian Judaism. But Chrysostom does seem to understand that, with the disaster, a new phase of the Kingdom began. Cf. J. McKenzie, JBC 43:165–70.

37 Since Titus destroyed Jerusalem in 70, Chrysostom's reckoning of three centuries is about correct. The point is, however, that the time passage is ample to prove Christ's predictions true.

you so rash and foolish as to keep up your shameless objections?

IV

We have said [889] enough to prove that the temple will never be rebuilt. But since the abundance of proofs which support this truth is so great, I shall turn from the gospels to the prophets, because the Jews put their belief in them before all others.[38] And from the words of the prophets I shall make it clear that the Jews will recover neither their city nor their temple in days to come. And yet the need was not mine to prove that the temple will not be restored. This was not my obligation; the Jews have the obligation to prove the opposite, namely, that the temple will be rebuilt. For the years that have elapsed stand by my side in the combat and bear witness to the truth of my words.

(2) Even though the outcome of events defeats them, even though they cannot prove in deeds what they maintain in words, even though they are simply making a rash boast, they have a right to present their testimony. The proof for my position is that the events of which I speak did actually occur: Jerusalem did fall and has not been restored after so many years. Their position rests on their unsupported words.

(3) Yet the burden of proof was on them to show that the city would rise again. This is the procedure for giving proofs in courts of law. Suppose two people are in dispute over some matter and the first party presents the claim for his position in writing, while the second party attacks his statement. The second party must then bring forward witnesses or other proofs in refutation of what is said in the written deposition; but the plaintiff need not do so. This is what the Jews must now do. They must produce a prophet who says that by all means Jerusalem will be rebuilt. For if there was going to be an end to the present captivity for you Jews, there was every

---

38 Chrysostom drew from the prophets proof for Christ's divinity because the pagans would accept the books of the Jews, who were Christ's enemies (cf. *Demonstration* 2 [PG 48.815]); here he draws arguments from the same source because the Jews put their belief in the prophets.

need for the prophets to foretell this, as is clear to anyone who has even so much as glanced at the prophetic books. For it was the custom of old among the Jews that, under inspiration from above, their prophets would foretell the good or evil things which were going to befall the people.[39]

(4) What was the reason for this? It was because the Jews were so arrogant and obstinate. They immediately forgot what God had done for them, they ascribed his kindness to demons and reckoned that his blessings had come from them. Even when the sea was divided for them, as they went forth from Egypt, and while other wonderful things were happening to them, they forgot the God who was performing these miracles and attributed them to others who were not gods. For they said to Aaron: "Make for us gods who will be our leaders."[40] And they said to Jeremiah: 'We will not listen to what you say in the name of the Lord. Rather we will continue doing what we had proposed: we will burn incense to the queen of heaven and pour out libations to her, as we and our fathers, our kings and princes have done. Then we had enough food to eat and we were well off; we suffered no misfortune But since we stopped burning incense to the queen of heaven and pouring out libations to her, we are in need of everything and are being destroyed by the sword and by hunger."[41] The inspired prophets, then, foretold what would happen to the Jews so that they would ascribe none of the events to idols, but would believe that both punishments and blessings always come from God: the punishment came for their sins, and the blessings because of God's love and kindness.

(5) So that you may learn that this is the reason [890] for the prophecy, hear what Isaiah, the most eloquent of prophets, had to say to the Jewish people. "I know that you are stubborn and that your neck is an iron sinew" (that is, unbending), "and your forehead

---

39 See J. McKenzie, "Prophet, Prophecy," DB 694–99, esp. 695.
40 Cf. Ex 32.1. The people request Aaron to make them gods in the form of idols to lead them; thus they show they are abandoning the leadership of Yahweh. Aaron weakly compromises and makes a calf like the Egyptian Apis and the Canaanite Baal. Cf. E. Power, CCHS 226.
41 Cf. Jer 44.16–18. G. Couturier, JBC 19:107, says that in 2–14 Jer ex-

bronze" (that is, incapable of blushing)."⁴² We, too, make a practice of giving the name 'bronze-faced to those who cannot blush. And Isaiah went on to say: "I foretold what things would come upon you before they took place and I let you hear of them."⁴³ Then he added the reason for the prophecy when he said: "So that you may never say: 'My idols did them, my statues and molten images commanded them.'"⁴⁴

(6) At another time some of the Jews who were quarrelsome and boastful and, even after the prophecies were fulfilled, were acting as impudently as if they had never heard them. Then the prophets not only foretold what would come to pass but even had witnesses of what they were doing. Again it was Isaiah who said: "Make reliable men my witnesses, Uriah the priest, and Zechariah, son of Jeberechiah."⁴⁵ And this was not all Isaiah did. He set his prophecy down in writing in a new book so that, after his prophecy was fulfilled, what he had written might bear witness against the Jews of what the inspired prophet predicted to them a long time before. This

---

plains the present miseries of the people: idolatrous practices have broken the covenant, and God has brought evil on Jerusalem and Judah. The people's interpretation is the exact opposite: the eradication of idolatry by King Josiah was the cause of these calamities. When "the queen of heaven" (Astarte, a Canaanite fertility goddess; cf. DB 66–67) had worshippers in Israel, prosperity existed. Only a return to her cult will assure the future.

42 Is 48.4. Verse 3 speaks of "things of the past," i.e., the idolatry of pre-exilic days. Even though these things were foretold and came to pass, Israel was stubborn, with iron sinew and bronze forehead. Cf. Jer 5.3; Ex 32.9; Dt 9.6. It is not rare for Chrysostom to insert explanations in a quotation as here, where the terms are strange and his explanations helpful.

43 Cf. Is 48.5. This refers back to "the things of the past" of verse 3.

44 Cf. ibid. 5 (the rest of the verse). The Babylonians attributed the conquest of Jerusalem to Bel-Marduc; the Israelites might be tempted to believe them. So Is shows that Yahweh had foretold it so that his people might not abandon their faith and confidence in him.

45 Cf. Is 8.2 (LXX); Chrysostom, with LXX, reads ". . . son of Barachiah." The witnesses give legal formality to his act of prophecy of destruction to come from Assyria. Uriah collaborated with Ahaz in profaning the temple (2 Kgs [4 Kgs] 16.10–16). Zechariah (called son of Jeberechiah in NAB) was probably the father-in-law of Ahaz (2 Kgs [4 Kgs] 18.2). Cf. F. Moriarty, JBC 16:20.

is why he did not simply write it in a book, but in a new book, a book capable of staying sturdy for a long time without easily falling apart, a book which could last until the events described in it would come to pass. [46]

V

I shall prove that this is true, and that God foretold everything which was going to befall the Jews. I shall do so not only from what Isaiah said but from all the things which happened to them, both good and bad. Indeed, the Jews three times endured bondage, very harsh and most severe; but none of these came upon them unpredicted. God saw to it that each captivity was prophesied. He carefully foretold the place, the duration, the kind, the form of their misfortune, the return from salvery, and everything else.

(2) First, I shall speak of the prediction of their slavery in Egypt. Surely, in speaking to Abraham, God said: "Know for certain that your posterity will be strangers in a land not their own; they shall be subjected to slavery and shall be oppressed four hundred years. But I will judge that nation which they shall serve, said God. And in the fourth generation they shall return here with great possessions."[47] Do you see how he mentioned the number of years? Four hundred. The nature of their slavery? He did not simply say: "They shall be subjected to slavery," but: "They shall be oppressed." Listen to Moses' explanation of their misfortune. He said: "No straw is supplied to your servants, and still we are told to make bricks."[48] And

---

46 Cf. Is 30.8. LXX reads, "on a tablet and in a book (or record)." The tablet was made of wood; the book was probably a leather scroll. Both would be durable and capable of lasting until the events described would come to pass.

47 Cf. Gn 15.13–16. E. Maly, JBC 2:59, points out that these verses are an insertion and break the continuity but that the author's sense of salvation history is profound: even 400 years do not really interrupt the plan of God, who is seen to direct all history toward his appointed goal. Chrysostom is more interested in indicating the place, duration, and kind of bondage the posterity of Abraham will undergo in Egypt.

48 Ex 5.16. They are being oppressed by intolerable working conditions and lack of necessary materials.

each day they were flogged so that you may learn the meaning of the words: "They shall be subjected to slavery and shall be oppressed." When He said: "I will judge that nation which they shall serve," He was speaking of the drowning of the Egyptians in the Red Sea, which Moses described in his canticle[49] when he said: "Horse and chariot he has cast into the sea." Then he also mentioned the manner of their return when he said that they will return here with great possessions: "Each of you take from his neighbor and comrade gold and silver vessels."[50] Since they had been subjected to slavery a long time and had received no pay, God permitted them to make this demand of the Egyptians even though their masters might be unwilling to pay.[51] And the prophet exclaimed and said: "And he led them forth laden with silver [891] and gold, with not a weakling among their tribes."[52] So here we have one bondage which was precisely predicted.

(3) Come now and let us turn our discussion to the second captivity. What one is that? The bondage in Babylon. Jeremiah certainly foretold it exactly when he said: "Thus says the Lord: Only after seventy years have elapsed for Babylon will I visit you and fulfill for you my promise to bring you back to this place. I shall change your bondage; I shall gather you from all the nations and all the places to which I have banished you, says the Lord, and bring you back to the place from which I have exiled you."[53] Do you see how here again

---

49 The canticle of Moses is the paean of victory in Ex 15.1–21. "Horse and chariot he has cast into the sea" comes from the opening verse of the paean.

50 Cf. Ex 3.22 and 11.2. According to Chrysostom, their long years of slavery are to be repaid in a spoliation of the Egyptians before their departure.

51 Cf. Ex 12.35–36. By the ten plagues Yahweh, the God of the Israelites, has proved his power. This (as verse 36 says) makes the Egyptians so well-disposed that they let their former slaves have the articles of silver and gold and clothing for which they asked (verse 35). Chrysostom overlooks this willingness of the Egyptians in his explanation of 3.22 and 11.2.

52 Ps 104(105).37. Verse 38 adds: "Egypt rejoiced at their going, for the dread of them had fallen upon it."

53 Apparently a conflation of Jer 29.10 and 14. Jer's revelation chiefly concerns the coming destruction of Jerusalem; he exhorts the people to repent and submit to the power of Babylon; he promises merciful treatment, if

He spoke of the city, the number of years, and the places from which and to which He was going to lead them?

(4) This explains why Daniel did not make his prayer for the Jews until he saw that the seventy years had elapsed. Who says so? It was Daniel himself, when he said: "I, Daniel, took care of the king's affairs. But I was appalled at the vision, nor was there anyone to understand it."[54] "And I understood in the Scriptures the counting of the years of which the Lord spoke to the prophet Jeremiah: that for the ruins of Jerusalem seventy years must be fulfilled. I turned to the Lord God, seeking to pray and entreat him with fasting, sackcloth, and ashes."[55]

(5) Did you hear how this bondage was foretold and how the prophet did not dare to bring his prayer and entreaty to God before the appointed time? He feared that his prayer might be rash and in vain. He was afraid he would hear what Jeremiah had heard: "Do not pray for this his people, and do not make demand of me for them for I shall not hear your voice."[56] But when he saw that the sentence pronounced against them had been fulfilled and that the time was summoning them to return, he did pray for them. And he did not merely pray, he made his entreaty with fasting, sackcloth, and ashes.

---

they do, and ultimate restoration. He was not believed; Nebuchadnezzar did exile many priests, prophets, and people to Babylon. Even King Jehoiakim was dragged there in chains (2 Chr [2 Par] 36.6). Jer 29.1–32 is a letter from Jer to these exiles, in which he promises them restoration after seventy years (cf. also 25.11). G. Couturier (JBC 19:78) seems to take this as an indefinite period; C. Lattey (CCHS 582) dates it from 605–537, reckoning sixty-nine years as seventy in round numbers.

54 Cf. Dn 8.27. The vision is that of the Ram and the He-Goat which the angel Gabriel explained (verse 17) as referring to the end of time, when God sits in judgment on his enemies (cf. verse 19). Perhaps in his shock Dn means he could not understand all the details of the vision.

55 Cf. Dn 9.2–3. NAB ad loc. says that Jer (25.11; 29.10) had prophesied a Babylonian captivity of seventy years, a round number signifying the complete passing away of the existing generation. Jer's prophecy was fulfilled in the capture of Babylon by Cyrus (539 B.C.) and the subsequent return of the Jews to Palestine. The author of Dn 9 is not satisfied with this fulfillment since it is not a full restoration of Zion; so he prays for further enlightenment. Chrysostom sees only obedience to a literal prophecy in Dn's action.

56 Cf. Jer 14.11–12, where Jer pleads for his people who have been misled

(6) The prophet acted toward God in a way quite common among men. When we see that a master has cast his slaves into prison for many serious crimes, we do not make a plea for them immediately, nor at the outset, nor at the beginning of their punishment. We let them be punished for a few days; then we go to the master with our plea and we have time working on our side. This is exactly what the prophet did. Although the penalty the Jews paid was not as severe as their sins deserved, nonetheless they did pay it. And it was only then that the prophet went to God to plead on their behalf.

(7) If you would like to hear it, let us listen to the prayer he made for them. He said: "I confessed and said, 'Lord great and awesome God, you who keep your covenant and your mercy toward those who love you and observe your commandments!' "[57] What are you doing, Daniel? When you intercede for those who have sinned and quarreled with God, are you talking about men who keep God's laws? Do those who transgress his commandments deserve pardon? What did Daniel say? "I am not making this prayer for their sake but for the sake of their forefathers, for the sake of Abraham, Isaac, and Jacob. The promise and pledge was made to those who kept God's commandments. These men, then, have no just claim to salvation; [892] this is why I mention their forefathers."[58]

(8) Daniel was not speaking of the Jews in bondage when he said: "You who keep your covenant and your mercy toward those who

---

by false prophets. But God's purpose is fixed and Jer is forbidden to pray for his people, as he is also in 7.16 and 11.14.

57 Cf. Dn 9.4. Verses 4–20 are a later addition; it is not the prayer of an individual but of the community. It is not a plea for enlightenment on the meaning of Jer's prophecy as the context would demand, but an acknowledgment of public guilt and a supplication for the restoration of Zion; cf. L. Hartman (JBC 26:30). The inspired prayer is written in much better Hebrew than is the rest of the book. Since Chrysostom would know it only in a Greek version, he could not be expected to have known that or to have suspected it as an intrusion.

58 These words, which Chrysostom puts in Dn's mouth, do echo some of the sentiments of verses 5–20.

love you and observe your commandments." That is why he immediately added: "We have sinned, acted lawlessly, done evil, and departed from your commandments and your laws. We have not obeyed your servants the prophets."[59] For there is one defense left to sinners after they have sinned: to confess their sins.

(9) Do you now please consider the virtue of the just man and the arrogance of the Jews. He who is conscious of no evil in himself pronounces a most severe judgment on himself when he says: "We have sinned, acted lawlessly, done evil." But those who were filled with ten thousand evils did quite the opposite when they said: "We kept your commandments; and now we call strangers blessed and evildoers are exalted."[60] Just men usually act modestly after they have done just deeds; the wicked generally exalt themselves after they have sinned. The man who was conscious of no wickedness in himself said: "We have acted lawlessly, we have departed from your laws"; those who are aware of the burden of ten thousand sins say: "We have kept your commandments." I tell you this so that we may shun the sinner and emulate the just.

VI

After he ran through their lawless acts, the prophet next spoke of the penalty they paid, because he wanted to use this to win God over to pity them. For he said: "And there came upon us the malediction recorded in the law of Moses, the servant of God, because we sinned."[61] What is that malediction? Do you wish us to read it?[62]

---

59 Dn 9.5–6.
60 Cf. Mal 3.14–15 (LXX), who sees the suffering of the just man and the prosperity of the evil. Chrysostom has Mal, the just man, confessing his sins while the sinful Jews profess to have kept God's commandments. The Christian must imitate the just and avoid the sinners' boastful lies; otherwise they, as the sinners, will feel God's punishments.
61 Cf. Dn 9.11. No effort is made to conceal or extenuate the people's guilt. All have sinned; the curses threatened for transgressors (Lv 26; Dt 28.15–68) have fallen on them. Their plight is hopeless but Dn pleads for God's compassion and forgiveness (9.17–19). Chrysostom looks here only at the people's sins and not at Dn's plea.
62 "Read" may here mean "recite," as in *Disc.* 2.3.9. A preacher may have

"If you will not serve the Lord your God, I shall lead forth against you a shameless nation, a nation whose tongue you will not understand, and you will be few in number."[63] The three boys in Babylon also made this same point clear when they showed that the kind of punishment visited upon them came about because of what they had done. They made confession to God for the sins of all Jews when they said: "You have handed us over to our enemies, lawless and hateful rebels, to an unjust king, the worst in all the world."[64] Do you see how God fulfilled the curse which said: "You will be few in number?" And the one which said. "I shall lead forth against you a shameless nation?"[65]

(2) This is the very thing which Daniel was hinting at when he said: "There came upon us evils such as never occurred under heaven according to what happened in Israel."[66] What evils were these? Mothers ate their own children. Moses foretold this, but Jeremiah shows that it came true. For Moses said: "The refined and delicate woman, so delicate and refined that she would not venture to put her foot upon the step, shall put her hand to the unholy table and eat her own children."[67] But Jeremiah shows that this came true

---

had a copy of the Scriptures in the pulpit, but so many of Chrysostom's quotations vary from the received text that we must conclude either that he is quoting from memory or using a LXX text different from the received, perhaps one familiar to him from his days in the school of Diodorus.

63 Cf. Dt 28.49–50 (LXX) which omits: "If you will not serve the Lord your God" and "and you will be few in number," and shows other variations. If Chrysostom did have a text before him, it was probably open to Dn and not Dt.

64 Dn 3.32. For their sins the people were given into the hands of their godless enemies, particularly Nebuchadnezzar, the most wicked of all. The text comes from the prayer of Azariah (Dn 3.25–45), which confesses the Israelites' sins and God's justice and begs for deliverance while the three boys are in the fiery furnace. Cf. *Disc.* 4.5.7–8.

65 Cf. again Dt 28.49–50.

66 Cf. Dn 9.12 (LXX).

67 Cf. Dt 28.56–57 (LXX). Again the text is altered and abbreviated. LXX reads: "She that is tender and exceedingly delicate among you, whose foot has not tried to step upon the ground because of her delicacy and tenderness shall look with an evil eye on her husband in her bosom, and her son and her daughter, and the afterbirth which comes out between her thighs, and the child which she will bear. For she shall eat them because of the

when he said: "The hands of compassionate women boiled their own children."[68]

(3) But even after he had spoken of the sins of those who had sinned and after he brought into the open the punishment they endured, he did not ask that this should save them. See, then, the prudence of the servant. For after he had made clear that they had not yet paid the penalty their sins deserved, nor had their sufferings discharged the debt for their offenses, he then fled to the mercy of God and the loving-kindness of his way and says: "And now, O Lord, our God, who led your people out of the land of Egypt, and made a name for yourself even to this day, we have sinned and acted against your law."[69] What he is saying is: "You did not save the Jews of old for their good actions [893] but because you saw their affliction and distress, because you heard their cry. In the same way, free us from our present evils because of your loving-kindness and because of that alone. We have no other claim to salvation."

(4) So he spoke and, after many a lament, he brought forward the city of Jerusalem, like a captive woman, and said: "Let your face shine upon your sanctuary. Give ear, O my God, and listen, open your eyes and see our ruins and the ruins of your city, in which your name is invoked."[70] For when he looked among the men and saw no man who could make God propitious, he turned to the buildings and brought up the city. He showed its desolation and, after he completed his discourse on these things, he made God propitious. And this became clear from the events which followed.

(5) But back to what I was talking about. For I must return again to the topic I proposed. Yet I had good reason for bringing in these digressions: I wanted to give your minds a brief breathing space, since they were growing weary from the constant conflicts with the

___

want of all things secretly in your distress and affliction, with which your enemy will afflict you in all your cities." This is the horrible climax of the terrible description of a siege. We read of such cannibalism also during a siege of Samaria (2 Kgs [4 Kgs] 6.28–30).
68 Lam 4.10. Cf. *ibid*. 2.20; Bar 2.3; Ez 5.10, as well as preceding note.
69 Cf. Dn 9.15.
70 Cf. *ibid*. 17-18.

Jews. But let me return to the point where I departed from my topic to speak of these matters. Let me prove that the evils which were going to overtake the Jews had been accurately predicted by God's inspiration. My discourse had already shown that those two captivities came upon the Jews neither by chance nor unexpectedly.

(6) It remains for me now to bring up the third captivity. After I have done that, I must speak about the bondage which now encompasses them; I must give clear proof that no prophet ever predicted that there would be any freedom or escape from the ills which now encircle them.

(7) What, then, is this third captivity? It is the bondage that came upon them in the days of Antiochus Epiphanes. After Alexander, king of the Macedonians, conquered the Persian king, Darius, he took over the kingdom. After Alexander died, four kings followed him to the throne. Antiochus was the son of one of Alexander's four successors. Many years later Antiochus burned the temple, laid waste the holy of holies, put an end to the sacrifices, subjected the Jews, and destroyed their whole state.[71]

VII

Daniel foretold all this with the greatest accuracy, even to the very day. He foretold when it would be, how, by whom, the manner of it, where it would find an end, and what change it would bring about. You will understand this better after you have heard the vision which the prophet set forth in the form of a parable. The ram is Darius, the Persian king; the goat is the Greek king, Alexander of Macedon; the four horns are Alexander's successors; the last horn is Antiochus himself. But it will be better for you to hear the vision itself.

---

71 Antiochus IV Epiphanes ("The Glorious") came to the Syrian throne in 175 B.C. and sought to Hellenize his whole empire including Israel. He plundered the temple in 168 B.C.; the following year he erected in the temple an altar to Zeus Olympios, the "abomination of desolation." He suppressed Jewish worship and religious practices. Cf. 1 Mc 1.20–67. This is the third bondage of the Jews.

(2) Daniel said: "For I saw in a vision and I was sitting at the river Ubal." (The spot in question he calls by a Persian name.) "And I looked up and saw standing by the Ubal a ram with his horns held high; and the one horn was higher than the other, and the high one mounted to the very heights. And I saw the ram butting toward the sea,[72] north, and south. No beast will stand before it, nor was there anyone to rescue a beast from its grasp; it did what it pleased and became very powerful. And as I sat, I understood."[73] He was speaking of the Persian power and domain which overran the whole earth.

(3) Next he spoke of Alexander of Macedon [894] and said: "Behold, a he-goat came from the southwest across the whole earth without touching the ground. And the goat had a horn to be seen midway between his eyes."[74] He then spoke of Alexander's encounter with Darius and the victory won by Macedonian might. "The goat came up to the horned ram, grew savage, struck the ram,"—I must cut short the account—"broke both his horns and there was no one to rescue the ram from his power."[75]

(4) After that Daniel spoke of Alexander's death and the four kings who succeeded him: "And at the height of its power the great horn was shattered, and in its place there came up four others, facing the four winds of heaven."[76] Daniel then passed from this point to the reign of Antiochus and showed that he came from one of those four when he said: "Out of one of them came one strong horn, and

---

72 The sea is the west.
73 Cf. Dn 8.2–5 (LXX), which reads Ubal (verse 2) for Ulai of NAB. This vision (of the Ram and the He-Goat) repeats the major portion of the preceding vision of the Four Beasts (7.1–27) but in a more explicit fashion.
74 Cf. ibid. 5. The horn is really Alexander; the goat is the Greek empire (cf. 21). "Without touching the ground" symbolizes swift advance, such as that of Cyrus (Is 41.3), whom the Lord used as his instrument to save Israel.
75 Cf. ibid. 6–7. The ram is Darius.
76 Cf. ibid. 8. "The horn was shattered," i.e., Alexander died (in Babylon in 323 B.C. at the age of 32). His kingdom was divided between four of his generals: Cassander (Macedonia), Lysimachus (Thrace and Asia Minor), Seleucus (Syria, Mesapotamia. and Persia), and Ptolemy (Egypt). Only Seleucus and Ptolemy figure in the history of the Jews.

it became very powerful toward the south and the east."[77] Daniel then went on to show that Antiochus destroyed the Jewish commonwealth and way of life when he said: "And through him the sacrifice was disordered by transgression; and it came to pass that he prospered. And the holy place will be laid waste and sin replaced the sacrifice. After the altar was destroyed and the holy places trampled underfoot, he set up an idol within and offered unlawful sacrifices to the demons; righteousness was cast to the ground. He both did this and prospered."[78]

(5) Then again, for a second time, he spoke of the same reign of Antiochus Epiphanes, the bondage, and the capture and desolation of the temple; this time, however, he gave the date of these events. He again began, toward the end of the book, with the empire of Alexander and described all the intervening accomplishments of the Seleucids and the Ptolemies in their wars against each other, the exploits of their generals, the stratagems, the victories, the armies, the battles fought on land and sea.[79] When he came to Antiochus he ended by saying: "His armed forces shall rise up, defile the sanctuary, and remove the continuity" (and by the continuity he meant the uninterrupted daily sacrifices) "and in its place they will put an abomination. By treachery they will lead off those who violate the covenant" (that is, the transgressors among the Jews whom they will remove and keep with themselves); "but the people who know their God shall take strong action" (he means the events in the time of the

77 Cf. ibid. 9. Seleucus soon strengthened the weak kingdom he inherited and extended its sway.
78 Cf. ibid. 11–12 (LXX) with additons and omissions. LXX reads: "And through him the sacrifice was disordered, and he prospered; and the holy place will be laid waste. And sin replaced the sacrifice and righteousness was cast down to the ground, and he did this and prospered." The rest is missing from LXX. The reference is clearly to the profanantion of the temple by Antiochus when he replaced the altar of holocaust with one for pagan sacrifice and erected the statue of Zeus Olympios, the "abomination of desolation" (Mt 24.15 and Mk 13.14). Cf. 1 Mc 1.20–54. Success crowns this campaign because Antiochus is Yahweh's instrument of punishment (cf. Dn 11.36).
79 Cf. ibid. 10.20–11.30.

Maccabees: Judas, Simon, and John). "And the wise men of the people will have understanding of many things but they will fall by the sword and by fire" (here again he describes the burning of Jerusalem) "and by exile and the plunder days. And when they fall, they will receive a little help" (he means that, in the midst of those evils, they will be able to draw a breath and rise from the dread things which have overtaken them), "but many will join them out of treachery. And they shall fall from the number of the wise."[80] He said this to show that even many of those who stood firm will fall.

(6) Next, Daniel gave the reason why God permitted them to be involved in such trials. What is the reason? "To purge them, to choose them, and to make them white until the time of the end."[81] This is why, said Daniel, God permitted these evils so as to cleanse them and to show who among them was genuine and approved. In telling of the same king's[82] power and might. [895] he said: "He shall do as he pleases, he shall exalt himself and become very powerful."[83] In speaking of the king's blasphemous spirit, he went on to say: "He shall utter excessive haughty thoughts against

---

80 Cf. *ibid.* 11.31–35 (LXX). For the continuity of morning and evening sacrifices cf. Ex 29.38–42; Nm 28.3–8; J. Huesman, JBC 3:83; F. Moriarty, *ibid.* 5:52. 2 Kgs (4 Kgs) 16.15 speaks of a morning holocaust and an evening sacrifice. Lv 6.2–6 gives the ritual for the daily holocaust. The abomination is the statue of Zeus Olympios. In LXX verse 35 reads: "And some of them that understand shall fall, to try them as with fire and to test them." (Cf. next note). The text of Dn says nothing of those who stand firm falling. Below (*Disc.* 5.8.4) those who "stand firm and attain" will be released from bondage.

81 Cf. Dn 11.35 (LXX), which continues: "that they may be manifested at the time of the end." Chrysostom's "make them white" comes much closer to JB "made white." Cf. Dn 12.10. P. Saydon (CCHS 641) says of verses 33–35 that those who remain loyal to God (1 Mc 2.42) will teach others what is right but many will perish despite the aid of the small band of Maccabees. Many joined the Maccabees but were insincere and betrayed their people. Of the sincere many will die but not as a punishment. Death will cleanse and purify them, as gold is purified by fire, until the time God has appointed.

82 I.e., Antiochus Epiphanes.

83 Cf. Dn 11.36. LXX, which continues "against every god," i.e., pagan gods such as Apollo and even Zeus Olympios, with whom Antiochus had identified himself.

the God of gods; he shall prosper until the wrath be accomplished."[84] Daniel was here making it clear that it was not of Antiochus' own will but because of God's wrath against the Jews that he
was so victorious.

(7) After Daniel told in many other passages what evils the
king would bring on Egypt and Palestine, how he would return, at
whose bidding, and under the pressure of what cause, the prophet
then recounted a change of fortune and said that, after enduring all
these evils, the Jews would find some aid from an angel sent to help
them.[85] "At that time there shall arise Michael, the great prince,
guardian over the sons of your people. It shall be a time unsurpassed
in distress since nations began on earth until that time. At that time
your people will escape, everyone who is found written in the
book."[86] By that he meant those deserving to be saved.

VIII

But I have not yet given a proof for the question I am investigat-
ing. What is that question? That God set a time limit for those
involved in these trials, just as he set a limit of four hundred years
for the exile in Egypt and seventy years for the bondage in Babylon.
Let us see, then, if he set any time limit for this third slavery. Where
can we find the answer to this? In what Daniel said in the verses

---

84 A continuation of 11.36. The king has exalted himself over the gods of his
fathers and the God of the Jews and his insolence toward God and his
worshippers will last as long as God is wrathful with his people. Cf. P.
Saydon, CCHS 641.
85 The angel Michael is probably the same one who overcomes the dragon in
Rv 12.7 and disputes with the devil over the body of Moses in Jude 9. In
Dn 10.21 he is guardian and protector of God's people.
86 Cf. Dn 12.1. Verses 1–3 give a magnificent conclusion to the revelation of
chapters 10–11. Despite the terrible sufferings in the eschatological crisis,
the elect of God will be saved. The passage is remarkable as the earliest
clear enunciation of belief in the resurrection of the dead. Cf. J. Hartman,
JBC 26:34. Even under Michael there will be another and more violent
persecution; this may predict the affliction of the righteous at the end
of the world. If so, the age of Antiochus merges insensibly into that of
Antichrist.

following those I discussed.

(2) Since he had heard of the many great evils which would befall the Jews--the burning of Jerusalem, the toppling of their state, the bondage of his people--he then wanted to learn what would be the end of these trials, and if there would be any change in their disastrous condition. So he asked the angel who had appeared to him and said: "Lord, what is to be the outcome of this?" "Come here, Daniel," he said, "because the words are to be kept secret and sealed" (indicating the obscurity of the words) "until the time of the end."[87] Then the angel mentioned the reason why God consented to these evils: "As long as many are chosen, made white, and purged, as long as the lawless act lawlessly, as long as all the unholy ones shall not understand and the holy ones do understand."[88]

(3) Next, in predicting the length of time these evils would last, Daniel's angel said: "From the time of the changing of the continuity."[89] The daily sacrifice was called the continuity, for what is continuous is frequent and unceasing. And among the Jews it was customary to offer sacrifice to God in the evening and about dawn each day; this is why they called that daily sacrifice a continuity.

(4) But when Antiochus came, he completely did away with this practice. That is what the angel meant when he said: "From the time of the changing of the continuity" (that is, from the time the sacrifice was abolished) "there shall be one thousand two hundred and ninety days,"[90] that is, three and a half years and a little more. Then to show that there will be an end and deliverance from these

---

87 Cf. Dn 12.8–9. Michael refuses to answer Daniel. The revelation is closed and sealed. What Daniel cannot now understand will be understood when the appointed time comes.

88 Cf. Dn 12.10. PG (48.895) reads: "the unholy ones shall understand," almost certainly in error. I have restored the negative to make what probably is a printer's omission accord with LXX. The point certainly seems to be that God permitted these evils for the sake of the wise (11.32, 35; 12.3), who will make themselves white and refine themselves through persecution. These will understand when their day of deliverance is approaching; the wicked will not. Cf. P. Saydon (CCHS 642).

89 Cf. Dn 12.11. I.e., the abolition of holocausts. See *Disc.* 5.7.5, above.

90 Dn 12.11.

woes, the angel went on to say: "Blessed is the man who stands firm and attains one thousand three hundred and thirty-five days,"[91] adding forty-five days to the one thousand and two hundred and ninety days. He did this because it happened that the conflict lasted a month and a half and in that time the victory became complete, as did also the deliverance of the Jews from the evils which weighed heavy upon them. And when he said: "Blessed is the man who stands firm one thousand three hundred and thirty-five days," [896] he revealed their deliverance. He did not simply say, "the man who attains," but "the man who stands firm and attains." The reason for this is that many of the unholy ones saw the change, but he does not call them happy; he calls blessed only those who gave witness during the time of troubles, who did not desert their religion, and who then found abatement of their ills. This is why he did not simply say: "the man who attains," but "the man who stands firm and attains."

(5) What could be clearer than this? Do you see how very carefully the prophet foretold their captivity and release from bondage? He gave the time not in terms of years, or months, but to the very day. That you may know that my words are not based on mere conjecture, come, let us bring in another witness to what I have said, a witness whom the Jews regard with the highest trust, I mean Josephus,[92] who has made their disasters a subject of tragic history and who has paraphrased the entire Old Testament. He was born

---

91 *Ibid.* 12. The time of distress was to last three and one-half years (7.25; 12.7) or 1150 days (8.14). L. Hartman (JBC 26:34) thinks that in verse 11 the number was increased (in a gloss) to 1290 because the persecution had not ended in 1150 days. Still later and for the same reason another glossator increased the number to 1335. Saydon (CCHS 642) thinks that 1290 and 1335 days point immediately to the Maccabean restoration, mediately to the Messianic restoration, ultimately to the final triumph of the righteous at the end of the world. Chrysostom's explanation at least has the virtue of more simple (and probable) guesswork.

92 Flavius Josephus (A.D. 37–ca. 100) was a Jewish statesman, soldier, and historian who wrote in Greek the *Jewish Antiquities* (to A.D. 66) and a *History of the Jewish Wars* (from the capture of Jerusalem in 170 B.C. by Antiochus Epiphanes to its capture by Titus in A.D. 70).

after Christ's coming and, in speaking of the captivity predicted by Christ, he also discussed this captivity and set forth Daniel's vision about the ram, the goat, the four horns, and the last horn which arose after the others. I do not wish anyone to be suspicious of what I have said; come, then, and let us compare his words with mine.

(6) Josephus praised Daniel and showed exceedingly high admiration for him, setting him above all the other prophets.[93] When he came to the story of Daniel's vision, he had this to say.[94] Daniel left us a book in which he made clear the accuracy and fidelity to truth[95] of his prophecy. For he tells us that after he and some companions had gone forth to a plain at Susa,[96] the metropolis of Persia, suddenly the earth quaked and shook violently.[97] His friends fled and he was left alone. He fell face down and was fixed fast to the spot leaning on both hands. Then someone touched him and at the same time ordered him to get up and see what would happen to his people after many generations.[98]

(7) Daniel then arose and was shown a large ram with many[99] horns growing from his head, but the last horn was the highest. Then

---

93 What Josephus says is that the other prophets foretold disasters and, hence, were in disfavor; Daniel was "a prophet of good tidings" and won the people's goodwill, "gained credit...for his truthfulness," and won the people's esteem for his godliness. See *Jewish Antiquities* 10.268 (trans. R. Marcus, Loeb Libr. *Josephus* 6.307).

94 What Chrysostom says in this and the six following paragraphs stems very largely from Josephus' *Jewish Antiquities* 10.269–76 (Loeb Libr. *Josephus* 6.307–11). In fact, editors have used Chrysostom's account to correct the text of Josphus where it was in doubt.

95 Literally, which cannot be distinguished (from truth).

96 Josephus says nothing of the vision in Dn 7. He also avoids the chronological problem presented by Dn 8.1, which states that the vision on the plain of Susa took place in the third year of Belshazzar's reign, i.e., two years after the vision of the Four Beasts which immediately precedes it. P. Saydon (CCHS 635) considers the date of the Susa vision to be an editorial insertion.

97 Neither the earthquake nor the friends mentioned in the next sentence are found in Dn 8.

98 The man who touched Dn is not mentioned until verse 17 (where he is apparently an angel), after the vision of the goat has been described.

99 In Dn 8.3 the ram has two great horns, the one larger and newer than the other.

he looked to the west and saw a goat borne through the air. The goat rushed at the ram, struck him twice with his horns, knocked him to the ground, and trampled on him. Next he saw the goat grown larger and putting forth a very large horn from his forehead.[100] This horn was broken off, but four others grew up, turned to the four winds. As Josephus told the story, Daniel saw a smaller[101] horn rise up from these and it grew strong. God, who showed Daniel the vision, was telling him that war would come upon his nation, that Jerusalem would be taken by storm, the temple would be pillaged, the sacrifices would be hindered and cut short, and that this would last for one thousand two hundred and ninety days.[102]

(8) Daniel wrote that he had seen these events in the plain at Susa; he also made it clear that God explained to him what he had seen in the vision. God said that the ram signified the empire of the Persians and Medes, and the horns, those who would hold royal power. He further said that the last horn signified that there would come a king who would [897] surpass those others in wealth and glory.[103] God then explained that the goat would be a ruler from among the Greeks who would twice clash with the Persian king, defeat him in battle, and take over all his empire.[104] The first large horn on the goat's forehead signified the first king. After this fell off, the growth of the four horns and the turning of each of these to the four regions of the earth was a sign that, after the death of the first king, who had neither sons nor family, his successors would divide the empire among them and would rule the world for many years.[105]

(9) And from these successors, the explanation continued, there would arise a king who would make war on the Jewish laws, take

---

100 In Dn 8.5 the goat had a great horn even before attacking the ram.
101 This smaller horn is Antiochus Epiphanes. LXX reads "strong."
102 See above, *Disc.* 5.7.1–5.8.5, where Chrysostom explains the prophecy, which he will now do again, following Josephus.
103 This sentence is not found in Dn 8.
104 The last part of this sentence (everything following the word "Greeks") is wanting in Dn 8.
105 Josephus and Chrysostom again add to Dn.

away their form of government, pillage their temple, and prevent their sacrifices from being offered for three years. And it did happen that the nation of our fathers underwent these sufferings under Antiochus Epiphanes, just as Daniel had seen many years before and had written would come to pass.[106]

IX

What could be clearer than this? Now it is time, unless you think I am making you weary, now it is time to come back to the question we proposed for investigation, namely, the Jews' present slavery and their bondage of today. This was the reason for going through all their exiles. Pay careful heed to me, for our contest is not concerned with ordinary, everyday matters. At the Olympic contests people have the patience to sit from midnight to noon waiting to see who will win the crown; they take the hot rays of the sun on their bare heads, and do not leave before the winners are decided. Our contest today is not for an Olympic prize but for an incorruptible crown. It would be a shame, then, for us to grow weary and give in to our fatigue.

(2) What I have said has sufficiently proved that the three captivities were predicted, the first lasting for four hundred years, the second for seventy, and the third for three and a half years. Now let us talk about the present bondage of the Jews. To show that the prophet also predicted this one, I shall offer as my witness that same Josephus, who is on the side of the Jews. Listen to what he says subsequent to his account of Daniel's vision. He said: "In the same manner Daniel also wrote about the empire of the Romans and that they would capture Jerusalem and devastate the temple."[107]

---

106 Chrysostom's paraphrase of Josephus (which started with *Jewish Antiquities* 10.268) stops here (at 10.276) but will presently continue by reference if not by paraphrase.

107 *Jewish Antiquities* 10.276 (trans. Loeb Library *Josephus* 6.311). Marcus, in a note *ad loc.*, says that Josephus' rabbinic contemporaries interpreted Dn 11–12 as a prophecy of Roman conquest of Jerusalem. This will lead to the fourth bondage, which will never end.

(3) Please consider that even if the man who wrote that was a Jew, he did not, on that account, let himself emulate the obstinacy of you Jews. After he said that Jerusalem would be captured, he did not dare to go on to say that it would be rebuilt, nor to mention a definite time for its restoration, because he knew that the prophet had not fixed a definite time. Yet when Josephus spoke previously of the victory of Antiochus and his devastation of Jerusalem, he did state how many days and years the captivity was going to last.[108] But Josephus said nothing of this sort about the bondage under the Romans. He wrote that Jerusalem and the temple would be despoiled, but he did not add that what had been devastated would be restored. For he saw that the prophet had not added anything about such a restoration. Josephus did say: "All these things, as God revealed them to him, Daniel left behind in his writings, so that those who read them and observe how they have come to pass must wonder that Daniel was so honored by God."[109]

(4) But let us consider where it was that Daniel said that the temple [898] would be despoiled. After he had made his prayer in sackcloth and ashes, Gabriel came to him and said: "Seventy weeks are cut short[110] for your people and for your holy city.'[111] Look,"

---

108 *Ibid.* 276 and cf. 271.
109 *Ibid.* 277.
110 Cf. Dn 9.24(LXX). "Cut short" seems here to mean "brought to a crisis or a decision." NAB translates "are decreed," as does JB. Vulgate reads "cut short."
111 Cf. Dn 9.24. Jer 25.11 and 29.10 had prophesied the restoration of Jerusalem and end of the Babylonian captivity. Cyrus did capture Babylon and the exiles did return. But Dn still lives during the persecution of Antiochus and sees the conditions of exile still existing. The angel Gabriel (cf. Dn 9.21) explains the seventy weeks as "seventy Sabbatical periods" or seventy times seven years or 490 years from Jeremiah's prophecy. He divides the 490 years into unequal periods of 49, 434, and 7 years; 49 until the anointing of Cyrus as king of Persia; 434 until Jerusalem is rebuilt and the murder of the high priest, Onias III, another anointed one; 7 for the persecution under Antiochus, his profanation of the temple, and the ruin of Jerusalem. Practically all exegetes now agree that the 490 years end with the end of Antiochus' persecution; they have abandoned the once common opinion that Dn 9.26–27 refer to the death of Christ. Chrysostom interprets the time not as the duration of the captivity but as

the Jews will say, "he did mention the time." Yes, but the time is
not the time of the captivity; what is mentioned is the length of time
after which the captivity is going to come upon them. It is one thing
to speak of how long the captivity will last and another thing to
state the number of years before it will arrive and be upon them.

(5) We read: "Seventy weeks are cut short for your people"; no
longer does God say: "for my people." And yet the prophet said:
"Let your face shine upon your people,"[112] but God thereafter was
estranged from them because of the bold crime they were going to
commit. Presently the prophet gave the reason: "Until transgression
will stop and sin will end."[113] What does he mean by the words:
"Until sin will end?" What the prophet is saying is that the Jews are
committing many sins, but the end of their evil deeds will be the day
they slay their Master. Christ also said this: "Fill up the measure of
your fathers."[114] "You killed your servants,"[115] he said. "Now
add to that the blood of your Master."

(6) See how the thoughts of Christ and Daniel agree, Christ said:
"Fill up"; the prophet says: "Until transgression will stop and sin
will end."[116] What does "end" mean? That no sin thereafter is left

the years before the fourth bondage of the Jews will begin with the final
destruction of the temple by Titus. Cf. L. Hartman, JBC 26:31.

112 Cf. Dn 9.17. LXX, NAB, and JB all read "on your desolate sanctuary" for
Chrysostom's "on your people."

113 Cf. ibid. 24. LXX lacks "until transgression shall stop," but it is found in
NAB and JB. P. Saydon, CCHS 637, takes the ending of sin as meaning
that sin will be shut up, sealed up, and thus prevented from doing any
harm. Chrysostom sees it as meaning that the Jews will commit the ultimate sin, the slaying of Christ.

114 Cf. Mt 23.32, i.e., by continuing to kill prophets. This chapter in Mt is
directed against the hypocrisy of the scribes and pharisees and invokes
woes upon them.

115 Chrysostom puts these words in the mouth of Christ, perhaps thinking of
Mt 23.30–31. Their protest of verse 30 is empty where they disclaim
responsibility for the acts of their fathers who murdered the prophets.
The situation of their fathers has reappeared and, in verse 31, their conduct shows they are worthy sons. In the parable of the vine-dressers
(21.35–38) their fathers killed the servants and now they will kill the son.
Cf. A. Jones, CCHS 893.

116 Cf. Mt 23.32 and Dn 9.24.

to commit. "And until everlasting justice will be introduced."[117] But what is everlasting justice except the justification given by Christ? "And until the sealing of the vision and the prophet and a holy of holies be anointed,"[118] that is, until prophecies shall cease. For this is what is meant by "to seal," namely, to bring anointing to an end, to bring vision to an end. This is why Christ said: "The law and the prophets until John."[119] Do you see how this threatens utter desolation and the payment for sins and acts of injustice? For God did not threaten that he will forgive the sins of the Jews but that he will execute vengeance upon then.

X

And when did this happen? When were prophecies completely done away with? When was anointing ended so as never again to return? Even if we be silent, the stones will shout out, because the voice of the facts is so clear. For we could not mention a time at which these predictions were accomplished other than the long and many years already past and the years which are going to be longer and more numerous still. Daniel put it more precisely when he said:

---

117 Cf. Dn *ibid.* (LXX), i.e., the recognition of God's supreme rights and fulfillment of the duties which derive from them. Chyrsostom gives it a Pauline interpretation (cf., e.g., Rom 1.17; 3.26; 2 Cor 5.21; Gal 2.21 etc.).

118 Cf. Dn 9.24 (LXX). To seal, as Chrysostom says, means to end; others, however, understand this to mean the fulfillment of vision and prophet (cf. P. Saydon, CCHS 637). The anointing of a holy of holies almost certainly refers to the consecration of the restored temple by Judas Maccabeus, although many Church Fathers applied it to Jesus. Cf. L. Hartman, JBC 26:31. NAB reads: "Then transgression will stop and sin will end, guilt will be expiated, everlasting justice will be introduced, vision and prophecy ratified and a most holy will be anointed."

119 Cf. Mt 11.13. The Jews believed that prophecy had ended with the closing of the canon of the prophetic books. Jesus (verse 10) applies the words of Mal 3.1 to John; this makes the Baptist as great as any prophet (verse 11). Verse 13 affirms that John terminates the Law and the prophets. If there will be no more prophets, God cannot predict or promise an end to bondage.

"And you will know and understand that from the going forth of the word of the answer that Jerusalem was to be rebuilt until the coming of an anointed leader, there will be seven weeks and sixty-two weeks."[120]

(2) Pay careful attention to me here, because here lies the whole question. The seven weeks and the sixty–two weeks make four hundred and eighty-three years, for he is here speaking not of weeks of days or months but weeks of years. From Cyrus to Antiochus Epiphanes and the captivity there were three hundred and ninety-four years.[121] However, Daniel makes it clear that he is not talking about the destruction of the temple under Antiochus but the subsequent destruction under Pompey, Vespasian, and Titus. He further extends the time and instructs us from what point we must start counting by showing us that our reckoning is not to start from the day of the return from captivity. From what point must we reckon? "From the going forth of the word of the answer that [899] Jerusalem was to be rebuilt."[122]

(3) Jerusalem, however, was not rebuilt under Cyrus but under

---

120 Arguing from the LXX reading of Dn 9.25, Chrysostom says that 483 years will pass "from the going forth of the word of the answer that Jerusalem will be rebuilt." He also says these years will encompass past and future. The going forth of the word, therefore, is not the divine communication through Jeremiah concerning the seventy years' captivity and return from exile, as exegetes usually understand, e.g. Jer 25.11–14; 29.10;30.18;31.38. The restoration of Jerusalem which Chrysostom understands (and will presently say) is that commissioned by Artaxerxes and carried out by Nehemiah (2 Ezr 2–3) ca. 445 B.C. Cf. Neh (2 Ezr) 2–3. Chrysostom does not here seem concerned with the identity of the anointed leader.

121 This reckoning is subject to difficulties since Cyrus reigned from 539 to 530 B.C. and Antiochus from 175 to 164. The point, however, seems to be that it was not 483 years and, therefore, the word of the answer did not go forth in the time of Cyrus to rebuild Jerusalem nor was Daniel talking about its destruction under Antiochus, but its subsequent destructions. This would mean a fourth bondage, which will never end.

122 Pompey captured Jerusalem after a seige in 63 B.C. Vespasian was Roman emperor A.D. 70–79. His son Titus, who was associated with him and succeeded him as emperor (79–81), captured Jerusalem in 70. Chrysostom's reckoning of Dn 9.25 from 445 B.C. would bring us to A.D. 38, which is too late for Pompey's capture and too soon for Titus', unless we allow 32 years for the rebuilding.

Artaxerxes, who was called the Long-handed.[123] For after the return of the Jews, Cambyses was ruler, then the Magians, and after
them Darius Hystaspes. Next came Darius' son, Xerxes, and after
him Artabanus. After Artabanus, Artaxerxes the Long-handed,
ruled Persia. During the twentieth year of his kingship Nehemiah
returned and restored Jerusalem. Ezra has given us an exact account
of this.[124] So then, if we count four hundred and eighty-three years
from this point, we will surely come to the time of the last destruction. And so it is that the prophet said: "It shall be rebuilt with
streets and a surrounding wall."[125] Therefore what he says is this:
after the city has been rebuilt and has recovered its own appearance
and form, count the seventy weeks from that point and you will see
the slavery which has not yet come to an end.

(4) To make still more clear this very point, namely, that the evils
which now grip the Jews will not come to an end, he goes on to say:
"After the seventy weeks[126] the anointing will be utterly destroyed
and there will be no judgment on it; he will destroy the city and the
sanctuary with the help of a leader who comes and they will be cut
off as in a deluge."[127] There will be no remnant left, nor a root to
grow up again, "until the end of a war which is brought to an end by
the vanishing of the people."[128]

(5) And again, in speaking of this slavery, he said: "The incense
and the oblation will be abolished and, furthermore, on the holy
place will be the abomination of desolation: and accomplishment

---

123 Plutarch, *Artaxerxes* 1, tells us he was so called because his right hand
was longer than his left. He ruled Persia from 465 to 423 B.C.
124 Cf. Neh (2 Ezr) 2–3.
125 Cf. Dn 9.25. Neh (2 Ezr) 6.15 says that it took fifty-two days to complete the wall. This is a far cry from the thirty-two years needed to square
Chrysostom's reckoning. However, rebuilding the entire city could take
that long.
126 LXX reads sixty-two for seventy, as do NAB and JB.
127 Cf. Dn 9.26 (LXX). The anointing might mean the anointed one and is so
translated in NAB and JB. LXX reads "there will be no judgment in him"
(i.e., the anointed). Chrysostom uses a feminine form of the pronoun,
probably referring to the city (a feminine noun in Greek). He must be
referring to Titus as the leader who comes to destroy city and sanctuary.
128 *Ibid.*

shall be given to the desolation until the end of time."[129] When you hear him say: "Until the end of time," what else is left for you Jews to look forward to? "And furthermore." What does this mean? "Furthermore," that is, in addition to what he has said, that is, in addition to the destruction of the sacrifice and the oblation, there will be some other greater evil. What is that evil? "On the holy place will be the abomination of desolation."[130] By the holy place he means the temple; by the abomination of desolation he means the statue set up in the temple by Antiochus, who destroyed the city.

(6) And he went on to say: "Desolation until the end." It is true that Christ came into the world according to the flesh long after the day of Antiochus Epiphanes, but when he prophesied the captivity to come, he showed that Daniel had predicted it. This was his reason for saying: "When you see the abomination of desolation which was spoken of by Daniel the prophet, standing in the holy place—let him who reads understand."[131] The Jews called every image and statue made by man an abomination. So by his veiled reference to that statue, Daniel showed both when and under whom the captivity would take place. As I showed before, Josephus also assured us that these words were spoken about the Romans.[132]

(7) What is there for me to say to you now that has not already been said? When the prophets predicted the other captivities, they spoke not only of the captivity but also of the length of time it was appointed for each bondage to last; for this present captivity, however, they set no time but, to the contrary, said that the desolation would endure until the end. And to prove that what they said is true, come now and let me offer as witnesses the events themselves.

---

129 *Ibid.* 27. Chrysostom reads "incense" for "sacrifice" of LXX.
130 *Ibid.* The "abomination of desolation" was the altar and statue of Zeus Olympios set up in the temple by Antiochus Epiphanes. See above, *Disc.* 5.6.7
131 Mt 24.15. Confr. note *ad loc.* states that we find one application of the prophecy in 1 Mc 1.54 (the statue of Zeus). The prophecy will be fulfilled a second time for Jerusalem but not necessarily in the same way. Lk 21.20 sees the "abomination of desolation" in the army which surrounded and destroyed Jerusalem.
132 See above, *Disc.* 5.9.2.

If the Jews had never attempted to rebuild the temple, they could say: "If we had wished to set our hands to the task and to begin to rebuild it, we could by all means have completed the task." But now I shall show that not [900] once, nor twice, but three times they did attempt it and three times, like wrestlers in the Olympic games, they were thrown to the ground. Therefore there can be no dispute or question but that the Church has won the victory crown.

XI

Yet what kind of men were they who set their hands to the task? They were men who constantly resisted the Holy Spirit, revolutionists bent on stirring up sedition. After the destruction which occurred under Vespasian and Titus, these Jews[133] rebelled during the reign of Hadrian and tried to go back to the old commonwealth and way of life. What they failed to realize was that they were fighting against the decree of God, who had ordered that Jerusalem remain forever in ruins.

(2) But it is impossible for a man to wage war on God and win. So it was that, when these Jews made their attack against the Emperor, they forced him again to destroy Jerusalem completely. For Hadrian came and utterly subdued them; he obliterated every remnant of their city. To prevent the Jews from making such an impudent attempt in the future, he set up a statue of himself. But he realized that, with the passage of time, his statue would one day fall. So he gave his own name to the ruined city and, in this way, burned on the Jews a permanent brand which would mark their defeat and testify to the impudence of their revolt. Since he was called Aelius Hadrianus, he ordained that from this name the city was to be called Aelia and to this day it is called by the name of the

---

133 The words: "After the destruction which occurred under Vespasian and Titus, these Jews" are not found in eight MSS, nor does Savile have them in his edition. If they are to be omitted, the text would read: "They rebelled during etc." Chrysostom then goes on to echo a sentiment from *Demonstration* 16 (PG 48.835): no one has destroyed what Christ has built; no one can rebuild what Christ has destroyed.

Emperor who conquered it and destroyed it.[134]

(3) Do you see the first attempt of the impudent Jews? Now look at the next. They tried the same thing in the time of Constantine. But the Emperor saw what they tried to do, cut off their ears, and left on their bodies this mark of their disobedience. He then had them led around everywhere, like runaway slaves and scoundrels, so all might see their mutilated bodies and always think twice before ever attempting such a revolt. "Yet these things happened very long ago," the Jews will say. But I tell you that the incident is well known to those of us who are somewhat on in years and are already old men.[135]

(4) But what I am going to tell you is clear and obvious even to the very young. For it did not happen in the time of Hadrian or Constantine, but during our own lifetime, in the reign of the Emperor of twenty years ago.[136] Julian, who surpassed all the emperors in irreligion, invited the Jews to sacrifice to idols in an attempt to drag them to his own level of ungodliness. He used their old way of sacrifice as an excuse and said: "In the days of your ancestors, God

---

134 Hadrian ruled as emperor from 117 to 138. There was a Jewish revolt against Rome under Bar-Cochba (a symbolic messianic name) who even founded a new kingdom and enjoyed initial success against the Romans (132–33). More than 500,000 Jews fell in the final Roman victory at Bethar (134). Jerusalem was destroyed and the new city, Aelia Capitolina, built in 135, towards the north, where the suburbs had been. A column was erected in Hadrian's honor on the temple mount. Temples and statues of Roman, Greek, and Phoenician gods defiled the old Holy City. Cf. Graetz 2.393–422 and *Demonstration* 16 (PG 48.834–35).

135 Constantine (ca. 274–337) did renew Hadrian's edicts against the Jews but, for the most part, was a stout defender of religious freedom. What Chrysostom says here (for which he claims eye-witnesses) can hardly have happened. Graetz makes no mention of any attempt to rebuild the temple or of the mutilation inflicted on the disobedient. Neither is mentioned in EJ (which is silent on attempts to rebuild the temple after Titus destroyed it). Eusebius has nothing on either event in his *Historia ecclesiastica* or his *De vita Constantini*. Chrysostom's witness seems both unique and suspect.

136 Julian the Apostate was emperor from 361 to 363 but in his short reign did much to restore paganism; he was favorable to the Jews and wished to reinstate their sacrificial system, which had disappeared with the destruction of the temple. Chrysostom treats this attempt to rebuild the temple in *Demonstration* 16 (PG 48.834–35).

was worshipped in this way."

(5) They refused his invitation, but, at that time, they did admit to the very things I just lately proved to you, namely, that they were not allowed to offer their sacrifices outside Jerusalem. Their answer was that those who offered any sacrifice whatsoever in a foreign land were violating the Law. So they said to the Emperor: "If you wish to see us offer sacrifices, give us back Jerusalem, rebuild the temple, show us the holy of holies, restore the altar, and we will offer sacrifices again just as we did before."

(6) These abominable and shameless men had the impudence to ask these things from an impious pagan and to invite him to rebuild their sanctuary with his polluted hands. They failed to see that they were attempting the impossible. They did not realize that if human hands had put an end to those things, then [901] human hands could get them back for them. But it was God who destroyed their city, and no human power could ever change what God had decreed. "For what God, the Holy One, has planned who shall dissipate? His hand is stretched out; who will turn it back?"[137] What God has reared up and wishes to remain, no man can tear down. In the same way, what he has destroyed and wishes to stay destroyed, no man can rebuild.

(7) I grant you that the Emperor did give you Jews back your temple and did build you an altar, just as you foolishly suspected he would. But he could not send down to you the heavenly fire from on high, could he? Yet if you could not have this fire, your sacrifice had to be an abomination and unclean.[138] This is why the sons of

---

137 Cf. Is 14.27 (LXX). LXX lacks "His hand is stretched out," which is found in NAB and JB. The sentiment which Chrysostom stresses is the same in *Disc.* 5.11.2 and *Demonstration* 16 (PG 48.835); cf. n. 133.

138 Cf. Lv 9.23–24. The fire was the holocaust fire, which was to burn perpetually (Lv 6.2–6), probably as a symbol of divine presence. The heavenly fire from on high is the fire issuing from the meeting tent which consumed the already burning offerings on the altar to the awe of the onlookers. The meaning of this theophany is clear: the ordination to the priesthood of Aaron and his sons and Aaron's holocausts are approved as sacred and acceptable to Yahweh. Cf. R. Faley, JBC 4:22.

Aaron perished; they brought in a foreign fire.[139]

(8) Nonetheless, these Jews, who were blind to all things, called on the Emperor for help and begged him to aid them in undertaking to rebuild the temple. The Emperor, for his part, spared no expense, sent engineers from all over the empire to oversee the work, summoned craftsmen from every land; he left nothing undone, nothing untried. He overlooked nothing but worked quietly and a little at a time to bring the Jews to offer sacrifice; in this way he expected that it would be easy for them to go from sacrifice to the worship of idols. At the same time, in his mad folly, he was hoping to cancel out the sentence passed by Christ which forbade the rebuilding of the temple. But He who catches the wise in their craftiness[140] straightway made clear to him by His action that the decrees of God are mightier than any man's and that works get their strength from the word of God.

(9) They started to work in earnest on that forbidden task, they removed a great mound of earth and began to lay bare the foundations. They were just about to start building when suddenly fire leaped forth from the foundations and completely consumed not only a great number of the workmen but even the stones piled up there to support the structure.[141] This put a stop to the untimely obstinacy of those who had undertaken the project. Many of the Jews, too, who had seen what had happened, were astonished and struck with shame. The Emperor Julian had been madly eager to finish the work. But when he heard what had happened, he was afraid that, if he went on with it, he might call down the fire on his

---

139 The foreign fire was profane; to use it was a crime against the cult. Lv 10.1–2 says that Aaron's sons, Nadab and Abihu, each took his censer, put fire in it and incense on the fire, and presented unlawful fire before Yahweh, fire which he had not prescribed for them. Then from Yahweh's presence a flame leaped out and consumed them. Cf. Nm 3.4. They had taken their fire from a place outside the altar area, whereas the censer fire was to be taken from the altar itself (Lv 16.12). See *Disc.* 4.7.6.

140 Cf. 1 Cor 3.19; Jb 5.13.

141 Cf. *Demonstration* 16 (PG 48.835). Graetz (2.600–601) explains the fire by natural causes. Compressed gases, trapped in the old temple's subterranean passages, were suddenly released and ignited when they came in contact with the air. Several workmen were killed.

own head. So he and the whole Jewish people withdrew in defeat.

(10) Even today, if you go into Jerusalem, you will see the bare foundation, if you ask why this is so, you will hear no explanation other than the one I gave. We are all witnesses to this, for it happened not long ago but in our own time. Consider how conspicuous our victory is. This did not happen in the times of the good emperors; no one can say that the Christians came and prevented the work from being finished. It happened at a time when our religion was subject to persecution, when all our lives were in danger, when every man was afraid to speak, when paganism flourished. Some of the faithful hid in their homes, others fled the marketplaces and moved to the deserts. That is when these events occurred.[142] So the Jews have no excuse left to them for their impudence.

XII

Are you Jews still disputing the question? Do you not see that you are condemned by the testimony of what Christ and the prophets predicted and which the facts have proved? But why should this surprise me? That is the kind of people you are. From the beginning you have been [902] shameless and obstinate, ready to fight at all times against obvious facts.

(2) Do you wish me to bring forward against you other prophets who clearly state the same fact, namely, that your religion will come to an end, that ours will flourish and spread the message of Christ to every corner of the world, that a different kind of sacrifice will be introduced which will put an end to yours? At least listen to Malachi who came later than the other prophets. Let me not at this time bring in the testimony of Isaiah and Jeremiah or the other prophets who came before the captivity. I do not want you Jews to say that their predictions came true during the bondage. Let me bring forward a prophet who came after the return from Babylon and after

---

142 Julian did persecute the Christians at Antioch after they had been accused of starting the fire in Apollo's temple at Daphne. See Downey, *History* 388.

the restoration of Jerusalem, a prophet who clearly predicted what was to happen to you.

(3) The Jews did return from Babylon, they did recover their city, they did rebuild their temple, and they did offer sacrifices. But it was only after all this that Malachi predicted the coming of the present desolation and the abolition of the Jewish sacrifices. This is what he said, speaking in God's behalf: "Shall I for your sakes accept your persons? says the Lord Almighty.[143] For from the rising of the sun, even to its setting, my name is glorified among the nations; and everywhere they bring incense to my name, and a pure offering. But you have profaned it."[144]

(4) When do you Jews think that this happened? When was incense offered to God in every place? When a pure offering? You could not mention a time other than the time after the coming of Christ. Suppose Malachi did not speak of our time, suppose he did not speak of our sacrifice but of the Jewish sacrifice. Then his prophecy will be opposed to the Law. Moses had forbidden the Jews to

---

143 Mal 1.9 (LXX) The first part of the verse says: "And now propitiate the face of your God and make supplication to him. These things have been done by your hands." The things done were the offering by careless priests of blind, lame, and sick animals, unfit for sacrifice (verses 7–8). Now the question is: Shall God accept you? Your sacrifices are polluted and of no avail. But God will be pleased by pure offerings from among the nations.

144 Cf. *ibid.* 11-12 (LXX) C. Stuhlmueller, JBC 23:63, says that in contrast to the polluted Israelite sacrifice stands a pure offering, a "sacrifice." LXX has "incense" for "sacrifice," and JBC points out that the Hebrew word is associated with incense but has a wider use. JB translates it "a sacrifice of incense." The new worship will be universal, and many interpretations have been given to this, e.g., Jews of the Diaspora, sacrifices of the gentiles, pagan recognition of Yahweh, Persian Zoroastrian worship, the unorthodox Jewish worship in Samaria, or in the heretical Jewish temple in Elephantine in Egypt. The Council of Trent, in a decree of the 22nd Session (Sept. 17, 1562; H. Denzinger–A. Schönmetzer, *Enchiridion symbolorum . . .* [ed. 32; Freiburg im B. 1963] no. 1742), states that Mal 1.11 refers to the Mass, the perfect sacrifice of the messianic era. Stuhlmueller holds that "the text looks forward to a ritual sacrifice of the messianic age, a fulfillment of the Mosaic rite, which will be offered by all men and accepted by God." This seems basically to be Chrysostom's position, too.

bring their sacrifice to any place other than that which the Lord God would choose, and then he confined their sacrifices to one particular place. If Malachi said that sacrifices were going to be offered everywhere and that it would be a pure offering, he was contradicting and opposing what Moses had said.

(5) But there is no contradiction nor quarrel. For Moses spoke about one kind of sacrifice, and Malachi later predicted another. What makes this clear? It is clear both from the prophet's words and also from many other indications. The first indication has to do with the place. For Malachi predicted that the sacrifice would be offered not in one city, as in the time of the Jewish sacrifice, but "from the rising of the sun even to its setting." The second indication has to do with the kind of sacrifice. By calling it "a pure offering," he showed the kind of sacrifice of which he spoke.

(6) A further indication deals with those who are going to offer this sacrifice. He did not say "in Israel," but "among the nations." He did not want you to think that the worship given in this sacrifice would be confined to one, two, or three cities; therefore, he did not simply say "everywhere," but from the rising of the sun, even to its setting. By these words he showed that every corner of the earth seen by the sun will receive the message of the gospel. He called it a "pure offering," as opposed to the old sacrifice, which was impure. And it was—not by its own nature but because of the disposition and intention of those who offered it. This is why the Lord said: "Your incense is loathsome to me."[145]

(7) And yet, in other respects, if you should put the two sacrifices side by side to compare them, you will find that the difference between them is so great and unmeasurable that, according to the nature of comparison, only this new sacrifice is properly called pure. Paul contrasted the old Law with the new Law of grace and said that the old Law had been glorified but is now without glory, because of the surpassing glory of the new Law.[146] I, too, would make so bold [903] as to say in this case that, if the new sacrifice should be

---

145 Is 1.13. Cf. *Disc.* 1.7.2 and 7.3.4.
146 Cf. 2 Cor 3.10.

compared to the old, only this new sacrifice would properly be called pure. For it is not offered by smoke and fat, nor by blood and the price of ransom, but by the grace of the Spirit.

(8) Now hear another prophet who made the same prediction and said that the worship of God would not be confined to one place, but that the time would come when all men would know him. It is Zephaniah who said: "The Lord shall appear to all nations, and will make all the gods of the nations waste away; then each from its own place shall adore him."[147] Yet this was forbidden to the Jews since Moses commanded them to worship in one place.

(9) You hear that the prophets foretold and predicted that men will no longer be bound to come from all over the earth to offer sacrifice in one city or in one place, but that each one will sit in his own home and pay service and honor to God. What time other than the present could you mention as fulfilling these prophecies? At any rate listen to how the gospels and the Apostle Paul agree with Zephaniah. The prophet said: "The Lord shall appear"; Paul said: "The grace of God our Savior has appeared to all men instructing us."[148] Zephaniah said: "To all nations"; Paul said: "To all men." Zephaniah said: "He will make their gods waste away;" Paul said: "Instructing us, in order that rejecting ungodliness and worldly lusts, we may live temperately and justly."[149]

(10) Again, Christ said to the Samaritan woman: "Woman, believe me, the hour is coming when neither on this mountain nor in

---

147 Cf. Zep 2.11 (LXX). Since Zep prophesied ca. 640–30, R. Murphy (JBC 18:12) states that this mention of the universal worship of Yahweh at this early date is to be considered suspect and a borrowing from Is 41.1, 5; 42.4, 10, 12; 49.1; 51.5. S. Bullough, CCHS 684, stresses only Yahweh's triumph over the false gods; he says nothing of his universal worship. The same text is quoted in *Demonstration* 17 (PG 48.836), where it is conflated with Zep 3.9.

148 Ti 2.11, where grace has appeared to all men in the Incarnation and redemptive work of Christ. Cf. 1 Tm 2.3–6;2 Tm 1.9–10.

149 Ti 2.12. R. Foster (CCHS 1150) states that instruction in the Gospel guides us continuously to regulate our lives by practicing piety, justice, self-restraint, i.e., by performing our duties to God ("godly"), to our neighbor ("justly"), and to ourselves ("temperately"). This is the practical bearing of the Incarnation on our conduct.

Jerusalem will you worship the Father. God is spirit, and they who worship [904] him must worship in spirit and in truth."[150] When Christ said this, he removed from us for the future the obligation to observe one place of worship and introduced a more lofty and spiritual way of worship.

(11) These arguments would suffice to establish that, for the future, there will be no sacrifice, no priesthood, no king among the Jews. Above all, the destruction of the city has proved all these points. But I could also bring forward the prophets as my witnesses, and they distinctly said the same thing. But I see that you have become weary with the length of my discourse; I am afraid that you may think I am foolish and rash to keep annoying you. For this reason I promise that I will speak to you on this same subject at another time.[151]

(12) Meanwhile, I ask you to rescue your brothers, to set them free from their error, and to bring them back to the truth. There is no benefit in listening to me unless the example of your deeds will match my words. What I said was not for your sakes but for the sake of those who are sick. I want them to learn these facts from you and to free themselves from their wicked association with the Jews. I want them then to show themselves sincere and genuine Christians. I want them to shun the evil gatherings of the Jews and their syna-

---

150 Jn 4.21,24. Cf. B. Vawter, JBC 63:77. Chrysostom gives a simple, but appropriate and correct application to a profound passage. Samaritans and Jews had long quarrelled over the proper place for sacrificial worship. Jesus shows that soon the question will be irrelevant; the old controversy is being superseded by a revelation that renders it an idle one (cf. 2.19). When salvation history has further progressed, it will be seen that the temple was superfluous to this history. (For this notion in Judaic thinking, cf. O. Cullmann, "L'opposition contre le temple de Jérusalem," New Testament Studies 5 [1959] 157–73.) "Spirit" in the biblical sense does not define God's nature so much as his life-giving activity. God is Spirit in that he gives the Spirit. So, too, God is light and love (Jn 1.5; 4.8). This explains how and why he must be worshipped in Spirit and truth, i.e., internally and according to his will, which has given his true worshippers his life, his light, his love.

151 Chrysostom will speak on the end of sacrifice and priesthood for the Jews on the following day in Disc. 6.5–6 and later in 7.2.1–5. He also spoke of it in Demonstration 16–17 (PG 48.834–38).

gogues, both in the city and in the suburbs,[152] because these are robbers' dens and dwellings of demons.[153]

(13) So then, do not neglect the salvation of those brothers. Be meddlesome, be busybodies, but bring the sick ones to Christ. In this way, we shall receive a far greater reward for our good deeds both in the present life and in the life to come.

And we shall receive it by the grace and loving-kindness of our Lord Jesus Christ, through whom and with whom be glory to the Father together with the Holy Spirit, the giver of life, now and forever, world without end. Amen.

---

152 Cf. *Disc.* 1.6.2.
153 Cf. *Disc.* 1.3.1; 2.3.5.

DISCOURSE VI

Although he had delivered a long homily against the Jews on the previous day, and had become hoarse from the length of his Sermon, he now delivered the following discourse.

ILD BEASTS ARE less savage and fierce [903] as long they live in the forests and have had no experience fighting against men. But when the hunters capture them, they drag them into the cities, lock them in cages, and goad them on to do battle with beast-fighting gladiators. Then the beasts spring upon their prey, taste human flesh and drink human blood. After that, they would find it no easy task to keep away from such a feast but they avidly rush to this bloody banquet.[1]

(2) This has been my experience, too. Once I took up my fight against the Jews and rushed to meet their shameless assaults, "I destroyed their reasoning and every lofty thing that exalts itself against the knowledge of God, and I brought their minds into captivity to the obedience of Christ."[2] And after that I somehow acquired

---

1 It is a truism that a captured beast after tasting a man's flesh becomes more blood-thirsty for human victims. As Chrysostom develops the analogy, he becomes the blood-thirsty beast and the Jews his human victims. His rhetoric is odd and hardly in the best taste by today's standards.

2 Cf. 2 Cor 10.4–5. Confr. note sees Paul's weapon as faith, which is above reason; everything opposing faith is wrong and must be set aside or destroyed. J. O'Rourke, JBC 52:33, sees the destruction of reasoning as the refutation of fallacious arguments raised against Paul's teaching. Knowledge of God is belief in and service of God. The minds, in the Pauline text, are the minds of those who think rightly and are taken captive because they bow to God's higher power through faith and submission to what Christ wills. For Chrysostom, as for Paul, preaching the word of God is a warfare

147

a stronger yearning to do battle against them.

(3) But what is the matter with me? You see that my voice has grown weaker and cannot again last for so long a time. I think that what has happened to me is much the same as what happens to a soldier in battle. He cuts to pieces a number of his foes, courageously throws himself against the enemy lines, [904] strews the ground with corpses, but then breaks his sword; disheartened by this mishap he must retreat to his own ranks. Indeed, what has happened to me is worse. The soldier who has broken his sword can snatch another from some bystander, prove his courage, and show how eager he is for victory. But when the voice becomes weak and exhausted, you cannot borrow another from somebody else.

(4) What shall I do, then? Shall I, too, run away? The power your loving assembly holds over me does not let me run away. I reverence and respect our father, who is here.[3] I reverence and respect your eagerness and earnestness. Therefore, I shall entrust the whole undertaking to his prayers and your charity and I will attempt what lies beyond my power.

(5) It is true that today's feast of the martyrs invites me to recount the conflicts they underwent. If I neglect this topic, if I strip and get ready to enter the arena against the Jews, let no one accuse me of choosing the wrong time for my discourse. The martyrs would find a discourse against the Jews more desirable than any panegyric of mine, since I could never make them more illustrious than they are.[4]

(6) What need could they have of my tongue? Their own struggles surpass our mortal nature. The prizes they won go beyond our powers and understanding. They laughed at the life lived on earth;

(cf. 1 Tm 1.18); but it is doubtful that Chrysostom achieved any signal victory over the Jews by winning them to faith in Christ, especially in the one day intervening between *Discourses* V and VI. *Discourse* V must have taken well over two hours to deliver; it is no wonder that, as the title to *Discourse* VI says, he was hoarse.

3 Bishop Flavian was present. Cf. *Disc.* 3.1.7 and n. 13.

4 Montfaucon (PG 48.904) notes that it was a feast of the martyrs. Simon (141 n. 1) says that this homily, given on a solemn feast day, replaced the panegyric of a martyr whom he identifies as Timotheus, who was particu-

they trampled underfoot the punishment of the rack; they scorned death and took wing to heaven; they escaped from the storms of temporal things [905] and sailed into a calm harbor; they brought with them no gold or silver or expensive garments; they carried along no treasure which could be plundered, but the riches of patience, courage, and love. Now they belong to Paul's choral band while they still await their crowns, but they find delight in the expectation of their crowns, because they have escaped henceforth the uncertainty of the future.[5]

(7) What need could they have of any words of mine? Therefore, they will find this topic more desirable than any panegyric of mine which, as I said before, will bring no increase to their personal glory. But it could be that they will derive great pleasure from my conflict with the Jews; they might well listen most intently to a discourse given for God's glory. For the martyrs have a special hatred for the Jews since the Jews crucified him for whom they have a special love. The Jews said: "His blood be on us and on our children";[6] the martyrs poured out their own blood for him whom the Jews had slain. So the martyrs would be glad to hear this discourse.

---

larly venerated at Antioch on September 8. Chrysostom, however, speaks of martyrs; if Simon is correct, Timotheus must have had companions in his martyrdom. There was a Timotheus from Antioch who was tortured and beheaded in a Roman prison in 311, but his feast was observed August 22, in the Western Chruch.

5 The 'choral band' (*choros*) Chrysostom has in mind may be formed of those declared by Paul (2 Tm 4.8) to have crowns awaiting them—all who "have looked with eager longing for the Lord's appearing." This passage indicates that Chrysostom, as well as the other Greek Fathers, shows some unsureness on the hereafter. We find two types of statements in their writings: they affirm that the souls of the just are with God and enjoy ineffable happiness; or they say that the just wait in great peace and certainty to receive their reward at the time of the resurrection and Last Judgment. The present passage follows the second position. Cf. A. Wenger, *Jean Chrysostome: Huit catéchèses baptismales inédites* (SC 50; Paris 1957) 231 n. 1 and ACW 31.271.

6 Mt 27.25. Chrysostom quotes the same text in *Disc*. 1.5.1. See notes *ad loc*. In attributing hatred of the Jews to the martyrs, he is no doubt reflecting the historical position on anti-Semitism of fourth-century Antioch.

II

If the present captivity of the Jews were going to come to an end, the prophets would not have remained silent on this but would have foretold it. I gave adequate proof of this when I showed that all their bondages were brought upon them after they had been predicted: the bondage in Egypt, the bondage in Babylon, and the bondage in the time of Antiochus Epiphanes. I proved that for each of these the Sacred Scriptures had proclaimed beforehand both a time and a place.[7] But no prophet defined a duration for the present bondage, although Daniel did predict that it would come, that it would bring total desolation, that it would change their old commonwealth and way of life, and how long after the return from Babylon it would come to pass.[8]

(2) But Daniel did not reveal that it would come to an end nor that these troubles would ever stop. Nor did any other prophet. Daniel did, however, predict the opposite, namely, that this bondage would hold them in slavery until the end of time.[9] The great number of years which have come and gone since that day are witnesses to the truth of what he said. And the years have shown neither trace nor beginning of a change for the better, even though the Jews tried many times to rebuild their temple. Not once, not twice, but three times they tried. They tried in the time of Hadrian, in the time of Constantine, and in the time of Julian. But each time they tried they were stopped. The first two times they were stopped by military force; later it was by the fire which leaped forth from the foundations and restrained them from their untimely obstinacy.[10]

(3) Now I would be glad to ask them a few questions. Why, tell me, did you recover your own country after spending so many years in Egypt? And after you had been again dragged away into Babylon,

---

7 Cf. *Disc.* 5.5.1–5.8.9.
8 Cf. *Disc.* 5.9.2–5.10.7.
9 Cf. *ibid.* (esp. 5.10.7).
10 For the attempt under Hadrian cf. *Disc.* 5.11.1–2; under Constantine, 5.11.3; under Julian, 5.11.4–9.

why did you come back to Jerusalem? Again, in the time of Antiochus, you suffered many evils, but you came back to your old state, you again recovered your sacrifices, your altar, your holy of holies, and all the rest, along with the dignity these things once had. But nothing such as this has happened in your present bondage. One hundred, two hundred, three hundred, four hundred years and many more than that have passed This is the five hundredth year up to our own day,[11] but we see no hint of such a change for the better on the horizon. What we do see is that the Jewish fortunes have completely collapsed; they do not even have a dream to show they might have [906] any expectation such as they had in their former captivities.

(4) Suppose the Jews should plead their sins as an excuse. Suppose they should say: "We sinned against God and offended him. This is the reason why we are not recovering our homeland. We did treat shamelessly the prophets who never ceased to accuse us, we did deny the blood-guilt of which the prophets spoke in tragic phrases,[12] but we will now confess and condemn ourselves for our own sins." If the Jews should plead this excuse, I will be glad to question each one of them again.

(5) Is it because of your sins that you Jews have been living for so long a time outside Jerusalem? What is strange and unusual about that? It is not only now that your people are living sinful lives. Did

---

11 In *Demonstration* 16 (PG 48.935) Chrysostom speaks more accurately of four hundred years. Here he is more the rhetorician than the chronologist.

12 The shameless treatment of the prophets by the Jews is summed up in the last Beatitude in Mt 5.11–12. There are few instances in the OT of prophets slain by the Israelites. In Mt 23.29–39, J. McKenzie (JBC 43:162) finds the argument by which the present generation of Jews is linked with its ancestors in killing the prophets somewhat involved and rabbinical in character. By disclaiming the actions of their fathers (verse 30), they confess they are sons of prophet-killers. By the Jewish conception of sonship, this designation (which they accept) shows that they share in the dispositions of those who killed the prophets. By "the blood-guilt of which the prophets spoke in tragic phrases" Chrysostom probably means the slaying of Christ and would have in mind such predictions as Is 53.5–9, which he will discuss below in *Disc* 6.5.1–4. He has already treated of this prophecy in *Demonstration* 4 (PG 48.819).

you, in the beginning, live your lives in justice and good deeds? Is it not true that from the beginning and long before today you lived with countless transgressions of the Law? Did not the prophet Ezechiel accuse you ten thousand times when he brought in the two harlots, Oholah and Oholibah, and said "You built a brothel in Egypt; you passionately loved barbarians, and you worshipped strange gods."[13]

(6) What about this? After the waters of the sea were divided, after the rocks were broken asunder, after so many miracles were worked in the desert, did you not worship the calf? Did you not try many times to kill Moses, now by stoning him, now by driving him into exile, and in ten thousand other ways?[14] Did you ever stop hurling blasphemies at God? Were you not initiated in the rites of Baal of Peor?[15] Did you not sacrifice your sons and daughters to demons?[16] Did you not make a display of every form of ungodliness and sin?

---

13 Cf. Ez 23.5–9. The verse does not occur as cited, but the whole chapter deals with the allegory of the two faithless sisters. NAB note points out that their names are symbolic; Oholah ("Here own tent") stands for Samaria; Oholibah ("My tent is in her") stands for Jerusalem. The reference seems to be to the schismatic temple and cult in Samaria as opposed to their authentic counterparts in Jerusalem, where originally the Ark of the Covenant was under a tent (cf. 2 Sm [2 Kgs] 7.2). Israel's apostasy to idols (harlotry) dated back to Egypt (cf. Ez 20.5–9); the love affairs with barbarians refer to political alliances which earlier prophets condemned because they showed lack of faith in God and put a greater value on profane power and wealth (cf. Hos 5.13; 7.11; 8.9–10; Is 7.1–9; 2 Kgs [4 Kgs] 16.7–8; Jer 4.30). Cf. A. Tkacik, JBC 21:55 and L. Hartman, "Ohola and Oholiba," NCE 10.666.

14 Miracles such as the manna (Ex 16) and the water from the rock (Ex 18) were performed in the desert before the incident of the molten calf (Ex 32). The Israelites constantly grumbled against Moses and were on the point of stoning him in Horeb (Ex 17.4).

15 Cf. Nm 25.1–5. F. Moriarty (JBC 5:48) says that the exact nature of the false worship offered to the Moabite gods is unknown but probably was connected with the fertility cults, which were widely practiced in the ancient Near East. In Hos 9.10 Baal-Peor is called the Shame. The submission of the stubborn Israelites to his cult is mentioned in Ps 105 (106).28, where it is linked with the plague and vengeance of Phinehas. Cf. *Disc.* 4.2.6.

16 Cf. Ps 105(106).37; 2 Kgs (4 Kgs) 16.3. See also *Disc.* 1.6.7 and 3.3.8.

(7) Did not the prophet, speaking in behalf of God, say to you: "Forty years I was offended with that generation, and I said: 'These always err in heart.' "[17] How was it, then, that at that time God did not turn himself away from you? How is it that after you slew your children, after your idolatries, after your many acts of arrogance, after your unspeakable ingratitude, that God even allowed the great Moses to be a prophet among you and that he worked wondrous and marvellous signs himself? What happened in the case of no human being did happen to you. A cloud was stretched over you in place of a roof; a pillar instead of a lamp served to guide you; your enemies retreated of their own accord; cities were captured almost at the first battle-shout. You had no need of weapons, no need of an army in array, no need to do battle. You had only to sound your trumpets and the walls came tumbling down of their own accord. And you had a strange and marvellous food which the prophet spoke of when he exclaimed: "He gave them the bread of heaven. Man ate the bread of angels: he sent them provisions in abundance."[18]

(8) Tell me this. In those days you were guilty of ungodliness, you worshipped idols, you slew your children, you stoned the prophets, and you did ten thousand dreadful deeds. Why, then, did you enjoy such great kindness and good will from Him? Why did He offer you such protection at that time? Now you do not worship idols, you do not slay your children, you do not stone the prophets. Why are you now spending your lives in endless captivity? God was not one kind of God then and a different kind now, was he? Is it not the same God who governed those past events and who brings to

---

17 Cf. Ps 94(95).10 (LXX). This verse is part of an answer to the charge of the wicked that Yahweh does not know the unfaithfulness of their forefathers in the journey to the Promised Land. But he does hear and see all and he will punish.
18 Cf. LXX Ps 77(78).24–25 Chrysostom here makes reference to the manna in the desert (Ex 16.4). Ex 13.21 speaks of the column of cloud and pillar of fire which guided the Israelites toward the Red Sea. All their military exploits here mentioned came under Joshua (Jos 1–12). The collapse of Jericho's walls may have been the result of an earthquake sent by God. The blowing of horns and the shouting were meant by God to test the people's obedience and faith in His promise. See NAB note on Jos 6.20.

pass what goes on today? Tell me this. Why did you have great honor from God when your sins were greater? Now that your sins are less serious, he has turned himself altogether away from you and has given you over to unending disgrace.

(9) If he turns away from you now because of your sins, he should have done so all the more in those days. If he put up with you when you were living lives of ungodliness, he ought to put up with you all the more now that you venture no such enormities. [907] Why, then, has he not put up with you? Even if you are too ashamed to give the reason, I will state it clearly. Rather, I will not state it, but the truth of the facts will do so.

(10) You did slay Christ, you did lift violent hands against the Master, you did spill his precious blood. This is why you have no chance for atonement, excuse, or defense. In the old days your reckless deeds were aimed against his servants, against Moses, Isaiah, and Jeremiah. Even if there was ungodliness in your acts then, your boldness had not yet dared the crowning crime. But now you have put all the sins of your fathers into the shade. Your mad rage against Christ, the Anointed One, left no way for anyone to surpass your sin. This is why the penalty you now pay is greater than that paid by your fathers. If this is not the reason for your present disgrace, why is it that God put up with you in the old days when you sacrificed your children to idols, but turns himself away from you now when you are not so bold as to commit such a crime? Is it not clear that you dared a deed much worse and much greater than any sacrifice of children or transgression of the Law when you slew Christ?[19]

III

Tell me this. Will you still dare to call him an imposter and lawbreaker? Will you not instead go off and bury yourselves somewhere, when you look the facts in the face, since their truth is so obvious? If Jesus were an imposter and lawbreaker, as you say he was, you should have been held in high honor for putting him to

---

19 See above *Disc.* 1.5.1 and nn.; 6.1.7 and n.

death. Phinehas slew a man and put an end to all God's wrath against the people.[20] The Psalmist said: "Then Phinehas stood up and propitiated him and the slaughter stopped."[21] He rescued a great many ungodly men from the wrath of God by slaying a single lawbreaker. This should have happened all the more in your case, if indeed the man you crucified was a transgressor of the Law.

(2) Phinehas, then, was held guiltless after he slew a lawbreaker; indeed, he was honored with the priesthood.[22] But after you crucified an imposter, as you say, who made himself equal to God, you did not receive esteem nor were you held in honor. Instead you suffered a more grievous punishment than you did when you sacrificed your children to idols. Why is this so? Is it not clear even to the dullest minds? You committed outrage on him who saved and rules the world; now you are enduring this great punishment. Is this not the reason?

3. Yet even today you abstain from blood which would defile you and you observe the sabbath. But at the time you slew Christ, you violated the sabbath.[23] God even promised, through Jeremiah, to spare your city if you would stop carrying burdens on the sabbath.[24] Look, you are observing this law now; you are not carrying burdens on the sabbath. But God is not reconciled to you on this account. Since that sin of yours surpassed all sins, it is

---

20 Cf. Nm 25.6–13 and *Disc.* 4.2.6–7.
21 LXX Ps 105(106).30 (cf. NAB 106.30).
22 Nm 25.13. His zeal, which to us seems intemperate, became proverbial. Sir (Ecclus) 45.23–25 says that because Phinehas met the crisis of his people and atoned for the children of Israel God made with him a covenant of friendship by which he and his descendants should possess the high priesthood forever.
23 This is difficult to understand. The Jews were very careful to have Jesus' execution over with before the Sabbath began. J. Hartman (JBC 3:88) notes that Ex 31.12–18 gives the most solemn OT statement regarding the Sabbath, which constitutes a token of the special covenant between Yahweh and Israel; it is this covenant which makes Israel holy. Of course Chrysostom knew this passage but it seems unlikely that he sees in Christ's crucifixion a desecration of this covenant and, therefore, a violation of the Sabbath.
24 Cf. Jer 17.21.

useless to say your sins are keeping you from recovering your homeland. You are in the grip of your present sufferings not because of the sins committed in the rest of your lives but because of that one reckless act. If this were not the case, God would not have turned his back on you in such a way, even if you had sinned ten thousand times. This is clear not only from all I have already said but from what I am now going to tell you.

(4) What is this? Oftentimes we have heard God speak to your fathers through the prophets and say: "You deserve countless evils. But I do this for my name's sake, that it may not be profaned among the nations."[25] And again: "It is not for your sakes that I do this, O house of Israel, but for my name's sake."[26] What God is saying is this: "You deserved heavier [908] vengeance and punishment. But so that no one may say that God let the Jews stay in the power of their enemies because God was weak and unable to save them, I am helping you and protecting you."

(5) Suppose Christ were a lawbreaker and you crucified him; suppose you had committed countless sins and much worse ones than the sins of your fathers. God would still have saved you to keep his name from being profaned. If Christ were a lawbreaker, God would not have let him be considered a great man, God would not want people putting the blame on Christ for your misfortunes. If God clearly overlooks your sins for his glory's sake, he would have done so all the more if you crucified a lawbreaker. He would have approved of this slaughter and would have blotted out your sins, many as they are. But when God clearly and completely turns himself from you, it is obvious that, by his anger and by abandoning you forever, he is proving even to the most shameless that he who was slain was not a lawbreaker, but the lawgiver who has come as the author of countless blessings. You acted outra-

---

25 Cf. Ez 36.22 (LXX). This whole chapter foretells the restoration of Israel, rebuilding of her cities, multiplication of her seed, the gift of a new heart and a new spirit. Yet this renewal will not be through her own merits but for the glorification of Yahweh's name among the Gentiles. Chrysostom's quotation of 36.22 seems to be a conflation.

26 Cf. *ibid.* 32, which also seems to be a conflated quotation.

geously against him and you are now held in indignity and dishonor. We worship him and, even though heretofore we were held in greater dishonor than all of you, now, through the grace of God, we are more venerable than all of you and are held in higher esteem.[27]

(6) But the Jews will say: "Where is the evidence that God has turned away from us?" Does this still need proof in words? Tell me this. Do not the facts themselves shout it out? Do they not send forth a sound clearer than the trumpet's call? Do you still ask for proof in words when you see the destruction of your city, the desolation of your temple, and all the other misfortunes which have come upon you? "But men brought these things upon us, not God." Rather it was God above all others who did these things. If you attribute them to men, then you must consider that, even if men were to have the boldness, they would not have had the power to bring these things to accomplishment, unless it were by God's decree.

(7) The barbarian came down upon you and brought all Persia with him.[28] He expected that he would catch you all by the suddenness of his attack and he kept you all locked up in the city as if you were caught in the net of a hunter or fisherman. Because God was gracious to you at that time—I repeat, at that time—without a battle, without a war, without a hostile encounter, the

---

27 This is reminiscent of *Disc* 1.2.1, where Chrysostom says that the Christians, who at first were dogs, have been raised to the adoption of sons while the Jews, who were sons, fell to the kinship of dogs.

28 Sennacherib, king of Assyria (not Persia) 705–681 B.C., on his accession was greeted with rebellion from Babylon and from Syria and Palestine. Babylon was quickly crushed and razed. Syria and Palestine, under Hezechiah and with help from Egypt, at first surrendered and paid tribute, but Sennacherib still moved on Jerusalem. The prayer of Hezechiah, the oracle of Isaiah promising deliverance, the extermination of 185,000 Assyrians by the angel of Yahweh are recounted in 2 Kgs (4 Kgs) 18.17–19.37 (cf. 2 Mc 15.22) and duplicated in Is 36.1–37.38. A shorter version is found in 2 Chr (2 Par) 32.1–23. See J. McKenzie, "Hezekiah," DB 357–59; "Sennacherib," DB 786. The "angel of the Lord" (2 Kgs [4 Kgs] 19.35) may be a pestilence (cf. 2 Sm [2 Kgs] 24.15–17), perhaps bubonic plague (cf. 1 Sm [1 Kgs] 5.6–9; 6.1–6).

barbarian king left one hundred and eighty-five thousand of his slain soldiers among you and fled, contented that he alone was saved. And God often decided countless other battles in this way. So also now, if God had not deserted you once and for all, your enemies would not have had the power to destroy your city and leave your temple desolate. If God had not abandoned you, the ruin of desolation would not have lasted so long a time, nor would your frequent efforts to rebuild the temple have been in vain.

IV

These are not my only arguments. I shall use other sources as well in my efforts to prevail upon you to agree that it was not by their own power that the Roman emperors did what they did.[29] They did what they did because God was angry with the Jews and had abandoned them. If the things that happened were the work of men, your misfortunes should have ended with the capture of Jerusalem and your disgrace should not have gone beyond it. Let me grant, according to your argument, that men demolished the walls, destroyed the city, and overturned the altar, [909] Was it the work of men that you have no more prophets? Men did not take away the grace of the Spirit, did they? Did men destroy the other things you held solemn, such as the voice from the propitiatory,[30] the power which came in the anointing,[31] the declaration

---

29 Vespasian and his son Titus, who destroyed Jerusalem and the temple in 70; Hadrian who rebuilt there a pagan city, Aelia Capitolina, in 135 after he razed Jerusalem to the ground; possibly also Constantine and Julian. See Introd. I 16; *Disc* 5.11.1–10; *Demonstration* 16 (PG 48.834–35).

30 The propitiatory or mercy-seat was a gold slab covering the Ark of the Covenant and probably means "place of atonement." Two facing cherubim overshadowed the mercy-seat with their outspread wings. Here Yahweh meets Israel and reveals his commandments (Ex 25.22). In Nm 7.89 Moses hears Yahweh's voice addressing him from above the propitiatory from between the two cherubim. See J. McKenzie, "Ark of the Covenant," DB 84–85; J. Huesman, JBC 3:71.

31 The purpose of anointing a person or thing was to make it sacred. Priests and kings were anointed, as were the meeting tent and its furniture and the Ark. The reference here would seem to be to the ordination of priests, Aaron and his sons, which Chrysostom will discuss below (*Disc.* 6.5.6–6.6.6).

made by the priest from the stones?[32]

(2) The Jewish religious way of life did not have all its origins from here below; the greater number and the more solemn things came from heaven above. For example, God permitted the sacrifices. The altar was from here below as were the faggots, the knife, and the priest.[33] But the fire which was going to enter the sanctuary and consume the sacrifices had its source from on high; no man carried the fire into the temple, but a flame came down from above and by this the ministry for the sacrifice was fulfilled.[34]

(3) And, again, if they ever had to know something, a voice came forth from the propitiatory, or mercy-seat, from between the cherubim, and foretold the future.[35] Again from the stones which were on the breast of the high priest, which they called the declaration, there came a sort of flashing which indicated the future.[36]

---

32 Ex 28.6—30 describes two of the priestly vestments: the ephod and breast-piece. NAB note states that the ephod seems to have been some sort of apron hanging from the priest's shoulders by straps (verse 7) and tied around his waist by the loose ends of the embroidered belt attached to it. The breastpiece was an embroidered linen pocket-like square attached to the ephod's shoulder straps and mounted with twelve precious stones symbolizing the twelve tribes of Israel. In the burse-like pocket were the Urim and Thummim (verse 30), the stones of declaration or decision, which the priest would draw or cast like lots and thus get a yes or no answer regarding God's decision in doubtful matters. Cf. J. McKenzie's articles in DB 241—42 (ephod); 106 (breastplate); 910 (Urim and Thummim). See also J. Huesman, JBC 3:79.

33 Ex 20.24—25 describes the most primitive altar of earth or uncut stone. Ex 27.1—8 describes a more elaborate altar, made of acacia wood with a bronze grating and left hollow (perhaps to be filled with earth); this may be substantially the type used in Solomon's temple (1 Kgs [3 Kgs] 8.64). The faggots were fuel for the altar fire for holocausts and incense. The knife was for slaughtering and flaying the animals destined for holocaust. The priesthood was hereditary, e.g., Aaron and his descendants or Levi and his; in any event priests were chosen from among men.

34 Cf. *Disc*. 4.7.6; 5.11.7; Lv 9.23—24.

35 More precisely, according to Ex 25.22, from the mercy-seat Yahweh will tell Moses all the commandments that he wishes him to give to the Israelites.

36 The "sort of flashing" is tantalizingly imprecise. At any rate the Urim and Thummim were lots of contrary meaning. J. Castelot, JBC 76:8, says that

Furthermore, whenever someone had to be chosen and anointed, the grace of the Spirit would wing its way down and the oil would run on the forehead of the elect. Prophets fulfilled these ministries. And many a time a cloud of smoke obscured the sanctuary.[37] To keep the Jews from continuing their shameless ways and attributing their desolation to men, God not only permitted the city to fall and the temple to be destroyed but he also removed the things which had their source from heaven above: the fire, the voice, the flashing of the stones, and all other such things.

(4) The Jews will tell you. "Men waged war on us; men plotted against us." When they say this, tell them that men would certainly not have waged war against them unless God had permitted it. Granted that men tore down your walls. Did a man keep the fire from coming down from heaven? Did a man stop the voice which was continually heard from the propitiatory? Did a man stop the declaration from the stones? Did a man put an end to the anointing of your priests? Did a man take away all those other things? Was it not God who withdrew them? Surely, this is clear to everybody. Why, then, did God take them away? Is it not obvious that he hated you and turned his back on you once and for all? The Jews will say: "By no means! The reason why we do not have these is because we do not have our mother-city." But why do you not have your mother-city? Is it not because God has abandoned you?

(5) Let us, rather, stop their shameless mouths with still more

<hr>

God's will had to be determined by a process of elimination going from the general to the particular, e.g., "If you draw Urim, I shall do so and so; if you draw Thummim, I shall do the opposite." Depending on which lot came forth, further determination would have to be made until a precise expression of God's will would be finally gotten. Cf., e.g., 1 Sm (1 Kgs) 14.41–42. The process sounds superstitious, but by eliminating human factors the suppliants proved their trust that God would manifest his will through his appointed representatives, the priests who drew the lots.

37 For the grace of the Spirit coming with anointing see 1 Sm (1 Kgs) 10.1,10 (where Saul is anointed by the prophet Samuel) and *ibid*. 16.13 (where Samuel anoints David). Priests also were anointed (cf. Ex 29.29; Lv 4.5). The clouds of smoke would come probably from the altar of incense.

proof. To do this, let me prove from the Scriptures themselves that the destruction of the temple was not the reason for destroying the ritual given to the prophets. The real reason was the wrath of God. And he is much more provoked to anger now, because of the Jews' mad rage against Christ, than he was when they worshipped the calf. Surely, when Moses was their prophet, there was neither temple nor altar. Even though they kept committing countless acts of ungodliness, his gift of prophecy did not desert him. To be sure, he was a great and noble man, but, in addition to him, there were again seventy other men who, at that time, were proclaimed as prophets.[38]

(6) This was true not only in Moses' day but also thereafter, when they had been given a temple and the rest of the ritual. Even after this temple was burned and they all had been led off to Babylon, Ezechiel and Daniel saw no holy of holies, stood beside no altar. But even though they were in the middle of a barbarian land and [910] in the midst of unclean transgressors of the Law, they were filled with the Spirit and foretold the future, predicting events far more numerous and marvellous than those prophesied by their predecessors. And they saw divine visions insofar as it was possible for them to see.[39]

---

38 Cf. Nm 11.16, 24—26. NAB note states that the seventy elders did not prophesy in the sense of foretelling the future but rather by speaking in enraptured enthusiasm. Such manifestations of mystic exaltation occurred in the early days of Hebrew prophecy (cf. 1 Sm [1 Kgs] 10.10—13; 19.20—24). The same charism is found in the early Church (Acts 2.10, 17; 19.6; 1 Cor 10.6). The person possessing this charism often manifested an abnormal state such as trance, frenzy, or rapture, but a true prophetic word was in every case a distinct gift received from God (cf. Dt 13.2—6). These seventy elders will now share Moses' authority as the spirit of Elijah was passed on to Elisha in 2 Kgs (4 Kgs) 2.9, 14. Cf. J. McKenzie, "Prophet, Prophecy," in DB 694—99 and B. Vawter, JBC 12:3—12.

39 The prophetic experience as described by the prophets is rich in imagery and symbolism, such as we find in Is 6.6—7 (the burning coal to purify his lips), Jer 1.9 (the Lord touches Jer's mouth and puts his word therein), Ez 3.1 (the eating of the scroll). The prophet is compelled to speak by a personal external will which he cannot overcome despite his own personal unwillingness. Like the mystics, they affirm the ineffability of the immediate experience of God and must use imagery and symbolism to describe it. In the vision, an object of daily experience becomes an object of pro-

(7) Tell me this. Why is it that you have no prophets now? Is it not clear that it is because God has turned his back on your religion? Why did he turn his back on you? It is again obvious that he did so because of him whom you crucified and because of your recklessness in committing that outrage. What makes this so obvious? It is obvious from this: when you Jews lived the life of ungodliness before, you got everything; now, after the cross, although you seem to be living a more moderate life, you endure a greater vengeance and have none of your former blessings.

V

The prophets clearly and distinctly put the truth before you so that you could learn the reason for your troubles. Hear how Isaiah predicted not only the blessings that will come to all through Christ but also your senseless arrogance. He said: "By his stripes we were healed,"[40] and by these words he foretold the salvation which has come to all through the cross. Then, to show the kind of men we are, he went on to say: "We had all gone astray like sheep, each turned aside on his own way."[41] In describing the manner of his execution on the cross, he said: "Like a lamb led to the slaughter or a sheep before the shearer, he was silent and opened not his mouth. In his humiliation his legal trial was taken

---

phetic significance. Especially in the later OT books the vision has become a literary form which allows the prophet to use imagery and symbolism to describe a genuine and profound experience in veiled language. Cf. DB 696–97,915.

40 Is 53.5. The identity of the Suffering Servant is much disputed: some see him as the people of Israel collectively, i.e., as the corporate personality of Israel; others see in him Deutero-Is himself, as a second Moses or other charismatic leader, who makes himself a sin offering, heals others through his innocent suffering, and brings judgment and righteousness through his death rather than by conquest. The corporate-personality-of-Israel theory seems best because the Servant in his person recapitulates the gifts and the mission of Israel. More than any other prophetic passage, Is 42–53 leads to the Gospels, and in NT the title "Servant" is often applied to Jesus. Chrysostom obviously follows the NT interpretation. See J. McKenzie, "Servant of the Lord," DB 791–94. Cf. Demonstration 4 (PG 48.819).

41 Is 53.6. Cf Demonstration (loc. cit.).

away."⁴²

(2) And where can we see that all these things came true? In Pilate's unlawful court of law. Although they testified to so many things against him, as Matthew said, Jesus made no answer to them. Pilate, the presiding official, said to him: "Do you hear what witness these men bear against you?"⁴³ And he made no answer but stood there silent. This is what the heaven-inspired prophet meant when he said: "Like a lamb led to the slaughter or a sheep before the shearer, he was silent." Then he showed the lawlessness of the law court when he said: "In his humiliation his legal trial was taken away." No one at that time cast a truly just vote against him, but they accepted the false testimony against him. What was the reason for this? Because he did not wish to proceed against them.

(3) If he wished to do so, he would have stirred up everything and shaken the world to its depths. When he was on the cross, he split the rocks, darkened the earth, turned aside the rays of the sun, and made night out of day over the whole world.⁴⁴ If he did this on the cross, he could have done it in the courtroom. Yet he did not wish to do it but, instead, showed us his mildness and moderation. This is why Isaiah said: "In his humiliation his legal trial was taken away." Then, to show that Jesus was not just anybody, he went on to say: "Who shall declare his generation?"⁴⁵ Who is this man of whom Isaiah said: "His life is taken from the earth?"⁴⁶ This is why Paul also said: "Our life is hidden with Christ in God. When Christ, our life, shall appear, then you too will appear with him in glory."⁴⁷

(4) But let me return to the topic which I proposed to discuss and prove, namely, that the Jews are enduring their present troubles

---

42 Is 53.7–8 (LXX). Verse 8 in NAB reads: "Oppressed and condemned he was taken away, and who would have thought any more of his destiny?" JB has: "By force and by law he was taken; would anyone plead his cause?" Cf. *Demonstration* (*loc. cit.*); 1 Cor 15.3; 1 Pt 2.24.
43 Cf. Mt 27.13.
44 Cf. Mt. 27.51.
45 Is 53.8 (LXX); cf. *Disc.* 1.1.1 (with n. 2).
46 Is 53.8 (LXX). This may be the origin of Mk 2.20.
47 Cf. Col 3.3–4.

because of Christ. It is time now to bring in my witness, Isaiah, who spoke these words. Where, then, did he say this? After he spoke of the trial, death, and ascension, after he said: [911] "His life is taken from the earth,"[48] he went on to say: "And I shall give the ungodly for his burial, and the rich for his death."[49] He did not simply say "the Jews," but "the ungodly." What could be more ungodly than those who first received so many good things and then slew the author of those blessings?

(5) If these prophecies have not been fulfilled, if you Jews are not now held in dishonor, if you are not now bereft of everything your fathers had, if your city did not fall, if your temple is not in ruins, if your disaster has not surpassed every tragedy, then you Jews should refuse to believe me. But if the facts shout out and prophecy has been fulfilled, why do you keep up your foolish and unavailing impudence?

(6) Where are the things you held as solemn, where is your high priest, where are his robe, his breastpiece, and stones of declaration?[50] Do not talk to me about those patriarchs[51] of yours who are hucksters and merchants and filled with all iniquity. Tell me, what kind of priest is he if the ancient oil for anointing priests no longer exists nor any other ritual of consecration? What kind of a priest is he if there is neither sacrifice, nor altar, nor worship?

---

48 Cf. Is 53.8 (LXX).
49 Ibid. 9 (LXX) and Demonstration 4 (PG 48.819).
50 Cf. Ex 28.4, 15–30 and above, Disc. 6.4.1–4.
51 Kraeling (137) mentions this reference by Chrysostom to Jewish patriarchs but says it is not clear whether he referred to the patriarch, properly speaking, the titular head of ecumenical Judaism, or to a provincial official analogous to the metropolitan bishop. Kraeling thinks that the latter is the more probable. The reputation of the Jews as merchants and moneylenders is perennial; Kraeling (158) speaks of the establishment of a chain of banks from Acco [sic] to Antioch by the Jews, Papos and Lulianus, as a factor in the attempt to rebuild the temple under Julian the Apostate. Downey, History 447, says that Ilasios, the ruler of the synagogue (archisynagōgos) of the Jewish community at Antioch, was sufficiently wealthy to make important financial contributions to the synagogue built by the community at Apamea in 391. Although the value judgment against the Antiochene patriarchs is Chrysostom's own, it well may reflect popular prejudice against the flourishing conditions of the Jewish community under Theodosius.

Do you wish me to speak of the laws governing the priesthood and how priests were consecrated in olden times? In this way you would find out that those among you who are today called patriarchs are not priests at all. They act the part of priests and are playing a role as if they were on the stage, but they cannot carry the role because they are so far removed from both the reality and even the pretense of priesthood.

(7) Recall how in those days Aaron was made a priest, how many sacrifices Moses offered, how many victims he slew, how he bathed Aaron, anointed the lobe of his ear, his right hand and right foot. Only then did Moses lead Aaron into the holy of holies; only then did he bid him remain there a set number of days. But it is worth your while to hear his very words. "This is the anointing of Aaron and the anointing of his sons."[52] "And the Lord spoke to Moses saying 'Take Aaron with his sons, their vestments, and the oil of unction, the calf for sin, and a ram, and gather together the community at the entrance of the meeting tent.' And Moses spoke to the whole assembly: 'This is the word which the Lord has commanded.' And after he brought them forward" (for I must cut the account short),[53] "he washed them with water, put the tunic [on Aaron], girded him with the sash, clothed him with the robe,[54] placed the ephod on him,[55] girded him and fastened it around him. He then set the breastpiece on him with the declaration of doctrine and truth on it, and put the miter[56] on his head, and on the miter, the gold plate.

52 Lv 7.35 (LXX). The entire chapter deals with the portion of the victim to be given to the priest. The anointing may mean the anointed part of the oblation and is translated in NAB as "the priestly share."

53 Lv. 8 describes the ordination of Aaron and his sons. Chrysostom telescopes the description somewhat but does recount the tripartite ceremony consisting of lustration, investiture, and anointing.

54 Of the priest's tunic we know only that it was brocaded and that the sash was of variegated work. The high priest also wore a one-piece violet robe with openings for head and arms; it reached to the knees and was adorned at the bottom with woven pomegranates and golden bells. Cf. J. Huesman, JBC 3:80.

55 For the ephod see above, n. 32.

56 For the breastpiece and the stones of declaration see also above, n. 32. The

Taking the anointing oil he sprinkled the altar with it and consecrated it and the vessels; the laver and its base he also consecrated.
And he poured some of the oil on Aaron's head and did in like
manner to his sons. And he brought forward the calf. After he
sacrificed it, when Aaron and his sons had put their hands upon it,
he took some of its blood and put it on the horns of the altar and
purified the altar. And he poured the blood on the base of the altar
and consecrated it by performing the rite of atonement over it. After
he burned portions of the calf, some within on the altar, others
outside the camp, he brought in a ram and offered it for a holocaust.
[912]

(8) And again he brought a second ram, the ordination ram.
Aaron and his sons laid their hands on it and Moses immolated it.[57]
He took some of its blood and put it on the lobe of Aaron's right
ear, the thumb of his right hand, and the big toe of his right foot.[58]
And he did the same thing to Aaron's sons. Then he took some parts
of the sacrifice and put them into Aaron's hands and those of
his sons and in this way he made the offering. And again he took
the blood and some oil and sprinkled Aaron and his vestments
with it, and his sons and their vestments.[59] He consecrated them

---

miter or turban (Ez 21.31) and the golden plate or diadem (2 Sm [2 Kgs]
1.10; 2 Kgs [4 Kgs] 11.12) are symbols of royal authority given the high
priest. The investiture is followed by the anointing of the high priest joined
with that of the dwelling, the altar and its furnishings, and the basin, which
served as a blood receptable. The anointing is followed by the ordination
sacrifices. Cf. JBC 4:20–21.

57 Lv 8 speaks of three sacrifices, all offered by Moses: a sin offering (verses
14–17), a holocaust (18–21), and a special ordination sacrifice (22–3).
The sin offering erases any uncleanness connected with the holocaust altar
and makes it suitable for sacred encounter between the divine and the
human. A ram was specified for the holocaust by a procedure prescribed in
the sacrificial code (Lv 1.10–13). The final sacrifice climaxed the ordination ceremony and marked the formal assumption of office. Cf. JBC 4:21.

58 This ritual may have symbolized the sanctification of the whole man by
anointing the extremities just as the altar was sanctified by spreading blood
on its outermost parts. It may also have been linked with service: the ears
receive instruction; the hands and feet carry it out. Cf. JBC 4:21.

59 This blood and oil sprinkling of the priests and vestments disturbs the
continuity of the passage and may be an interpolation. The exact purpose
of this second consecration is not clear since Aaron and his sons have

and ordered them to cook the flesh at the entrance to the tent of meeting and to eat it there. And he said: 'You shall not go forth from the entrance to the tent of meeting for seven days until the day when the day of your ordination is complete.'"[60]

(9) Moses said that by all these rites Aaron was ordained, purified, and consecrated, and that they appeased God. But we find none of these today: no sacrifice, no holocaust, no sprinkling of blood, no anointing with oil, no tent of meeting where they must sit for a definite number of days. This makes it obvious that the priest among the Jews today is unordained, unclean, under a curse, and profane; he only provokes God's wrath. If a priest could not be ordained in any other way than by these rites, and these rites no longer exist, then there is no possible way that their priesthood could have continued to exist. You see that I was right when I said they had gotten somewhere far off and had been far removed from both the reality and even the pretense of the priesthood.

VI

We can also learn from other sources how awesome was the dignity of the priesthood. Indeed, there was a day when some wicked and evil men revolted against Aaron, quarreled with him over his position in the community, and tried to drive him from his leadership. Moses, the mildest of men,[61] wanted to persuade them by the facts themselves that he had not brought Aaron to the leadership because he was a brother, relative, or member of his family, but that it was in obedience to God's decree that he had entrusted the

---

already been anointed. Perhaps the stress here is on the anointing of their vestments as symbols of their priestly office. Cf. JBC 4:21.

60 The whole passage is from Lv 8.1–33. The cooked meat and bread offered in this final sacrifice (Chrysostom omits the bread) were to be eaten as sacred food, i.e., within the sacred confines that same day (cf. Lv 7.15). But the ordination observance was to continue for seven days during which at least the sin offering was to be repeated daily (Ex 29.36–37).

61 Cf. Nm 12.3, which states that Moses was by far the mildest man on the face of the earth, i.e., he was one of the pious, who lived a humble and God-fearing life. The term must not be confused with weakness. Moses is aware of his own limitations (cf. Ex 3.11; 4.10–13).

priesthood to him. So he ordered each tribe to bring a staff, and Aaron was instructed to do the same.[62]

(2) When each tribe had brought a staff, Moses took all of them and put them inside the meeting tent. Once he had put them there, he gave orders that they await the decision of God which would come to them through those staves.[63] Then all the other staves kept their same appearance, but a single one—Aaron's—blossomed and put forth leaves and fruit. So the Lord of nature used leaves instead of letters to teach them that he had again elected Aaron.[64]

(3) God said in the beginning: "Let the earth bring forth vegetation,"[65] and he stirred up its power to bear fruit; in Aaron's day, he also took that dry and fruitless wood and made it blossom without earth or root. That staff was thereafter a proof and witness both of the wickedness of those men and of God's choice. It uttered no word, but the very sight of it, in tones clearer than any trumpet's call, urged every man never to attempt such things as did Aaron's foes.

(4) Not only in this case but at another time and in another way God made clear his choice of Aaron. Many men conspired against Aaron in their lust for the leadership for which God selected him. (And leadership is the kind of thing many men fight over and desire.) Moses ordered them to bring their censers, put incense in them, [913] and to wait for a decision from heaven. As they were burning their incense, the earth split apart and gulped down all their sup-

---

62 Cf. Nm 17.16–18. "Staff" means both "staff" and "tribe." The family of Aaron is symbolized by the staff or rod. This incident teaches the pre-eminence of the house of Aaron and the tribe of Levi; it is another indication of the persisting tension between the Levites and the secular tribes. Cf. F. Moriarty, JBC 5:32.

63 Cf. Nm 17.19–22.

64 Cf. ibid. 23–25. The overnight blossoming of the staff was characteristic of the almond branch, which in Jer 1.11 symbolizes the swift coming of divine judgment. Its blossoms sometimes appeared during winter and carried a promise that spring was not far off. Cf. JBC 5:32. God had first chosen Aaron and his descendants for the priesthood in Ex 29.9 and Lv 1.5.

65 Gn 1.11.

porters, and a flame from heaven consumed those who had taken up their censers.[66]

(5) Moses did not want anyone to forget, with the passage of time, what had happened. Nor did he want men of a later day to remain ignorant of God's wondrous decision. Therefore, he gave orders that those bronze censers be picked up and beaten into plates for the altar.[67] Just as the very sight of the voiceless staff sent forth a voice, so these bronze plates would speak to all men thereafter, to exhort and advise them never to imitate the madness of those men of old, for fear that they might suffer the same judgment.

(6) Do you see how priests were chosen in former days? But everything that goes on among the Jews today is a ridiculous sport, a trading in shame, filled with outrages beyond number. Tell me, then. Do you let yourself be led by these men who stubbornly oppose God's laws in their every word and deed? Do you rush to their synagogues?[68] Are you not afraid that a bolt of lightning may come down from above and consume your head? Even if a man is not a thief himself but is seen in a den of robbers, he pays the same penalty as they. You do know this, do you not? But why talk about robbers and their crimes?

---

66 Nm 16 combines two distinct rebellions: one effected by Korah and 250 malcontents who revolted against the religious leadership of Moses and Aaron and were punished by fire (*ibid*. 1–11; 16–24); the revolt of Dathan and Abiram was political, against Moses' civil leadership, and the rebels were swallowed up in an earthquake (*ibid*. 12–15; 25–34). The censers belong to the Korah revolt. Cf. the NAB notes on this chapter.

67 Since the censers of Korah and his followers had been touched by fire from the Lord, they could no longer be put to profane use; hence Moses had them collected and hammered into plates to cover the altar (cf. Nm 17.1–5). Ex 21.1–8 describes the altar of holocausts which had these bronze plates fastened over the planks from which the altar was made. This covering was a perpetual reminder and warning that no one but the priests, the descendants of Aaron, was to come close to the altar of Yahweh to offer incense to him. Cf. JBC 5:32.

68 During the exile and dispersion of the Jews, a cult centered around the temple was impossible; the synagogue was organized as a substitute for maintaining Jewish unity in faith and worship. It was not a house where the deity dwelt but a meeting house for prayer, study, and holding services on the sabbath and feasts. It was furnished with an ark, in which the scrolls of the law were kept, a tribune for the speaker or reader, a table, lamps,

(7) Surely you all know and remember the time when some evil tricksters in our midst tore down the statues.[69] You remember how not only those who did this reckless deed but also those who were seen simply standing there when it happened were all arrested and dragged off to court together. And you remember that they all paid the supreme penalty. Tell me, then. Are you all agog to run off to a place where they outrage the Father, blaspheme the Son, and reject the Holy Spirit, the giver of life? Are you not afraid, do you not shudder to set foot inside those profane and unclean places? Tell me. What defense or excuse will you have since it is you who have thrust yourself into ruin and perdition, since it is you who have hurled yourself from the precipice?

(8) Do not tell me that the Law and the books of the prophets are there. These do not make it a holy place.[70] Which is the better thing? Is it better to have the books there or to speak out the truths they contain? Obviously it is better to speak out these truths and to keep them in your heart. Tell me, what about this? The devil quoted Scripture.[71] This did not make his mouth holy, did it? You cannot say it did, since the devil kept on being the devil. What about the demons? Just because they spoke out and proclaimed: "These men are servants of the most high God and they proclaim to you a way of salvation,"[72] do we on this account rank them among the apostles?

---

and trumpets for ceremonial use. It gave rise to a religion which was primarily a faith and way of life existing without a temple or a temple cult. See J. McKenzie, "Synagogue," DB 855–56. Nonetheless, Chrysostom considered it not only a grave threat to Judaizing Christians but as a dwelling place of demons (cf. *Disc.* 2.3.5).

69 Chrysostom delivered a series of twenty-one homilies *On the Statues* which give a vivid picture of the days of terror following the overthrowing and mutilation of the statues of Theodosius and his family by a mob in Antioch in 387. Many were executed for this crime against the crown. The point here is that guilt by association suspended due process, and Judaizing Christians may expect to be punished by God for sharing in the rites of the synagogue.

70 Cf. *Disc.* 1.5.2–6. *Disc.* 1.6.1 makes the same point about the temple of Serapis.

71 Cf. Mt 4.6, where the devil supports his temptation of Christ by quoting Ps 90(91). 11–12.

72 Acts 16.17. The words are spoken by a girl possessed of "a spirit of divination," in the Greek: "having a *python* spirit." *Python* originally designated

By no means! Just as before, we keep right on turning our backs on them and hating them.

(9) If spoken words do not make the mouth holy, does the presence of the Scriptures make a place holy? But how could this be right? This is my strongest reason for hating the synagogue: it does have the Law and the prophets. And now I hate it more than if it had none of these. Why is this? Because in the Law and the prophets they have a great allurement and many a snare to attract the more simple-minded sort of men. This is why Paul drove out the demon which did not remain silent but spoke out. As the author of Acts says: "Being very much grieved, he said to the spirit, 'Go out of her.' "73 Why? Because the demon kept shouting: "These men are servants of the most high God."74

(10) As long as the demons remained silent, they did not deceive people by their words; when they spoke out, they did so with the intention of enticing many of the simpler sort [914] into listening and heeding them in these other matters. The demons wish to open the door to their deceits and to create confidence in their lies. And so they give some admixture of truth, in the same way that those who mix lethal drugs smear the lip of the cup with honey to make the harmful potion easy to drink.75

(11) This is why Paul was very much grieved and why he hurried to stop up the demons' mouths when they took to themselves a dignity which ill became them. This is why I hate the Jews. Although they possess the Law, they put it to outrageous use. For it is by

the dragon or serpent guarding the Delphic oracle and slain by Apollo. Later the word came to mean "spirit of divination" and even "ventriloquist." The point is that her speaking the truth does not make her any less possessed than the possession of the Scriptures makes the synagogue a holy place.

73 Cf. Acts 16.18. Paul's command is "in the name of Jesus Christ," which is the powerful source of redemption. Chrysostom omits the phrase. Usually the inference from physical restoration to redemption is the didactic intent of healing-stories. Of course Chrysostom's oratorical purpose centers around the girl's demon of divination, which might attract the unwary.
74 Acts 16.17.
75 Cf. e.g., Horace, Sermones 2.1.56, where a spendthrift son kills his old crone mother by poison (hemlock) mixed with honey.

means of the Law that they try to entice and catch the more simple-minded sort of men. If they refused to believe in Christ because they did not believe in the prophets, the charge against them would not be so severe. As it is, they have deprived themselves of every excuse because they say that they do believe in the prophets but they have heaped outrage on him whom the prophets foretold.

VII

In short, if you believe the place is holy because the Law and the books of prophets are there, then it is time for you to believe that idols and the temples of idols are holy. Once, when the Jews were at war, the people of Ashdod[76] conquered them, took their ark, and brought it into their own temple. Did the fact that it contained the ark make their temple a holy place? By no means! It continued to be profane and unclean, as the events straightway proved. For God wanted to teach the enemies of the Jews that the defeat was not due to God's weakness but to the transgressions of those who worshipped him. And so the ark, which had been taken as booty in war, gave proof of its own power in an alien land by twice throwing the idol to the ground so that the idol was broken.[77] The ark was so far from making that temple a holy place that it even openly attacked it.

(2) Look at it in another way. What sort of ark is it that the Jews now have, where we find no propitiatory, no tables of the law, no holy of holies, no veil, no high priest, no incense, no holocaust, no sacrifice, none of the other things that made the ark of old solemn and august?[78] It seems to me that the ark the Jews now have is no

---

76 The Israelites, who carried the Ark into battle against the Philistines, were vanquished; the Ark was taken as booty to the town of Ashdod and put in the temple of Dagon. Cf. 1 Sm (1 Kgs) 4.5.1–2.

77 The Philistines found the Ark a hostile trophy. On two successive days the image of Dagon was overturned (perhaps by an earthquake) and the second time the image was found by the people of Ashdod without head or hands; only the stump stood. Cf. 1 Sm (1 Kgs) 5.4–5.

78 The old Ark had the mercy-seat as its cover and contained the tablets of the Law. It was probably destroyed with Solomon's temple in 587 B.C.

better off than those toy arks which you can buy in the market place. In fact it is much worse. Those little toy arks cannot hurt anybody who comes close to them. But the ark which the Jews now have does great harm each day to those who come near it.[79]

(3) "Brethren, do not become children in mind, but in malice be children,"[80] and rescue from their untimely anguish those who are frightened by these things. Teach them what should really terrify them and make them afraid. They should not be terrified by that ark but they should be afraid that they will bring destruction to the temple of God.[81] How will they destroy the temple of God? By constantly rushing off to the synagogue, by a conscience which is inclined toward Judaism, and by the untimely observance of the Jewish rites.

(4) "You who would be justified in the Law have fallen away from grace."[82] This is what you must fear. On that day of judgment you must be afraid of hearing him who will judge you say:

---

under Nebuchadnezzar, when the Israelites were exiled to Babylon. In Solomon's temple the Ark reposed in the holy of holies, which was separated from the holy place or sanctuary by a veil. In Herod's temple the holy of holies was entirely empty and totally dark; it was entered only once a year—by the high priest on the Day of Atonement. Here also it was separated from the holy place by a veil; the rending of this veil on Good Friday (Mt 27.51; Mk 15.38) signified the access of all people to God through the death of Jesus.

79 The synagogues at Antioch must have contained not only the ark or chest in which the scroll of the Law was kept but also some replica of the Ark of the Covenant as a reminder of the Jewish faith and way of life. Just as crucifixes and statues of the saints may have been for sale in the market place (as they are in stores today), so, too, there were probably on sale "little toy arks" such as the mezuzahs, small cases holding rolled-up scrolls inscribed on one side with the text of Dt 6.4–9 and 11.13–21, and on the other with the name of God, to be attached to door posts.

80 1 Cor 14.20. The verse continues: "and in mind mature." The whole chapter deals with the gift of tongues and prophecy (which is a superior gift). The Corinthians had a childish attachment to the gift of tongues, and Paul is telling them that the Christian must strive to be like a child in moral innocence but always mature in judgment. Chrysostom is urging the mature Christians to rescue their Judaizing brethren from their childish terror of the synagogue's Ark.

81 I.e., their own souls. In baptism they had become temples of God and dwelling places for the Spirit. Cf. ACW 31.57 and 232.

82 Cf. Gal 5.4. See also *Disc.* 2.2.1; 2.3.8.; 8.5.5. Those who adopt Jewish

"Depart, I know you not."[83] "You made common cause with those who crucified me. You were obstinate toward me and started up again the festivals to which I had put an end. You ran to the synagogues of the Jews who sinned against me. I destroyed the temple and made ruins of that august place together with all the awe—inspiring things it contained. But you frequented shrines that are no better than hucksters' shops or dens of thieves."

(5) The cherubim [915] and the ark were still there, the grace of the Spirit still abounded in the temple when Christ said: "You have made it a den of thieves"[84] and "a house of business."[85] And He said this because of the trangressions and blood-guilt of the Jews. Now, after the grace of the Spirit has abandoned them, after all those august solemnities have been taken away, they are still stubborn with God and carry on their irreligious rites. What worthy name can we find to call their synagogues?

(6) The temple was already a den of thieves when the Jewish commonwealth and way of life still prevailed. Now you give it a name more worthy than it deserves if you call it a brothel, a stronghold of sin, a lodging-place for demons, a fortress of the devil, the destruction of the soul, the precipice and pit of all perdition, or whatever other name you give it.

(7) Do you wish to see the temple? Don't run to the synagogue; be a temple yourself. God destroyed one temple in Jerusalem but he reared up temples beyond number, temples more august than that old one ever was. Paul said: "You are the temple of the living

---

customs, such as circumcision and observance of feasts, obligate themselves to the whole Jewish way of life. But this is not to follow the way of truth taught in the Gospel.

83 Cf. Lk 13.27.

84 Mt 21.13. Chrysostom is wrong about the cherubim and the Ark, which were probably destroyed with the temple before the Babylonian captivity. The Ark is not mentioned in NT except in Heb 9.4, where it is spoken of as a type of the heavenly tabernacle, and in Rv (Apoc) 11.19, where it appears in the heavenly temple.

85 Jn 2.16. In the synoptic account Jesus' wrath seems to be directed against the dishonesty of the traffickers in the temple; in Jn the emphasis is rather on the very institutions which Jesus opposes. The sacrificial system of Judaism has made a market place of the temple. Cf. B. Vawter, JBC 63:65.

God."[86] Make that temple beautiful, drive out every evil thought, so that you may be a precious member of Christ, a temple of the Spirit. And make others be temples such as you are yourselves. When you see the poor, you would not find it easy to pass them by. When any of you see some Christian running to the synagogue, do not look the other way. Find some argument you can use as a halter to bring him back to the Church. This kind of almsgiving is greater than giving to the poor, and the profit from it is worth more than ten thousand talents.[87]

(8) Why do I speak [916] of being worth more than ten thousand talents? Or worth more than the whole visible world? A human being is worth more than the whole world. Heaven and earth and sea and sun and stars were made for his sake.

(9) Consider well, then, the dignity and worth of the man you save. Do not think lightly of the care you show to him. Even if a man gives away more money than you can count, he does not do as great a thing as the man who saves a soul, leads it from its error, and takes it by the hand along the road to godliness. The man who gives to the poor takes away the poor man's hunger; the man who sets a Judaizing Christian straight, wins a victory over godlessness. The first man gave consolation to the poor; the second put a stop to reckless transgression. The first freed the body from pain, the other snatched a soul from the fires of hell.

(10) I showed you the treasure; do not forsake the profit. You cannot dare put the blame on your poverty or excuse yourself because you are indigent. The only expense is one of phrases; the only cost is one of words. Therefore, let us not shrink back from the task but, with all the zeal and desire we possess, let us go hunting for our brothers. Even though they be unwilling, let us drag them into our own houses, let us sit down with them at table and put a meal before

---

86 Cf. 2 Cor 6.19.

87 Chrysostom often speaks of almsgiving, linking it with prayer, temperance, holiness, and other good works. See ACW 31.38, 114–18, 175, 185–6, 239–40, 279, 291, 325. Here correction of a Judaizing brother is greater than almsgiving and brings an almost usurious profit because of the value of the human soul which is saved. Cf. *Disc.* 7.6.4.

them. Let us do this so that after they have broken their fast[88] before our eyes, after they have given us a full and sufficient guarantee of their conversion and return to better ways, they may help both themselves and us to a share in eternal blessings through the grace and loving-kindness of our Lord Jesus Christ, through whom and with whom be glory to the Father together with the Holy Spirit, now and forever, world without end. Amen.

---

88 Judaizing Christians frequented not only the synagogues but also the homes of the Jews, where they would feast and fast with them. Here, Chrysostom suggests that stronger Christians search out the weak ones, bring them to their homes, serve them a meal which will break the fast they have been keeping with the Jews. In *Disc.* 8.5.2–6 he suggests that the stronger Christians go to the homes of those who are weak and attempt to bring them back to the Church, after convincing them of their error.

DISCOURSE VII

I

AVE YOU HAD ENOUGH [915] of the fight against the Jews? Or do you wish me to take up the same topic today? Even if I have already had much to say on it, I still think you want to hear the same thing again. The man who does not have enough of loving Christ will never have enough of fighting against those who hate Christ. Besides, there is another reason which makes a discourse on this theme necessary. These feasts of theirs are not yet over; some traces still remain.

(2) Their trumpets were a greater outrage than those heard in the theaters; their fasts were more disgraceful than any drunken revel. So, too, the tents which at this moment are pitched among them are no better than the inns where harlots and flute girls ply their trades.[1] Let no one condemn me for the boldness of my words; it is

---

1 Trumpets were blown at the great annual feasts of Passover, Pentecost, and Tabernacles. Here the reference, as in *Disc.* 1.1.5, is probably to the New Year (Rosh Ha-Shanah) on the first of Tishri (Sept.–Oct.). Chrysostom has compared the synagogue to the theater before. See *Disc.* 1.2.7 and Introd. III 18. The fasts then would be the Ten Days of Penitence between the New Year and the Day of Atonement. See EJ 15.1001. This period was not a drunken revel except insofar as it is possible to be drunk without wine. See *Disc.* 8.1.5 where Chrysotom states that the fasting of the Jews is more disgraceful than any drunkenness. The tents refer to the feast of Tabernacles (Sukkot), which fell on the fifteenth of Tishri and lasted a week during which the Jews danced and "made merry before the Lord" (cf. Lv 23.33–43). See *Disc.* 1.1.5; DB 863–64 and EJ 15.495–501. EJ 6.1195 says that the Monday after Sukkot was a fast day to atone for possible sins committed while in the state of drunkenness and gluttony during the holidays. In *Disc.* 1.3.1 Chrysostom compares the synagogue to a brothel as well as a theater.

177

the height of boldness and outrage not to suspect the Jews of these excesses. Since they stubbornly fight against God and resist the Holy Spirit,[2] how can we avoid the necessity of passing such sentence upon them?

(3) This festival used to be a holy one when it was observed according to the Law and at God's command. But this is no longer true. All its dignity has been destroyed because it is observed against God's will.[3] Those who, above all others, treat the Law and the ancient festivals with the least respect are the very ones who are ready today to observe the Law and festivals more than anyone else. But we are the ones who honor the Law above all others, even if we let it rest like a man who has grown old and infirm, even [916] if we do not drag it, gray with age, to the arena,[4] even if we do not force it to enter the contests which are not suited to its years. In my past discourses I gave adequate proof that today is not the day of the Law nor of the old commonwealth and the old way of life.[5]

(4) But come now, let me investigate what remains to be discussed. I did enough to complete my task when I proved from all the prophets that any such observance of ritual outside Jerusalem is transgression of the Law and a sacrilege.[6] But they never stop whispering in everybody's ear and bragging that they will get their city back again. Even if this were true, they could not escape the charge of transgressing the Law.[7] But I gave you abundant evidence to prove that the city will not be restored nor will they get back their old commonwealth and way of life.

---

2 Cf. Acts 7.51. *Disc.* 1.2.3; 4.4.3.
3 Both good and evil depend on God's will. See *Disc.* 1.7.6; 4.1.6–4.2.7.
4 Literally, "the broad-jump pits."
5 Cf. *Disc.* 4.4.6; 5.1.3–9; 5.9.1–5.11.10; *Demonstration* 16–17 (PG 48.834–38).
6 Cf.*Disc* 4.4.4–4.5.6; 5.1.5; 5.4.1. Again we must recall that this injunction is often anachronistic in Chrysostom. There could have been no observance in Jerusalem until the Jews possessed that city and a temple. There were other sanctuaries and places of worship prior to that time, although Dt 12.5 gives a law of one sanctuary linked with the one God of Israel. Cf. J. Castelot, JBC 76:39–54.
7 Cf. *Disc* 6.2.1–9.

(5) Once that has been proved, there is no room for disagreement on any of the other points. For example, neither the form of sacrifice, nor of the holocaust, nor the binding force of the Law, nor any other aspect of their old commonwealth and way of life can stand. To begin with, the Law commanded that three times each year every male go up to the temple.[8] But they could not do this once the temple was destroyed. Then, too, the Law commanded that sacrifices be offered by the man afflicted with gonorrhea, the leper, the woman in her menstrual period, the woman who had given birth to a child.[9] But this is impossible since the place no longer exists nor is there an altar to be seen. The Law commanded them to sing sacred hymns but, as I showed before, the place they were living in pre-

---

8 Cf. Ex. 14-17. The three pilgrimages specified are for the feast of unleavened bread (immediately after Passover), the grain harvest (Pentecost), and the fruit harvest (Tabernacles). Cf. also Ex 34.18–26; Lv 23; Dt 16. Of course, there is no mention of the temple in any of these passages. Verse 17 says: "Thrice a year shall all your men appear before the Lord," i.e., at a sanctuary. After the Jews occupied Jerusalem, the temple was the sanctuary.

9 Cf. Lv 15.1–15, which deals with gonorrhea; 16–17, with the loss of semen whether voluntary or not; 18, with sexual relations whether licit or not; and 19–30, with the menstrual flow. The loss of seed through gonorrhea and the normal or abnormal menstrual flow required both ritual purification and the offering of two turtledoves or two pigeons, one as a sin offering, the other as a holocaust. Intercourse (verse 18) required purification by bathing but no offering. The loss of seed or blood was looked on as a diminution of the life principle and involved exclusion from Israel's cultic life prior to purification. The purification for leprosy is much more complicated and is recounted in ch. 14. The purification after childbirth (Lv 12) required the mother to remain sequestered from the sacred for thirty-three days after a son's circumcision; she was unclean for fourteen days after the birth of a daughter and then had to wait sixty-six days before making her purification offerings. Whether the child was son or daughter, the offerings were a lamb for holocaust and a pigeon or turtledove for the sin offering. If the mother could not afford a lamb, she might present two pigeons or two turtledoves, as did the Blessed Mother of Jesus (Lk 2.24). The uncleanness came neither from conception nor childbirth; in delivery, the mother's vitality (linked with her blood) was diminished, and thus she was objectively separated from Yahweh, the source of life, until her integrity was restored by purification. Cf. R. Faley, JBC 4:27–33.

vented them;[10] the prophets condemned them and said [917] they were reading the Law and making their confession of praise to God in a foreign land.[11] Since they could not even read the Law outside Jerusalem, how could they observe it outside Jerusalem?

(6) This is why God threatened them and said: "I shall not visit your daughters when they commit fornication nor your daughters-in-law when they commit adultery."[12] What does this mean? First, I shall read[13] to you the old Law and then I shall try to make his meaning clearer. What, then, does the Law say? "If a woman transgresses against her husband, disdaining and disregarding him, and if someone sleeps with her the sleep of intercourse, and if she escapes the eye of her husband and there is no witness against her, nor is she caught in the act, or if a spirit of jealousy comes over her husband when she has not been defiled. . ."[14]

(7) This is what the Law means. If a woman commits adultery and her husband suspects it, or if he suspects her when she has not committed adultery, but there is no witness nor conception to prove the suspicion, "he will bring her to the priest and take along barley meal as an offering for her."[15] Why, I ask, must it be barley meal

---

10 Cf. *Disc.* 4.5.9 and Ps 136(137).3–4 See also *Demonstration* 17 (PG 48. 835–36).

11 Cf. Am 4.5(LXX) and *Demonstration* 17 (PG 48.836). LXX varies considerably from NAB and JB. However, in all three the tone is caustic because the Israelites were rendering religion farcical by making ritual an end in itself. Although it seems clear that Chrysostom had this text in mind, his application of it is quite different from that which Amos seems to have intended.

12 Cf. Hos 4.14 (LXX). Again Chrysostom misconstrues the meaning. The chapter is an indictment of the priests (verses 4–19) who have involved themselves in the idolatry and orgiastic fertility rites of the Baalistic sanctuaries (cf.1Kgs [3 Kgs] 14.23; Jer 2.20) located on high hills and green groves (as the first part of verse 13 says), where they have practiced the ritual prostitution of the Canaanite shrines and even introduced it into the sanctuaries dedicated to Yahweh. Cf. NAB note *ad loc.*

13 Again there is doubt whether Chrysostom reads or recites the passage from Nm. The latter is more probable because of the variations (e.g., omissions and transpositions) in the Greek text as he gives it. In fact he does not complete the sentence until the following paragraph.

14 Cf. Nm 5.12–14 (LXX).

15 Cf. *ibid.* 15. "For her" may mean "for his jealousy regarding her."

rather than fine flour or the meal of wheat? Since what happened was a source of pain, accusation, and wicked suspicion, the form of the sacrifice imitated a household disaster.[16] This is why the Lord said: "You will not pour oil on it nor put frankincense over it."[17] "Then" (for I must cut the account short) "the priest shall lead her forward and will take pure water in an earthen vessel; he will pick up some of the dust which is on the floor and throw it into the water; he will make the woman stand, will make her swear an oath, and he will say to her: 'If you did not transgress so as to become defiled for your husband, be immune from the water of reproof. But if you did transgress and you are defiled, if someone other than your husband did have intercourse with you, may the Lord make of you an execration and a curse among your people.' "[18]

(8) What is the meaning of "an execration and a curse"? As the saying goes; May what happened to that poor woman not happen to me! " 'By the Lord causing your belly to swell and the water that brings a curse will enter your belly to make it swell.'[19] And the woman will say: 'Amen, Amen.' And it will come to pass, if the woman is defiled, that the water of the curse will enter her belly to make it swell, and the woman will be an execration. If she is not

16 Fine flour was the usual offering (Lv 5.11) while barley was the food of the poor (cf. the five barley loaves of Jn 6.9). Since the suspected wife's ordeal also involves her husband, Chrysostom thinks of it as a "household disaster." The barley sacrifice seems quite in keeping with the domestic misfortune which occasioned it, since the alleged crime is like a disaster where the very bread would be taken from the family's mouth. Furthermore, the Hebrew family shared in the guilt of an offending member because it owed him protection. Cf. DB 273.

17 Cf. Nm 5.15. Oil and frankincense were omitted from all sin offerings but added to a token offering. Cf. Lv 2.2 and NAB note, which explains this offering as a "reminder." Nm 5.15 (LXX) continues by explaining the omission of oil and incense because the offering is a sacrifice of jealousy, a sacrifice of memorial, recalling sin to remembrance. NAB gives as the reason: "since it is a cereal offering of jealousy, a cereal offering for an appeal in a question of guilt."

18 Cf. ibid. 15–21. NAB note on verse 21 gives the meaning: if the woman is guilty, her name would be used in curses and oaths to invoke a similar misfortune on another person or oneself.

19 This is a Yahwist variation on trial by ordeal. An archaic practice has been transformed into a ceremony consistent with faith in God. The Israelite

defiled, she will be unharmed and will conceive offspring."[20] Once the Jews had gone off into bondage, none of these things could be done because there was no temple, no altar, no Meeting Tent, no sacrifice to be offered. Because this was the case, when God threatened them, he said: "I shall not visit your daughters when they commit fornication nor your daughters-in-law when they commit adultery."[21]

II

Do you see that the Law takes its force from the place? And since the city is gone, there can no longer be a priesthood. There can be no emperor if there are no armies, no crown, no purple robe, none of the other things which weld together an empire. So, too, there can be no priesthood if sacrifice has been destroyed, if offerings are forbidden, if the sanctuary has been trampled into the dust, if everything which constituted it has disappeared. For the priesthood depended on all these things.

(2) As I said before, it was enough for my purpose to prove that neither the sacrifices, nor the holocausts, nor the other purifications, nor any other part of the [918] Jewish commonwealth and way of life would return. It was enough, finally, to prove that the temple will never rise again. Now that it is no more, everything has been taken away; if something ritualistic seems to be going on, it is against the Law and a reckless crime. In the same way, once I have proved that the temple will never be restored to its former state, I have at the same time also proved that the rest of the ritual of worship will not return to its former condition, that there will be no priest, there will be no king. If not even a commoner of Jewish blood was al-

---

ritual ascribes punishment of the woman, if guilty, to Yahweh and not to some magical effect of the water she was forced to drink. Cf. F. Moriarty, JBC 5.15.

20 Cf. Nm 5.21–28. The citation continues here from the point where it left off at the end of the preceding paragraph.

21 Cf. Hos 4.14 (LXX).

lowed to be a servant to foreigners, it would be all the more forbidden for their king himself to be subject to others.

(3) But since my effort and zeal are here devoted not only to stopping up the mouths of the Jews but also to instructing your loving assembly, come now and let me take another authority and prove this same point. Let me prove that both the sacrifices of the Jews and their priesthood have so completely ended that they will never again return to their former status.

(4) Who says this? That great and wonderful prophet, David. He made it clear that the one kind of sacrifice would be abolished and another brought in to take its place when he said: "Many are the wondrous works you have done, O Lord my God: and in your thoughts there is no one like to you. I have declared and I have spoken."[22] See how wise the prophet is. He said: "Many are the wondrous works you have done," and he stood aghast at God's power to work miracles. But he did not go on to tell us about the creation of the things we see: of heaven, earth, and ocean, of water and fire; he did not tell us of those strange marvels which happened in Egypt, or of any other miracles like those. What did he say were wondrous works? "Sacrifice and oblation you did not desire."[23]

---

22 Ps 39(40).6. Chrysostom quotes from this Ps three times in *Demonstration* 8 (PG 48.823–24) and fourteen times in the present homily (7.2.4, 6, 7, 9; 7.3.1, 2; 7.4.1). The psalmist put his trust in God alone in the preceding psalm; God has heard his cry, put a new song in his mouth, and shown that many will turn from idolatry to trust in Him (Ps 39[40].2–6). Their deliverance is connected with God's wondrous deeds of salvation history.

23 *Ibid.* 7. Chrysostom takes this as a rejection of both pagan and Jewish sacrifice; what the psalmist says is that God prefers obedience to any of the four types mentioned: sacrifice, oblation, holocaust, sin offerings. Dedication and commitment are the only adequate responses to God, but the principle of sacrifice is not rejected. There is a similar emphasis in Am 5.21–27, where NAB note says that God does not condemn ritual worship in itself but the cult whose exterior rites have no relationship to interior morality and justice. Cf. *Disc.*1.7.1–2, where Chrysostom quotes Am 5.21 and 23 as well as Is 1.13 to prove that God abhors sacrifice. He also cites Is 1.10–12 in *Disc.* 4.6.2–3 to prove that the Jews were offering sacrifices which God never required of them. As NAB note on verse 11 points out, no matter how numerous the sacrifices, they were unacceptable unless the worshipper had the right dispositions. But again the principle of sacrifice is not rejected.

(5) What do you mean, David? Is this a strange marvel? No, he said. For this was not the only thing he saw. Inspired by heaven, he saw with prophetic eyes how God would lead the nations to him; he saw how those who were nailed to their gods, who worshipped stones, who were worse off than brute beasts suddenly looked up and recognized the Master of all creation; he saw how these men put aside their foul worship of demons and gave pure and bloodless worship to God. At the same time he saw that the Jews, too, who were even more imperfect than the pagans, would put aside their worship through sacrifices, holocausts, and other material things and be led to our way of life. And he pondered on God's ineffable loving-kindness which surpasses all understanding; he stood aghast at how greatly things had changed, how God had reshaped them, how he had made men from demons into angels, and how he had introduced a commonwealth and way of life worthy of heaven.

(6) All this was to take place after the old sacrifice had been abolished and after God had brought into its place the new sacrifice through the body of Christ. This is why David stood aghast and marvelled and said: "Many are the wondrous works you have done, O Lord my God."[24] To show that he made this whole prophetic prediction in behalf of Christ when he said: "Sacrifice and oblation you did not desire,"[25] David went on to say: "But a body you have fitted to me."[26] By this he meant the Lord's body which became the common sacrifice for the whole world, the sacrifice which cleansed our souls, [919] canceled sin, put down death, opened

---

24 Cf. Ps 39(40).6.

25 *Ibid.* 7.

26 *Ibid.* NAB reads: "but ears open to obedience you gave me;" JB: "you opened my ear," with a note that "opened" literally means "dug out," i.e., God sees to it that his servant knows his will. Rahlfs' LXX reads: "you fitted me with ears," but notes a variant, "a body," found in the three principal MSS (Vaticanus, Sinaiticus, Alexandrinus). Heb 10.5, quoting the Ps, reads: "you fitted to me a body," interprets it as messianic and as annulling the first covenant to establish the second. Chrysostom follows Heb both in reading and interpretation here and in *Demonstration* 8 (PG 48.824), where he immediately adds Ps 17(18).44–45: "A people whom I knew not have served me. As soon as they heard, they obeyed me." The combination of texts there shows that obedience is better than sacrifice.

heaven, gave us many great hopes, and made ready all the other things which Paul knew well and spoke of when he exclaimed: "Oh, the depth of the riches and of the wisdom and of the knowledge of God! How incomprehensible are his judgments and how unsearchable are his ways."[27]

(7) David, then, foresaw all this when he said: "Many are the wondrous works you have done, O Lord my God."[28] He went on to say, speaking in the person of Christ: "In holocausts and sin offerings you had had no pleasure,"[29] and then continued: "Then I said, Behold I come."[30] When was "then"? When the time was ripe for more perfect instructions. We had to learn the less perfect lessons through his servants, but the loftier lessons which surpass the nature of man we had to learn from the Lawgiver himself.

(8) This is why Paul said: "God, who at sundry times and in varied ways spoke in times past to the fathers by the prophets, last of all in these days has spoken to us by his Son, whom he appointed heir of all things, by whom also he made the world."[31] And again, John said: "For the Law was given through Moses; grace and truth came through Jesus Christ."[32] And this is the highest panegyric for the Law, namely that it prepared human nature for the Teacher.

(9) But he did not want you to look on him as a new God or any kind of innovation. Hear what he said: "In the head of the book it is written of me."[33] What he meant was this: "Long ago the prophets

27 Rom 11.33, also cited in *Disc.* 1.1.1.
28 Cf. Ps 39 (40).6.
29 *Ibid.* 7 and Heb 10.5.
30 Cf. Ps 39 (40).7 and Heb 10.7, where the words are quoted as if addressed by the Son to the Father, as is the case with the whole passage from Heb (5—9).
31 Cf. Heb 1.1—2.
32 Jn 1.17. B. Vawter, JBC 63:46, points out that this theme of the figures represented by Moses and the Law fulfilled in the realities coming from Christ is frequent in Jn; cf. e.g., in 6.31—33.
33 Ps 39(40).8 and Heb 10.7. Chrysostom conceives of the book as a scroll which was unrolled little by little. In *Demonstration* 8 (PG 48.824) he says this text makes two points clear: first, He is to come; second, He is to come after the sacrifices have been rejected. But this would be clear only if Chrysostom had repeated the first part of verse 7: "Sacrifice and oblation

foretold my coming and at the beginning of the Scriptures they opened them a little to give men a glimpse of the knowledge that I am God."

III

And so, at the beginning of creation, when God said: "Let us make mankind in our image and likeness,"[34] he was revealing to us in a rather obscure way the divinity of his Son, to whom he was then speaking. Later on the Psalmist showed that this new religious way of life did not contradict the old, but that it was God's will that the old sacrifice be abolished and the new sacrifice replace the old. The new was an extension of the right way of worship; it did not oppose or fight with the old. He showed this when he said: "In the head of the book it is written of me," and added: "That I should do your will, O my God; I have desired it and your law in the midst of my heart."[35] And when he explained what God's will was, he made no mention of sacrifice or holocausts or offerings or toil and sweat, but said: "I have declared your justice in a great assembly."[36]

(2) What does he mean when he says: "I have declared your justice?" He did not simply say: "I have given," but, "I have declared." What does this mean? That he has justified our race not by right actions, not by toils, not by barter and exchange, but by grace alone. Paul, too, made this clear when he said: "But now the justice of God has been made manifest independently of the Law."[37] But

---

you did not desire" (Heb 10.5), or had included: "in holocausts and sin offerings you had no pleasure" (Heb 10.6), which he omits from the *Demonstration.*

34 Gn 1.16.

35 Ps 39(40).8–9.

36 *Ibid.* 10.

37 Rom 3.21. We are justified through faith in Christ. The Mosaic Law had nothing to do with this new manifestation of God's justice, at least directly (cf. Gal 2.19). The Christian dispensation of salvation is independent and

the justice of God comes through faith in Jesus Christ and not through any labor and suffering. And Paul took up again the testimony of this Psalm when he spoke as follows: "For the Law, having but a shadow of the good things to come, and not the exact image of the objects, is never able by the sacrifices which they offer continually, year after year the same, to perfect those who draw near. Therefore in coming into the world, he says: 'Sacrifice and oblation you wished not, [920] but a body you have fitted to me.' "[38] By this he meant the entrance into the world of the Only-begotten, the dispensation through the flesh.[39] For this is the way he came to us. He did not change place for place—how could he since he is everywhere and fills all things—but he was made visible to us through the flesh.

(3) Here we are fighting not only against the Jews but also against the pagans and many heretics. So let me uncover for you the deeper meaning here; let me search out the reason why Paul mentioned this text when he had countless testimonies to show that the Law and the old commonwealth and way of life are no longer productive. He did not cite this text simply by chance but he did it with good reason and ineffable wisdom. Everybody would agree that he had on this subject other testimonies, both of greater length and more vehe-

---

destined to supersede the Law (Rom 10.4). Cf. J. Fitzmeyer, JBC 53:37–38.

38 Heb 10.1 and 5; cf. Ps 39(40).7. "Shadow" is used in the sense of the foreshadowing of what is to come through Christ (cf. Col 2.17); the image in some way shares the reality of what it represents. So the annually repeated sacrifices on the Day of Atonement could not remove sin; they simply foreshadowed the sacrifice of Christ. Verse 5 attributes the words of the psalm to the Son at his Incarnation. Recall that the psalm is not a repudiation of the Jewish ritual but a statement of its relative inferiority to obedience. Since Christ expressed his obedience to God's will by offering his body in death, the LXX reading ("body" for "ears") is particularly applicable to him. Cf. M. Bourke, JBC 61:57–58. Chrysostom does not doubt the Pauline authorship of Heb. Important differences (stylistic, structural, even theological) from other Pauline works, however, make it likely that the author was a Jewish Christian of Hellenistic background (ibid. 61:2–3).

39 The Incarnation, by which the Father's eternal plan was realized and made manifest in the Son, who will reestablish all things both in heaven and on earth. Cf. Eph 1.3–10.

ment, if he had wished to bring them forward.

(4) For example, Isaiah said: "I have no pleasure in you. I have had enough of whole-burnt rams. I desire not fat of fatlings and blood of bulls and goats, not even if you come into my sight. Who required these things at your hands? If you offer me wheaten flour, it is in vain. Incense is an abomination to me."[40] And again, in another place: "I did not call you now, Jacob, nor, Israel, did I make you weary. You did not honor me with sacrifices nor did you worship me with your gifts; I did not weary you with frankincense, nor did you get incense for me with silver."[41] And Jeremiah said: "Why do you bring me incense from Sheba and cinnamon from a far country? Your holocausts have not pleased me."[42]And again: "Heap up your holocausts upon your sacrifices and eat up the flesh."[43] And another prophet said: "Take away from me the sound of your songs: I will not hear the canticle of your harps."[44] And again, there

---

40 Cf. Is 1.11–13 (LXX). The words: "I have no pleasure in you" are not found in LXX nor is verse 11 cited this way in *Disc.* 4.6.3, which conforms to LXX. However three MSS and Savile here read: "Isaiah showed that their sacrifices were hateful when he spoke in the person of God and said: 'What care I for the number of your sacrifices etc.' " with the LXX. In verse 12 Chrysostom omits "you shall be no more admitted to tread my court" of LXX. Again Isaiah is condemning the abuse, but not the institution, of sacrifice, although Chrysostom would have it that God detested the sacrifices of the Jews.

41 Cf. Is 43.22–24 (LXX). C. Stuhlmueller, JBC 22:21, notes that God's invectives are delivered in courtroom style (but will be followed by forgiveness). The prophet (Deutero-Is) shifts from pre-exilic days, when sacrifices were offered as if they were the very essence of religion (Is 1.11–15), into the exile when sacrifice was impossible. The spirit of the past, which gloried in elaborate ritual, continues into the present and burdens God with its offenses. But it is not God's responsibility that Israel despairs over its deprivation of temple sacrifice and all "human" means of expiation. Israel's complaints are making God weary. Both Israel and God are weary but for different reasons: Israel is weary of its loss of sacrifice, God of their complaints. Of course Chrysostom understands the passage as a divine condemnation of sacrifice.

42 Cf. Jer 6.20 (LXX). G. Couturier, JBC 19:23, notes that Jer here refers to luxury offerings imported from Arabia. Again Chrysostom looks on the text as a prophetic indictment against exterior cult.

43 Jer 7.21. The indictment continues.

44 Am 5.23 (LXX). P. King, JBC 14:19, indicates the place of song and music in ritual. While sacrifice was being offered, hymns were sung to the accompaniment of instruments. Cf. *Disc.* 1.7.2, where Chrysostom quotes

was another text, where the Jews were saying: "Will the Lord receive it in place of holocausts if I give my first-born for my wickedness, the fruit of my body for the sin of my soul?"[45] And the prophet reproved them and said: "It has been announced to you what is good and what the Lord God requires of you, that you love mercy, do judgment and justice, and be ready to walk behind your God."[46] David also spoke in the same vein when he said: "I will not take calves from your house nor goats from your flocks."[47]

(5) When Paul had so many testimonies in which God surely rejects those sacrifices, the times of the new moon, the sabbaths, the festivals, why did he omit all these and mention just that one text?[48] Many of the infidels and many of the Jews themselves who are now doing battle with me maintain that their commonwealth and way of life was not abolished because it was imperfect or its place taken by a greater way of life—I mean ours—but because of the sinfulness of those who offered the sacrifices in those days. And Isaiah certainly did say: "If you stretch out your hands, I will turn away my eyes from you: and if you multiply your prayers, I will not hear."[49] Then, to give the reason for this, he went on to say: "For your hands [921] are full of blood."[50] These words are not an accusation made against the sacrifices; they are an indictment of the sinfulness of those who offered them. God rejected their sacrifices because they offered them with bloodstained hands.

(6) Again, when David said: "I will not take calves from your

---

this verse to prove God's hatred and rejection of the Jewish festivals as well as their danger for Judaizing Christians.

45 Cf. Mi 6.7 (LXX). NAB note says here that through Canaanite influence the abominable practice of human sacrifice had been introduced under impious kings (2 Kgs [4 Kgs] 16.3; 21.6) such as Ahaz and Manasseh.

46 Mi 6.8 (LXX). In verse 6 the people had asked the prophet how they should worship the Lord and had proposed various forms of sacrifice. Here is Micah's answer (cf. Dt 26.16; Zec 7.9; Mt 23.23).

47 Ps 49(50).9.

48 I.e., Rom 3.21 and Heb 10.1,5. In *Disc.* 4.5.6 Chrysostom speaks of the observances of sacrifices, sabbaths, and new moons as unessential.

49 Is 1.15. The gesture of prayer, with hands outstretched and palms open toward heaven, is rejected because the hands are bloodstained with crime. Cf. F. Moriarty, JBC 16:8.

50 Is 1.15.

house nor goats from your flocks,"[51] he went on to add: "But to the sinner God said: 'Why do you declare my justices and take my covenant in your mouth? You hated discipline and cast my words behind you. If you saw a thief, you ran along with him and you threw in your lot with adulterers. Your mouth abounded with injustice and your tongue wrapped up deceits in your words. You sat down and spoke slander against your brother and set a stumbling— block for your mother's son.' "[52] This makes it clear that in this instance God did not simply reject sacrifices, but that he rejected them because those who offered them were adulterers and thieves and plotted against their brothers. So these enemies of mine maintain that, since each prophet accuses those who offer the sacrifices, his prophecy is saying that this is the reason why God rejected their sacrifices.

IV

This is what my opponents say to me. But Paul dealt them a knockout blow and said enough to shut their shameless mouths when he cited as his witness the text I discussed.[53] When Paul wished to prove that God had rejected the old commonwealth and way of life, because it was imperfect, and that he had rendered it inoperative, he took as his testimony that text in which no accusation is made against those who offered the sacrifices. He used a text

---

51 Ps 49(50).9. In verses 7–15 Yahweh gives a discourse on sacrifice, the point of which is that sacrifices cannot control God for "all the animals" (verse 10) are his. He does not rebuke the people for the number of their sacrifices (8). But he has no need of sacrifice; he is independent of all things because all things belong to him. What he asks is the people's personal involvement and commitment in the liturgical sacrifices. Cf. R. Murphy, JBC 35:66.

52 Cf. Ps 49(50).16–20. Verses 16–23 give a second discourse on true obedience, which condemns the insincerity of the wicked man and his sins of theft, adultery, and calumny. Cf. JBC 35:66.

53 Heb 10.5–7 and Ps 39(40).7–9.

which makes it clear that the sacrifice was in itself imperfect. For the prophet David made no accusation against the Jews; he simply said: "Sacrifice and oblation you did not desire, but a body you fitted to me: in holocausts and sin offerings you had no pleasure."[54] (2) In explanation of this text Paul said: "He annuls the first covenant in order to establish the second."[55] If David had said: "Sacrifice and oblation you did not desire," and then said no more, their argument would have some place to defend itself. But since he also said: "But a body you fitted to me," and showed that another sacrifice was brought in to replace it, he left no hope for the future that the old sacrifice would return. And in explaining this, Paul said "Through this offering we have been sanctified in the will of Christ;"[56] and also: "If the blood of bulls and goats and the sprinkled ashes of a heifer sanctify the unclean for the cleansing of the flesh, how much more will the blood of Christ, who through the Holy Spirit offered himself unblemished, cleanse our conscience from dead works?"[57] This gives us abundant proof, then, that those

---

54 Cf. Ps 39(40).7 and Heb 10.5−6.
55 Cf. Heb 10.9. The author of Heb looks on God's preference for obedience rather than sacrifice as a repudiation of OT sacrifices and their replacement by the voluntary self-offering of Christ.
56 Ibid. 10. M. Bourke, JBC 61:58, states that the offering is the will of God, carried out by Christ, that he offer in death the body which God has fitted to him. The offering of Jesus' body is the same as the shedding of his blood. Each expresses the total self−offering of Christ. Chrysostom has inverted the two parts of the verse without appreciable difference in meaning.
57 Cf. Heb 9.13−14. M. Bourke, JBC 61:53, points out that in the Old Law the blood of the sacrifices (Lv 16.3, 14, 15), the sprinkled ashes (Nm 19.9, 17−19), and lustral waters (ibid.) conferred external ritual purity on those defiled by touching corpses, bones, or graves (ibid. 19). Chrysostom reads verse 14 as I have translated it, but NT reads "through the eternal spirit," which Bourke says is neither the Holy Spirit nor the divine nature of Jesus but "the life which cannot be destroyed" of 7.16, where the emphasis is on Christ's eternal priesthood in contrast with the transitory OT priesthood. The structure of Heb 9 favors this because it shows that the earthly sanctuary is a type of the heavenly sanctuary (6−10) where Christ is high priest and victim (11−14) through whom redemption comes by a new covenant (15−17). Verse 14 emphasizes the eternity of Christ's one and only sacrifice as contrasted with the annually repeated sacrifices on the Day of

old rituals have stopped, that a new rite has been brought forward to replace them, and that the old will not hereafter be restored.

(3) What is left to discuss now? For some time I have been anxious to prove to you that their kind of priesthood has disappeared and will never return. Let me make this expressly clear from the Scriptures themselves. First I must preface this with a few remarks, so that my explanation of what the Scriptures say may be even more obvious.

(4) On his return from Persia, Abraham begot Isaac; Isaac then begot Jacob; Jacob begot the twelve patriarchs[58] from whom arose the twelve tribes—or, rather, the thirteen, [922] because, in Joseph's place, his two sons, Ephraim and Manasseh, became leaders of tribes.[59] A tribe was named after each of Jacob's sons: for example, the tribe of Ruben, of Simeon, of Levi, of Judah, of Naphthali, of Gad, of Asher, of Benjamin.[60] So also in Joseph's case, his two sons, Manasseh and Ephraim, gave their names to two tribes; one was called the tribe of Ephraim and the other the tribe of Manasseh. Of these thirteen tribes all but one had fields and large incomes, all but one tilled the fields and devoted themselves to all the other secular pursuits. But the tribe of Levi was honored with the priesthood; it alone was freed from secular work. They did not till the farms, nor follow trades, nor do anything else of the sort, but devoted their attention exclusively to the priesthood.[61] From all the people they received tithes of wine and wheat and barley and everything else; all gave them tithes and this was their income. No one from any other tribe could ever become a priest. From this tribe—I

Atonement. If we keep this in mind, Chrysostom's *a fortiori* argument, which logically concludes only to the superior cleansing power of Christ's sacrifice, may be extended to include, as Chrysostom does, the end of the old ritual (which will never be restored) and its replacement by a new (and eternal) rite. Furthermore, OT blood sprinkling produced only ritual cleanness; the purifying power of Christ's sacrifice extends to the defiled conscience and purifies it from dead works, i.e., the sins which caused spiritual death.

58 Cf. Acts 7.8; Gn 17.10; 21.2–4; 25.24–26; 29.32; 35.22.
59 Cf. Gn 48.5. Jacob adopted the two sons of Joseph.
60 Cf. Ex 1.2–4. Chrysostom omits Issachar, Zebulun, and Dan.
61 Cf. Nm 18.1–6, 21.

mean the tribe of Levi—came Aaron, and, by succession, his descendants received the priesthood; no one from another tribe ever
became a priest. And so these Levites received tithes from the rest
and, in this way, supported themselves.[62]

(5) But in the time of Abraham, before the day of Jacob and
Isaac, before the coming of Moses, when the Law had not yet been
written, when the priesthood did not clearly belong to the Levites,
when there was no Meeting Tent or temple, before the division of
the people into tribes, before Jerusalem existed, before anyone at all
had yet taken control of the government among the Jews, there was
a man named Melchizedek, a priest of the Most High God. This
Melchizedek was at the same time both priest and king; he was to be
a type of Christ, and Scripture makes clear mention of this.[63] For
Abraham attacked the Persians, rescued his nephew Lot from their
hands, seized all the spoils, and was returning from his mighty victory over his foes. After describing those events the Scripture had
this to say about Melchizedek. "Melchizedek, the king of Salem,
brought out bread and wine, for he was a priest of the Most High
God. He blessed Abraham and said, 'Blessed be Abraham by the
Most High God, creator of heaven and earth; blessed be the Most
High God who has delivered your enemies into your hand.' Then
Abraham gave him a tenth of everything."[64]

(6) If, then, any prophet clearly says that after Aaron, after that
priesthood, after those sacrifices and oblations, there will rise up
another priest, not from Levi's tribe but from another tribe from
which no one ever became a priest, a priest not according to the

---

62 Cf. *ibid.* 21–32.
63 Cf. Gn 14.18 and Heb 7.1–3, where Melchizedek's non-Levitical priesthood is a type of Christ's. He is without father or mother because they are
not mentioned in OT. M. Bourke points out that, in accordance with a
principle of rabbinic exegesis, what is not mentioned in the Torah does not
exist. Since the OT does not speak of Melchizedek's ancestors, birth, or
death, he and his priesthood are eternal. But the author of Heb knows that
no priest, except Jesus, remains forever (7.24). His interest in Melchizedek
is solely in his "eternal" priesthood and his superiority to Levitical priests,
two points which he prefigures and which are verified in Jesus. Cf. JBC
61:38–39.
64 Cf. Gn 14.18–20.

order of Aaron but according to the order of Melchizedek, it is just as clear that the old priesthood has ceased to exist and another, a new priesthood has been brought in to take its place. If the old priesthood were going to remain effective, it would have to be called a priesthood according to the order of Aaron and not according to the order of Melchizedek. Did any prophet speak of this new priesthood? Yes, that same prophet who before spoke about the sacrifices and who was speaking of Christ when he said: "The Lord said to my Lord: 'Sit at my right hand.' "[65]

V

[923] To prevent anyone from suspecting that this was said about some ordinary man, it was not Isaiah nor Jeremiah, nor any prophet who was a common man that said it, but King David himself. But a king cannot call any man his Lord; it is God alone whom he can call Lord. If David were a common man, perhaps one of those shameless people would have said that he was talking about a mere human being. But now, since David was a king, he would not have called a man his Lord. If David were talking about some ordinary person, how could he have said that this person sat at the right hand of that ineffable and mighty Majesty? That would have been impossible. But of this person David said: "The Lord said to my Lord: 'Sit at my right hand till I make your enemies your footstool.' "[66]

---

65 Ps 109(110).1. Chrysostom has no doubt about the Davidic authorship and interprets the psalm as referring to Christ; his messianic dignity makes him king, royal priest, and victor over his foes. If the author is not David but a court poet, verse 1 would mean "Yahweh said to my master [the king]," and the psalm would proclaim an oracle given to David by God.

66 *Ibid.* Mt 22.44 shows similar certainty of Davidic authorship, but the purpose of Ps 109(110) is to suggest the mystery of his person and his transcendent superiority to David. The command to sit suggests the enthronement of the new king in a place of honor, at the right hand of God. Vic-

(2) Then, to keep you from thinking that this person was weak and powerless, David went on to say: "With you is the principality in the day of your strength."[67] And he made it still clearer when he said: "From the womb before the daystar I begot you."[68] But no mere man was begotten before the daystar. "You are a priest forever, according to the order of Melchizedek."[69] He did not say: "According to the order of Aaron." So ask the Jews why David brought in another priest, according to the order of Melchizedek, if the old priesthood was not going to be abolished.

(3) At any rate, see how Paul made this still clearer when he came to this text. After Paul said of Christ: "As he [David] says also in another place, 'You are a priest forever according to the order of Melchizedek,' "[70] the Apostle went on to say: "On this point we have much to say, and it is difficult to explain it."[71] After he reproved his disciples[72] —but I must cut the account short—he went on to tell them who Melchizedek was and to tell the story. "He met Abraham returning from the slaughter of the kings and blessed

---

tory over his enemies is also promised. The image of the footstool belongs to the courtly style. Cf. R. Murphy, JBC 35:126. NAB note says that vanquished enemies had to permit their victor to put his feet on their prostrate bodies as a sign of their submission. NAB also states that the psalmist addresses the Messiah as his superior; therefore he must be David's superior and not merely David's son or descendant. Cf. also Acts 2.34–35; 1 Cor 15.25; Heb 1.13; 10.13.

67 Cf. Ps 109(110).3. See JBC 35:126, which states that the text is corrupt and translation problematical. Chrysostom follows LXX.

68 Ps 109(110).3. Both in the first portion of the verse and here the emphasis is on the strength and mysterious birth of the king. As in Ps 2.7, the king is Yahweh's son. The daystar is the morning star (cf. Is 14.12); the implication is that of generation from eternity.

69 Cf. Ps 109(110).4. R. Murphy, JBC 35:126, states that the king is, as it were, successor to Melchizedek in his royal and priestly function. NAB note *ad loc.* indicates that there are three points of resemblance between Melchizedek, the prophetic type, and Christ, who fulfilled this prophecy: both are kings as well as priests, both offer bread and wine to God, and both have their priesthood directly from God and not through Aaron.

70 Heb 5.6.

71 *Ibid.* 11.

72 *Ibid.* The reproof is that they "have grown dull of hearing." They must be again taught the rudiments of the word of God because they have become as those in need of milk and not of solid food (verse 12).

him; to whom Abraham divided the tithes of all."[73] Then, to give some insight into Melchizedek, the type, he said: "Now consider how great this man is, to whom even Abraham the patriarch gave tithes of all."[74] He did not say this for no purpose but because he wanted to show that our priesthood is much greater than the Jewish priesthood. And the excellence of the realities is shown beforehand in the very types which foreshadow them.

(4) Abraham was the father of Isaac, the grandfather of Jacob, and the ancestor of Levi, for Levi was Jacob's son. The priesthood among the Jews began with Levi. So this man Abraham was the ancestor of the Levites and the Jewish priests. But in the time of Melchizedek, who is the type of our priesthood, Abraham had the rank of a layman. Two things make this clear. First, he gave tithes to Melchizedek, and it is the laymen who give tithes to the priests. Second, he was blessed by Melchizedek, and laymen are blessed by priests.[75]

(5) We again see the excellence of our priesthood when we find Abraham, the patriarch of the Jews, the ancestor of the Levites, receiving a blessing from Melchizedek and giving tithes to him. Surely the Old Testament says that Melchizedek blessed Abraham and exacted a tenth part from him. And Paul brought these very points to the fore and then said: "Consider how great this man is."[76] Who is "this man"? Paul told us. Melchizedek, "to whom even Abraham their patriarch gave tithes from the best portions of the spoils."[77] "And indeed they who are of the [924] priestly sons of Levi have a commandment to take tithes from the people, that is,

---

73 *Ibid.* 7.1–2. LXX of Gn 14.20 does not make clear who gave tithes to whom. The author of Heb, by adding Abraham as subject of the verb, makes obvious his understanding of who the donor was.

74 Cf. *ibid.* 4. The tithes recall the tenth part of all products of the land to be paid to the Levites, the priestly tribe (cf. Nm 18.20–32), according to the Mosaic Law. In Heb 7.12 the author will say that the connection between Law and priesthood is so close that the passing of the priesthood involves the passing away of the Law on which it was based. Cf. JBC 61:39.

75 Gn 14.18–20.

76 Heb 7.4.

77 Cf. *Ibid.*

from their brethren, though these also have come from the loins of Abraham."[78]

(6) What Paul means is this. He said that the Levites, who were priests among the Jews, received a commandment, according to the Law,[79] to take tithes from the other Jews. Although they all were descended from Abraham, both the Levites and the rest of the people, nonetheless the Levites took tithes from their brothers. But Melchizedek, who was not of their descent, because he was not a descendant of Abraham, and who was not of the tribe of Levi but from another nation, exacted a tenth part from Abraham, that is, he took tithes from him.

(7) Not only this, but he did something further. What is that? He again blessed Abraham, even though it was Abraham who had received the promises.[80] What does this show? That Abraham was much inferior to Melchizedek. How can this be? "Beyond all contradiction, that which is less is blessed by the superior,"[81] so that, unless Abraham, the ancestor of the Levites, were inferior to Melchizedek, Melchizedek would not have blessed him, nor would Abraham have given tithes to Melchizedek. But Paul wished to show that, because of the excellence of Melchizedek, that inferiority might have continued, so he went on to say: "Even Levi, the receiver of tithes, was also, so to speak, made subject to tithes, through Abraham."[82]

(8) What does he mean by "was made subject to tithes"? Although Levi was not yet born, through his father, he, too, gave tithes to Melchizedek. As Paul said: "He was still in the loins of his father when Melchizedek met him."[83] This is why Paul was careful to say:

---

78 Cf. *ibid.* 5 and Nm 18.21.
79 Cf. Heb 7.5. Chrysostom omitted the phrase "according to the Law" in his citation just above, but it is found in Heb 7.5.
80 Cf. Heb 7.6 and Gn 17.1–22.
81 Heb 7.7. This contradicts what is said in OT (cf. Jb 31.20; 2 Sm [2 Kgs] 14.22); perhaps the author of Heb is here giving a liturgical rule rather than a general principle. Cf. JBC 61:39.
82 Heb 7.9. Levi here represents both Jacob's son and the priestly tribe descended from him. Cf. JBC 61:39.
83 Heb 7.10.

"So to speak." He went on to tell why he said this. "If then perfection was by the Levitical priesthood (for under it the people received the Law), what further need was there that another priest should rise, according to the order of Melchizedek, and said not to be according to the order of Aaron?"[84]

(9) What is it that Paul meant? He meant this. If the Jewish religion was perfect, if the Law was not a foreshadowing of future blessings but had been efficacious in every respect, if it was not going to yield to another Law, if the old priesthood was not going to disappear and make way for another priesthood, why did the prophet say: "You are a priest forever according to the order of Melchizedek"?[85] He should have said: "according to the order of Aaron." This is why Paul said: "If then perfection was by the Levitical priesthood, what further need was there that another priest should rise, according to the order of Melchizedek, and said not to be according to the order of Aaron."[86]

(10) This surely made it clear that the old priesthood was ended and that another much better and more sublime priesthood had been brought in to replace it. When we admit this, we should also agree that another way of life suited to the new priesthood will be brought in and another Law given, and clearly this is ours. Paul prepared us for this when he said: "When the priesthood is changed, it is necessary that a change of law be made also, for the author of these is one."[87]

---

84 *Ibid.* 11. The perfection here mentioned is not that of priestly consecration but is the power to forgive sin. The Law was given to Israel as a means of union with God; the Levitical priesthood was the instrument by which the Law was meant to achieve its purpose. Cf. JBC 61:40 and NAB note *ad loc.*
85 Ps 109(110).4.
86 Heb 7.11.
87 *Ibid.* 12. The truth here expressed is peculiar to the situation of Israel where the priesthood and the Mosaic Law were inseparably linked. The priesthood was the basis on which the Law was given to the people. Hence, the passing away of the priesthood involves the passing away of the Law. Cf. JBC 61:40. The words "for the author of these is one" are italicized in the PG Greek text as part of the scriptural quotation and were so understood by Erasmus, the Latin translator. However, they are not found in Heb 7.12. Perhaps these words give Chrysostom's reason why a change in priesthood necessitates a change in Law.

(11) Many of the prescriptions of the Law were devoted to the ministries of the priesthood, and the old priesthood has been abolished. Since another priesthood was brought in to replace the old, it is clear also that a greater Law had to be brought in to replace the old. To make clear who it was of whom these words were spoken, Paul said: "For he of whom these things are said is from another tribe, from which no one has ever done service at the altar. For it is evident [925] that our Lord has sprung out of Judah, and Moses spoke nothing at all about priests when referring to this tribe."⁸⁸

(12) Christ clearly is sprung from that tribe, namely the tribe of Judah; Christ surely is a priest according to the order of Melchizedek; Melchizedek is surely much more venerable than Abraham. Then we must also admit from every angle that one priesthood is being brought in to replace another and that it is much more sublime than the old priesthood. If the type was such, if it was more magnificent than the Jewish priesthood, the reality which it foreshadowed is itself still much more magnificent. This is the point which Paul was making when he said: "And it is yet far more evident if there arise another priest, according to the likeness of Melchizedek, who has become so not according to the Law of carnal commandment, but according to a life that cannot end."⁸⁹

(13) What did Paul mean when he said: "Not according to the Law of carnal commandment, but according to a life that cannot end"? He meant that none of Christ's commandments are carnal commandments. He did not order the sacrifice of sheep and calves; he ordered us to worship God through the virtue of our lives; as our reward for this, he set the prize of a life that cannot end. And again, after we had died as the price of our sins, he came and raised us up;

---

88 Heb 7.13–14 "He of whom these things are said" is, of course, Jesus, the priest according to the order of Melchizedeck of Ps 109(110).4. The author of Heb knows and accepts the tradition that Jesus was of the family of David (cf. Rom 1.3). He does not share the Qumran community's expectation of a priestly messiah belonging to the Levitical family of Aaron and of a royal messiah descended from Judah through David. See R.E. Brown, "The Messianism of Qumran," *Catholic Biblical Quarterly* 19 (1957) 53–82. Judaism probably had no expectation such as that of the author of Heb. Cf. JBC 61:40.

89 Heb 7.15–16. The Law of carnal commandment, according to current

he saved us by freeing us from a double death: the death from sin and the death of the flesh. Since he came bringing us such gifts, Paul said: "Not according to the Law of carnal commandment, but according to a life that cannot end."[90]

VI

I have, therefore, now proved what was left to be proved. I have proved that, because the priesthood was changed, it was reasonable and necessary that there also be a change of Law. And again I was able to prove this very point by bringing forward as my witnesses the prophets. They testified that the Law will be changed, that the old commonwealth and way of life will be transformed for the better, and that never again will a king arise for the Jews.

(2) But I must say only as much as my audience can listen to and heed; I must not crowd everything together and say it all at once. Therefore, I will store up the rest for another occasion and, for the present, I will stop my instruction at this point. But let me first exhort your loving assembly to keep in mind what I have said and to connect it up with what I said before. And what I asked you before, I shall now ask you again. Rescue your brothers and show great concern for our members who have grown negligent. I do not under-

---

exegesis, is the legal requirement (cf. Nm 3.3, 10) which provided that OT priestly succession be confined to Levites who were of the family of Aaron. The life that cannot end is the life Jesus possesses because of his resurrection. He is priest by virtue of his exaltation (5.5–6) rather than because of his divinity. The Aaronic priesthood was not confirmed by oath; Jesus' was (7.20–25), and he will have no successor in that eternal priesthood. Cf. JBC 61:41. Although Chrysostom's explanation is somewhat simplistic, it has the merit of showing that the purifying power of Christ's priesthood and sacrifice not only surpasses the Aaronic ritual purification but extends to man's double death, from his sin and in his flesh. Chrysostom's exegesis seems to fit Heb 9.13–14 (see above Disc. 7.4.2) better than 7.15–16.
90 Heb 7.16.

take this great task just to hear myself talk or to enjoy the tumult of your applause; I do it to bring those who have been cut off back to the path of truth.

(3) Let no one say to me: "I have nothing in common with him;[91] I would be lucky to manage well my own affairs." No one can manage his own affairs if he does not love his neighbor and work for his salvation. This is what Paul meant when he said: "Let no one seek his own interests, but those of his neighbor."[92] He knew that your own interests lie in what benefits your neighbor. You are in good health, but your brother is sick. So then, if you are in your right mind, you will be distressed over him who is in distress and you will, in this matter, follow the example of that blessed soul who said: "Who is weak, and I am not weak? Who is made to stumble, and I am not inflamed?"[93]

(4) If we find joy in tossing down a couple of obols[94] and spending a little [926] money on the poor, what great pleasure will we reap if we can save men's souls? What recompense will we enjoy in the life to come? Certainly, in this world, as often as we run into these men, we will derive great pleasure from meeting them, because we recall the good turn we did for them. When we see them in the next world before the dread tribunal of judgment, we will experience a great confidence. When the unjust, the greedy, the plunderers, and those who have inflicted countless evils on their neighbors go before this tribunal and see their victims — and they surely will see

---

91 Selfishness is no excuse for ignoring the Judaizing Christians. Cf. *Disc.* 4.7.1. Chrysostom urged the stronger brethren to hunt them down in *Disc.* 1.8.5–7 and 6.7.10, to rebuke them sharply in 2.3.7–9, and to be meddlesome and interfere with their brother's wrongdoing in 4.7.9 and 5.12.13.
92 1 Cor 10.24. Cf. *ibid.* 33. Charity is the supreme law which must regulate the Christian's behavior.
93 2 Cor 11.29. Charity further demands that the Christian be righteously angry at what causes others to fall. The Greek verb ("I am inflamed") implies that Paul suffers as though being burned alive when members of the Church are led into sin. Cf. J. O'Rourke, JBC 52:40. Chrysostom cites the same text in *Disc.* 4.7.10 to urge the Christians to realize that they, too, suffer when their fellow members, the Judaizing Christians, are rotting with disease.
94 Two obols (coins) would be worth about a nickel.

them, as Christ says, and as is clear from the story of the rich man and Lazarus[95] — they will not be able to open their mouths nor to say a word in their own defense. They will be overwhelmed with the great shame of their condemnation and will be swept off from the sight of their victims into the rivers of flame.

(5) But when those who taught and instructed their neighbors in this life stand before the tribunal, they will see those whom they saved pleading in their behalf. And they will be filled with great confidence and trust. Paul made this clear when he said: "We are your boast, as you will also be ours."[96] Tell me, when will this be? "In the day of our Lord Jesus Christ."[97]

(6) And, again, Christ gave good counsel when he said: "Make friends for yourselves with the mammon of wickedness, so that when you fail they may receive you into the everlasting dwellings."[98] You see that much confidence will come to us from those to whom we have done good in this life. But if there are so many prizes, such great recompense, such ample repayment for the money we spent on others, how will we fail to gain many great blessings when we help a soul? Tabitha clothed widows and aided the poor and came back to life from the dead.[99] If the tears of those to whom she did good brought her departed soul back to her body— and this before the day of resurrection—will not the tears of those

---

95 Cf. Lk 16.19–31.
96 Cf. 2 Cor 1.14.
97 Cf. *ibid.* Chrysostom understands this as the Last Judgment at the second coming of Christ. Cf. 1 Cor 1.8.
98 Lk 16.9. This is a moralization to the parable of the unjust steward (*ibid.* 1–13). Mammon means that in which one puts his trust (cf. verses 10–12). Confr. note says the mammon of wickedness is riches, which lead men to sin. C. Stuhlmueller, JBC 44:120, explains verse 9 thus: "Use prudently the wealth which you have, in order to ensure your status within the final age; remember that wealth tends to lead men to dishonesty. When earthly goods fail, you will be welcomed into the everlasting tents [i.e., dwellings] of the Kingdom of God." He also notes that some Greek texts read "when you fail," as does Chrysostom, whose exegesis of the text is substantially the same.
99 Cf. Acts 9.36–41. Peter is the agent in this miraculous story, which bears some resemblance to that of Jesus' restoration to life of the daughter of Jairus (Lk 8.40–42, 49–56).

whom you rescued and saved do something to help you? The widows who stood around Tabitha's corpse pointed out that she who had died was alive. In the same way, those whom you saved in this life will stand around you on the day of judgement. They will snatch you from the fire of gehenna[100] and see to it that you enjoy His loving-kindness in abuudance.

(7) Knowing, then, what we now know, let us not be roused to fervor only for the present hour; fan the fire you now have, go forth, and spread salvation over the city; even if you do not know them, get busy and find those who have this sickness. I shall be all the more eager to speak to you when I have found out from your very deeds that I did not scatter my seed on rocky ground. And you yourselves will be more eager to practice virtue. In money matters, the man who has made a profit of two gold pieces gets a greater enthusiasm to collect and amass a profit of ten or twenty pieces. This happens, too, in the matter of virtue. The man who has succeeded in doing a good deed gets some encouragement and motivation from doing this right action. The result is that he will undertake other good deeds.

(8) Let us, then, rescue our brothers and store up beforehand pardon for our sins. Much more, let us first store up abundant confidence and, before all else, let us see to it that God's name is glorified. To do this, let us take our wives, children, and households and go out after this game and quarry.[101] Let us drag from the snares of the devil those [927] whom he has made captive to his will. And let us not stop until we have done everything in our power to rescue them, whether they heed or reject our words. But it would be impossible, if they are Christians, for them not to heed us.

(9) Still, I do not want you to have even the excuse that they would not heed you. Let me say this. If you pour out many words and do everything in your power and still see that he refuses to heed you, then bring him to the priests. By the help of God's grace the priests will surely overcome their quarry. But it will all be your doing, because it was you who took him by the hand and led him to

---

100 See J. McKenzie, "Gehenna," DB 299–300. Cf. *Disc.* 1.7.10 and 8.5.5.
101 Cf. *Disc.* 1.8.5–7; 2.1.3–5; 6.7.10.

us. Let husbands talk to their wives and wives to their husbands, fathers to their children and friends to friends.

(10) Let the Jews learn how we feel. Let it also become known to those who side with the Jews, even though they pretend to be ranked with us. [928] We have an eager and vigilant concern for our brothers who have deserted over to the Jewish side. When the Jews find this out, it will be they, rather than we, who thrust out those of our number who frequent their synagogue. I should say, there will be no one hereafter who will dare to flee to them, and the body of the Church will be unsullied and pure.

(11) It is God's will that all men be saved and come to a knowledge of the truth.[102] May he give you strength for this hunt and may he lead them back from this error. May he save us all together and make us worthy of the kingdom of heaven for his glory, since it is fitting that his be the glory and the power for ever and ever. Amen.

---

102 Cf. 1 Tm 2.4.

DISCOURSE VIII

ONE IS THE FASTING [927] of the Jews,[1] or rather, the drunkenness of the Jews.[2] Yes, it is possible to be drunk without wine; it is possible for a sober man to act as if he is drunk and to revel like a prodigal. If a man could not get drunk without wine, the prophet would never have said: "Woe to those who are drunk not from wine;"[3] if a man could not get drunk without wine, Paul would never have said: "Do not be drunk with wine."[4] For he said this as if there were a possibi-

---

1 If *Discourses* IV–VIII constitute a series, this sermon would have been given after the Ten Days of Penitence and the Monday following Sukkot, probably in the year 387. Cf. Introd. III 25. Given the content of the sermons already delivered, what now remains is to reclaim and rehabilitate those who have fallen into the Judaizing trap.

2 In *Disc.* 1.2.5 the Jews' hardness of heart came from a gluttony and drunkenness which made them reject Christ's yoke when they should have been fasting; now their fasting is untimely and an abomination (cf. *Disc.* 1.2.6). Those who fasted in Isaiah's day (cf. Is 58.4–5) should have been properly contrite instead of drunk with anger; now when the Jews fast, they dance in the marketplace and go to licentious excesses. Their pretext is that they are fasting, but they act like men who are drunk (cf. *Disc.* 1.2.7). Note that their drunkenness does not come from wine.

3 Cf. Is 29.9. The chapter deals with the Assyrians' assault on Jerusalem, but the invaders will fail because of Yahweh's protection. In her blindness and drunkenness (which makes her stagger, but not from strong drink) Jerusalem refuses to believe God's revelation that she will be saved. F. Moriarty, JBC 16:49, says that Judah's moral lethargy and persistent refusal to listen to conscience will inevitably lead to the loss of all moral sense.

4 Eph 5.18.

lity of getting drunk some other way. And it is possible. A man can be drunk with anger, with unseemly desire, with greed, with vainglory, with ten thousand other passions. For drunkenness is nothing other than a loss of right reason, a derangement, and depriving the soul of its health.[5]

(2) Therefore, I would not be making too strong a statement if I should say that we find a drunkard not only in the man who is a heavy drinker of strong wine but we also find one in the man who nurtures some other passion in his soul. For the man in love with a woman who is not his wife, the man who spends his time with prostitutes, is a drunkard. The heavy drinker cannot walk straight, his speech is rude, his eyes cannot see things as they really are.[6] In the same way, the drunkard who is filled with the strong wine of his undisciplined passion is also unsound of speech; everything he utters is disgraceful, corrupt, crude, and ridiculous; he, too, cannot see things as they really are because he is blind to what he sees. Like a deranged man or one who is out of his wits, he imagines he sees everywhere the woman he yearns to ravish. No matter how many people speak to him at gatherings or banquets, at any time or place, he seems not to hear them; he strains after *her* and dreams of his sin; he is suspicious of everything and afraid of everything; he is no better off than some trap-shy animal.

(3) Again, the man in the grip of anger is drunk. In the same way as the other drunkards, his face becomes swollen, his voice grows rough, his eyes are bloodshot, his mind is darkened, his reason is

---

5 The notion of a man being drunk without wine is a favorite with Chrysostom. The ravages of passion are just as bad as the ravages of drink. There are parallel passages (which argue from the same two texts: Is 29.9 and Eph 5.18) in, e.g., *De Statuis* 1 (PG 49.22) and *De resurrectione Domini* (PG 50.434–36). The latter is particularly graphic and is quoted (along with others) in ACW 31.255–59. The worst thing is that drunkenness is a self-chosen demon, which robs a man of reason and leads not only to the pains of hell but to what is worse, the loss of God.

6 The drunkard is worse off than the demoniac. We can pity the demoniac but feel only anger and vexation at the drunkard because his condition is the result of his own negligence. Cf. ACW 31.256.

submerged, his tongue trembles, his eyes are out of focus, and he does not hear what is really said. His anger affects his brain worse than strong wine; it stirs up a storm and causes a distress that cannot be calmed.

(4) But if the man in the grip of passion or anger is drunk, this is all the more true of the impious man who blasphemes God, [928] who goes against his laws and never is willing to renounce his untimely obstinacy. This man is drunk, mad, and much worse off than insane revelers, even if he does not seem aware of his condition. And this is the characteristic which most marks a drunkard: he has no awareness of his unseemly behavior. This, in fact, is the special danger of madness: those who suffer from it do not know they are sick. So, too, the Jews are drunk but do not know they are drunk.

(5) Indeed, the fasting of the Jews, which is more disgraceful than any drunkenness, is over and gone. But let us not stop thinking ahead for our brothers, let us not consider that our concern for them is now no longer timely. See what soldiers do. Suppose they have met the enemy and routed them. As they return from pursuing the foe, they do not immediately rush back to camp. First they go back to the battlefield to pick up their fallen comrades. They bury the dead but, if they see among the corpses men who are not mortally wounded but are still breathing, they give them as much first aid as they can, they pick them up, and carry them back to their camp. Then they extract the dart, call the physicians, wash away the blood, apply remedies to the wounds, and by giving them every care, they bring the wounded back to health.

(6) Therefore, we must do the same. By God's grace, we made the prophets our warriors against the Jews and routed them. As we return from pursuing our foes, let us look all around to see if any of our brothers have fallen, if the fast has swept some of them off, if any of them have shared in the festival of the Jews. Let us bury no one; let us, however, pick up every fallen man and give him the treatment he needs. In battles between armies of this world, a soldier cannot bring back to life or recover for further service a comrade who has fallen once and for all and died. But in a battle of this war of ours, even if a man has been mortally wounded, if we have good

will and the help of God's grace, we can take him by the hand and lead him back to life. Unlike a casualty in war, here it is not a man's body that dies, but his will and his resolution. And it is possible to restore to life a will that has died; it is possible to persuade a dead soul to come back [929] to its own proper life and to acknowledge again its Master.

II

We must not grow weary, my brothers, we must not become exhausted, we must not lose heart. Let no one say: "We should have done all we could to put them on their guard before the fast. Now that they have fasted, now that they have sinned, now that their transgression is complete, what use is there in helping them now?"

(2) If anyone knows what it means to look out for his brothers, he also knows that he must look out for them and show this concern now more than ever. We must not only put them on their guard before they sin but we must also extend a helping hand after they have fallen. Suppose God had done that from the beginning; suppose he had put us on our guard only before we sinned; suppose, after we had sinned, he had given us up and let us lie where we had fallen from one end of our life to the other. Then no one of us would ever have been saved.

(3) But God does not act that way. He loves men, he is kind to them, he desires their salvation above all things. And so he looks out for them even after they have sinned. He put Adam on his guard, too, before he sinned. He said to Adam: "From every tree in the garden you will eat; but from the tree of the knowledge of good and evil do not eat; for on the day you eat of it, you will surely die."[7]

---

7 Gn 2.16–17 (LXX). E. Maly, JBC 2:25, says that the whole meaning of the garden is that man's happiness is consequent on his remaining subject to God. For the Semites, "knowledge" means to experience in any way. Good and evil, as terms of polarity, signify a totality; hence, the experience is a total one, although not necessarily in the moral sense. E. Sutcliffe, CCHS 185, points out that verse 17 has been understood in two ways: either as a

God put Adam on his guard by giving him every warning he would need: he showed him the ease of fulfilling the law, the liberality of what it permitted, the harshness of the future punishment, and the speed with which it would come. For God did not say: "After one, two, or three days," but, "on the very day you eat of it, you will surely die."[8]

(4) God looked out for Adam very carefully; he instructed him, exhorted him, and gave him many blessings. But even so, Adam disregarded his commands and fell into sin. Still God did not say: "What good will it do now? What is the use of helping now? He ate the fruit, he fell into sin, he transgressed the law, he believed the devil, he dishonored my commandment, he was wounded, he became subject to death and died, he came under the judgment. What need have I to speak to him now?"

(5) But God said none of these things. Rather, he came immediately to Adam, spoke to him, and consoled him. Again God gave Adam another remedy—the remedy of toil and sweat.[9] God kept right on doing everything and exerting himself until he raised up fallen nature, rescued it from death, led it by the hand to heaven, and gave it greater blessings than it had lost. By the things God

---

threat of immediate death, which God did not carry out because the sinners were not obstinate; or the threat of subjection to the law of death since the sinners would no longer have access to the tree of life (3.22). He thinks the Hebrew text suggests the first.

8 Gn 2.17. Here Chrysostom also seems to understand the text as a threat of immediate death; where, in the next paragraph, he states that God did not say that Adam "became subject to death and died," we have a rhetorical device. God did not say it because he intended to console Adam and rehabilitate him by the remedy of toil and sweat. So, if it is a threat of immediate death, God does not carry it out because Adam was not obstinate and God desires all sinners to be saved.

9 Cf. Gn 3.17–19. Cf. E. Maly, JBC 2:28, who states that these verses indicate a constant biblical theme: nature's involvement in salvation history (cf. e.g., Ps 28[29]; Is 11.6–9). Man is cursed through the earth, which will bring forth thorns and thistles. There is no proportion between man's labor and its results. Man's natural lot is death, which comes, but not immediately, as the result of sin. Sin produces man's death, but life continues through man's labor, which is part of his punishment for sinning. God is both just and merciful.

himself did, he taught the devil that he would reap no profit from his plot. Satan had succeeded in driving men from Paradise but he would soon see them in heaven mingling with the angels.

(6) In the case of Cain, God did the same thing. Before Cain's great sin, God spoke plainly to him, warned him, and said: "You sinned; stop it. His [Abel's] refuge is in you and you will rule over him."[10] See God's wisdom and understanding. He said: "Because I have honored Abel, you are afraid he will take from you the privilege of the first-born; you are afraid he will take the first place, which is due to you."[11] For the first-born necessarily had a more honored position than the second-born. So God said: "Take courage, do not be afraid, feel no anguish over this. His refuge is in you, and you [930] will rule over him."[12] This is what God meant: "Stay in the honored position of the first-born; be a refuge, a shelter, and a protection for your brother. But do not jump to bloodshed; do not

---

10 Cf. Gn 4.7 (LXX). The full verse reads: "Did you not sin if you brought [your sacrifice] properly but failed to divide it properly? Stop it. His refuge is in you [or: his submission is to you] and you will rule over him." It is true that in the LXX text the negative is the first word in the sentence and separated from the conclusion ("you sinned") by the two conditional clauses. But Chrysostom has a disconcerting habit of quoting a text in part and often out of context. The LXX reading is far from that of NAB and JB; it must come from a corrupted text of obscure meaning.

11 Chrysostom's paraphrase looks to Gn 4.5, where Cain's offering is rejected and Abel's accepted. Cf. *Disc.* 1.7.3. JB note *ad loc.* states that the theme of the preference of the younger over the older runs through the bible and demonstrates the freedom of God's choice, his contempt for earthly standards of greatness, and his regard for the lowly. But 4.7 (LXX) suggests that Cain sinned in the way he offered his sacrifice and, hence, Abel's was preferred although Cain retained his rights of primogeniture.

12 Cf. Gn 4.7. The whole Cain and Abel incident is filled with anachronisms: civilization is well developed (verse 2); sacrifice has been instituted (3–4); other peoples exist who may threaten Cain's life (14–15). The Yahwistic tradition may have moved the story back to the beginnings of man to give it more universal meaning: man's revolt against God leads to his revolt against his fellow man; the crime of murder confirms the fallen state of man; God is just in his punishment of sin but merciful in applying his justice (15). Cf. E. Maly, JBC 2:30 and JB note *a* on p. 19.

come to that impious act of murder." Even so, Cain did not listen, he did not stop, he did not commit that murder, he did bathe his hand in blood from his brother's throat.[13]

(7) But then what happened? God did not say: "Let him go now. What further use is there in helping him? He did commit the murder, he did slay his brother. He scorned my advice; he dared to do that mad and unforgiveable deed of slaughter. Even though I was looking out for him, instructing him, counseling him, even though he enjoyed such benefits from me, he drove all these from his mind and paid them no heed. Let him go, then, and be hereafter cast from my sight. He has deserved no consideration from me."

(8) God neither said nor did anything like that. Instead, he came again to him, corrected him, and said: "Where is your brother Abel?"[14] When Cain said he did not know, God still did not desert him but he brought him, in spite of himself, to admit what he had done. After Cain said: "I do not know," God said: "The voice of your brother's blood cries to me."[15] What God was telling Cain was that the very deed proclaimed who the murderer was. And what did Cain say? "My guilt is too great to be forgiven. If you drive me from the land, I shall also be hidden from your face."[16]

---

13 Gn 4.8 merely states that Cain slew Abel; 4.11 speaks of "your brother's blood." That Cain cut Abel's throat is probably a rhetorical invention to make the crime more graphic.

14 *Ibid.* 9.

15 *Ibid.* 10. E. Maly, JBC 2:32, compares Lv 17.11–14 to show that for the ancients life was in the blood. Since human life comes from God in a special way (Gn 2.7), human blood spilled by a creature will cry out to its rightful Lord. Chrysostom's rather simplistic explanation may look to the first part of verse 10: "And the Lord said, 'What have you done?' " The author of Heb (12.24) speaks of the sprinkling of (Jesus') blood "which speaks better than Abel."

16 Cf. Gn 4.13–14 (LXX). E. Maly, JBC 2:32, points out that banishment from the land meant banishment to the desert places, where outlaws and demons dwell. Since Yahweh lives in a special way among his people, Cain's banishment will involve loss of God's presence, without which Cain will lose his protection and, hence, his life will be endangered.

(9) What Cain meant was this. "I have committed a sin too great for pardon, defense, or forgiveness; if it is your will to punish my crime, I shall lie exposed to every harm because your helping hand has abandoned me." And what did God do then? He said: "Not so! Whoever kills Cain shall be punished sevenfold."[17] What God said was this: "Do not fear that. You will live a long life. If any man does kill you, he will be subject to many punishments." For the number seven in the Scriptures means an indefinitely large number. So, then, Cain was stricken with many punishments—with torment and trembling, with grief and discouragement, with paralysis of his body. After he had undergone these penalties, as God put it: "Whoever kills you and frees you from these punishments will draw the same vengeance upon himself."

(10) The punishment of which God spoke seems to be excessively harsh but it does give us a glimpse of his great solicitude. God wanted men of later times to exercise self-control; therefore, he designed the kind of punishment which was capable of setting Cain free from his sin. If God had immediately destroyed him, Cain would have disappeared, his sin would have stayed concealed, and he would have remained unknown to men of after days. But as it is, God let him live a long time with that bodily tremor of his. The sight of Cain's palsied limbs was a lesson for all he met; it served to teach all men and exhort them never to dare do what he had done, so that they might not suffer the same punishment. And Cain himself be-

---

17 Gn 4.15. Both JB note *ad loc.* and JBC 2:32 see in this the institution of tribal blood—vengeance. Desert tribes were restrained from indiscriminate killing only by fear of the vengeance which would be exacted by the tribe or clan of the murdered one. Cain is to bear a mark or token which, according to JB, is not a brand of shame but a protecting sign to indicate that Cain belongs to a clan which will exact blood for blood. Since given by God, it is a sign of divine protection. Chrysostom makes no mention of the mark but must mean this sign when he says that Cain was stricken with many punishments of body and mind. These ailments are blessings in disguise since they not only punish him but can protect him and free him from his sin. They also serve to deter both Cain and others from committing further murders.

came a better man again. His trembling, his fear, the mental torment
which never left him, his physical paralysis kept him, as it were,
shackled. They kept him from leaping again to any other like deed
of boldness; they constantly reminded him of his former crime;
through them he achieved greater self-control in his soul.

III

As I was speaking, it occurred to me to bring up a further
question. Cain confessed his sin and condemned what he had done;
he said his crime was too great to be forgiven [931] and that he
deserved no defense. Why, then, could he not wash away his sins?
The prophet Isaiah said: "Be the first to tell your iniquities, that you
may be justified."[18] Why, then, was Cain condemned? Because he
did not tell his sins as the prophet commanded. Isaiah did not simply
say: "Tell your iniquities." What did he say? He said: "Be the first
to tell your iniquities."

(2) The question here is this. It is not simply a matter of telling,
but of being the first to tell and not waiting for an accuser to convict
you. But Cain did not tell first; he waited for God to accuse him.
And then, when God did accuse him, he denied it. After God had
once and for all given clear proof of what he had done, Cain then
told his sin. But this is no longer a confession.

(3) Therefore, beloved, when you commit sin, do not wait for
another man to accuse you but, before you are accused and indicted,
do you yourself condemn what you have done. Then, if someone

---

18 Is 43.26 (LXX). As verses 26–27 NAB has: "Speak up, prove your innocence! / Your first father sinned; your spokesman rebelled against me;" and
JB: "State your own case and prove your innocence. / Your first father
sinned, your mediators have rebelled against me." Neither has in verse 26
the word "first," which is essential to Chrysostom's argument, and this
word may have come into existence in the Bible MS known to Chrysostom
through a copyist/translator's error. The latter, seeing "first" (*prōtos*) in
the following verse (27—only LXX has the plural "first [fathers]"), may
have unconsciously entered it also in verse 26, thereby giving to "tell your
iniquities" the sense "be the first to tell your iniquities."

accuses you later on, it is no longer a matter of your doing the right thing in confessing, but of your correcting the accusation which he makes. And so it is that someone else has said: "The just man begins his speech by accusing himself."[19] So it is not a question of accusing but of being the first to accuse yourself and not waiting for others to accuse you.

(4) Peter certainly sinned gravely in denying Christ. But he was quick to remind himself of his sin and, before anyone accused him, he told of his error and wept bitterly.[20] He so effectively washed away his sin of denial that he became the chief of the apostles and the whole world was entrusted to him.

(5) But I must get back to my main topic. What I said has given us sufficient proof that we must not neglect or scorn our brothers who fall into sin. We must put them on their guard before they sin and we must show great concern for them after they have fallen. This is what physicians do. They tell people in good health what can preserve their health and what can ward off every disease. But if people have disregarded their instructions and have fallen sick, physicians do not neglect them but, especially at that time, they look out for the patients so that they may free them from their ailments.

---

19 Prv 18.17 (LXX). This is the first part of 17, which continues: "but when he has entered upon the attack, his adversary is convicted [or reproached]." Again Chrysostom uses a half-verse out of context to bolster an argument on which the full text has no bearing.

20 Cf. Mt 26.69–75; Mk 14.66–72; Lk 22.54–62; Jn 18.16–18, where Peter's denial is recounted. His fall had been predicted by Jesus (Mt 26. 33-35; Mk 14.26–31; Lk 22.31–34; Jn 13.37–38). His excessive self-confidence led him to a more grievous sin; the others were scandalized but Peter, despite his special protestations of loyalty, denied Christ three times before dawn of the following day. Here is a demonstration of common human weakness and a warning that infidelity lies very close to the surface. However, Peter, the Rock, neither concealed nor excused his lapse but found quickly the remedy of repentance and was rewarded with the Keys to the Kingdom.

(6) And Paul certainly did this too. Incest is a sin and serious transgression which is not even found among the pagans. But Paul did not scorn the man who had committed incest. Even though this man rebelled and refused to be cured, even though he kicked about and was unmanageable, Paul led him back to health and he did it in such a way as to unite him again to the body of the Church.²¹ Paul did not say to himself: "What good would it do? What would be the use? He committed incest, he has sinned; he does not want to give up his licentious ways; he is puffed up and boastful and has made his wound incurable. So let us be done with him and leave him in the lurch."

(7) Paul said none of these things. The very reason why he showed great concern for this sinner was that he saw the man had slipped into unspeakable wickedness. So Paul never gave up frightening him, threatening him, punishing him both through his own efforts and with the help of others. Paul left nothing undone, nothing untried until he brought the man to acknowledge his sin, to see his transgression. And, at last, Paul freed the man from every stain of sin.

---

21 The reference is to 1 Cor 5.1–5, where Paul says that a report has reached him (at Ephesus) that a man has his father's wife. Paul must not mean the man's own mother (or he would have said so) but his stepmother. Nor can we tell whether the woman's husband was alive or dead, whether stepson and stepmother were married, nor whether, if married, they had been wed before the stepson's conversion. In any event, such a union was regarded as incestuous and was contrary to Roman law (which was the law of Corinth) and Jewish law (cf. Lv 18.8; 20.11). Obviously, Paul also, by his apostolic authority, forbids such unions. Paul's censure is aimed chiefly at the authorities of the Corinthian Church. Since the letter is sent from Ephesus, what Chrysostom says in this and the following paragraph amounts to a rhetorical exaggeration. Actually, Paul excommunicates the man. Using terms from the Mosaic code (cf. Dt 17.7; 19.19; 22.24), he commands that the man be excluded from the community and be delivered to Satan to be afflicted physically, even unto death (cf. 1 Tm 1.20). But the purpose of the punishment and sentence passed by Paul is curative: that the sinner's spirit may be saved on the day of our Lord Jesus Christ. Cf. R. Kugelman, JBC 51:27; W. Rees, CCHS 1088.

(8) Now you do [932] the same thing Paul did. Imitate the
Samaritan in the gospel who showed such concern for the man who
had been wounded. For a Levite passed that way, a Pharisee passed
by, but neither of them turned to the man lying there. They just
went their way and, like the cruel, pitiless men they were, they left
him there. But a Samaritan, who was in no way related to this man,
did not hurry past but stopped, took pity on him, poured oil and
wine on his wounds, put him on his own animal, and brought him to
an inn. There he gave some money to the innkeeper and promised
him more for taking care of a man who was in no way related to
him.[22]

(9) He did not say to himself: " What do I care about him? I am a
Samaritan. I have nothing in common with him. We are far from the
city and he cannot even walk. What about this? Suppose he is not
strong enough to make the long journey. Am I going to bring in a
corpse, will I be arrested for murder, will I be held accountable for
his death?" Many a time people go along a road and see men who
have been wounded but are still breathing. But they pass them by

---

22 Cf. Lk 10.30–35. The parable of the Good Samaritan is found only in Lk.
To appreciate its significance one must recall the attitude of Jews toward
Samaritans. Sir (Ecclus) 50.25 refers to the Samaritans as loathsome and
not even a nation; Jn 4.9 states that Jews do not associate with Samaritans;
in Jn 9.48 the Jews call Jesus a Samaritan and possessed by a devil. In
telling the story Chrysostom omits the detail that a priest (a representative
of the religious leaders of the people) as well as a Levite passed by the
wounded man. He adds the Pharisee (omitted in Lk) or perhaps substi-
tutes him for the priest. The parable has always been a common field for
allegory: Christ as the Good Samaritan; the wounded man as the human
race robbed and despoiled by the devil; oil and wine, the sacraments; the
inn, the Church, etc. (cf. R. Ginns, CCHS 954). Chrysostom would see the
Samaritan as the stronger brethren; the wounded man as the Judaizing
Christian; the robbers as the Jews who have mortally hurt their victim's
soul by their demonic proselytizing; the oil and wine as the word of
instruction; the mildness, and patience of the brethren as an ointment and
bandage which will cure their own wounds as well as those of their victim-
ized fellow members; the Pharisee and Levite as those who are too selfish
to become involved.

not because they are stingy with their money, but because they are afraid that they themselves may be dragged into court and held accountable for the murder.

(10) That gentle and benevolent Samaritan feared none of these things. He scorned all such fears, put the man on his own beast, and brought him to an inn. He did not think of any of these things — neither the danger, nor the expense, nor anything else. If the Samaritan was so kind and gentle to a stranger, what excuse would we have for neglecting our own brothers when they are in deeper trouble? For those who have just observed the fast have fallen among robbers, the Jews. And the Jews are more savage than any highwaymen; they do greater harm to those who have fallen among them. They did not strip off their victim's clothes nor inflict wounds on his body as did those robbers on the road to Jericho. The Jews have mortally hurt their victim's soul, inflicted on it ten thousand wounds, and left it lying in the pit of ungodliness.

IV

Let us not overlook such a tragedy as that. Let us not hurry past so pitiable a sight without taking pity. Even if others do so, you must not. Do not say to yourself: "I am no priest or monk; I have a wife and children. This is work for the priests; this is work for the monks." The Samaritan did not say: "Where are the priests now? Where are the Pharisees now? Where are the teachers of the Jews?" But the Samaritan is like a man who found some great store of booty and got the profit.

(2) Therefore, when you see someone in need of treatment for some ailment of body or soul, do not say to yourself: "Why did so-and-so or so-and-so not take care of him?" You free him from his sickness; do not demand an accounting from others for their negligence. Tell me this. If you find a gold coin lying on the ground, do you say to yourself: "Why didn't so-and-so pick it up?" Do you not rush to snatch it up before somebody else does?

(3) Think the same way about your fallen brothers; consider that tending his wounds is like finding a treasure. If you pour the word of instruction on his wounds like oil, if you bind them up with your mildness, and cure them with your patience, your wounded brother has made [933] you a richer man than any treasure could. Jeremiah said: "He who has brought forth the precious from the vile will be as my mouth."[23] What could we compare to that? No fasting, no sleeping on the ground, no watching and praying all night, nor anything else can do as much for you as saving your brother can accomplish.

(4) Consider how frequent and numerous are the sins you commit with your mouth. How many obscene things has it said? How many blasphemies, how many abuses has it uttered? If you give some thoughts to this, you will surely never hesitate to look out for your fallen brother. By this one good deed you can cleanse every stain from your mouth. Why do I say cleanse? Because you will make your mouth as the mouth of God. And what honor could be equal to that? It is not I who make this promise to you. God himself said it. If you bring back one person, he said, your mouth will be cleansed and holy, as my mouth is.

(5) So let us not neglect our brothers, let us not go around saying: "How many kept the fast? How many were filched away from us?" Rather, let us show our concern for them. Even if those who observed the fast are many, you, my beloved, must not make a show and a parade of this calamity in the Church; you must cure it. If someone tells you that many have observed the fast, stop him

---

23 Cf. Jer 15.19 (LXX). The context of the chapter is that Jeremiah laments because Yahweh has forsaken him, but God renews and confirms the prophet's mission in verse 19, when he says: "If you will return, then will I restore you and you will stand before my face; if you will bring forth the precious from the vile, you shall be as my mouth." What is precious is God's word; the vileness is either that of Jeremiah himself or of the people. Chrysostom would seem to see the sorry state of the Judaizing Christians as the vile and the reward to be reaped by their rescuers as the precious. Or he may mean that the wounded Christians are precious and the Jews are the vile robbers who wounded them. In either case, the rescuer is recompensed by becoming "as God's mouth." No other good work is comparable to this.

from talking so that the rumor may not get around and become public knowledge. You say to him: "For my part, I don't know of anyone who observed it. You are mistaken, sir, and deceived. If you see two or three filched away, you say that these few are many." So stop this accuser from talking. But you must also see to it that you show your concern for those who were snatched away. Then you will keep the Church safe from a double hurt: first, by preventing the rumor from making the rounds and, secondly, by bringing back to the sacred fold the sheep who were snatched away.

(6) Therefore, let us not go around asking: "Who fell into sin?" Let our only zeal be to set straight those who have sinned. It is a dangerous practice and a terrible thing only to accuse your brothers and not to come to their aid, to parade in public the sins of the sick and not to cure them. Let us, then, get rid of this wicked practice, my beloved, for it leads to no small harm.

(7) Let me tell you how it does this. Somebody hears you say that there were many who observed the fast with the Jews and, without any further investigation, he spreads the story to somebody else. And the second man, without inquiring into the truth of the rumor, again tells it to still another. Then, as the evil rumor little by little grows greater, it spreads a great disgrace over the Church. And this does no good for those who have fallen away; in fact, it causes considerable harm both to them and to many others.

(8) Even if those who did fall are few in number, we make them a multitude by the multitude of our rumors; we weaken those who resisted and we give a push to those on the point of falling. If one of our brothers hears the rumor that a large number joined in keeping the fast, he will be more inclined to be careless himself; again, if it is one of the weak ones who hears the story, he will rush to join the throng of those who have fallen. Even if many have sinned, let us not join with those who rejoice at this or any other evil. If we do, we make a parade of the sinners and say that their name is legion. Rather, let us stop the rumormongers and keep them from spreading the story.

(9) Do not tell me that those who observed the fast are many. Even if they are many, you must set them straight. I did not expend all these words for you to accuse many, but for you to make the

many few and to save even these few. Therefore, do not put [934] their sins on parade, but treat their wounds. Some people parade rumors about and have time only for that. They see to it that the number of those who have sinned is judged to be large even if only a few have fallen. In the same way, if people reprove the rumor-mongers and shut their mouths, if they show concern for those who have fallen, no matter how many they be, it is no hard task for them to set the sinners straight. And furthermore, they keep those rumors from doing harm to anyone else.

(10) You have heard David's lament for Saul when he said: "How the mighty have fallen. Tell it not in Gath, publish it not in the streets of Ashkelon so that the daughters of foreign tribes may not rejoice, so that the daughters of the uncircumcised may not exult in arrogance."[24] If David did not wish the matter paraded in public so that it might not be a source of joy to his foes, so much the more must we avoid spreading the story to alien ears. Rather, we must not spread it even among ourselves for fear that our enemies may hear it and rejoice, for fear that our own may learn of it and fall. We must hush it up and keep it guarded on every side. Do not say to me, "I told so-and-so." Keep the story to yourself. If you did not manage to keep quiet, neither will he manage to keep his tongue from wagging.

V

What I say applies not only to the actual observance of the fast but also to ten thousand other sins. Let us not only ask if many were

---

24 2 Sm (2 Kgs) 1.19–20. "How the mighty have fallen" (which is repeated in verse 27) is a characteristic type of expression in lamentations. "The mighty" include not only Saul but his sons as well. Verse 20 forbids all to spread the story of the disaster in the Philistine towns. In the final chapter of 1 Sm (1 Kgs) there is a graphic account of the Philistines' rout of Saul's forces, his wound and the slaying of his three sons. When Saul's armor-bearer would not kill him, Saul chose suicide (so infrequent among the Israelites) to avoid torture and shameful death. But his foes decapitated his corpse, put his armor in the temple of Astarte, and hung his body on the wall of Bethshan from where it was later taken down and burned. Certainly this story would have brought joy to Saul's Philistine foes in Gath and Ashkelon, two towns far from the scene of slaughter.

filched away; let us ask how we may bring them back. Let us not exalt our enemies' side and destroy our own. Let us not show that they are strong and that our side is weak. Let us do quite the opposite. Rumor can often destroy a soul but, just as often, it can lift it up; it can put zeal in a soul where there was none and, again, it can destroy the zeal that was there.

(2) So I urge you to increase the rumors which exalt our cause and show its greatness, but not the rumors which spread shame on the community of our brothers. If we hear something good, let us broadcast it to all; if we hear something bad or evil, let us keep that hidden among ourselves and do everything we can to get rid of the evil. Therefore, let us now go forth, let us get busy and search for the sinner, let us not shrink back even if we must go into his home. If you do not know him, if you have no connection with him, get busy and find some friend or relative of his, someone to whom he pays particular attention. Take this man with you and go into his home.

(3) Do not blush or feel ashamed. If you were going there to ask for money or to get some favor from him, you would have reason for feeling ashamed. If you hurry there to save the man, no one can find fault with your motive for entering his home. Sit down and talk with him. But start your conversation on other topics so that he does not suspect that the real purpose of your visit is to set him straight.

(4) Say to him: "Tell me, do you approve of the Jews for crucifying Christ, for blaspheming him as they still do, and for calling him a lawbreaker?" If the man is a Christian, he will never put up with this; even if he be a Judaizer times without number, he will never bring himself to say: "I do approve." Rather, he will stop up his ears and say to you: "Heaven forbid! Be quiet, man." Next, after you find that he agrees with you, take up the matter again and say: "How is it that you attend their services, how is it you participate in the festival, how is it you join them in observing the fast?" Then accuse the Jews of being obstinate. Tell him about their every transgression which I recounted to your loving assembly in the days just past. Tell him of their transgressions connected with the place, the

time, [935] and the temple, and how the prophets gave proof of these in their predictions. Show him how the whole ritual of the Jews is useless and unavailing. Show him that they will never return to their old commonwealth and way of life and that they are forbidden to fulfill, except in Jerusalem, what the old life demanded.[25]

(5) Furthermore, remind him of gehenna.[26] Remind him of the test he will undergo before the Lord's dread tribunal of judgment. Remind him that we will give an accounting for all these things and that no small punishment awaits those who dare to do what he is doing. Remind him that Paul said: "You who are justified in the Law have fallen away from grace."[27] Remind him of Paul's threat: "If you be circumcised, Christ will be of no advantage to you."[28] Tell him that, as is the case with circumcision, so, too, the fasting of the Jews drives from heaven the man who observes the fast, even if he has ten thousand other good works to his credit. Tell him that we have the name of Christians because we believe in Christ and not because we run to those who are His foes.

(6) Suppose he uses the cures which the Jews effect as his excuse; suppose he says: "They promise to make me well, and so I go to them." Then you must reveal the tricks they use, their incantations, their amulets, their charms and spells. This is the only way in which they have a reputation for healing; they do not effect genuine

---

25 This is a sketchy summary of *Discourses* IV–VII and may indicate an intrinsic bond between IV–VIII, so that they would all belong to the same series. Of course many of these themes also occur in *Discourses* I–II, which certainly belong together and probably to a similar series given the preceding year. See Introd. III 10–11; 23–25.

26 For gehenna cf. *Disc.* 1.7.9; 7.6.6; below, 8.8.11.

27 Cf. Gal 5.4. Chrysostom quotes the text in the same way in *Disc.* 2.2.1; in 2.3.8 he has: "Those who are justified in the Law have fallen away from grace;" in 6.7.4 he reads: "You who would be justified" etc. In all instances he omits the clause: "You are estranged from Christ." Again he uses the text against Judaizing Christians.

28 Gal 5.2. Cf. *Disc.* 2.1.4–5; 2.2.1–2. Just as the Galatians had to choose either Christ and freedom or the Law and slavery, so the Judaizing Christians must choose between Church and synagogue.

cures.[29] Heaven forbid they should! Let me go so far as to say that even if they really do cure you, it is better to die than to run to God's enemies and be cured that way. What use is it to have your body cured if you lose your soul? What profit is there that you find some relief from your pain in this world if you are going to be consigned to eternal fire?

(7) So that no Jew may say he will cure you, listen to what God said: "If there arise among you a prophet or dreamer of dreams who gives you a sign or wonder, and if the sign or wonder of which he spoke comes to pass, and if he says: 'Let us go and worship other gods,' do not listen to that prophet; for the Lord, your God, is testing you to see if you love the Lord, your God, with all your heart and with all your soul."[30]

(8) What God means is this. Suppose some prophet says to you: "I can raise a dead man to life or cure a blind man. But you must obey me when I say: 'Let us worship demons, or let us offer sacrifice to idols.'" Then, suppose the man who said this can cure a blind man or can raise a dead man to life. God said that you must not heed him because of these signs and wonders which he works. Why? Because God is testing you, he permitted that man to have this power. It is not that God does not know your thoughts but that he is giving you a chance to prove if you really love him. And there are men who are

---

29 Kraeling (157) says the Jews had an enviable reputation for effecting cures from sickness and for expelling démons from persons possessed. As evidence he refers to the present passage for the cures and to *Disc.* 1.7.5–6 for expelling demons, but neither seems to support his statement. Simon (141) says that the rabbis enjoyed a solid reputation as physicians and magicians and suggests that they did use amulets. Chrysostom states that their cures are· not genuine. He will now compare the Jewish physicians to false prophets, who work wonders but then urge the people to idolatry.
30 Cf. Dt 13.2–4 (LXX). Chrysostom cites the same verses to the same purpose in *Disc.* 1.7.7–8. Dt 13 deals with different forms of temptation to practice Canaanite idolatry. In 18.22 unfulfilled prophecies prove a prophet false. The converse, as we see here, is not necessarily true; the prophet must also be tested by his doctrine (cf. Gal 1.8) and fidelity to Yahweh. It is also a test of the Israelites' fidelity, as were their travails in the desert (Dt 8.2). Cf. R. MacKenzie (CCHS 267); J. Blenkinsopp (JBC 6:36).

eager to drag us away from our Beloved. Even if they show dead men brought back to life, the man who truly loves God will not stand apart from God because he has seen such signs and wonders.

(9) If God said this to the Jews, he says it all the more to us. We are the ones he led to a greater life of virtue. He opened the door for us to rise again. He gave the command to us not to love our dwelling here on earth but to keep all our hopes aimed at the life to come.[31]

VI

But what are you saying? Is it that a bodily ailment is afflicting you and crushing you? You have not suffered as many ills as did blessed Job. You have not endured even the slightest part of his pain. First, he lost the whole throng of his flocks, his herds, and every other possession.[32] Then the whole chorus of his children was snatched off.[33] And all this happened on a single day, so that not only the nature of his calamities but also the unbroken succession of his losses might crush this athlete down to earth.

(2) After all that, [936] he received a lethal blow on his body, he saw worms swarming forth from his flesh, he sat naked on a dung hill,[34] a public spectacle of disaster for all men there to see, Job the just, truthful, God-fearing man who kept himself aloof from every evil deed. And his troubles did not stop there. All day, all night, he suffered distress, and a strange and unusual hunger assailed him. He

---

31 Cf. 2 Cor 4.16–17 and 5.2. The trials of this earthly life are nothing when compared to the rewards of eternal life. The "dwelling" is our earthly body, which is subject to suffering. This leads Chrysostom into the example of Job's patience under crushing bodily ailments.

32 Cf. Jb 1.13–17 (LXX). In a single day Job finds he has passed from wealth to utter destitution; this is a severe test to his virtue.

33 Cf. ibid. 18–19. Here the test is still more severe. The word "chorus" is well chosen because his sons and daughters were killed when a tornado collapsed the house where they were enjoying a festive banquet. In Ad eos qui scandalizati sunt (PG 52.522) Chrysostom compares the present life to a wrestling school where the athletes are exercised with many toils so they will be ready for the contests and prepared for the grips of their enemies.

34 Cf. Jb 2.7–8 (LXX). LXX does not here mention the worms. NAB speaks

said: "I see my food is a stench."[35] Each day he was reproached,
scoffed at, mocked, and ridiculed. He said: "My servants and the
children of my concubines have risen up against me, my dreams are
filled with terror, my thoughts are tossed with constant storms."[36]
(3) But his wife promised him freedom from all these things when
she said: "Speak some word against the Lord and die." [37] What she
meant was: "Curse God and you will be freed from the troubles

----

of "severe boils" and JB of "malignant ulcers." R. MacKenzie, JBC 31:15,
says Job is smitten with some unnamed and disfiguring disease, which
causes him continuous pain and sleeplessness and makes him a disgusting
sight. Chrysostom's reference to worms (or maggots) comes from 7.5. E.
Sutcliffe (CCHS 423) cites a physician who diagnoses the symptoms as
indicating true leprosy, smallpox, or more probably a very extensive
erythema. For "on a dung hill" of LXX, NAB reads "among the ashes,"
i.e., of a community dump. Either would seem to imply his exclusion from
human society. Cf. JBC 31:15.

35 Cf. Jb 6.7 (LXX). LXX reads *bromon* (wild oats) and, in apposition, has
hōsper osmēn leontos, "as the odor of a lion." Chrysostom, who cites only
the first half of the verse, reads *ŏrōmon* (stench) for *bromon*. The verse
comes in Job's first reply to Eliphaz, in which Job reaffirms his innocence,
describes his pain, and makes a pathetic appeal to God, which is mingled
with reproaches for the unkind treatment he has received. Cf. JBC 31:28.

36 There is no one text giving the words Chrysostom here puts into the mouth
of Job. Jb 19.16–19 (LXX) reads: "I called my servant and he heeded me
not; but my mouth entreated him. And I made supplication to my wife, I
summoned the sons of my concubines and fawned on them. But they
rejected me forever; whenever I rise up, they speak against me. When they
saw me, they abhorred me: the very people whom I loved rŏse up against
me." *Ibid*. 7.14: "You frighten me with dreams and terrify me with visions." The latter is very close to NAB and JB; the former verses show
considerable differences. In 19.17 the sons would have to be those of his
concubines; all his legitimate children were reported killed in 1.19.

37 Jb 2.9 (LXX). JBC 31:15 says that, as Job's wife sees it, God has now
shown himself to be Job's enemy and he should express that fact before he
dies. NAB note says that Job has nothing to hope for from God and,
therefore, nothing to live for. Chrysostom's explanation uses the Greek
verb *blasphēmein*, to speak impiously or irreverently of God., i.e., to curse
God (which is the reading of NAB and JB). She feels that then God will
punish him with death. Cf. *Disc*. 1.7.11, where 2.9 is quoted as here and
again it is suggested that blasphemy will bring death to Job and free him
from his disaster.

which oppress you." Did her advice change the mind of that holy
man? It did just the opposite; it gave him great strength so that he
even reproached his wife. He chose to feel pain, to endure hardship,
and to suffer ten thousand terrible things rather than curse God and
so find release from his terrible troubles.[38]

(4) The man who had been thirty-eight years in the grip of his
infirmity used to rush each year to the pool and each year he was
driven back and found no cure. Each year he would see others cured
because they had many to take care of them. But he had no one to
put him in the water ahead of the others and so remained in the
constant grip of his paralysis. Even so, he did not run to the sooth-
sayers, he did not go to the charm-users, he did not tie an amulet
around his neck, but he waited for God to help him. That is why he
finally found a wonderful and unexpected cure.[39]

(5) Lazarus wrestled all his days with hunger, disease, and poverty, not only for thirty-eight years but for his whole life. At any rate,
he died while he was lying at the gateway of the rich man, scorned,
scoffed at, famished, laid out before the dogs for food. For his body
had grown too weak to scare away the dogs who came and licked his
wounds.[40] Yet he did not search for a soothsayer, he did not tie

---

38 Cf. Jb 2.10 and *Disc.* 1.7.11.
39 Cf. Jn 5.1–9 for the cure of the man at the pool of Bethesda. The moving
   of the water probably came from greater activity by the underground
   spring which fed the pool. There are inconsistencies between the accounts
   of Chrysostom and Jn. Chrysostom has the man rushing to the water, being
   driven back, and finding no cure although he sees others cured. In Jn 5.7 he
   needs help to be put into the water (but has none) and only one is cured
   each time the waters are troubled (5.4). The inconsistencies seem only
   rhetorical. The important thing is that the paralytic, like Job, is patient and
   does not use magical means to recover his health. For demonic cures cf.
   Introd. II 37–38 and *Disc.* 1.7.5–11. In his homily *In paralyticum* (PG
   51.52–53) Chrysostom goes on to Jn 5.14, where Jesus finds the cured
   paralytic in the temple and says: "You are cured. Sin no more lest something worse befall you." From this apparent censure Chrysostom sees
   Christ's providence and clemency; he did not make a parade of the paralytic's sins. He performed the cure in the sight of all but he gave his
   exhortation and counsel in private.
40 Cf. Lk 16.19–22 for the story of Lazarus and the Rich Man. Chrysostom
   makes the same point as with the paralytic.

tokens[41] around his neck, and he did not resort to the charm-users, he did not call in those skilled in witchcraft, nor did he do anything he was forbidden to do. He chose to die from these troubles of his rather than betray in any small way his life of godliness. (6) Look at the torments and sufferings those men endured! What excuse will we have if for our fevers and hurts we run to the synagogues, if we summon into our own house these sorcerers, these dealers in witchcraft? Hear what the Scripture says: "My son, if you come to serve the Lord, prepare your soul for trial, put straight your heart, and be steadfast. Be obedient to him in sickness and in poverty. As gold is tested in the fire, so the chosen man is tested in the furnace of humiliation."[42]

(7) Suppose you flog your servant. Suppose, that, after you have dealt him thirty or fifty lashes, he then loudly demands his freedom, or that he flees from your control to take refuge with men who hate you. Suppose that he then incites them against you. Tell me this. Can he get you to forgive him? Can anyone offer a defense in his behalf? Of course not.

(8) But why? Because it is a master's duty [937] to punish his servant. And this is not the only reason. If the slave had to run away, he should not have gone to enemies who hated his master; he should have gone to his master's true friends. You must do the same. When you see that God is punishing you, do not flee to his enemies, the Jews, so that you may not rouse his anger against you still further.

---

41 The tokens are amulets on which, according to Simon (143), were inscribed demons' names associated with the names of angels, e.g., Raphael and Raphuphael. Chrysostom, in his *Baptismal Instructions* gives many warnings against, and examples of, amulets, omens, charms, and incantations; see ACW 31.esp. 189–91, 337–38.

42 Cf. Sir (Ecclus) 2.1–2a, 5 (LXX). Chrysostom's "Be obedient to him in sickness and in poverty" (which fits Job, the paralytic, and Lazarus) is not found in LXX. Perhaps Chrysostom inserts these words as a rhetorically suitable substitute for verses 2b–4, which say, in effect, that our service to God must be sincere and faithful. The point is that man must serve the Lord in trials and be tested in the fire of humiliation, as were Job, the paralytic, and Lazarus.

Run instead to the martyrs, to the saints, to those in whom he is well pleased and who can speak to him with great confidence and freedom.[43]

(9) But why talk about slaves and masters? If a father flogs his son, the son cannot do what the slave did, nor can he deny his relationship to his father. Suppose the father flogs his son, suppose he keeps him from his table, suppose he drives him from his house, and punishes him every way he can. Both the laws of nature and those established by man command the son to be brave and endure all this. No one ever excuses the son if he refuses to obey his father and put up with the punishment. Even if the boy who was flogged lifts his voice in ten thousand bitter laments, everybody tells him that it was his father who flogged him, that his father is his master and has the power to do whatever he wants, that the son must meekly endure it all.[44]

(10) So, then, slaves put up with their masters and sons put up with their fathers even though the punishments they get often do not fit the fault. Will you refuse to put up with God when He corrects you? Is he not more your master than your master is? Does he not love you more than any father? When he interferes and does something, it is not done from anger. He does everything for your own good. If you get some slight illness, will you reject him as your master and rush off to the demons and desert over to the synagogues? What pardon will you find after that? How can you call

---

43 God is our master, we are the slaves whose sins deserve punishment; we must not run to the Jews, who hate the master, but to the martyrs, who are his friends and will plead for us. "Rush to the martyrs" is probably to be taken almost literally, i.e., go to their tombs and look there for your cure. Simon (151) thinks that it is not a question of any martyrs but of local saints whose tombs can be touched. At Antioch this would mean above all others the tomb of the Maccabees. He would, then, understand this sentence to mean: "Do not go to the Jewish synagogue but to the old synagogue, which has been converted into a church dedicated to the Maccabees, where their tomb still is." Cf. Introd. II 34–38.

44 Here God is not only master but father. He has the right to punish a disobedient son, who must endure the punishment.

on Him for help again? Who else will be able to plead your cause even if he could speak with the freedom and confidence of a Moses? There is no one.[45] (11) Do you not hear what God said to Jeremiah about the Jews? "Do not intercede for this people because even if Moses and Samuel shall stand (before my face), I will not listen to them."[46] That is how far some sins go beyond forgiveness and how incapable of defense they are. Therefore, let us not draw down such anger on ourselves. Even if the Jews seem to relieve your fever with their incantations, they are not relieving it. They are bringing down on your conscience another more dangerous fever. Every day you will feel the sting of remorse; every day your conscience will flog you. And what will your conscience say? "You sinned against God, you transgressed his Law, you violated your covenant with Christ. For an insignificant ailment you betrayed your faith. You are not the only one who has suffered this ailment, are you? Have not others been much more seriously ill than you? Still no one of them dared commit such a sin. But you were so soft and weak that you sacrificed your soul. What defense will you make to Christ? How will you ask for his help in your prayers? With what conscience will you set foot in the church? With what eyes will you look at the priest? With what hands will you touch the sacred banquet?[47] With what ears will you listen to the reading of the scriptures there?"

---

45 Cf. *Disc.* 1.4.1–3; 1.7.5–10.
46 Cf. Jer 7.16 which Chrysostom conflates with 15.1 (where he omits "before my face"). The first part (7.16) opens a short speech which deals with idolatry, especially the fertility cult of the Mesopotamian goddess Astarte. The second part (15.1) shows how irrevocable God's decision to reject the Jews can be; he will refuse to hear the prayers of even Moses and Samuel, who have always been considered great intercessors for their people (Ex 32.11–14; Nm 14.11–25; 1 Sm [1 Kgs] 7.5–9; 12.19–23; Ps 98 [99].6). Cf. G. Couturier, JBC 19:48.
47 This is a clear reference to self-communication. If not universal, it was the common practice in the early Church for the communicant to receive both the sacred species from his own hands. Theodore of Mopsuestia describes it in his *Baptismal Catecheses* 16.27–28 (trans. Harkins, ACW 31.330). See R. Tonneau and R. Devreesse, *Les homélies catéchètiques de Théodore de Mopsueste* (Studi e Testi 145; Vatican City 1949) 577–79. Also see F.

VII

Every day your reason will sting you and your conscience will flog you with these words. What kind of health is this when we have such thoughts in our minds to accuse us? But if you put up with your fever for a little while, if you scorn those who want [938] to chant over you an incantation or tie an amulet to your body, if you insult them roundly and drive them from your house, your conscience will immediately bring you relief like a drink of water. Even if the fever recurs time and time again, even if it is burning up your body, your soul brings you a solace that is better and more profitable than any relief from water or perspiration.

(2) Even if you recover your health after the incantation, the thought of the sin you committed leaves you worse off than those who are tossed with fever. And if you are the one who has the fever now, if you are the one who suffers ten thousand torments, you will be better off than any healthy man, because you have gotten rid of those foul sorcerers. Your reason will exult, your soul will rejoice and be glad, your conscience will praise you and voice its approval.

(3) And what will your conscience say? "Well done, well done, good man. You are the servant of Christ, you are the man of faith, the athlete of the godly life. You chose to die in torment rather than betray the life of godliness entrusted to your care. You will stand with the martyrs on that day.[48] The martyrs chose to be flogged and torn on the rack that God might hold them in honor. So you chose this day to be flogged and racked with fever and wounds

---

Reine, *The Eucharistic Doctrine and Liturgy of the Mystagogical Catecheses of Theodore of Mopsuestia* (Studies in Christian Antiquity 2; Washington 1941) 182–85.Chrysostom alludes to the practice in his baptismal instructions (ACW 31.177–78). Cyril of Jerusalem gives the most explicit description of self-communication in his *Catechesis* 23.21–22 (PG 33.1124–25; trans. Harkins, ACW 31.330; A.A. Stephenson, FC 64 [Washington 1970] 203).

48 I.e., by choosing death rather than reject Christ to accept his foes, you gave witness to him, you laid down your life for him; you will, therefore, stand among his martyrs when he comes to the day of Judgment.

rather than submit to profane incantations and amulets. Because you nurture yourself with these hopes, you will not feel the torments which assail you."

(4) If this fever does not carry you off, another one surely will; if we do not die now, we are sure to die later. It is our lot to have a body doomed to die. But we do not have this body so that we may heed its passions and take to ourselves a life of godlessness, but that we may use its passions for the godly life. If we live the sober life, this corruption, this same mortal body will become the basis for our honor and will give us great confidence not only on that day[49] but also in the present life.

(5) So, go ahead and insult those sorcerers roundly and drive them from your house. Everybody who hears of it will praise you and marvel at you. People will say one to the other: "So and so was sick and in pain. Time and time again people came to him and urged him, exhorted him, and advised him to subject himself to magic incantations. He did not give in but said: 'It is better to die the way I am than to betray my faith and the godly life.' " Those who hear these words will applaud him long and loud; they will be astounded and give glory to God.

(6) Do you not think this will be more rich in honor than many statues, more brilliant in its magnificence than many portraits, more remarkable in its distinction than many dignities? Everyone will praise you, everyone will count you happy, everyone will crown you with the victor's wreath. And they will be better themselves, they will experience a return to zeal, they will imitate your courage. If somebody else does what you did, you will carry off the reward because it was you who gave him his start, it is you whom he emulates.

(7) Your good deeds will not only bring praise to you but also rapid release from your sickness. The nobility of your choice will win God to even greater good will; all the saints will rejoice at what you have done; they will pray for you from the bottom of their

---

49 Again, the day of Judgment.

hearts. If such courage brings these rewards in this life, consider what reward you will receive in heaven. In the presence of all the angels and archangels, Christ will come forward, take you by the hand, and lead you to the middle of that stage. Everyone will listen when he says:

(8) "This man was [939] once gripped by fever. Many people urged him to be rid of his ailment, but, for my name's sake and because he feared he might offend me in some way, he scorned these people and thrust aside those who were promising to cure him in that fashion.⁵⁰ He chose to die of his illness rather than betray his love for me."

(9) If Christ leads to the center of this stage those who gave him to drink, who clothed and fed him, he will do this all the more for those who endured fevers for his sake. Giving food and clothing is not the same thing as submitting to a long continuing disease. To submit to the disease is a much greater thing. And the greater the suffering, the more glorious will be the reward.⁵¹

(10) In sickness and in health, let us rehearse for this day and talk about it one to the other. If we find ourselves in the grip of a fever we cannot endure, let us say to ourselves: "What about this? If someone brought a charge against me and I was dragged into court, if I were tied to the whipping post and my sides were torn with

---

50 I.e., by incantations, amulets, sorcery, and magic.
51 Cf. Mt 25.31–46. The usual title given to this passage is "The Last Judgment." J. McKenzie, JBC 43:177, finds this designation misleading because this scene (which has no parallel in the other gospels) is an imaginative one in which the core of Jesus' moral teaching is set. E.g., the corporal works of mercy are found in 35–36. The theological theme is love for neighbor based on the identity of Jesus with men; in the last analysis this love determines whether men are good or bad. If their love is active, failure to reach moral perfection is rare and will be forgiven. But there is no substitute for active love. Chrysostom makes this active love for neighbor less important than bearing witness to Christ by enduring pain rather than offending him. In his *Baptismal Instructions*, Chrysostom shows Christ as the Judge of the games who leads the neophyte into the arena, forgives his sins, and joins forces with him in the fight against the devil (cf. ACW 31.183, 334–35).

lashes, would I not have to put up with it at any rate, even though I would get no profit or reward?"

(11) Now let us ponder on this. Suppose there is set before you a reward for your patience and endurance; suppose the reward is large enough to encourage your fallen spirit. "But my fever is severe," you say, "and hard to bear." Then compare your fever to the fire of gehenna. You will surely escape that fire if you show great endurance in putting up with your fever.[52]

(12) Remember how many sufferings the apostles endured. Remember that the just were constantly afflicted. Remember that blessed Timothy had no rest from his illness, but lived with his disease from one end of his life to the other. Paul made this clear when he said: "Use a little wine for your stomach's sake and your frequent infirmities."[53] That just and holy man took in hand the superintendence of the world, brought the dead back to life, drove out demons, and cured ten thousand ailments in others.[54] If he experienced such terrible sufferings, what defense will you have for groaning and grieving over ailments which will last only for a time?

(13) Did you not listen to the Scripture? It says: "Whom the Lord loves he chastizes; and he scourges every son whom he receives."[55] How many times and how many men have yearned to receive the crown of martyrdom? In this you have a perfect martyr's

---

52 For gehenna see *Disc.* 1.7.9; 7.6.6; 8.5.5.
53 1 Tm 5.23. G. Denzer, JBC 57:29, suggests that out of a spirit of asceticism Timothy drank only water. For reasons of health Paul urges him to take some wine because he apparently suffered from a weak stomach, which may have been the cause of his frequent ailments. See J. McKenzie, "Timothy," DB 892–93.
54 If these wonderful works are not rhetorical exaggerations, they must belong to his work with Paul, whose intimate and trusted associate he was.
55 Prv 3.12 (LXX). Heb 12.6, quoting the text the same way, urges the Hebrews to constancy, even to the point of blood in the struggle with sin. In Prv 3.11–12 the point seems to be that for the wise man suffering is an education, not a punishment. Chrysostom seems to follow the author of Heb because he is urging those who seek demonic cures rather to endure a death which will, in fact, be a martyrdom for Christ.

crown. A martyr is made not only when someone is ordered to offer sacrifice but chooses to die rather than offer the sacrifice. If a man shuns any practice, and to shun it can only bring on death, he is certainly a martyr.[56]

VIII

So that you may know that this is true, remember how John [the Baptist] died, from what motive, and why. Remember, too, how Abel died. Neither John nor Abel saw an altar with its fire, nor a statue standing before them. They heard no voice commanding them to offer sacrifice. John only reproached Herod and had his head cut off;[57] Abel merely honored God with a more excellent sacrifice than his brother did, and Cain slew him.[58] They were not deprived of martyr's crowns, were they? Who would dare to say that? The very way they died is enough to make everyone agree that they belong in the front ranks of the martyrs.

(2) If you are looking for some divine proclamation about these two men, listen to what Paul said. He made it clear that his words are the words of the Holy Spirit when he said: "I think that I also have the Spirit of God."[59] What [940] then, did Paul say? He began with Abel and told how Abel offered to God a more excellent sacrifice than Cain, and through his faith, though he is dead, he yet

---

56 In choosing death rather than illicit means of cure, a man gives witness to his love for God and, hence, is as much a martyr as those who have died rather than sacrifice to idols. Cf. *Disc.* 8.7.3–9.

57 Cf. Mt 14.1–12 and Mk 6.14–29 for the story of Herod's beheading of John the Baptist. Josephus, *Jewish Antiquities* 18.116–19 (trans. L. H. Feldman, Loeb Libr. *Josephus* 9.81–85) adds some details. The reproach, of course, was that Herod was living in open adultery with Herodias, his brother's wife.

58 Cf. Gn 4.3–8. *Disc.* 1.7.3 says that God accepted Abel's offering and rejected Cain's. *Disc.* 8.2.6 quotes in part verse 7 (LXX), which suggests that Cain's offering was imperfect because he had failed to divide it properly. Hence, it was rejected and Cain slew Abel. The point Chrysostom here makes is that both the Baptist and Abel are true martyrs although neither died rather than sacrifice to idols.

59 1 Cor 7.40. These words end a whole chapter on marriage and celibacy and

speaks.⁶⁰

(3) Then Paul continued his account down through the prophets and came to John. After he said: "They were put to death by the sword, and others were tortured,"⁶¹ after he recounted many and different modes of martyrdom, he went on to say: "Therefore, let us also, having such a cloud of witnesses surrounding us, put away every encumbrance and run with patience."⁶² Do you see that he also called Abel a martyr, along with Noah, Abraham, Isaac, and Jacob? For some of these died for God's sake in the same way that Paul spoke of when he said: "I die daily";⁶³ they died not by dying but only by their willingness to endure death.

(4) If you do this, if you reject the incantations, the spells, and the charms, and if you then die of your disease, you will be a perfect martyr. Even though others promised you relief along with an ungodly life, you chose death with godliness. And I have spoken these words to those boastful talkers who say that the demons do effect

---

conclude a verse which suggests that widows will be more happy (blessed) if they remain unmarried. W. Rees, CCHS 1090, thinks that the words Chrysostom quotes may mean that Paul, as well as others, have authority to speak in Christ's name. He further thinks that this is an ironical understatement aimed at some dissidents in Corinth, who falsely claimed such authority. Chrysostom also seems to mean that Paul has authority to speak in Christ's name.

60 Cf. Heb 11.4. M. Bourke, JBC 61:63, says that OT does not say that Abel's sacrifice was motivated by faith. Verse 6 says that without faith it is impossible to please God; in Gn 4.4 God has no regard for Cain's sacrifice but is pleased with Abel's—hence Abel must have faith because he pleased God. The words "though he is dead, he yet speaks" may allude to Gn 4.10; more probably they simply indicate the enduring witness to faith given by Abel's example.

61 Cf. Heb 11.37, which is conflated with *ibid.*35.

62 Cf. *ibid.*12.1. W. Leonard, CCHS 1170, states that "Therefore" is very emphatic. Therefore, i.e., because the honor roll of ch. 11 summons a dense cloud of witnesses who tell of the victories of faith, let us, like athletes ready ourselves for the race, do our part. They lived before Christ and had to wait for our age—the fulness of time—to receive the promises and come to the perfection of glory their faith and martyrdom had earned.

63 1 Cor 15.31. Cf. Rom 8.36, which quotes Ps 43(44).23: "For your sake we are put to death all the day long." J. Fitzmeyer, JBC 53:93, says that Paul

cures.[64] To learn how false this is, listen to what Christ said about the devil: "He was a murderer from the beginning."[65] God says he is a murderer; do you rush to him as you would to a physician?

(5) Tell me this. When you stand indicted before God's tribunal, what reason will you be able to give for considering the Jews' witchcraft more worthy of your belief than what Christ has said? God said that the devil is a murderer; they say that he can cure diseases, in contradiction to God's word. When you accept their charms and incantations, your actions show that you consider the Jews more worthy of your belief than God, even if you do not say it in so many words.

(6) If the devil is a murderer, it is clear that the demons who serve him are murderers, too. What Christ did has taught you this lesson. At any rate, he gave the demons leave to enter into the herd of swine and the demons drove the whole herd down the cliff and drowned them.[66] He did this so that you might know that the demons would have done the same thing to human beings and would have drowned them if God had allowed them to do so. But he restrained

---

quotes the psalm to show that tribulations are no proof that God does not love the persecuted; rather they are a sign of His love. W. Rees, CCHS 1097, thinks that 1 Cor 15.31 shows that Paul was in constant danger at Corinth and that, therefore, some Corinthians had said of him: "He dies daily." Now he reminds them of their words. Chrysostom's explanation seems equally or more probable. Of the examples he mentions, only Abel was actually slain. Noah (Heb 11.7) is shown as warning his contemporaries of imminent disaster and urging them, unsuccessfully, to repent. The event was a condemnation of their unbelief but a vindication of Noah's faith. Paul has already proposed Abraham as a prototype of the Christian believer (Rom 4.3). In Heb 11.8–9, Abraham's faith is proved by obeying God's command to migrate to Canaan (Gn 12.1,4) and by his confidence that his descendants would possess the land although he would only be a sojourner in it (Gn 15.16,18). The faith of Isaac and Jacob, heirs of the same promise (cf. Gn 26.4; 35.12), is mentioned in passing.

64 Cf. *Disc.* 1.7.11.

65 Cf. Jn. 8.44 and NAB note *ad loc.* B. Vawter, JBC 63:112, says this is true because it was through the devil that death first entered the world (cf. Gn 3.3–4; Wis 2.24). This makes him the enemy of the life which Jesus came to bring and the father of those Jews who seek to kill him.

66 Cf. Mt. 8.28–34; Mk 5.1–17; Lk 8.26–37, esp. 32.–33. In 31 the demons

the demons, stopped them, and permitted them to do no such thing. Once they had gotten power over the swine, the demons made quite clear what they would have done to us. If they did not spare the swine, it is all the more sure they would not have kept their hands off us. Therefore, beloved, do not be swept off by the deceits of the demons but stand firm in your fear of God.

(7) But how will you go into the synagogue? If you make the sign of the cross on your forehead, the evil power that dwells in the synagogue immediately takes to flight.[67] If you fail to sign your forehead, you have immediately thrown away your weapon at the doors. Then the devil will lay hold of you, naked and unarmed as you are, and he will overwhelm you with ten thousand terrible wounds.

(8) What need is there for me to say this? The way you act when you get to the synagogue makes it clear that you consider it a very serious sin to go to that wicked place. You are anxious that no one notice your arrival there; you urge your household, friends, and

---

(whose name is Legion) beg not to be sent to the abyss, which is either the abode of the dead (cf. Rom 10.7; Ps 106[107] .26) or the final prison of Satan (cf. Rv 20.3). Although aware that this is their ultimate destiny, they beseech Jesus not to send them there yet. When they enter the swine, the herd is destroyed. J. McKenzie, JBC 43:60, commenting on Mt 8.32, thinks that this implies that the demons perish, too, even "before the time" (verse 29), i.e., the appointed time for the eschatological consummation, when God will destroy every hostile power (cf. 1 Cor 15.24–25). Chrysostom's point is that if the demons destroyed the swine, how much more ready would they be to destroy men if God were to permit it. He uses the same argument in *Disc.* 1.7.5.

67 In his *Baptismal Instructions,* Chrysostom explains that, just before baptism, the catechumen has his forehead anointed and marked with the sign of the cross; this checks all the frenzy of the Evil One, for he is blinded by the sight and does not dare to look but runs away. Whatever threshold the Christian crosses, he must renounce Satan and make the sign of the cross on his forehead. It is a weapon which renders man or demon incapable of harming him (cf. ACW 31.169,191). For the sign of the cross as a protection, cf. J. Daniélou, *The Bible and the Liturgy* (Notre Dame 1956) 56–57. In *Demonstration* 9–10 (PG 48.825–27) Chrysostom speaks beautifully of the cross as a symbol and the eagerness with which people seek relics of the true cross.

neighbors not to report you to the priests. If someone does report you, you fly into a rage. Would it not be the height of folly to try to hide from men [941] your bold and shameless sin when God, who is present everywhere, sees it?

(9) Are you not afraid of God? Then, at least, stand in some awe and fear of the Jews. How will you look them in the eye? How will you speak to them? You profess you are a Christian, but you rush off to their synagogues and beg them to help you.[68] Do you not realize how they laugh at you, scoff at you, jeer at you, dishonor you, and reproach you? Even if they do not do it openly, do you not understand that they are doing this deep down in their hearts?

IX

Tell me, then. Will you put up with their jibes? Will you tolerate them? Suppose you had to suffer incurable ills; suppose you had to die ten thousand deaths. Would it not be much better to endure all that rather than have those abominable people laugh and scoff at you, rather than live with a bad conscience?

(2) My purpose in speaking is not to have you hear this for yourselves; I want you also to work to cure those who have this sickness. They are feeble in their faith, and for this I blame them. I also blame you for your unwillingness to set the sick ones straight. It is not in question that, when you come here to church, you listen to what is said; you leave yourself open to condemnation when you fail to follow through with action the words you hear.

(3) Why are you a Christian? Is it not that you may imitate Christ and obey his Laws? What did Christ do? He did not sit in Jerusalem and call the sick to come to him. He went around to cities and towns and cured sickness of both body and soul. He could have stayed sitting in the same place and still have drawn all men to himself. But he did not do this. Why? So that he might give us the example

---

68 Cf. *Disc.* 1.3.3–1.4.7; 1.6.7–8; 7.6.10.

of going around in search of those who are perishing.
(4) He gave us another glimpse of this example in the parable of
the shepherd.[69] The shepherd did not sit down with the
ninety-nine sheep and wait for the lost one to come to him. He
went out himself and found it. And after he found the lost sheep, he
lifted it to his shoulders and brought it back. Do you not see that a
physician does this same thing? He does not force patients who are
confined to bed to be brought to his home. The physician himself
hurries to the homes of the sick.

(5) You must do this, too, beloved. You know that the present
life is short; if we do not earn our profits here, we will have no
salvation hereafter. Gaining a single soul can often erase the burden
of countless sins and be the price which buys us life on that day.[70]
Ponder on this question. Why were we sent prophets, apostles, just
men, and often even angels? Why did the only-begotten Son of God
come among us himself? Was it not to save men? Was it not [942] to
bring back those who had strayed?

(6) You must do this with all the strength you have. You must
devote all your zeal and concern to bringing back those who have
strayed. At every religious service let me keep exhorting you to do
this; whether you pay attention or not, I will not stop saying it.
Whether you listen or not, it is God's law that I fulfill this ministry.
If you listen to me and do what I say, I will keep on doing this and
feel great joy. If you disregard it and become indifferent to what I

---

69 Cf. Mt 18.12–14; Lk 15.4–6. J. McKenzie, JBC 43:127, points out that
the parable has different forms and applications in Mt and Lk. In Mt it
illustrates Jesus' admonition to the "greater" disciples not to despise the
"little ones," i.e., the simpler disciples (cf. 18.1 and 10). In Lk the parable
is Jesus' answer to the charge that he fraternizes with tax collectors and
sinners. The one strayed sheep may have fallen and must be sought; it is the
Father's will that not even one should perish. In Lk Jesus takes the responsibility as his own; in Mt the responsibility belongs to the shepherds in the
Church. Chrysostom combines both: Jesus goes out after the lost sheep but
so, too, the shepherds, the stronger brethren, must not despise the weaker
disciples but seek out those who may be in danger.
70 Cf. above *Disc.* 8.7.9 and n. See also *Disc.* 4.7.9–11 and 7.6.3–9. Again,
that day is the Day of Judgment.

say, I will keep on saying it but I will feel great fear instead of joy. (7) If you disobey, it will involve no risk for me hereafter. I have fulfilled my part. Even if there will be no danger for me because I have carried out my full fair share, I will feel sorrow for you when you are accused on that day.[71] Even listening to me will be fraught with danger, when you fail to follow up my words with your deeds.

(8) Hear, at any rate, how Christ both reproved the teachers who buried the meaning of his message but how he also terrified those whom they taught. For after he said: "You should have deposited my money with the bankers," he went on to add: "And on my return I should have demanded it back with interest."[72]

(9) What Christ showed by the parable was this. After hearing a sermon (for this is depositing the money), those who have received the instruction must make it produce interest. The interest from the teaching is nothing other than proving through deeds what you have been taught through words. Since I have deposited my money in your ears, you must now pay your teacher back the interest, that is, you must save your brothers. So, if you should just keep holding on to what I said and produce no interest by action on your own part, I am afraid that you will pay the same penalty as the servant who

---

71 The notion that whether the people heed or not, the preacher's main work is done once he has instructed his flock is a common one in Chrysostom. If he fails, he will grieve for the remiss. If his words are fruitful, it will bring him joy and increase his zeal to plant the seed of further instruction. Cf. e.g., *Disc.* 1.8.3. But failure is not imputable to him. A farmer may be deceived by the soil and return with empty hands and find no consolation for his toils. So long as a preacher has done all he should, he is abundantly recompensed for his labor since God grants him generous payment whether the disciples listen or not. But the preacher looks on their laxity as his own personal loss. (Cf. ACW 31.93–94, 263).

72 Cf. Mt 25.27. The parable of the talents (*ibid.* 14–30) is paralleled by the parable of the gold pieces in Lk 19.11–27. There are differences in detail between Mt and Lk but the point is the same in both. The slaves who trade with the money double the investment; the timid slave buries his sum in the earth–he loses nothing but gains nothing. For Chrysostom investing the money is to act on his words and produce the interest of rescuing Judaizing Christians. He expresses similar sentiments in *Disc.* 4.7.8–9; 6.7.8–10.

buried his talent in the ground. And for this he was bound hand and foot and cast into the darkness outside,[73] because the words he heard brought no profit to others.

(10) So that we may not have this happen to us, let us imitate the servant who received five talents and the one who received two.[74] Whatever you will be asked to spend to save your neighbor, be it words, money, bodily pain, or anything else whatsoever, we must not shrink back or hesitate. Then each of us, in every way, will multiply proportionately the talent given him by God. Then each of us will be able to hear those happy words: "Well done, good and faithful servant; because you have been faithful over a few things. I will set you over many; enter into the joy of your Master."[75] May we all gain this by the grace and loving-kindness of our Lord Jesus Christ through whom and with whom be glory and power to the Father together with the Holy Spirit, world without end. Amen.[76]

---

73 Here Chrysostom has borrowed from the parable of the marriage feast, where the king told his servants to take the man without a wedding garment and "bind his hands and feet and cast him forth into the darkness outside" (Mt 22.13). He has applied this to the parable of the talents: "But as for the unprofitable servant, cast him forth into the darkness outside" (Mt 25.30). No doubt, the similarity of sentiment caused either a conflation or a substitution. The end of Chrysostom's sentence gives the point of both the parable of the talents (Mt) and of the gold pieces (Lk) .

74 Cf. Mt 25.15. Each servant received according to his ability but both doubled the investment and received equal rewards. Cf. *ibid*. 20–23.

75 *Ibid*. 21. J. McKenzie, JBC 43:176, says the reward of fidelity is the commission of greater responsibility; the admission to the joy of the master means that the slave is admitted to intimate association with his owner. A. Jones (CCHS 897) sees an allegorical application: The faithful servant shares with Jesus (cf. 25.34) the joy of the Father's kingdom and apparently (cf. verses 21, 23) is associated with the King's administration of the earthly kingdom so long as it lasts.

76 A note of Montfaucon's (PG 48.942) states that after the "Amen" two MSS have: "Our Father, St. Chrysostom, with God's help, has concluded his sermons *Against the Jews*, which are six in number." One MS says: "... which are five in number." See Introd. III 6.

INDICES

GENERAL INDEX

Aaron, 111 n., 168, 169 n.,
199 n.
anointing of, 165 n., 166
holocausts of, 93 n., 138 n.,
139 n.
ordination of, 158 n., 165,
166, 167
priesthood of, 138, 159 n.,
165, 168 n., 193, 194,
195, 198, 200 n.
sons of, 139, 159 n.
staff of, 168
Abel, 26, 27 n., 210, 211, 234,
235, 236 n.
Abihu, son of Aaron, 139 n.
Abiram, revolt of, 169 n.
abomination
of desolation, 120, 122, 123n.,
134, 135
Jewish fast and ritual, 9, 26,
27, 73 n., 138, 188,
205 n.
synagogue, 19
Abraham, 113, 116, 192, 193,
195, 196, 197, 199, 235,
236 n.
abrogate, lv, lix, 5 n.
Adam, 89, 208, 209
adultery, 25 n., 37, 43, 180,
182, 190 n., 234 n.
Aelia, 136

Aelia Capitolina, xxviii, 136,
137 n., 158 n.
Aelius Hadrianus, 136
Ahab, 74, 75
Ahaz, 25 n., 112 n., 189 n.
Albert, P., xxiv n., 3 n.
Alexander the Great, 120, 121,
122
Alexandria, 60 n.
School of, xxiii
Allegory, 5 n., 152 n., 216 n.
Altaner, B., lix
altar, xxv n., 27, 42, 63, 67,
122, 138, 139 n., 151,
158, 159, 161, 164, 166,
169, 177, 182, 199
of holocaust, 93 n., 122 n.,
138 n., 159 n., 169 n.
of incense, 93, 160 n.
invisible, 23
pagan, 234
to unknown god, 105
to Zeus Olympios, 120 n.,
135 n.
Amos, 180 n.
amulet, xli, xlvi, 29 n., 222,
223 n., 226, 227 n., 230,
231, 232 n.
anachronism, 65 n., 82 n.,
178 n., 210 n.
angel, 2, 30, 40 n., 87, 99,

253

255

pagan, 51 n., 152
ritual
  Jewish, xxxv, xl, xlvi, l, 20, 23, 32, 57 n., 58, 77, 84, 86, 87 n., 91, 97 n., 98, 161, 173, 178, 180 n., 187 n., 188 n., 191 n., 192, 222
  prostitution, 180 n.
  purification, 179 n., 200 n.
  worship, 26 n., 182, 183 n.
robbers, 49, 216 n.
  Jews, 217, 218 n.
synagogue a den of, xxxix, 10, 15, 19, 145, 169
Rock (Peter), 214 n.
Rosh Ha-Shanah, xl, 3 n., 4 n., 71 n., 72 n., 177 n.; see Year, New
rumor, 219, 220, 221

sabbath, 22 n., 32, 54, 58, 60, 63, 66 n., 86, 87 n., 155, 169 n., 189
sacred, 22 n., 23 n., 28 n., 57, 91, 93 n., 138 n., 158 n., 167 n., 179, 219
  banquet, 45, 78 n., 229
  books, 19, 20, 21, 105
sacrifice, 23, 26, 27, 28 n., 35, 67, 122, 139, 141 n., 193, 199, 210 nn., 234
  of children, 25, 58, 154, 155
  Christ's, 142, 184, 186, 191, 192 n., 200 n.
  Jewish, xlviii, 57, 81, 82 n., 84, 85, 86, 87, 88, 89, 90, 91, 93, 120, 123 n., 125, 138, 141, 142, 144, 159, 164, 165, 166, 167, 172, 179, 181, 182, 183, 187, 188, 189, 190
  sacrificial, 60, 61, 93 n., 137 n., 144 n., 166 n., 174 n.
Saducees, xxxi
Salem, 193
salvation, 6, 11, 13 n., 31, 32, 36 nn., 37, 38 nn., 39, 44, 60, 94, 95, 116, 119, 145, 162, 170, 186 n., 201, 203, 208, 239
  history, xxxiii, 27 n., 113 n., 144 n., 183 n., 209 n.
Samaria, 199 n., 141 n., 152 n.
Samaritan, 88 n., 144 n.
  Good, xlix, 216, 217
  woman, 143
Samuel, 160 n., 299
sanctuary, 23 n., 28 n., 131 n., 178 n., 179 n., 180 n., 191 n.
  temple, 199, 122, 134, 138, 159, 160, 173 n., 179 n., 182
Sanhedrin, xxxii, 106
Satan, 210, 215 n., 237
Saul, 160 n., 220
Savile, H., xxxi n., lii, 136 n., 188 n.
Saydon, P., 123 n., 124 n., 126 n., 127 n., 131 n., 132 n.
Schatkin, M., xliv, lv, 157 n.
Schwartz, E., xxvi n.
scribe, xlv n., 131 n.
Scripture, xxii, xxiii, xxiv, xli,

266

271

INDEX OF HOLY SCRIPTURE

(Books of the Old Testament)

273

11.2: 114
12.15: 49 n.
12.15-20: 53 n.
12.35-36: 114 n.
13.21: 93 n., 153 n.
14-17: 179 n.
14.24: 93 n.
15.1: 114
15.1-21: 114 n.
15.11: 105
16: 152 n.
16.4: 153 n.
17.4: 152 n.
18: 152 n.
19.16-18: 93 n.
20.24-25: 159 n.
21.1-8: 169 n.
23.14-17: 179 n.
25.22: 158 n., 159 n.
27.1-8: 159 n.
28.4: 164 n.
28.6-30: 159 n.
28.7: 159 n.
28.15-30: 164 n.
28.30: 159 n.
29.9: 168 n.
29.29: 160 n.
29.36-37: 167 n.
29.38-42: 123 n.
31.12-18: 155 n.
32: 152 n.
32.1: 111
32.9: 112 n.
32.11-14: 229 n.
33.19: 27 n.
34.18-26: 179 n.

Leviticus
1.5: 168 n.
1.10-13: 166
2.2: 181
4.5: 160 n.
5.11: 181 n.
6.2-6: 93 n., 123 n., 138 n.
7.15: 167 n.
7.35: 165
8: 165 n., 166 n.
8.1-33: 167 n.
8.14-17: 166 n.
8.18-21: 166 n.
8.22-23: 166 n.
9.23-24: 93 n., 138 n., 159 n.
9.24: 93 n.
10.1: 93 n.
10.1-2: 139 n.
10.2: 93 n.
12: 179 n.
14: 179 n.
15.1-15: 179 n.
15.5: 13 n.
15.16-17: 179 n.
15.18: 179 n.
15.19-30: 179 n.
16.3: 191
16.12: 93 n., 139 n.
16.14: 191 n.
16.15: 191 n.
16.29: 4 n.
16.29-34: x1 n.
17.11-14: 211 n.
18.8: 215 n.
20.11: 215 n.
23: 179 n.
23.6: 53 n., 66 n.
23.15-21: 82 n.

16.17: 179 n.
17.7: 215 n.
18.22: 30 n., 223 n.
19.19: 215 n.
22.24: 215 n.
23.18-19: 23 n.
26.16: 189 n.
28.15-68: 117 n.
28.49-50: 118
28.56-57: 118
30.19: 31
32.1-43: 8 n.
32.15: 8
32.15-18: 8 n.
32.17: 25 n.
32.18: 8 n., 58
33.5: 8 n.

Joshua
1.12: 153 n.
6.20: 153 n.

Judges
6.21: 93 n.

1 Samuel (1 Kings)
2.22: 23 n.
4: 172 n.
5.1-2: 172 n.
5.4-5: 172 n.
5.6-9: 157 n.
6.1-6: 157 n.
7.5-9: 229 n.
10.1: 160 n.
10.10: 160 n.
10.10-13: 161 n.
12.19-23: 229 n.
14.41-42: 160 n.

16.13: 160 n.
19.20-24: 161 n.
31: 220 n.

2 Samuel (2 Kings)
1.10: 166 n.
1.19-20: 220
1.20: 220
1.27: 220
7.2: 152 n.
12.1-12: 75 n.
12.5-6: 76 n.
14.22: 197 n.
24.15-17: 157 n.

1 Kings (3 Kings)
8.64: 159 n.
14.23: 180 n.
16.29-22.39: 74 n.
18.21: 80
18.28: 76 n.
18.38: 93 n.
20.35-38: 74
20.35-43: 74 n.
20.39-42: 76
29.42: 76
22.34-38: 76 n.

2 Kings (4 Kings)
1.10-14: 93 n.
2.3: 75 n.
2.9: 161 n.
2.14: 161 n.
2.23: 76 n.
6.28-30: 119 n.
11.12: 166 n.
16.3: 25 n., 152 n., 189 n.
16.7-8: 152 n.

277

279

281

22.11-13: 64 n.
22.13: 241 n.
22.44: 194 n.
23.12: 56 n.
23.23: 189 n.
23.29-39: 151 n.
23.30-31: 131
23.32: 131
24.1-23: 109 n.
24.2: 99 n.
24.15: 122 n., 135
25.7-13: 64 n.
25.14-30: 8 n., 64 n., 240 n.
25.15: 241 n.
25.20-23: 241 n.
25.21: 241
25.23: 241 n.
25.24-30: 94 n.
25.27: 240
25.30: 241 n.
25.31-46: 232 n.
25.34: 241 n.
25.35-36: 64
25.44-45: 64 n.
25.45: 48-9
26.3: 101 n.
26.6-13: 101 n.
26.9:101
26.10: 101
26.13: 101
26.17: 54 n.
26.17-19: 66 n.
26.33-35: 214 n.
26.69-75: 214 n.
27.13: 163
27.25: 18 and n., 149
27.51: 163 n., 173 n.
27.56: 102 n.

27.61: 102 n.
28.1: 102 n.

Mark
2.20: 163 n.
5.1-17: 236 n.
6.14-29: 234 n.
10.11: 43 n.
13.14: 122 n.
14.6: 101 n.
14.8-9: 101 n.
14.12: 54 n.
14.12-16: 66 n.
14.26-31: 214 n.
14.66-72: 214 n.
15.38: 173 n.
15.42: 66 n.

Luke
2.14: 2
2.24: 179 n.
4.24: 19 n.
8.2: 102 n.
8.26-37: 236 n.
8.31: 236-37 n.
8.32-33: 236 n.
8.40-42: 202 n.
8.49-56: 202 n.
10.30-35: 216 n.
11.24-26: 24 n.
13.27: 174
13.34: xxxi n.
14.11: 56 n.
15.4-6: 239 n.
16.1-13: 202 n.
16.9: 202
16.10-12: 202 n.
16.18: 43 n.

285